'*Developments in French Politics 6* is e
now! This fresh, engaging compendium
a period of tremendous political transfc
to date. Yet its judicious coverage, hig
reference will certainly ensure its si
moment.'

– Lorna Milne, *University of St Andrews, UK*

'This volume provides a welcome guide to the complex, and sometimes
disturbing, politics of a country that plays a central role in the European
Union. Its portrait of how France is grappling with the kind of problems that
now grip many western democracies is illuminating for everyone concerned
about such issues.'

– Peter A. Hall, *Harvard University, USA*

'The editors have marshalled together a superb set of chapters. This is a
perfect starting point for thinking about the continuities and changes that
have marked out the Macron era in France and the years preceding his arrival
at the Élysée Palace. Essential reading for anyone wanting to understand
contemporary France.'

– Christopher Bickerton, *University of Cambridge, UK*

'*Developments in French Politics 6* is a must-read for understanding the complex challenges confronted by all contemporary democracies. The high quality multi-generational team of international researchers deliver an
unprecedented, innovative and cutting-edge analysis of "transformation and
resistance" in twenty-first-century Fifth Republic France.'

– Amy G. Mazur, *Washington State University, USA*

'For those seeking to understand the key changes and continuities in French
politics and society since 2014, this latest volume in the *Developments* series
brings together an expert team to parse the issues and trends that define this
compelling polity. For country specialists and generalists alike, the book
provides an excellent map of France's contemporary political landscape,
domestically and globally. It represents the state of the art in the study of the
country, its population and its institutions.'

– Jocelyn Evans, *University of Leeds, UK*

'An insightful and timely guide to the forces shaping contemporary France,
and the challenges facing Emmanuel Macron.'

– Sophie Pedder, *author of*
Revolution Française: Emmanuel Macron and the Quest to
Reinvent a Nation *and Paris Bureau Chief for* The Economist, *France*

DEVELOPMENTS TITLES AVAILABLE FROM RED GLOBE PRESS

Helen Drake, Alistair Cole, Sophie Meunier and Vincent Tiberj (eds)
Developments in French Politics 6

Maria Green Cowles and Desmond Dinan (eds)
Developments in the European Union 2

Richard Heffernan, Colin Hay, Meg Russell and Philip Cowley (eds)
Developments in British Politics 10

Erik Jones, Paul M. Heywood, Martin Rhodes and Ulrich Sedelmeier (eds)
Developments in European Politics 2

Stephen Padgett, William E. Paterson and Reimut Zohlnhöfer (eds)
Developments in German Politics 4*

Gillian Peele, Christopher J. Bailey, Jon N. Herbert, Bruce E. Cain and B. Guy Peters (eds)
Developments in American Politics 8

Stephen White, Paul Lewis, and Judy Batt (eds)
Developments in Central and East European Politics 5*

Stephen White, Richard Sakwa and Henry E. Hale (eds)
Developments in Russian Politics 9*

* Rights: world excluding North America

DEVELOPMENTS IN FRENCH POLITICS 6

HELEN DRAKE

ALISTAIR COLE

SOPHIE MEUNIER

VINCENT TIBERJ

 macmillan international HIGHER EDUCATION  RED GLOBE PRESS

First published 2021 by
RED GLOBE PRESS

Red Globe Press in the UK is an imprint of Macmillan Education Limited, registered in England, company number 01755588, of 4 Crinan Street, London, N1 9XW.

Red Globe Press® is a registered trademark in the United States, the United Kingdom, Europe and other countries.

ISBN 978-1-352-01129-6 hardback
ISBN 978-1-352-00775-6 paperback

This book is printed on paper suitable for recycling and made from fully managed and sustained forest sources. Logging, pulping and manufacturing processes are expected to conform to the environmental regulations of the country of origin.

A catalogue record for this book is available from the British Library.

A catalog record for this book is available from the Library of Congress.

The editors collectively dedicate the book to the memory of Robert Elgie (1965–2019), an author in two previous volumes (2004 and 2013) and a very substantial figure for the study of contemporary France in comparative perspective. Robert's untimely death leaves us all deeply saddened.

CONTENTS

LIST OF FIGURES AND TABLES

Figures

Tables

LIST OF ABBREVIATIONS

ADF	*Association des départements de France*
AFP	Agence France-Presse
AMF	*Association des maires de France*/Association of Mayors of France
AN	*Assemblée nationale*/National Assembly
ARF	*Association des Régions de France*/Assembly of the Regions of France
ARS	*Agences régionaux de santé*/Regional health agencies
BAC	*Brigade anti-criminalité*/Anti-crime Brigade
CCNE	*Comité consultatif national d'éthique*/National Advisory Council on Bioethics
CET	*Cotisation économique territorial*/Territorial economic contribution
CEVIPOF	*Centre d'étude de la vie politique française*
CFDT	*Confédération démocratique du Travail*/Democratic Confederation of Labour
CGT	*Confédération général du Travail*/General Confederation of Labour
CICE	*Crédit d'impôt pour la compétitivité et l'emploi*/Tax Credit for Competitiveness and Employment
CISE	Italian Centre for Electoral Studies
CNCDH	*Commission nationale consultative des droits de l'homme*/National Consultative Commission for Human Rights
COP21	Conference of Parties 21/United Nations Climate Change Conference
CRS	*Compagnie républicaine de Sécurité*/Republican Security Force
CTC	*Collectivité territoriale de Corse*/Corsican Territorial Authority
DFP6	*Developments in French Politics 6*
DILCRAH	*Délégation interministérielle à la lutte contre le racisme, l'antisémitisme et la haine anti-LGBT*/Interministerial Delegation against racism, antisemitism and anti-LGBT hate
EELV	*Europe Écologie-les Verts*/Europe Ecology – the Greens
EP	European Parliament
EPCI	*Établissement public de coopération intercommunale*/Inter-communal public authority
ESS	European Social Survey
EU	European Union
FDI	Foreign Direct Investment
FI/LFI	*France insoumise*/Unbowed/Untamed France
FN	*Front national*/the National Front

G7	Group of Seven
GDP	Gross Domestic Product
GND	*le Grand Débat national*/the Great National Debate
IFOP	*Institute d'études opinion et marketing en France et à l'international*
IGPN	*Inspection général de la police nationale*/General Inspectorate of the National Police
INSEE	*l'Institut national des statistiques et des études économiques* / National Institute of Statistics and Economic Studies
ISF	*Impôt de la solidarité sur la fortune*/Solidarity wealth tax
LGBT	Lesbian, gay, bisexual and transgender
LGBTQ	Lesbian, gay, bisexual, transgender and queer/questioning
LMPT	*la Manif pour Tous*/Out for All
LO	*Lutte ouvrière*/Workers' Struggle
LR	*les Républicains*/the Republicans
LREM	*la République en Marche* (also LRM)/Republic on the Move
LRM	*la République en Marche* (also LREM)/Republic on the Move
LTI	Longitudinal Tolerance Index
MAPTAM (law)	*la modernisation de l'action publique territoriale et d'affirmation des métropoles*/Modernisation of territorial public policy and the *métropoles*
MEP	Member of European Parliament
MNR	*Mouvement national républicain*/National Republican Movement
MODEM	*Mouvement démocrate*/Democratic Movement
MP	Member of Parliament
NATO	North Atlantic Treaty Organization
NGO	Non-governmental organization
NOTRE (law)	*Nouvelle organisation territoriale de la République*/new territorial organisation of the Republic
NPA	*Nouveau Parti anticapitaliste*/New Anticapitalist Party
OECD	Organisation for Economic Co-operation and Development
OFCE	*Observatoire français des conjonctures économiques*/French Economic Observatory
PaCS	*Pacte civil de solidarité*/Civil Solidarity Pact
PCF	*Parti communiste français*/French Communist Party
PR	Proportional representation
PS	*Parti socialiste*/Socialist Party
PVV	*Partij voor de Vrijheid*/Party for Freedom
RAPFI	*Rapport au Politique des Français issus de l'Immigration*/How immigrant-born French relate to politics
RN	*Rassemblement national*/National Rally
RPR	*Rassemblement pour la République*/Rally for the Republic
SME	Small and medium-sized enterprise
SNCF	*Société nationale des Chemins de Fer français*
TEO	*Trajectoires et origines*/Trajectories and Origins
TV	Television
UDC	Swiss People's Party or Democratic Union of the Centre

LIST OF ABBREVIATIONS

UDF	*Union pour la démocratie française*/Union for French Democracy
UK	United Kingdom
UMP	*Union pour un mouvement populaire*/Union for a Popular Movement
UN	United Nations
US/USA	United States of America
VAT	Value added tax
WTO	World Trade Organization
WWII	World War Two
YVM	Yellow Vests Movement

ABOUT THE AUTHORS

Camille Bedock has been a CNRS researcher in the Centre Emile Durkheim in Sciences Po Bordeaux since October 2018. Before that, she was a FNRS postdoctoral researcher in the Centre for the study of Politics (Cevipol) of the Université Libre de Bruxelles (2016–18) and a temporary lecturer in Sciences Po Bordeaux (2014–16). She has a PhD from the European University Institute of Florence in Social and Political Science (2014). She works on the determinants and processes of democratic reforms in consolidated democracies, on the views of citizens about their political systems, and on party system change in France and Southern European democracies. In 2017 she published a book entitled *Reforming Democracy: Institutional Engineering in Western Europe* with Oxford University Press. Her works can be found in journals such as the *European Political Science Review, Government and Opposition, Representation, French Politics,* and the *Revue française de science politique.*

Alistair Cole is Professor of Politics and Head of the Department of Government and International Studies at Hong Kong Baptist University. He obtained a 1st in Government and History from the LSE (1980, awarded the Bassett Prize for Political Science) and a D. Phil from Balliol College, Oxford (1986, funded by a BA grant). He held positions in Oxford, Caen, Aston, Keele and Bradford before being named as Professor of European Politics at Cardiff University, Wales, UK, in 1999. From 2015 to 2019, Alistair Cole was Professor of Political Science at the Institute of Political Studies, Lyon, France. He has published extensively, mainly in the field of French, British and European politics. He has published 20 books (6 single author monographs, 6 co-written monographs, 8 edited or co-edited books), 67 refereed journal articles, 25 professional articles and 62 chapters in edited books. His latest book – *Emmanuel Macron and the Two Years that Changed France* – was published by Manchester University Press in May 2019.

Sylvain Crépon is Associate Professor in Political Science and member of the IRJI (Institute for Interdisciplinary Legal Research) at the University of Tours. His work, mostly based on qualitative surveys, focuses on nationalist and populist movements, renewals of racism and also religious controversies in France and Western Europe. On the subject of the *Front National* (now *Rassemblement National*), he is co-editor, with Alexandre Dézé and Nonna Mayer, of *Les faux semblants du Front national. Sociologie d'un parti politique* (2015) Paris, Presses de Science Po, and author of *Enquête au cœur du nouveau Front national* (2012) Paris, Nouveau Monde éditions.

Helen Drake is Professor of French and European Studies and Director of the Institute for Diplomacy and International Governance (IDIG) at Loughborough University London. Previously at Loughborough University's Midlands campus, she has published on contemporary France, France's relations with the European Union, questions of political leadership, the history of European Studies as an academic discipline, and Brexit. From 2012 to 2018 she chaired the UK's University Association for Contemporary European Studies, UACES. From 2013 to 2016 she held a Jean Monnet Chair of European Integration and from 2017 to 2019 ran two research projects on Brexit: one (28+ Brexits) studying the real UK-EU negotiations, the other using simulated Brexit negotiations as a way of raising awareness in UK schools of the stakes of Brexit. In 2010 Helen was named *Chevalier dans l'Ordre des Palmes Académiques* by the French government for services to French culture and language and in 2017 received the Innovation in Academia Arts and Culture Award from the University of Kent, UK. She is a member of the Scientific Council of ESSCA (École de Management) Angers, France, and of the Expert Committee for the research network Alliance Europa, Pays de la Loire, France.

Christopher Hill (FBA) is Emeritus Professor of International Relations at the Department of Politics and International Studies (POLIS) of the University of Cambridge, and an Emeritus Fellow of Sidney Sussex College. He has held chairs at the LSE, Cambridge and SAIS Bologna. His most recent publications are: *The Future of British Foreign Policy: Security and Diplomacy in a World after Brexit* (Polity, 2019); *International Relations and the European Union*, 3rd ed. Edited with Michael Smith and Sophie Vanhoonacker (OUP 2017); *Foreign Policy in the Twenty-First Century* (Palgrave Macmillan, 2016); and *The National Interest in Question: Foreign Policy in Multicultural Societies* (OUP 2013).

Nicolas Lebourg is researcher at CEPEL (CNRS-University of Montpellier) and Research Fellow on the Transnational History of the Far Right project (George Washington University). He is a member of the steering committee of the VIORAMIL (Violence and Militant Radicalism) programme of the French National Research Agency and also participates in COSPRAD (Scientific Committee on Radicalization Processes). He researches into the European far right (publishing with Jean-Yves Camus (2017) *Far-Right Politics in Europe*, Cambridge, Harvard University Press); the transnational far right (author of (2019) *Les Nazis ont-ils survécu ?*, Paris, Seuil); and the French far right (co-author with Joseph Beauregard (2012), *François Duprat, l'homme qui inventa le Front National,* Paris, Denoël).

Nonna Mayer is CNRS Research Director Emerita at the Centre for European Studies and Comparative Politics of Sciences Po Paris (CEE). Her main fields of research are racism and anti-Semitism, electoral behaviour and radical right populism. She chaired the French Political Science Association

(AFSP) from 2005 to 2016. She is editor of the series *Contester* at the *Presses de Sciences Po*, which is focused on changes in modes of collective action. Since 2011 she has co-led (with S.Cohen) the joint CEE-CERI methodological research seminar *Les sciences sociales en question. Grandes controverses en sciences sociales*. Member of the National Consultative Commission for Human Rights (CNCDH) since 2016 and part of its standing group on racism, she coordinates the research team in charge of the annual CNCDH Barometer on racism. She is the co-author, with E. Druez, of the French contribution to a five-country research project on antisemitism and immigration in Western Europe (Mayer and Druez, 2018). She is also supervisor of the French fieldwork for the EU-funded 'ReligSpace' research project (European Research Council, 2019). Her recent publications include: Mayer, N., Michelat, G., Tiberj, V., Vitale, T. (2020) *Le regard des chercheurs*; and *La lutte contre le racisme, l'antisémitisme et la xénophobie. Année 2019*, Paris: *La Documentation française*, pp.33–121 (all publications available at https://www.sciencespo.fr/centre-etudes-europeennes/fr/publications/733).

Sophie Meunier is Senior Research Scholar at the Princeton School of Public and International Affairs, Princeton University, and Co-Director of the EU Program at Princeton. She is the author of *Trading Voices: The European Union in International Commercial Negotiations* (Princeton University Press, 2005) and *The French Challenge: Adapting to Globalization* (Brookings Institution Press, 2001), winner of the 2002 *France-Ameriques* book award. She is also co-editor of several books on Europe and globalization, most recently *The Politics of Interest Representation in the Global Age* (Cambridge University Press, 2014) and *Speaking with a Single Voice: The EU as an Effective Actor in Global Governance?* (Routledge, 2015). Her current work deals with the politics of Foreign Direct Investment in Europe, notably Chinese investment. She was made *Chevalier des Palmes Académiques* by the French Government.

Susan Milner is Professor of European Politics and Society at the University of Bath. Her research interests cover social and employment policy and employment relations. She is currently researching policies to tackle gender pay gaps in France and the UK, which will continue during a Leverhulme Major Research Fellowship in 2020–22.

Rainbow Murray is Professor of Politics at Queen Mary University of London. Her primary research interests are political institutions (parliament, government, political parties, elections and informal institutions) and political inclusion (with a particular interest in gender). She has a long-standing love of French politics and has written extensively about France, both in scholarly outputs and through expert commentary. Her first monograph focused on gender parity within French political parties, while more recent work has explored representation within the *Assemblée nationale*. Her work has been published in journals including the *American Political Science Review*, the *European Journal of Political Research*, the *Political Research Quarterly*, *West European Politics*, *French Politics*, *Modern & Contemporary France*, and *Parliamentary Affairs*.

Romain Pasquier is CNRS Research Professor (*Directeur de recherche*) at the *Centre de recherche sur l'action politique en Europe*, Institute of Political Studies, University of Rennes. Specialist of regional governance and decentralization in Europe, he obtained in 2010 his *Habilitation à diriger des recherches* at the *Centre d'études européennes* in Sciences-Po Paris. In 2000–01, he was Jean Monnet Fellow at the Robert Schuman Centre, European University Institute of Florence. He obtained his PhD in 2000 from the University of Rennes. From 2008 to 2017, he was a guest researcher and professor in several universities (Exeter, Aberystwyth, Montreal, Seville, Miami). He is chief scientific advisor of the Institute of Territorial Governance and Decentralization (Paris) and since 2015 has supervised the Chair "Territoires et mutations de l'action publique" at Sciences-Po Rennes. In 2012, Pasquier was an expert for the DG Regio of the European Commission where he supervised an evaluation of the implication of sub-state authorities in processes of continental or sub-continental integration. In 2019, Pasquier wrote a report for the OECD on Decentralisation and Regionalisation in Portugal. Since 2010 he has published and edited ten books and more than fifty articles and chapters in his field of research (http://scholar.google.fr/citations?user=wr1apSkAAAAJ&hl=fr).

Bruno Perreau is the Cynthia L. Reed Professor of French Studies at the Massachusetts Institute of Technology. Perreau received his PhD in political science from the University of Paris Panthéon-Sorbonne, and taught at Sciences Po and at the University of Paris Val de Marne. He was a member of the Institute for Advanced Study, Princeton; a research associate at the University of Cambridge (Jesus College); a fellow at Stanford Humanities Center; a visiting scholar at the University of California, Berkeley and a fellow at the Center for Advanced Study in the Behavioral Sciences (Stanford). He received awards from the British Academy, the European Commission, the European University Institute, the French Government and the American Council of Learned Societies. Since 2012, he has been affiliated with the Center for European Studies, Harvard, and the THEMA lab, University of Lausanne. Perreau is the founding chair of the MIT Global France Seminar. He is the author of ten books on political institutions and ideas, bioethics, gender in translation and queer theory. He has recently published *The Politics of Adoption* (MIT Press, 2014), *Queer Theory: The French Response* (Stanford University Press, 2016), *Les Défis de la République* (co-edited with Joan W. Scott, Presses de Sciences Po, 2017), and *Qui a peur de la théorie queer ?*

(Presses de Sciences Po, 2018). He is currently working on a new book on minority politics in France and in the US.

Yann Raison du Cleuziou is a senior lecturer in political science at the University of Bordeaux where he is attached to the Montesquieu Research Institute. He is president of the French Association of Social Sciences of Religions. His research focuses on the history and political sociology of contemporary French Catholicism. After working on the political engagement of the clergy on the far left in the 1960s and 1970s, he is now working on Catholic conservative activists engaged in nationalist, populist or anti-gender struggles. He has showed how, in a context of the collapse of religious practice, Catholicism has been reconstituted by those who are most successful in transmitting the faith and who are also, tendentially, the most conservative. The secularization of society therefore paradoxically leads to a desecularization within the Church. He has conducted several qualitative and quantitative surveys in order to renew the description of the internal divisions in Catholicism. Primary works include: (with Nicolas de Brémond d'Ars), *French Catholics and Their Church. Pluralism and Deregulation*, Washington (DC), CRVP, 2015; *De la contemplation à la contestation. La politisation des dominicains de la Province de France (années 1940–1970)*, Paris, Belin, 2016; *Une contre-révolution catholique. Aux origines de La Manif pour tous*, Paris, Seuil, 2019.

Vincent Tiberj is Full Professor and Researcher at the Emile Durkheim Center, and Dean of Research at Sciences Po Bordeaux. Between 2002 and 2015, he was a research fellow at the *Fondation nationale des sciences politiques* (FNSP) (National Foundation of Political Science), first in CEVIPOF, and then in the *Centre d'études européennes* (CEE) (Center for European Studies). His publications include: *Les citoyens qui viennent* (Paris: PUF, 2017); *Sociologie plurielle des comportements politiques* (Paris: Presses de Sciences Po, 2017); as editor with Olivier Filleule, Florence Haegel, and Camille Hamidi; *Des votes et des voix. La France des urnes de Mitterrand à Hollande* (Paris: Champ social éditions, 2013); *La crispation hexagonale. France fermée contre France plurielle, 2001–2007* (Paris: Plon/FJJ, 2008); *Français comme les autres? Enquête sur les citoyens d'origine maghrébine, africaine et turque* (Paris: Presses de Sciences Po, 2005), co-authored with Sylvain Brouard. A specialist in political psychology and in the analysis of electoral and political behaviours in France, Europe and the United States, Tiberj's work focuses on the reasoning of 'ordinary' citizens' and the political sociology of social and ethnic inequalities, as well as on xenophobic prejudices and value systems. Since 2009, he is also associated with the annual CNCDH Barometer on racism CNCDH.

Emilie Tran was born in Cambodia of Chinese (Teochew) descent and was educated in France. Her PhD in History and Civilization is from the *Ecole des Hautes Etudes en Sciences Sociales*, Paris. Since 2000, she has been living in Greater China (Shanghai, Macao, Hong Kong). She has taught at the University of Macau, the Hong Kong University of Sciences and Technology, and the University of Saint Joseph where she was also the Coordinator of the Department of Public Administration and International Relations, and Dean of the Faculty of Administration and Leadership. She joined Hong Kong Baptist University in 2016 as the Coordinator of European Studies (French Stream). Having researched on China's elite politics and the formation of Chinese Communist Party cadres, she shifted her research in the mid-2010s from China's domestic politics to China's external relations and foreign policy. At that time posted in Macao SAR, she studied China's foreign policy and soft power towards Portuguese-speaking countries. Now she focuses on China-Europe relations, Chinese diaspora and investments in Europe and France in particular. Since 2018, Emilie is one of the 443 *Conseillers Consulaires*, elected through direct universal suffrage, who represent the overseas French; her constituency is the French in Hong Kong and Macao.

1 TRANSFORMATION AND RESISTANCE IN FRENCH POLITICS

Alistair Cole, Helen Drake, Sophie Meunier and Vincent Tiberj

Introduction

Developments in French Politics Six (DFP6) is the latest in the long-running series on contemporary France. It brings together a combination of scholars from various generations and countries, each expert in their own domain. It presents the most recent and innovative research that is consistent with the need to reach and teach a readership that spans students, specialists, educated professionals and generalists. Such inter-generational and inter-cultural exchange has always been one of the key achievements of the 'Developments In' series. This volume, moreover, interprets French politics and society through particular events or processes that are situated mainly in the very contemporary period; but it also builds upon our received knowledge about France. In these respects, the study takes its place alongside both the five previous 'Developments In' volumes on France, as well as other scholarship offering meta-studies of one type or other of contemporary French politics (Elgie et al., 2018; Evans and Ivaldi, 2018; Demossier et al., 2020).

Insofar as it focuses on a specific period, DFP6 covers the years from 2014 to 2020. This period stretches from mid-way through François Hollande's presidency (2012–17) to the mid-point of Emmanuel Macron's term in the Elysée (2017–22). However, the book does not over-emphasize either the Hollande or Macron presidencies in and of themselves as defining or distinctive moments of change – that would be overly deterministic and would give too much importance to these presidential figures. Indeed, France's presidency and its presidential elections are a source of distrust, since they create such unrealistic expectations (Grossman and Sauger, 2017). We will see that many of the developments covered in this volume (in relation to Catholicism, racism or new forms of family, for example) evolved largely irrespective of changes of president.

Nonetheless, we take seriously the claim of the incumbent president that we are witnessing if not a 'revolution' (Macron, 2016) in French politics, then at least a transformation. A 'Developments In' volume typically addresses a series of questions that *are* pertinent to a particular period in time, but which also have a more general significance for the country in question. The current volume is shaped by the intensity of these questions in the light of Macron's claims that they represent a transformative transition from an old to a new world (a 'new' world envisioned, that is, before the Covid-19 crisis hit). The traditional 'Developments In' analytical frame of continuity and change is thus reformulated in this volume in terms of transformation and resistance. This is a dichotomy framed more specifically by Macron and his supporters as the onward march of 'progressives' (a term usually used for describing the left) against recalcitrant 'populists' castigated as troublemakers or recalcitrant 'Gauls' on the wrong side of history. This binary, for Macron, replaces the traditional left–right political dyad, and Chapters 3, 4 and 5 tackle these claims in detail, as we discuss below.

Many Western democracies also experienced political upheavals at about the same time as Macron's election in 2017 (viz. Brexit in the UK and Trump in the US). What is specific to the French case is that, while Macron's victory was part of the same trend, it also seemed to spare France a manifestly populist moment, at least for now. Yet one important question, addressed in Chapters 2 and 11 of this volume, is the extent to which popular resistance – such as the Yellow Vests movement – to Macron's style (a mix of traditional technocracy and innovative entrepreneurship) constituted a populist rejection of representative democracy per se, or the expression of demands for greater citizen inclusion in the democratic process of public policy-making.

In addressing their subject matter, the following chapters offer a wide variety of methodological, conceptual and theoretical perspectives; many of the 13 chapters in this volume also offer original data. Indeed, the originality, significance and rigour of the volume as a whole lie in the authors' autonomy to develop their own webs of meaning from the events they reconstitute. Contributors thus embrace in the following chapters a variety of normative positions towards, for example, liberalism in all its forms; towards topical and sensitive issues of societal change including real-world, intellectual struggles with normativity itself (in the form of political correctness and dissent); towards universalist, republican ambition on the part of policy-makers, and the defence of specific ideas, interests and institutions on the part of a range of stakeholders. The hypothesis shared nonetheless by all of these chapters is that French politics *is* experiencing a form of transformation, marked by the ebbing of older partisan structures and central cleavages, by challenges to the foundations of its republican model and by a re-evaluation of France's place in Europe and the world. The process is neither smooth, nor linear – and indeed, resistance is key to the process of change itself.

France has not been alone in experiencing a breakdown of such traditional structures during this period. Accordingly, we situate this volume's scholarship in comparative perspective, showing what has been both a shared experience in many Western democracies and what has been a uniquely French response. Throughout the volume, we draw implicit and explicit comparisons with other countries, either to elucidate the distinctiveness of France, or to demonstrate its convergence with other countries, or some combination of the two. Related to this challenge is how to address the problem of the level of analysis. In a book on contemporary French politics, it is natural to take the nation – France and Frenchness – as the main unit of analysis; but what does this signify in reality? Do we understand France as a united and unified nation? Or do we prefer to reason in terms of its diversity? We land on terrain where we are impelled to include in our reasoning the reality of spatial core–periphery dynamics, and to endeavour to understand French politics from a bottom-up perspective, in localities, cities and regions. Likewise, we acknowledge the value of taking the perspective of particular groups (such as immigrants) or specific issues (such as Catholicism, or sexual politics) when constructing our analyses.

Furthermore, France is part of an interconnected system of European and global governance that further disturbs the superficial neatness of our unit of analysis. France as an object of study cannot easily be removed from its global context. Crises and developments with their origins outside of the country inevitably spill over and influence domestic French developments; recent examples would include the 2016 election of Donald Trump as US President, the UK's withdrawal from the EU (Brexit), the climate emergency and the rise of populism in democratic nations and, of course, Covid-19. French presidents such as Macron, as Hollande before him, have explicitly acknowledged the lack of clear distinction between the internal and the external, with Hollande claiming that 'I no longer make the distinction between foreign policy (*politique extérieure*), European policy and domestic (*nationale*) policy. It is the same idea (*conception*), the same method and the same objectives: growth, justice and employment' (Elysée, 2012, cited in Drake, 2013, p. 139). Over time, this admission of porosity has arguably become part of the existential danger for the Fifth Republic; in the case of Macron, it has fed into a vision of sovereignty as necessarily relocating to the European level of governance. This fact of French governance is reflected, moreover, in our selection of chapters that tackle France's external challenges precisely by emphasizing the interconnectedness of external and internal, foreign and domestic action (see Chapters 12 and 13 in this volume).

Each chapter tackles the issue of transformation and resistance in recent French politics from its own distinctive angle such that the volume, collectively, addresses three broad, inter-related clusters of questions. In the remainder of this chapter, we offer several interpretations of these three categories of developments in French politics. First are those questions related specifically to trust and mistrust in political parties and the presidency. Second are those linked to the Republic: its fragilities and its defences. Third and finally are those concerning the re-casting of France's position in Europe and the world.

Political parties and the presidency in question

The rise and fall of political parties is not, by itself, a new phenomenon. The history of the French party system is peppered with examples of parties that have withered away, such as the French Radicals in the Fourth Republic, and Christian Democracy and the Communist Party in the Fifth Republic. The Fifth Republic itself has accommodated varying phases of party competition, including the ascendancy of Gaullism (1959–74) and the gradual challenge to its domination within the centre and right; the slow emergence of the left–right bipolarization as a structuring mode of party competition (1962–78); the rise of the FN from 1982 onwards, introducing a new player and shattering the symmetry of the *quadrille bipolaire*; and the rise and withering of other new parties and movements such as political ecology. But the earthquake–volcano metaphor appeared particularly apposite to describe the 2017 elections (Cole, 2019). As Bedock and Murray demonstrate in Chapters 3 and 4, respectively, those elections challenged the future survival of such mainstream parties as the Socialists on the left and the Republicans on the right. The analysis contained in Chapters 3 and 4 is not just a case of why individual parties die (Mack, 2010), but also one of partisan and electoral realignment (Martin, 2000) and of a fracturing of the left–right cleavage structure.

Left, right or something new?

This putative reshaping of the French party system is therefore a key development in the period covered by this book. Chapters 3, 4 and 5 (by Bedock, Murray, and Crépon and Lebourg respectively) each deal, from different perspectives, with the possibility that the traditional left–right political cleavage has been supplanted by something different: by a progressive versus patriot fault line; by a division between supporters of an open versus a closed society; by an enduring battle between *liberté* and *égalité*. All the authors agree that the traditional parties were severely disrupted by the 2017 elections when neither of the traditional, presidential parties representing France's social-democratic and centre-right traditions – the Socialist Party (PS) and the Republicans (LR) respectively – won through to the second round of the presidential elections, and suffered serious losses in the parliamentary contests too.

On the one hand, the transformation wrought by the 2017 presidential election was particularly deep, with the implosion of several of the traditional mainstream parties, first and foremost the Socialist and Republican parties. On the other hand, it is easier to identify the acceleration in 2017 of a process of *dealignment* than a clear process of *realignment*. For example, while we can identify the decline of the traditional parties, it is far from certain that the newcomers, starting with Macron's *La République en Marche* (LREM) and Jean-Luc Mélenchon's *la France Insoumise* (FI), have fundamentally changed the nature of party choice or the partisan game. Moreover, it is premature to consign LR in particular to the history books, since it continues to occupy a strategically important position on the centre and central right of French politics. Despite the scandals, its 2017 presidential candidate François Fillon was not far from qualifying for the second round; and both LR and PS incumbent mayors performed credibly in the 2020 municipal elections, unlike their LREM counterparts who failed almost everywhere to win municipal office. Furthermore, *Europe Ecologie-Les Verts* (EELV) could yet become the new leading organization of a left which still exists for the electorate (Tiberj, 2017), one of the numerous lessons of the 2017 election being that an underdog can get elected. As for the 2019 European and 2020 municipal elections, they pointed to a revival of the post-materialist and environmental issue areas that have resurfaced regularly since the first breakthrough of the Greens (then *Les Verts,* now *Europe Ecologie-Les Verts*) in the 1984 European elections (Cole and Doherty, 1995). The greening of the agenda of all the main parties represents another way of breaking the mould, by acting on agendas, rather than party structures.

Alongside these systemic questions, the depth of mistrust towards political parties per se emerges as a constant of all surveys carried out in France over the past decade, and most notably the CEVIPOF's trust barometer (CEVIPOF, 2020). Trust in parties is at a dangerous low, given that parties are essential intermediaries of democratic politics. Indeed, part of Macron's argument in favour of transformation lay in his belief that parties had failed as democratic actors; his own route to electoral victory was via a movement named as such: *La République en Marche.* He is not the first president to have been sceptical of the role of parties in French democracy; founder Charles de Gaulle ensured that parties were constitutionally bound to uphold the *nation.* Nor is it unusual in France to see parties labelled anything but 'party': 'movements', 'fronts', 'rallies' and 'unions' all, to the present day, point to France's history of fractured and fissiparous political alliances; to Thomas Carlyle's 'great men' seeking to rally their political troops around their persona; and to the episodic calls for solidarity between nominally different groupings.

Old wine in new bottles

At the same time, the frequency of re-branding exercises can itself exacerbate underlying mistrust in political parties since there is a long French tradition of designing new labels for old bottles, and of 'parties' changing their name for perceived political advantage. Macron's LREM, for example, counts a significant number of recycled Socialists and Republicans, and senior civil servants (Dolez et al., 2018). The most flagrant example of nominal instability is the Gaullists – the original presidential-rally-style party, defined by loyalty to a leader. They have changed their name on six occasions, usually reflecting a shift in leadership (*Rassemblement du peuple français, Union pour la nouvelle République, Union des démocrates et des républicains, Rassemblement pour la République, Union pour un mouvement populaire, Les Républicains*). As discussed in Crépon and Lebourg's Chapter 5, moreover, name change is certainly seen as a solution to a real problem in the case of the *Front national* (National Front or FN, now RN); the FN label being indelibly associated with founder Jean-Marie Le Pen, the far-right creator of the party in 1972. Marine Le Pen's success in imposing the new name, *Rassemblement national* (RN/National Rally), was fraught with legal and political dangers: the new name was already patented, and her movement was deeply divided over the decision. The intention, however, was to use the name change to broaden political appeal and enter one day into a coalition government (as yet, still a work-in-progress).

Newcomers, breaking the mould or claiming to, are the furthest from the party label. Recent examples include *En Marche!*, *la France Insoumise*, and *Génération.s* – all of which claim to mobilize beyond party, in social movements, citizens' committees or via social media. In the case of Macron and LREM, the novelty extends into parliament itself. Murray in Chapter 4 identifies the emergence of a new class of inexperienced LREM deputies and points to their difficulties in learning and mastering the rules of the parliamentary game. Moreover, the parliament since 2017, she demonstrates, is certainly more diverse in terms of generations and links to business, but not in terms of social stratification. By achieving close to gender parity from the outset, on the other hand, LREM is well placed to maintain a gender balanced cohort of deputies. Less novel however is that, while the arrival of political novices into parliament produced a temporary change in working patterns, this was soon followed by a return to the practices of previous cohorts once the new generation discovered what it actually took to be a deputy. After an initial period, LREM deputies began spending more time in their constituencies and less time in the chamber; and were proposing more amendments to legislation, and showing reduced willingness to toe the party line come what may. By May 2020, LREM had lost its absolute majority in the National Assembly as another set of (17) party deputies peeled away to form an 'independent' grouping in the chamber, declaring themselves to belong neither to the majority, nor the opposition.

The choice of more flexible organizational forms is partly a reaction to the loss of trust in traditional party organizations: the three formations mentioned above all had some links with the PS, through politicians, party managers or electors. But they are also more adapted to new forms of political mobilization, as demonstrated during the 2017 campaign by the mastery of new means of political communication such as YouTube by candidates Mélenchon and Macron. On the other hand, the capacity for such movements to capture town halls and local government seats is in the main untested (as confirmed in the 2020 municipal election).

More generally, this weakening of partisan underpinnings has contributed to broader institutional challenges facing the French Fifth Republic as it enters its seventh decade. The weakening of the main parties and of their ability to aggregate social interests is central to any discussion of a broader crisis of institutional capacity. However, it is essential not to confuse the snapshot of a given point in time with a relentless, inevitable movement. For all the relabelling and remodelling, by mid-term in the first Macron presidency, *En Marche!* and its founder had demonstrated their inability to absorb the discontent and protest which broke out very early on in Macron's presidency in the form of the Yellow Vests (*gilets jaunes*) movement, discussed by Tran in Chapter 11. Was the French presidency in peril?

Presidential authority in question

By the time of the 2017 elections, as discussed by Drake and Cole in Chapter 2, the French presidential office manifestly was suffering from diminished political capacity and prestige: successive presidents had failed to incarnate the presidential office and live up to the expectations of their electoral campaigns. The formal presidency had by then become 'faster' (Cole, 2012), thanks to the 2000 reform that aligned the presidential with the parliamentary five-year term. Not only that, but the turnover of French presidents was also speeding up: neither Nicolas Sarkozy nor François Hollande enjoyed the authority to underpin a second term in office. How could this faster, shorter presidency accommodate Emmanuel Macron, France's youngest and most apolitical president?

Framed as a form of individual political leadership *against* existing parties and lax institutional practices, as he saw them, Macron's leadership arguably bore some similarities with the types of populist leaders he explicitly targeted. Rather like Mélenchon or Le Pen, he criticized existing parties and the establishment and called for a direct relationship with the people – as entirely permitted by the Constitution. Macron's first three years in office demonstrated the dangers inherent in dismissing the 'old world' of parties and associations. As Cole and Pasquier show in Chapter 8, for example, the deliberate undermining of the *corps intermédaires*, in the form of elected mayors or regions, weakened Macron's capacity to withstand the Yellow Vest protests, as examined both by Drake and Cole in Chapter 2 and by Tran in Chapter 11. Ignoring civil society for so long arguably contributed to the low social acceptability of the president and his reforms amongst the population as a whole.

Similarly, as Milner discusses in Chapter 10, Macron's early reforms focused on reducing the state regulation of employment, giving more flexibility to businesses to regulate labour, shifting the management of social security funds from social partners to the state, and transferring funding from payroll contributions to general taxation. Milner describes Macron's reform programme as driven by a vision of France as a 'competition state' (Cerny, 1997; Genschel and Seelkopf, 2014), with reforms justified by a discourse of globalization, priority given to lowering taxes on business, and state investment channelled into skills, innovation and productivity. Such intervention was led by executive power vested in a presidential incumbent, Macron, who commanded an absolute parliamentary majority and seemed determined to side-line trade unions' veto powers.

By the second anniversary of Macron's election (6 May 2019), there were signs of diminishing leadership returns and unresolved tensions. Part of the problem lay at the heart of the Macron enterprise itself, and in particular in its emphasis on process – his 'movement' – over project. He made a virtue of not governing with civil society, identified as one of the forms of blockage in France. But his refusal to engage with the usual social partners, not even the reformist trade union, the CFDT (*Confédération démocratique du Travail*), whereas his government appeared to be particularly pro-business, undermined Macron even in the eyes of many of his own *En Marche!* deputies. Above all, it was the Yellow Vests crisis that demonstrated the weakness of Macron's linkages within civil society, which directly challenged his personal style, perceived to be out of touch, arrogant and overly condescending. As for Macron's claim to be the Master of Time (*maître des horloges*), the Yellow Vest movement forced the president to backtrack repeatedly, which was symbolically important in terms of losing control of a tightly controlled agenda. However, such policy 'U-turns', alongside Macron's listening exercises explored in Drake and Tran's chapters, can also be read as evidence of a leader learning heuristically from experience to the point of admitting to mistakes, something to which Macron had ever more frequent recourse as the challenges and crises amassed.

The forces that were superficially occluded by such a highly politicized and unusual presidential election in 2017 – mistrust towards political parties and the presidency, as seen above, and social divisions – clearly lay close to the surface and were exposed by the momentum of the *gilets jaunes*' response to increased taxes on fuel, and by the more traditional forms of protest – against pension reform – that gathered strength from late 2019 up to the point of the Covid-19 crisis. If successful political leadership requires the ability to 'align the planets' (in Macron's own expression), such harmony is always precarious, and political leadership is always contingent on context. Any attempts to disrupt the 'operating system' of the political order, as discussed in Chapter 2, is a high-risk strategy in a country such as France where history is very much part of the present.

These developments point to our second broad theme, namely the unpicking of thin republican universalism.

Transforming republican universalism?

The traditional model of French politics and society placed republican values of equality, centralization and solidarity at their core (Raymond, 2006; Chabal, 2015). We label these as thin universalist values, as they are widely disseminated and accepted in traditional representations of French political culture; they are also invoked by those claiming recognition or legitimacy. However, although they may well be broadly diffused and implicitly understood, they are equally and essentially contestable. The ebbing of and negotiation with firm republican certainties, thus, cut across several chapters in the book and take on a number of forms.

First, republicanism is sometimes used as a register of a heavily ethnicized version of Frenchness. In the case of the National Front/Rally, Crépon and Lebourg argue strongly in Chapter 5 how Marine le Pen's strategy to reshape the FN (as was) under her leadership involved her 'steering towards the republican norm', in particular with regard to matters of race. In Le Pen's understanding, legitimacy would be won by aligning with, not challenging, norms readily associated with French republicanism, in order to isolate the Muslim 'other'. In a similar vein, Raison du Cleuziou, in Chapter 6, demonstrates how 'symbolic Catholicism' has found its way back into politics on the right of the political spectrum via activism and appeals to its Christian 'cultural heritage', which in France still 'retains privileges which place it above other religions in the Republic'. The reference to the Republic here is important, insofar as the separation of Church and State recognized the Catholic religion as that of the vast majority of French people and, in practice, the Republic continues to finance the edifices of Catholicism (for example, local government assistance for the upkeep of churches). At the heart of this development is resistance to changing sexual and family mores, changes deemed by conservative Catholics to represent a dangerous 'secularization of family values', and which saw the mobilization of social movements (such as *Sens Commun*) at the time of the 2017 presidential elections. In these two apparently different cases, the Christian and Catholic dimensions of French republicanism underpin specific political, social and religious beliefs.

Indeed, in Chapter 7, Bruno Perreau shows how 'new thinking about new families' in France has challenged norms at the heart of the Christian, Catholic dimensions of French republicanism. This particularly concerns notions of what constitutes 'a family' in the light of reproductive technologies (especially medically assisted procreation) that impel debate on 'equality (between families) and freedom (to choose how one becomes a parent)'. Perreau demonstrates the serious limitations, however, of policy approaches that restrict debate to questions of medical bioethics, when the broader picture is one of 'a major transformation of [France's] family way of life' that includes civil unions (PaCS) and rising numbers of children born to couples choosing no formal, civil status. Central to French republicanism, from this perspective, is the 'sacralizing [of] the fertile body as the nation's treasure' which has made for a struggle for the recognition of sexual minorities. For Perreau, the time has come in France to move beyond narrow bioethics to a 'technopolitical' era that 'places users, patients, multinational families, and minorities at the centre of the making of laws'.

Similarly, in a second perspective on the challenges for French republicanism, Pasquier and Cole, in Chapter 8, question the sustainability of republican norms that ever diverge from the realities of social practices in the field of territorial relations. They juxtapose the traditional understanding of the Republic's mission to centralize and standardize, with the real-life developments that reveal a much more differentiated – even customized – reality at regional and local levels. This process, which has been gathering pace over 30 years, has been both encouraged and challenged by the Macron period in office, following what the authors describe as the 'half-hearted rationalization' of the Hollande presidency. During that five-year term, for example, the map of French regions was significantly altered, reducing the number of regions from 26 to 18, yet 'without genuinely addressing the question of the capacity to act, or of the new relationship to be developed between the central state and the new regions'. They do identify the 'argument of financial constraint, and the need to control public expenditure' as a thread running through territorial governance reform before and during Hollande's presidency. In contrast, they see Macron's approach as a more complex, heuristic attempt to both consolidate central state strategic control, and liberate the potential of local difference. They note the challenge of accommodating these developments within the language of republicanism, and point to the dangers of short-term, political instrumentalization of the local and the regional levels of governance in France.

The third dimension here is that of the French Republic's notionally 'colour-blind' approach to questions of racial and ethnic diversity that typically mask realities of everyday experiences of prejudice and discrimination. Mayer and Tiberj, in Chapter 9, bring extensive, original data to bear on the question of racial prejudice in multicultural France, and their findings are significant. On the one hand, they identify and track both the 'slow decline of prejudice in France' and the shared characteristics between those anti-minority prejudices that do still exist, and which point towards a more 'general, ethnocentric-authoritarian vision of society'. On the other hand, and while they detect a more tolerant society overall, their extensive research points to growing gaps in tolerance between the young and educated, and the old and uneducated. They also identify, not unlike Cole and Pasquier's conclusions above, an ambiguity in Macron's approach to diversity at the heart of France's republican reality; a stance which they predict could alienate both the tolerant and the intolerant amongst French voters.

A fourth aspect of French republicanism concerns the tension between social order and social protest. The Yellow Vest movement of 2018–19 – dissected by Tran in Chapter 11 – was not just about renewing with a traditional repertoire of the street: the violent, persistent demonstrations targeted the symbols of state authority itself, most spectacularly the Arc de Triomphe on the Champs Elysées. Indeed, the 2014–20 period as a whole was marked by sporadic outbreaks of violence in an almost continual pattern of social street protest. These included the demonstrations against the *Loi El Khomri* in 2016 under President Hollande, when Emmanuel Macron was Minister of the Economy and Industry; the *gilets jaunes* themselves (these protests were still continuing, albeit less regularly and on a diminished scale, over a year after the movement first started in December 2018), and the mass strikes of the type observed against pension reform in December 2019 and January 2020. As Milner concludes in Chapter 10, 'the escalation of conflict over pensions suggests that the remainder of the Macron presidency will be clouded by unrest and social division'. Such turmoil was brought to an abrupt halt by the intensity of the Covid-19 crisis, and its resumption waited in the wings for Macron at the time of writing.

In a fifth and final perspective on the fabric of French republicanism, the secular, lay Republic is described by Hill in Chapter 13 as an object of community-based hatred for some Muslim communities in the suburbs. Hill demonstrates convincingly how choices made by the French people through their elected representatives about how the country should be run – such as that on the Muslim veil – have consequences for French foreign policy, promoting links between the domestic opponents of the lay Republic and enemies of the West (in this case France) abroad. French citizens have been forced to realize that events far from home are reverberating within their country in the form of the dramatic and tragic terrorist attacks that punctuated so violently Hollande's and – increasingly, albeit on a different scale – Macron's years in power.

These chapters all engage, then, in different ways, with the meaning of the Republic and republicanism in the face of what we might call 'post-republican realities'. In the book carrying that title, Cole and Raymond (2006) describe the ideal type French republican model as being one constructed on universal values and beliefs, rather than the reality of competition between interests; on discursive framings of the general interest that discourage diversity; on corporatist professional dynamics that frame their own demands in terms of the general interest, and on the importance of respecting abstract rules (while negotiating exceptions to them). Our authors' research collectively provides rich evidence that such a model has been gradually unpicked over the past three decades, and that this decline of republicanism as a political doctrine has left a void that newcomers have sought to fill. Indeed, as seen above, the 2017 elections saw the disintegration of a party system based on the traditional republican parties of the left and right; and the first years of the Macron presidency brought serious challenges to the stability of the institutions at the heart of the republican state. The chapters in this volume also demonstrate the flipside of the coin: namely that transformations provoke resistance, and that resilience can take the form of strengthening retrograde politics and policies that themselves find refuge in the appeal to the Republic.

Transforming relationships: France, Europe and the World

In 2015–18, the French Republic appeared to be in literal, physical danger as a result of repeated terrorist attacks. The list of these terror events (explored in Chapter 13) is long, beginning with the murderous attacks on an editorial meeting of the satirical newspaper *Charlie Hebdo* in January 2015, followed the next day by the murder of two policemen and four customers of a Jewish supermarket Hyper Casher, both in Paris; the Bataclan and other Paris sites in November 2015 which killed and injured so many people; Nice in July 2016, also a large-scale slaughter; and since then, other smaller-scale terrorist attacks in St Etienne du Rouvray, Marseille, Carcassonne, Paris, Levallois-Perret, Strasbourg and Lyon. On 11 January 2015, France staged a mass demonstration in solidarity with French republican values: this was the largest outbreak of public emotion since the 1945 Liberation. The vast majority of French Muslim civic and religious leaders were prompt to condemn the attacks (Geisser, et al., 2017), apart from the leaders of a handful of radical mosques (in Lyon, for example). But the *Je Suis Charlie* movement that emerged from the events of January 2015, and which identified in solidarity with the victims of the attack, also prompted a new debate over the nature and the limits of the freedom of expression in France: had *Charlie Hebdo* gone too far in its satirical depictions of Mohammed? Did the internet security law, which followed a few months later and which authorized phone tapping, internet trawling and other measures including a prolonged state of emergency, contradict the spirit of 11 January by adopting an authoritarian approach to defend democracy from its adversaries? Since the attacks of January 2015, the threat of terrorist violence has never been far away and as Hill demonstrates in Chapter 13, it points to its interconnectedness with France's past and present global role.

That role lends itself to analysis through our twin lenses of transformation and resistance: against the backdrop of a long decade (2007–20) of European crisis – of the Eurozone, Europe's failings to handle migration flows, Brexit, and then the Covid-19 crisis of 2020 – we can see transformation through events themselves and also by design, in the case of Macron's insistence on shaking up the European Union order. We can see French initiatives for policy change meeting resistance from its neighbours including Germany, and we see Macron's repeated attempts to reconceptualize European order encounter if not resistance, then much surprise, at least publicly, on the part of his counterparts.

In the case of the decade of economic crisis that followed the collapse of Lehman Brothers in 2008, the collective EU response to the crisis had involved the imposition of tighter controls for those euro-member states in great difficulty – Greece, Spain, Portugal, Ireland, Cyprus – against a series of rescue loans with tough economic conditions attached. These political responses produced changes in the very nature of European governance in the form of major moves to a more fiscally integrated Europe from 2009 to 2014; and the heightening of European Commission oversight of national budgets given quasi-constitutional status in the 2012 Fiscal Compact treaty. And these changes laid bare a line of territorial tension between a number of financially rigorous Northern European countries, and the perceived 'laxists' in Southern Europe, with France oscillating between the two. One side effect of the economic crisis, and the euro-zone crisis in particular, was to weaken the (social-democratic) linkage of the European Union with a European social model whose ambition is to ensure more than residual social rights. France's Socialist President Hollande (2012–17) was unable to ensure either a renegotiation of the Fiscal Compact Treaty upon arrival in office, despite his promises to do so, or a supply-side relaunch thereafter, and these failings exacerbated existing depictions of France as a 'flawed democracy', as discussed by Drake and Meunier in Chapter 12. Milner, in Chapter 10, moreover, points to the ongoing 'constraints of Eurozone governance' as a particular danger zone for Macron's domestic agenda of socio-economic reform.

A second dimension of Europe's crisis was the existential angst of Brexit following the UK's decision by referendum on 23 June 2016 to 'leave' the European Union. Led on the EU side by European Commissioner Michel Barnier and his task force, any divisions between member states were kept firmly under wraps for the entire duration of the three-and-a-half year period leading to the conclusion of the so-called New Withdrawal Agreement and Political Agreement (www.gov.uk/government/publica-tions/new-withdrawal-agreement-and-political-declaration) in December 2019 (the divorce), and in fact during the subsequent negotiations between the two sides on the 'Future Relationship with the EU' (www.gov.uk/government/publications/our-approach-to-the-future-relation-ship-with-the-eu), talks ongoing still at the time of writing. Of the EU27, French President Macron was at the forefront of those using Brexit as a domestic political argument against those 'populist" forces that he believed threatened the European project with disintegration. Brexit was taken rather as a model to avoid, as chaos engulfed British domestic politics after the 2016 referendum. It served as a scarecrow against would-be *souverainistes*, in Paris in particular, and Drake and Meunier, in Chapter 12, explore the limitations of this framing of Brexit for Macron and his supporters in the 2019 European Parliament elections.

Migration formed the third challenge to the cohesion of the EU. In 2015, controversies were centred on the 'Balkans route' trodden by refugees fleeing civil war in Syria (especially) and Afghanistan and arriving in Greece before beginning a dangerous journey through the Balkans (Montenegro, Serbia, Croatia and Slovenia), with the ultimate objective of reaching Germany or the UK. The initial response of German Chancellor Merkel – *Wir schaffen das* (we can do this) – was interpreted as being one of generosity towards people in need, in accordance with a basic humanitarian norm. But this call for humanism was immediately rejected by a strong part of European public opinion as an invitation for migrants to keep coming to Europe, whatever the physical dangers. The first most critical phase was concluded with the negotiation of an agreement between the EU and Turkey in November 2015, whereby Turkey would retain refugees from war-torn Syria in return for massive financial aid. Closing the Balkans route in 2015 greatly reduced migration through this particular route, but the gap was filled by Libya, a failed state riven by competing warlords, one incapable of policing the movement of (economic and political) migrants. At the end of the 2014–19 period, the crisis appeared every bit as profound as that of the euro. Moreover, its roots lay outside of the control zone of the EU itself, being the product of war in Syria and Afghanistan, economic misery in Africa or Bangladesh, fleeing from dictatorship in Eritrea or from chaos in Libya (Bourreau and Pascual, 2019). Drake and Meunier, in Chapter 12, note how France under François Hollande did not during this time play a leadership role, despite the extent to which he took solace in foreign affairs.

For his part, once elected president, Macron prioritized, in his pitch to the world at large, a broad, European vision. In his seminal Sorbonne speech of September 2017 (Macron, 2017d), the French President called for no less than a European relaunch – a transformation by any other name – characterized by a more integrated foreign, security and defence policy; a budget for the Eurozone; measures to tackle the democratic deficit at the EU level (reforms of the European parliament, the introduction of EU-wide constituencies for the European elections; a new democratic dialogue across Europe) and a Europe that 'protects' its citizens (reforms of the posted workers' directive) and its industries (from Chinese takeovers, notably). These positions were a powerful restatement of French preferences, namely to ensure political supervision of the governing mechanisms for the euro; to facilitate transfers from richer countries (especially Germany) to poorer ones, in the name of economic convergence and solidarity, and to endow the EU with new fiscal resources. Success in extending the domestic message to the European level was rather mixed during Macron's first three years in office, as discussed in Chapter 12. There was a tentative reform of the posted workers directive, and there were modest moves towards creating a budgetary instrument for the euro-zone, though this fell far short of the fully fledged budget advocated by Macron. On the other hand, Macron's grand design encountered obstacles, not least from Germany, with the unexpected exception in May 2020 of a bilateral, Franco–German proposal to draw on EU-level debt to the tune of €500bn in support of regions of the EU worst affected by the Covid-19 crisis.

The extent to which Macron succeeded in articulating his domestic and European reforms 'in tandem' (Chapter 12) was very much a work-in-progress at the time of writing, in mid-2020. The 2019 European Parliament (EP) election was cast by the French presidency as a success: yes, his 'progressives' came second to Marine le Pen's 'nationalists', but the latter did not increase their share of the EP's seats, and the only other party to come anywhere near Macron's were the Ecologists (*Europe-Ecologie-les Verts* – EELV), reflecting the saliency of the environment, part of a Europe-wide movement. EELV polled 13.47 per cent, making it the third political force and gaining in legitimacy and credibility from its dissociation from the PS. Within days of the 2019 European election, President Macron played a master hand, as he virtually imposed the choice of the President of the Commission (Ursula van der Leyen, rather than Manfred Weber), propelled Belgian ally Charles Michel to be Head of the Council and successfully lobbied for compatriot Christine Lagarde as President of the European Central Bank. Macron appeared to benefit from the new constellation of forces at the European level (the closing years of German chancellor Merkel, the self-exclusion of the UK, and the isolation of Salvini's Italy), although the subsequent rejection by the EP of French nominee to the European Commission, Sylvie Goulard, by the EP diminished somewhat the leadership dynamic in favour of Macron.

Moving beyond Europe, President Macron made strong early claims in terms of transformation in the field of foreign and external relations (Cole, 2019) and of the necessary disruption of existing relationships. Such was the spirit of the claim, in an interview with the *Financial Times* (2020), that NATO was 'brain dead', and of his advocacy of moves to a more integrated European defence capacity. One observer went so far as to identify 'France's moment in EU and world affairs' (Laidi, 2019). In this area, as in the others, however, was this more a question of style than substance? At the very least, there is a capacity-expectations gap. Macron restored a measure of French prestige, but was largely absent in the Middle East, was confronted with an ambitious China in Africa and Asia and maintained an increasingly difficult and fractious relationship with US President Trump. There might have been a transformation of style (by comparison with his predecessor) but there was no fundamental shift in balance of international force in favour of France or any other European power. And then came Covid-19. In its early stages at least, the Covid-19 crisis demonstrated the extent of European divisions: between traditional allies such as France and Germany, as well as in relation to outside parties (first and foremost China and the United States). Whether the crisis also presented new opportunities to pursue a more expansive, joined-up European agenda lies beyond the limits of this work. Turning back to France, the Covid-19 crisis gave a new sense to the idea of disruption, but this was one that challenged Macron's mantra of *en même temps*, which might best be described as the poised and reasoned arbitration between alternatives and the adoption of hybrid solutions. The crisis shook the foundations of trust in the political regime (Goar, 2020) and presented unprecedented challenges for society (after a two-month total lockdown of the population) and the economy (which sank into economic recession, in France as elsewhere).

Conclusion: transformation and resistance

In his 2016 book *Revolution*, Emmanuel Macron made the theme of transformation into the central idea of his presidential platform. Though essentially contested and under-specified, we use this concept as the central one that ties together the various clusters of chapters in the book. Let us be clear: transformation is considered as a discursive claim, rather than an objective reality to be measured scientifically (this claim would require a different exercise altogether).

The chapters each engage in their own way with the theme of transformation. In recent decades, various attempts have been made to describe an elusive transformation of French society. In the 1980s, Mendras celebrated the Second French Revolution (Mendras, 1987), at around the same time as Furet and Rosanvallon (1988) identified the end of the French exception. These studies reflected the optimism of the age, as France finally caught up with its century (Hoffmann, 1994), or adapted to (neo-liberal) global economic order after the early Mitterrand years (MacClean, 1996). By the turn of the century, however, France was being described as in decline (Baverez, 2005; Smith, 2003) or even in freefall (Drake, 2004). In the third edition of the current series, Levy, Cole and Le Galès (2008) identified the transition from Chirac to Sarkozy as a 'half-way house'. If we fast-forward one decade, the very contemporary binary rejection of the 'old world' that underpins *En Marche!* and the Macron enterprise indicates a firmer direction of travel (though one that remains deeply ambivalent). None of these attempts to frame continuity and change is satisfactory, yet each contributes something. The France that we observe in Macron's first mid-mandate is one that is sufficiently robust to provide a clear distinctive model, yet also one that continues to demonstrate difficulty in adapting to external transformations.

The tensions between these forces of transformation and resilience are articulated in distinctive ways in the various chapters. Chapter 2 discusses Macron's disruptive political leadership as a force for transformation, while Chapter 3 provides a detailed analysis of how Macron won the 2017 election. Chapter 4 analyses the transformation of the party system and the new political career opportunity structures produced by the victory of *En Marche!*, while Chapter 5 charts the changing political and policy dynamics of the FN/RN by comparing Jean-Marie Le Pen and daughter Marine's stewardship of the movement. Chapters 6 (Catholics) and 7 (new family modes) engage with very different types of religious and bio-ethical transformations, with their accompanying zones of resistance. Chapter 8 discusses the uneven and incremental changes in local and regional governance over the past decade, while Chapter 9 dispels various myths of the nature of tolerance and racism in French society. Chapters 10 (on socio-economic policy) and 11 (on the Yellow Vest movement) consider two very contrasting movements and moments within the Macron presidency, lying at different ends of the transformation–resistance spectrum. Chapters 12 and 13 offer a set of concluding judgements on the European, external and foreign policy dimensions of transformation.

Overall, our collective analyses show scepticism of evidence of a shift in the political system. As Evans and Ivaldi (2018, p. 16) argue in their analysis of the 2017 French elections: 'The very forces which led to this unprecedented electoral result continue to push against the new executive and its legislature, and (…) it is by no means certain that the renewal of French politics that its victors have claimed is indeed a renewal, or can form a stable basis for a new democratic life in the country'. We are inclined to agree with this statement. To take transformation literally would imply understanding history as a teleological process (with a beginning, a middle and an end) rather than an iterative one or as an eternal recommencement. We prefer to reason in favour of understanding French politics as a complex eco-system, influenced by specific political traditions, institutional practices, political discourses, social forces and external actors and actions, yet capable of adaptation and perpetual evolution.

2 CAN THE FRENCH PRESIDENCY SURVIVE? POLITICAL LEADERSHIP IN CRISIS

Helen Drake and Alistair Cole

This chapter takes as its subject the first three years of Emmanuel Macron's presidency (2017–20), as well as the leadership of Macron's immediate predecessor, François Hollande, French President from May 2012 to May 2017. In late 2019, the Macron presidency was already being recast by its protagonists as a performance in two acts, the *Before* and the *After,* to denote what the political executive was hoping would be a successful pivot away from the intense opposition and resistance that met central planks of Macron's project of transformative 'revolution' within two years of the new president taking office (Macron, 2016b). As a matter of fact, the *After* never arrived, since France, in keeping with the rest of the world, was struck in early 2020 by the Covid-19 virus pandemic. The disease caused excess mortality despite the cancellation of elections and the placing of the entire population of metropolitan and overseas France in lockdown for months, with severe restrictions on personal freedoms and the closing of borders to all but essential traffic. The French economy entered a deep recession (*Le Monde*, 8/4/20), and within a matter of just a few weeks, the task of leading France had become unexpectedly yet more complex and uncertain.

The chapter starts with a review of the French presidency at the moment of Macron's election in May 2017. From that snapshot in time, it looks back to the balance sheet of his predecessor François Hollande and forward to the first three years of Macron's presidency. In keeping with conventional approaches to the study of the French presidency (Elgie, 2013), these parts of the chapter focus on the president's formal power and powers relative to other institutions, bodies and forces, including the prime minister and government and the president's parliamentary majority; these are what Hoffmann (1990, p. 82), in his study of President de Gaulle, referred to as the president's 'supports'. Beyond those relations, moreover, lie the connections between the presidency, on the one hand, and on the other, intermediary bodies such as organized capital and labour, local and regional power bases. Presidents also have to manage contact with public opinion, the media and 'the street' (Reynolds, 2020). Sometimes, they also find themselves forced to respond to amorphous threats and crises, such as the terrorist attacks that plagued Hollande's presidency, climate change, the global health crisis of 2019 onwards and, on a different scale, the fire that almost destroyed the iconic cathedral Notre Dame in Paris in April 2019. Success or failure in managing this dynamic set of relations conditions a French President's formal capacity to lead a national project or implement a programme of policy change. Already by the time of Macron's election, there were signs that the authority of the presidential function was on the wane. Hollande did not even seek a second term in office, such were the meagre sources of authority remaining by the end of his term; his predecessor President Sarkozy had fought but failed to secure one. Macron went on to encounter serious, widespread resistance in the country at large, and a loss of trust early on in his mandate. In the annual IPSOS-SOPRA-STERIA (2018) survey on French attitudes towards institutions, for example, the French presidency was trusted by only 34 per cent of respondents in 2018, down from 44 per cent one year earlier and well below the degree of confidence expressed in local mayors (68 per cent).

How are we to understand this decline in presidential authority, when formally the French President's resources remained intact, if not enhanced, since the 2008 constitutional reforms, which as Elgie points out (2013, p. 23), benefited the president at the expense of the prime minister? We extend our perspective, in the following section, to address broader questions of political leadership that shed light on the French presidency, in particular the Macron mandate. Notably, neither Hollande nor Macron incarnated the charismatic form of leadership that is deemed to underpin genuine transformation. In contemporary times, charisma is typically understood as the expression of the leader's *je ne sais quoi* which defies objective description. That 'something' harkens back to the religious nature of the sacred bond between the charismatic leader and their followers. In Hollande's case, the explicit quest for 'normality' eschewed the very idea of such a connection. On the face of it, Macron fits more closely the easy stereotype of the charismatic leader (his youth, his looks, his luck, his fortune). Yet in the foreword to the paperback edition of her biography of Macron (2019, p. xviii), Pedder points to the 'stupefying degree of loathing for the president, and the violence that this unleashed'. In the absence of charisma, relations between leaders and the led must be perpetually made and remade on a transactional basis, and both presidents encountered repeated resistance that corroded their capacity to act, let alone lead and transform France. If not charismatic, we ask whether Macron is nonetheless a 'disruptive' leader (Drake, 2018, 2020). We understand disruption as essentially transformation *without the politics* in the sense of strong partisan or ideological identification. In the business world, it has come to mean the rejection of existing business models and the asking of new questions: (why) does business have to be done *like this*? In its intent, disruption is to business as revolution is to politics. Lichfield (2020) memorably described Emmanuel Macron as a 'revolutionary in a suit, not a politician', and Macron himself invoked the prospect of 'revolution' in his 2016 campaign volume (Macron, op. cit.).

In our conclusions, we return to our opening question: can the French presidency survive? Both Hollande and Macron presided in an age characterized by the sway of populists promising facile solutions to complex problems (Dignan, 2019; Fieschi, 2019). Macron explicitly styled his own leadership as a battle to hold these populists at bay. But this strategy was not without its own perils, invoking as it does a 'Manichean division between [...] the "good democrats" and the "evil populists"' (Mudde, Cas and Rovira Kaltwasser, 2018 in Drake, 2020, pp. 16–17). Speculating over whether Marine Le Pen will campaign for the 2022 presidency or not, and her chances of winning if she does, seems beside the point if it is the presidency itself that is in question: the French electorate by 2022 will have elected and rejected a hyperactive president (Sarkozy), a normal president (Hollande) and, perhaps, Macron too. Since the presidency is umbilically entwined with the Republic that in 2018 celebrated (remarkably quietly) its 60th anniversary, its demise would spell uncertain futures for French democracy. We end with reflections on the lessons from crisis – terrorism for Hollande, Covid-19 for Macron – for French political leadership and the Fifth French Republic.

The French presidency in 2017

The diminishing of French presidential authority contrasts with the considerable constitutional, institutional and historical resources of the office. Since 1962, the constitution of the Fifth French Republic provides for the direct election of the president, who as commander-in-chief, is constitutionally bound to guarantee national independence and ensure the integrity of the French territory. By arbitrating between other powers, he (there has yet to be a female president of the Fifth Republic) also guarantees the continuity of the state (*Conseil Constitutionnel*, n.d.). At the heart of this arbitration is the relationship between the president, the prime minister and government. The president nominates the prime minister and, in practice, can remove him or her from office (the Fifth Republic has known only one female prime minister, Edith Cresson, who served for just 11 months in 1991–02). The prime minister is in charge of the government, which 'determines and implements' national policy, but it is the president who chairs the Council of Ministers. The government and prime minister are responsible to parliament, which can, however, be dissolved by the president (in consultation with the prime minister and leaders of the two houses of parliament, the National Assembly and Senate).

This regime has been classified as a semi-presidential hybrid (Duverger, 2000; Elgie, 2013) and has provided for considerable variation over time in the *power* of a president, as distinct from his constitutional and institutional *powers*. From 1965 to 2002 the direct election of the president usually encouraged a left–right bipolar partisan competition for the conquest of the key institutional office (see Chapters 3 and 4 in this volume). Once elected, a president therefore depended on his partisan support in parliament – his parliamentary majority – to support his government and endorse his presidential programme. Under the original terms of direct election, the presidential term was seven years (*le septennat*), compared with a five-year term for parliament. At two points in the past (1986–88 and 1993–95), facing parliamentary elections in year five of the *septennat*, the president – François Mitterrand – had to 'cohabit' for the remainder of his term with a prime minister, government and parliamentary majority from opposing political camps. In 1997, President Jacques Chirac called early elections which he lost, taking him into a full *five* years of cohabitation. During this time, the constitution was revised to reduce the presidential term from seven to five years (*le quinquennat*), thus aligning the presidential and parliamentary electoral cycles. The reform also provided for the presidential election to precede the parliamentary contest, thereby consolidating the institutional ascendancy of the presidency. Because both the presidential and parliamentary elections were held in 2002, the second Chirac presidency had the luxury of enjoying a clear, five-year horizon without having to face national elections. Sarkozy repeated the feat in 2007, as did Hollande in 2012 and Macron in 2017. Cole (2012) notes how the shorter presidential term logically invites a 'fast' presidency, exacerbating ambient trends – 24-hour rolling news cycles; social media – of speed and short-termism.

During the periods of cohabitation in particular, but even when the president does enjoy partisan support, historical and informal sources of presidential power are vital crutches of presidential authority. These resources include the myth of heroic leadership (Hoffman, 1967), which took root in the days of Charles de Gaulle's presidency (1959–69). Since history 'looms large in contemporary France' (Drake, 2011, p. 8), this is a narrative which still offers a route for presidents, however formally diminished, to solemnly incarnate national unity. This pertains not only in times of crisis, but in the so-called 'reserved domain' of foreign policy and international affairs. Nowhere is the Gaullist framing of the French President's role as incarnating 'greatness' more relevant than in the sphere of foreign policy, lent credibility because of France's status as the leading continental military power with its own independent nuclear force. In the EU too, France accustomed itself early on to playing a leading role, and no French President to date has deviated from this rule.

How did Presidents Hollande and Macron activate or squander these resources, and to what effect?

François Hollande: the limits of a 'normal' presidency?

François Hollande's presidency was blighted from the start by his inability to control the Socialist Party that had taken him into power. As former party leader, Hollande had not repaired the fault lines in the party (over Europe, for example, and economic policy) that went on to weaken and fracture his presidential majority in parliament for the duration of his *quinquennat*. In turn, Hollande found himself drawing tactically on his constitutional right to switch prime ministers mid-course as a method of balancing the factions he faced. This was not a recipe for stable government.

Party and parliament in rebellion

Indeed, and almost from the outset, President Hollande's actions were contested by a group of PS rebels able to muster the support of between 30 and 50 deputies – *les frondeurs* – in the National Assembly (the lower house), and who came close to calling into question the government's parliamentary majority. The image of disharmony was increased by the lack of discipline on the part of the coalition partners which Hollande had drawn, or had hoped to draw, into government. From the outset, neither the Left Party, nor the Communist Party participated in the first of Hollande's administrations, the Ayrault government. The decision of *Europe Ecologie-les Verts* (*EELV*) to then withdraw from this government in 2014 signalled a turning point for the president, both politically and in terms of policy focus, with Manuel Valls appointed to replace Ayrault as premier in April 2014. Valls was much less tolerant with party indiscipline, or of open challenges to his authority. Faced with the continuing rebellion of *la fronde*, the Valls government used the restrictive article 49, clause 3 of the constitution to ensure the adoption in 2015 of none other than the *Loi Macron*, an umbrella law containing several – mainly symbolic – measures of economic liberalization. The experience of Ayrault and – especially – Valls in fact renewed with a constant in the history of the French left in governmental power: challenged from its left by rebellious deputies and the extra-parliamentary party organization and from its right by forces convinced that the left could never govern with credibility. The Hollande presidency became equated with a sense of drift, of weak government and of Socialist Party internal dynamics continuing to play themselves out within the government (Davet and Lhomme, 2016).

These were unfortunate developments given Hollande's avowed intention to strengthen the collective operation of the executive by rehabilitating the role of the premier, cast as a simple collaborator under Sarkozy. Similarly, the desire to restore a parliamentary vision of democracy, a stance both in line with the traditional PS critique of the overly presidential character of the Fifth Republic and articulated to distinguish Hollande from his predecessor, Sarkozy, had the effect of strengthening the *frondeurs*. This was a development that had been exacerbated by the primaries organized in 2011 to designate the Socialists' candidate for the 2012 elections and where the leading candidates were, in practice, deemed to represent a faction within the party, and hence became untouchable. This was the case notably of Arnaud Montebourg, the prophet of anti-globalization, who criticized the Ayrault and Valls governments, even while serving as minister.

The normality trap

Hollande's past as a party leader arguably left him more attuned to engineering compromises in party conferences when in opposition than engaging in the exercise of presidential authority when in power. In addition to this occupational hazard, Hollande's 2012 candidacy itself was based on his political positioning as being a 'normal' candidate and president, a style deliberately adopted to be the counterpart of the flamboyant Sarkozy (Cole, 2017). Once elected, however, Hollande was trapped by this frame of normality. During the 2012 presidential campaign, normality was presented as an ethical standard, even more than as a way of conceiving presidential practice. It included a commitment to keep Hollande's private life out of the public domain, but the public jealously displayed by Valerie Trierweiler, his former partner, destroyed this aspiration very early on. Subsequently, Hollande's use of *gendarmes* to cover his visits to Trierweiler's successor, Julie Gayet, for example, or the state secrets disclosed to journalists, were deemed to be inappropriate acts for a French President (Davet and Lhomme, 2016). Hollande's political judgement was then called into question by a succession of scandals involving leading figures of the Socialist-led government (Amar, 2014). By far the most important scandal was that of Jérôme Cahuzac, the Budget Minister whose reputation for integrity was shattered by evidence of a secret bank account in Switzerland (despite his repeated denials).

Even Hollande recognized retrospectively the shortcomings of his construction of the 'normal' president, misunderstood by an important fraction of the population and falling short of the idea of the presidency as an 'elective monarchy' (Hollande, 2018, pp. 26–8). Normality was also an inauspicious leadership mode for times that were anything but normal, *viz* the aftermath of the 2008–09 financial crisis and the large-scale terrorist attacks wreaked on France in 2015 and 2016. To some extent in those circumstances, Hollande demonstrated an ability to rise above normality and to the occasion, appearing as the embodiment of national unity in the mass rallies of 11 January 2015 in defence of the Republic after the attacks on *Charlie Hebdo*, and in the convoking of the Congress in Versailles (see Elgie, 2013, p. 22 for this instrument) just days after the 13 November 2015 outrage (the murders at the Bataclan nightclub and vicinity). At the end of December 2015, Hollande obtained some of his best poll ratings since taking office. The year 2016, however, brought fresh challenges to the president's authority: a lack of parliamentary support forced him to abandon a constitutional reform that would have allowed French nationals convicted of terror offences to be stripped of their French nationality; and terror struck again in Nice, on the very day – 14 July – that France was celebrating its national Bastille Day. The state of emergency declared after the 2015 attacks was prolonged and accompanied Hollande through the remainder of his term.

Leadership on the world stage

With further regard to the more symbolic aspects of the presidential role, Hollande took solace in European and foreign affairs, the traditional 'reserved domain' of the French President (Howorth, 2013; and see Chapters 12 and 13 in this volume); in Hoffmann's terms, these were his 'balancing tactics' (1990, p. 82). Hollande grew into the role of president in part as war leader: from 2012 to 2017 France intervened in Mali and the Central African Republic and participated in air strikes in Iraq and Syria. In terms of its soft power, Hollande's team successfully managed the global environment conference, the COP 21, which brought leaders across the world to Paris in December 2015 to pledge their commitments to control global warming and save the planet. But his attempts to reorient the EU in a less 'liberal' direction, however, and to assert an alternative, more growth-inspired path did not amount to much, and the traditionally central Franco–German relationship was undermined by disagreements over economic policy, the growing imbalances between the French and German economies, controversies over fiscal policy (the support from France and Italy for monetary easing put into place by the ECB at the height of the euro-crises of 2012 and 2015) and attitudes towards the euro-crisis in general and Greece in particular. These difficulties were counterbalanced by some successes at EU-level brinksmanship (avoiding a 'Grexit' in 2015 and curbing Russia's territorial ambitions in its near neighbourhood via the 2015 Minsk agreement).

Ultimately, Hollande's reputation suffered from the ambiguities of the 2012 campaign itself, from the lasting impression of a lack of coordination within the executive and in relations with the Socialist-led majority and, above all, by perceptions of a poor policy record, marked notably by the failure to control unemployment. In terms of political style and exercise of the presidency, Hollande's governing method – social democrat and partnership-based – did not fit easily with the speed required for effective decision-making under the 'fast' presidency. In 2016, faced with the prospect of another round of primary elections to designate the candidate who would contest the 2017 presidential elections on the left, Hollande drew his own conclusions and declined to enter the race: the first time that an incumbent French president had 'abdicated' in this way.

In the heat of that 2017 campaign, Hollande's achievements were overlooked. It is possible to propose a more favourable reading of his presidency. He went a good way towards modernizing France's social relationships (the introduction of gay marriage). His economic liberalization measures (the

2014 Competitiveness Pact-CICE) boosted investment, began to reconcile the business community and helped to restore France's competitiveness. He addressed stubborn issues of decentralization (see Chapter 8) and introduced tough measures to bring public finances under control (see Chapter 10). He performed an important role in foreign policy and EU affairs, as seen above (and in Chapters 12 and 13). And he embodied national unity in a genuinely presidential way in the aftermath of the terrorist attacks of 2015. As memory fades, and the circumstances of his departure wither, some historians will be inclined to rehabilitate Hollande, perhaps the last Socialist president of the Fifth Republic.

Emmanuel Macron – Jupiter in the house

Emmanuel Macron's election in 2017 was a mixture of *luck* (no mainstream party succeeded in taking their candidate to the second round of the elections, and his opponent Marine Le Pen and her party were normalized in many respects but still constituted a perceived threat to democracy for sufficient numbers of voters), *ability* (for example his display of competence and self-control in the TV debate face-off between himself and Marine Le Pen on 3 May 2017) and successful *campaign tactics* (the momentum and scale of his movement, *En Marche!*). Macron had no track record of substantial party affiliation, nor significant leadership experience: in comparison with the majority of his opponents, he was an unknown, untested political quantity. He *was* acknowledged to be a risk-taker: not even his fiercest adversary could contest his appetite for risk, as demonstrated by giving up his position as Economy, Industry and Digital Minister in 2016 to launch himself into the risky venture of *En Marche!* Resigning from the civil service to be able to contest the campaign points in the same direction. Some common themes that emerge in early studies of the early days of the Macron mandate, moreover, were the president's personal qualities of determination, resolution and brilliance, coupled with the notion of 'the killer' who wrong-footed his previous political boss, President Hollande, by standing for election (Besson, 2017; Couturier, 2017; Prissette, 2017; Sirinelli, 2017; Bourmaud, 2017; Pedder, 2018).

Back to the future: Gaullism restored?

Formally speaking at least, the new president held the key levers of political power necessary for a strong presidency: a decisive victory against Marine Le Pen in the second round of the presidential election (66 per cent), an absolute majority in parliament for his party following the June 2017 elections, a fragmented parliamentary opposition and a coalition of political support that spanned the traditional parties and from which he drew his first government. On these foundations, he rapidly amassed new resources in the form of a tightly knit band of loyal followers (including Ismael Emelien, Julien de Normandie, Christophe Castaner, Alexis Kohler inter alia), all devoted to their leader, and acting as guarantors of the core legitimacy of Macronism as they saw it, and gatekeepers to Macron himself. In these ways, Macron soon developed a presidential practice that renewed with traditional visions of the Fifth Republic, whereby the president was involved in almost everything: for example, appointments in the public sector media, the functioning of the justice system, the details of economic management, movements in the civil service and so on.

In the first months in office, furthermore, Macron adopted a model of governing most obviously associated with de Gaulle, namely policy-making by decree (*ordonnances*), as well as broadening the government beyond party politicians to include high civil servants and representatives of civil society and the professions. There are other similarities between Macron and the early Gaullist period, not least in Macron's sidestepping of party politics and the old political cleavages in favour of the creation of a new presidential movement to support the action of the individual. During his first year in office, in other words, Emmanuel Macron invested the presidency with renewed energy and strengthened the claim to understanding leadership, from a strategic institutionalist perspective, as a process of control of one institution over another (Elgie, 1995). Macron also had a theory of power that he publicly articulated at the time of his campaign. This guided his interpretation of the presidency from the outset, and subsequently became somewhat notorious, providing a rich seam of material for political satirists. In an interview with the business news magazine *Challenges*, Macron had commented (Macron, 2016a) that whereas his predecessor, Hollande, did not believe in a 'Jupiterian' president, he, Macron, did not believe in a 'normal' president. The metaphor stuck, despite Macron's protest that he never actually claimed to be the Jupiter of French presidents, and it did have the advantage of functioning as an image of his own creation, rather than allowing a critical media to dictate a negative image, as in the case of Hollande and 'Flamby': a damaging nickname invented by opponents to describe François Hollande as being as soft and wobbly as the popular dessert of that name.

The Macron presidency began without delay with a series of 'big bang' decrees reforming France's labour legislation, which, the new president argued, was necessary to open up the economy. Labour law enshrined in the Code du Travail was, he pronounced, 'obsolete and unsuited' to the contemporary world of work (Macron, 2018). Far-reaching reform of labour law formed part of a wider programme of deregulation, complemented by tax reductions and overhaul of the social security system, in order to reduce public debt and encourage business investment. This early policy intervention was led by executive power vested in a leader able to command an absolute parliamentary majority, as seen above.

Simultaneously, the new president fully inhabited his constitutional right to pilot and personalize France's European and international policy, investing this too with energy and symbolism. As for his predecessors, key foreign and defence policy decisions and initiatives taken were taken at the Elysée, either by Macron or in regular meetings with the chiefs of staff (Guisnel, 2018). From the very beginning of his mandate, Macron was rather more than a traditional French foreign policy president, however: he was admired elsewhere as a model of dynamic, youthful and reformist political leadership, rather like Justin Trudeau in Canada.

Leading but not governing?

Cole (2019) has written how during the first year in office, and unlike his predecessors, Macron was able to conceive of European, international and global economic pressures less as external constraints with negative implications for French identity and sovereignty and more as a set of endogenous opportunities that would feed back positively into his programme of domestic transformation. This core message of transformation as a modified form of revolution, the title of his 2016 book, focused on political elites and the need to reform and modernize the political system. It implied strategic thinking, if not a coherent political project in the usual sense. Drake (2020) and Stephens (2019) have both referred to Macron's Cassandra-like habit of unveiling his vision of the future, warts and all, to interlocutors not necessarily thrilled at the prospect. In this, former French ambassador Gérard Araud has described Macron (and Barack Obama) as a 'hyper-realist in a world of passion' (2019; and see Chapter 12 in this volume).

Far-sightedness and long-term thinking rely for their implementation on robust governance structures and practices, over and above loyalty to the 'chief'. In this, the Macron method and its tendency to sidestep tried and tested actors and routines (be they traditional party politics or other transmission belts of power and influence that link the national with sectoral, regional and local interests, such as locally elected mayors, regional presidents, trade unions) showed its flaws early on. In other words, the president made a virtue of not governing with civil society, identified as one of the forms of blockage in France. One plank of Macron's thinking was in fact to inject the 'immobilism' of old governance habits with new energies, such as higher standards of political ethics, a rationalized National Assembly (see Cole, 2019, p. 79) and greater diversity in political personnel, beginning with the membership of Macron's parliamentary party, LREM. The new president spelt out these changes in explicit terms on the first occasion that he availed himself of his constitutional right to convene both houses of parliament in the form of Congress, at Versailles, on 3 July 2017 (*EM!*, 2017); at the time of writing, however, much of this institutional innovation remains largely a dead letter (see Chapter 4 in this volume).

In practice, the task of governing, coordinating and managing, as distinct from leadership, has been an Achilles' heel for the president. The relationship with Prime Minister Édouard Philippe (May 2017 to July 2020 when he was replaced by Jean Castex in a government reshuffle), by all accounts relatively constructive, provided important cover, but cracks in the system have shown. For example, the aspiration to higher standards of political conduct (conceived in the wake of the criminal cases brought against former Presidents Chirac and Sarkozy for financial wrong-doing and the fall from grace of former Prime Minister and 2017 presidential candidate François Fillon over the misuse of public funds in 'Penelopegate' – see Chapter 3) was undermined by a particular scandal that emerged from within the very heart of the Elysée in July 2018. The scandal broke when videos of Alexandre Benalla, one of President Macron's key security advisors, were published by *Le Monde*, allegedly showing Benalla roughing up protestors during the 1 May 2018 demonstrations in Paris. The scandal cast light on the malfunctioning of the security services under Macron and the willingness of his advisors to take the law into their own hands. It was interpreted in the press as symptomatic of a leadership style based on the primacy of a network of personal loyalties to the exclusion of professional and political influences from outside the inner circle.

More serious in its impact on presidential authority was the president's routine dismissal of the 'old world' of parties, associations and other *corps intermédiaires*. His refusal, for example, to even engage with the reformist trade union, the *Confédération démocratique du Travail* (CFDT), undermined Macron in the eyes of many of his own *En Marche!* deputies. This is a leadership approach that has weakened the institutional thickness of the Fifth Republic, with, arguably, the effect of harming the social acceptability of Macron's reform programme amongst the population as a whole. Nowhere was this risk more exposed than in the *gilets jaunes* movement (see below; and also Chapter 11 in this volume) that erupted in late November 2018, compounded a year later by the lengthy strike action in opposition to proposed pensions reform. Above all, the Yellow Vests crisis demonstrated the weakness of Macron's linkages within civil society, which directly challenged his personal style, perceived to be out of touch, arrogant and overly condescending. How can we understand this dysfunctional breach between leader and led at the heart of the French Fifth Republic? A symptom of contemporary leadership struggles far from confined to the case of Emmanuel Macron and the French presidency?

Leadership in crisis? The French presidency in perspective

It can be argued that the study of political leadership, at least within political science, still favours the analysis of 'formal power relationships' over the informal, since the former 'are observable and measurable in a way that informal power relationships are not' (Baturo and Elkink, 2018, p. 506). The downside for the authors is that '[t]hese studies tend to overlook the importance of informal power structures, personal relations and processes not measured by a purely institutional approach (…)' (ibid.). We did describe above how President Macron relied on extra-institutional circles of collaborators, 'informal power structures' in their own right, and we saw the limitations of these when the going got tough. But in hollowing out tried and tested political routines, and in the absence of a well-established, substantive presidential party on which to rely to diffuse the presidential message and disseminate support, did Macron the president become significantly reduced to Macron the individual? Personalization of the French presidency is nothing new (Gaffney, 2015), but it carries risk in a context and in an age where the relational aspect of leadership has become so fraught. Leaders' relations and interactions with their various constituencies *do*, nonetheless, lend themselves to analysis in a more meaningful way than the observation of personal traits and characteristics, particularly when these are taken out of context.

Fitting in or standing out?

For example, today's leaders must relate to fast-moving social and societal norms, even fashions, that transcend any one leadership mandate. They must engage with France's 'hybrid media system' which, while 'not all-powerful', is nonetheless comprised of 'powerful communication actors' (Kuhn, 2020, p. 244). Similarly, Cole (2019) points to the pressures of celebrity politics, or '*pipolisation*', to use the French neologism, on Presidents Hollande and Macron alike. It is a phenomenon that involves the breaking down of the traditional distinction between public and private. Former President Sarkozy appeared to relish the opportunity to share his private life and loves with the French people, and the image of the 'bling-bling' president stuck. François Hollande's quest to embody an alternative 'normality' involved, in practice, embarrassing personal revelations at the pen of his former partner Valérie Trierweiler (see above) and by his own indiscretions in conversation with investigative journalists (Davet and Lhomme, 2016). In the case of Emmanuel Macron, the president's private life was more strategically curated, to the point where it can be argued that Brigitte, Macron's spouse, played an important role in the overall political enterprise of 'Macronism', and that together, Brigitte and Emmanuel Macron formed a coherent political household, akin to that of the Pompidou family at an earlier period (Derrien and Nedelec, 2017). However, President Macron's initial attempt to forge a new, formalized role of 'first lady' for his wife, complete with its own budget, which was for him a show of transparency, was decried by his critics as a distasteful and wasteful innovation, and he did not pursue it (*The Guardian*, 2017). Institutional innovation on this point had eluded him.

In other regards too, President Macron bucked the trend. Aged 39 when he became president, he was younger than the previous most youthful French President, Valéry Giscard d'Estaing (1974–81), and he played up this fact, as we saw above in the matter of foreign policy. With regard to familial and sexual norms too – married to a woman 26 years older to form a blended family – Macron is perhaps a man more of his times than any French President before him (Drake, 2020). Moreover, Macron very publicly embraces – flaunts, even – those areas where he could be said to transgress the norms associated with a French President, with regard, for example, to his fluent and unabashed use of the English language. Here, it has been argued, he has broken a taboo, particularly given his use not just of the English language, but English *business* speak (Chapuis, 2018).

Language and communication are fields rich in resources – and pitfalls – for any leader, and the French President is no exception. Macron did not leave this to chance. He articulated and initially followed an explicit communications strategy which saw him staying out of the fray of 24/7 running commentaries: his first televised interview only took place in October 2017. Some deemed it to be a 'catastrophic' approach (Chapuis, op. cit.). This is to overstate the case, but nevertheless, such a de Gaulle-style preference for rare public appearances and portentous speeches was increasingly difficult to maintain, as reforms gathered pace and, with them, wide-scale resistance, in particular in the form of the *gilets jaunes* movement which erupted in late 2018 (see Chapter 11); and crises were on the horizon too. In April 2019, as Macron and his government wrestled with the Yellow Vests' demands, Notre-Dame Cathedral burned to within minutes of collapse; the following month, in the elections to the European Parliament, LREM tailed the RN in second place; and by the end of the year, France was on the brink of its most serious health crisis ever: the outbreak of Covid-19.

Lessons in leadership

Faced with intractable opposition at large, populist rivals in the political sphere and/or in the midst of crisis, what options does a leader have? The answer lies in part in their formal resources, and we saw above how Macron's leadership style had to an extent hollowed out certain of those traditional forms of support (a cohesive presidential party and parliamentary majority, relays of elected officials throughout the territory amongst others and legitimacy and credibility as career politician). Hollande, for his part and in his memoirs (Hollande, 2018), describes his own leadership style as that of a social-democratic transactional leader: a style that posited a preference for formal consultation over open confrontation. Hollande's celebrated capacity for synthesis was developed over years as First Secretary of the Socialist Party, and involved an intimate knowledge of PS networks and of the changing centre of gravity within the party (Raffy, 2011). In the Macron administration, it can be argued that there was a weak culture of negotiation and a determination to avoid the logic of transaction. All parties might have been involved in round table talks over the labour or pensions reform, for example, but such partnership was limited to negotiating details of implementation, rather than genuinely co-producing public policy. Earlier, the reform of the national railway, the SNCF, and the legal statute of railway workers, was announced as a big bang, rather than a compromise as a result of negotiation.

Beyond these methods of governing lies the leader's relationships with those that they lead, nominally at least, in which reside much of the legitimacy of a leader's authority. The concept of charisma as articulated by Max Weber refers to legitimacy conferred on a leader by virtue of the followers' belief in the leader's vocation to lead. The bond was a matter of faith, and all its mysteries, not dissimilar to mediaeval distinctions between the king's physical, mortal body and the eternal, 'body politic' that he represented (Manow, 2010). Appetites for this form of revered authority figure have by and large in contemporary democracies been displaced into the realms of celebrity worshipping and royalism, and the term is typically reduced to mean a 'strong' leader, or one with appealing qualities (subjectively ascribed). But the scapegoating of political leaders (the blame-game), the criticisms of them for being both too distant and not-like-us (Macron, for example, on account of his wealth) and, on other occasions, too coarse and ordinary (in Macron's case, for using blunt, insensitive language about the unemployed, for example) are vestiges of the myths of leadership that included sacrifice (today's scapegoats) and relied on a sense that the leader was different, but legitimately so (see Grint, 2010).

Macron's ability, unfortunate or otherwise, to switch between these different linguistic registers is matched by his confidence to experiment more broadly with modes of communication beyond the limited register of televised addresses, media interviews and press conferences. In the face of the intense *gilets jaunes* resistance sparked in late 2018 by proposed hikes on fuel tax and following a halt in the legislative programme, the president, in a *Letter to the French* (Elysée, 2019), launched a listening exercise to address the grievances of the Yellow Vests, namely the Great National Debate. Tran, in Chapter 11 of this volume, provides a highly critical analysis of the scope and effects of this exercise, which nonetheless merits closer attention.

We have posited elsewhere (Drake, 2018) that Macron's approach to leadership bears resemblance to a style popularized as 'disruptive', a notion typically applied in the business world to describe new entrants into mature markets. Central to the idea (see Dignan, 2018) is *process*: disruption is an attack on the business model or operating system of the status quo. Translated into the political arena, to call Macron a disruptive leader is to point out, as Hoffmann (1990, p. 89) wrote of de Gaulle, that perhaps 'he [is] almost as concerned with showing the proper road as with reaching the destination'. In Macron's case, this 'proper road' ploughs through existing distinctions, or categories, typically thought of as sacrosanct. This would fit with criticism of Macron as having no overarching political project, where a 'project' is traditionally a requirement if not a defining characteristic of aspiring French Presidents. It makes sense of the nomenclature of his movement – *en marche* meaning 'in movement'. It provides context for his much derided verbal tic – *'et en même temps'* ('and at the same time') – whereby he rejects, seeks to transcend or even efface existing binary distinctions (such as between left and right in politics or between social protection and economic dynamism).

Successful disruption in business is also deemed to rely on a mode of leadership where leaders are open to learning and to sharing authority with the rest on the basis of the soft skills of emotional intelligence, including humility and optimism. These are elements that lend themselves to subjective interpretation and bias, but evidence does exist that Macron can draw on reserves of such human qualities (*Le Monde,* 2017). Even policy U-turns and tactical retreats (viz. constitutional reform) can be construed as heuristic methods of movement, and these lead to the image of an apolitical president attempting to revolutionize France without due regard for the depth of its political culture. Macron's political discourse is as emotional as it is rational (ibid.), and his love of France explicit; but after three years, his presidential authority based on a challenge to the 'operating system' of French politics was in serious trouble – perhaps 'the theory of disruption has no place in politics' (Drake, 2018). Could a crisis save the presidency?

Conclusions: can the French presidency survive?

The *Financial Times* reported that, in his interview with the paper in the midst of the Covid-19 coronavirus pandemic and 'when asked what he [Macron] has learnt about leadership, he candidly admits that it is too early to tell where this global crisis will lead. Mr Macron says he has deep convictions about his country, about Europe and the world, and about liberty and democracy, but in the end the *qualities that are needed in the face of the implacable march of events are humility and determination'* (*Financial Times,* 2020, our emphasis). More prosaically, the French response to the crisis saw President Macron focusing on solemn messages of national unity (his 13 April 2020 television address was watched by over 35 million French people), while turning for action to precisely the matrix of vertical and horizontal instruments of power and governance that he had formerly seemed to overlook.

What other options does France have to bring French institutions, including the presidency, in line with its people and its times? Voices in favour of a Sixth French Republic less centred on presidential authority do exist amongst France's political parties, even if they are not in the majority. In the 2017 presidential election campaign Jean-Luc Mélenchon, leader of *France Insoumise* on the left of the political spectrum, was placed fourth with 19.58 per cent of the votes on a programme that clearly advocated for a change of regime. A new constitution drafted by a constituent assembly would usher in a Sixth Republic, which would provide for a 'permanent control' by the people in the form of referenda proposing the destitution of any elected official, right up to and including the president (Corlay, 2017). This was a position long held by Mélenchon and was representative of a typical preference, on the French left, for a more distributed form of authority within the French Republic. The Socialist Party for its part, in the figure of the heavily defeated Benoît Hamon in the 2017 campaign, argued for a less president-centric regime that he deemed 'immature in relation to the democratic demands of French society' (quoted in Corlay, ibid.). In contrast, François Fillon, for LR, branded any notion of institutional change as the sign of a failing regime, although both he and Marine Le Pen, for the RN, envisioned greater recourse to referendum and a reduced number of deputies and senators in parliament.

Macron's own preferences were for 'political renewal' by amendment of the existing 1958 Constitution. The thrust of the proposed constitutional modification was proposed in July 2018 in a bill designed to deliver democracy that was 'more representative, accountable and efficient' (*Vie publique*, 2020a). Macron's intention had been to 'strengthen the quality of legislative procedure' (*Elysée*, 2017; see Chapter 4 in this volume too) by numerous means, including introducing a measure of PR in elections to the National Assembly, reducing the number of parliamentarians by 40 per cent in total and limiting the number of times a parliamentarian could stand for election. Progress stalled on the bill in July 2018 and, a year after that, came back to parliament in revised form as the bill for 'the renewal of democratic life' (*Vie publique*, 2020b), in response to the findings of the Great National Debate. Amongst other changes, PR would count for 20 per cent and not 15 per cent of the total seats in the National Assembly, and the scope of a form of citizens' democratic participation known as the 'shared initiative referendum' was extended. The bill had yet to become law by mid-2020. 'Citizens' consultations', on the other hand – on climate change, on the future of Europe and on life after Covid-19 – did take place.

Beyond these more formal scenarios for change, it is possible that France has outgrown its presidency, in all its most recent heroic, 'speedy', normal and Macronian incarnations. In a crisis, moreover, it is not uncommon to see leadership revert to the norm of 'hegemonic masculinity' (Geva, 2020) that privileges action, decisiveness, certainty and (overbearing) confidence – the 'determination' without the 'humility' that Macron identified as key. Such constructions of masculinity can be found in the repertoire of women leaders as well and are associated with the legitimation mechanism of charisma (Geva, ibid.). Leadership responses to international shocks, including Brexit and now Covid-19, have already been the object of enquiry into the extent of gendered responses to crisis (Guerrina et al., 2018; *The Guardian*, 2020), and in this respect it is hard to disagree with arguments that claim that 'the French presidency [has] been constructed and consolidated as a masculine institution' (Achin and Lévêque, 2017, p. 279). In this light, Emmanuel Macron's promises of renewal must be set alongside the possibility that 'the normalising power of the presidential institution may well limit the revolution being announced' (op. cit., 288); and beyond the case of President Macron lies the possibility that the French presidency itself has outlived its cultural shelf-life, with respect to norms of gender, but not only.

In Michel Houellebecq's 2015 novel *Soumission,* as a final consideration here, France, in 2022 and after a second Hollande term, elects its first Muslim president by way of an electoral pact between mainstream parties to keep the far right out of the presidency. He subsequently transforms the Fifth Republic into an Islamic republic. Looking beyond Houellebecq's own mindset and notoriety, the fictional scenario invokes the idea that repeated, protracted crises of leadership may ultimately bring forth what political anthropologists identify as 'tricksters': characters intent on subverting the system that brought them to power (Horvath, Szakolczai and Marangudakis, 2020). Neither Hollande nor Macron could be described as such since each in his way sought to shore up, not tear down, the 'indivisible, secular, democratic and social' Fifth Republic by restoring authority to the presidency as they saw fit. In Macron's version of disruptive leadership, the presidency was a vehicle for transforming France, not the target of attack. In seeking to normalize the presidency, Hollande did not intend to define it out of existence. Faced with crisis in the form of the 2015 terror attacks Hollande mobilized the presidency to restore a palpable sense of national unity – but it was short-lived. President Macron's authority in the crises he encountered was arguably more tenuous; it is too soon to tell for certain. If tricksters are waiting in the shadows to pounce on the resources of the French presidency to contort the Republic out of its current shape, then reforming the presidency, and with it the distribution of political authority more widely, seems more urgent than ever.

3 UNDERSTANDING THE UNEXPECTED: EMMANUEL MACRON'S VICTORY IN THE 2017 FRENCH PRESIDENTIAL ELECTION

Camille Bedock

The 2017 French presidential election attracted considerable attention. After the 2016 Brexit vote in the UK, the election of Donald Trump in the USA, and in a context of increasing support for radical and populist movements, Emmanuel Macron appeared as the embodiment of the potential success of liberal values and pro-European support, all the while rejuvenating the political elite. In the aftermath of his victory, hagiographic accounts of his election flourished and underlined a triumph against all odds of a young prodigy with an impeccable curriculum vitae, owing everything to his optimist and audacious vision and shining personality, his rejection of the 'old world' of sclerotic political parties, and his ability to embody France's aspirations to trust civil society and youth and *finally* reform itself (Besson, 2017; Couturier, 2017, Prissette, 2017). Obviously, these a posteriori reconstructions are inaccurate, incomplete and biased when seeking to understand the reasons behind Macron's success. In reality, his electoral victory was largely unexpected, as he entered politics only in mid-2016 after having left his post as Minister of the Economy and created from scratch a new political movement, *En Marche!*. The year 2017 also saw the acme of support for the National Front in a French presidential election, and marked the surge of a radical left protest vote. More generally, the 2017 French electoral sequence represents the culmination of a progressive reshuffle undergone by the French party system over the previous few years.

The traditional French governing parties, like most of their European counterparts, had since 2008 been under considerable stress in a context of economic crisis, anti-establishment attitudes and the rise of protest politics. In that context, Macron represented a rather original mix of anti-establishment protest on the one hand, and mainstream politics on the other. In a national context characterized by a distrust of the political elite, Macron built his success on a call for a radical reshuffle of the party system that he characterized as in a stage of sclerosis. This claim resonated largely with the call of both the radical left and right who both reviled the mainstream parties (the Socialist Party and the Republicans). Although this stage was set early on in the campaign, no one, before early 2017, would however have bet on Macron's chances of victory.

The situation changed dramatically when the leading mainstream Republican candidate, François Fillon, selected after a largely followed primary election, and who was largely expected to win, started to fall in the polls after revelations of alleged ethical misconduct on his side. Amid evidence of the fictitious employment in parliament of various members of Fillon's family over the previous decades; and accusations of similar wrongdoing by Marine Le Pen and her party, the then National Front, Emmanuel Macron saw his support growing rapidly.

In other words, the 2017 French electoral sequence should be read through two opposed readings: a structural one and a contingent one. On the one hand, one could interpret the victory of Emmanuel Macron and of *En Marche!* in the legislative elections as the result of long-term trends already at work for several years in France and other European countries: the decline of traditional government parties at the expense of more radical alternatives; the growing relevance of a cleavage opposing liberal and pro-European values against an anti-elite, Eurosceptic bloc; the complete reshuffle of the existing party systems. On the other hand, this unexpected victory also resulted from a very unusual political campaign characterized by two elements: the organization of open primaries; and corruption scandals. The primaries of the right and the centre, and later on of the *'Belle alliance populaire'* ('Great Popular Alliance' regrouping the Socialist Party and other small Green and left parties), led to the emergence of two candidates, each of which polarized their camp: François Fillon on the right, and Benoît Hamon on the left. Corruption scandals, for their party, played a central role in the 2017 outcome and decisively weakened the main challenger from the Republicans, François Fillon, and also Marine Le Pen, to a lesser extent.

After detailing the main electoral lessons that can be drawn from the 2017 electoral sequence and the main dividing lines of the French electorate, this chapter analyses in turn the structural and contingent causes that can explain the extent to which the French electoral order was overturned in 2017. It concludes by examining hypothetical scenarios for the restructuring of the French political space.

The 2017 French electoral sequence: the end of the 'world of yesterday'

In his final biographical book, the Austrian author Stefan Zweig dwelt on the 'world of yesterday' crumbling before his eyes. In many regards, the 2017 French electoral sequence constituted the end of a long era for

French politics, marked in particular by the weakening of the two political forces that had alternated in power since 1958 (the Socialist Party, and the Republicans, Tables 3.1 and 3.2); and by the surge of Emmanuel Macron and his political movement *En Marche!*. After securing the first place with 24.1 per cent of the vote in the first round of the presidential election ahead of Marine Le Pen, the candidate of the National Front, Macron won 66.1 per cent of the votes in the second round (33.9 per cent for Le Pen on a 74.5 per cent turnout). Macron then managed to obtain a comfortable parliamentary majority in the legislative elections for the party that by then had renamed itself *La République en marche* (LREM, 'The Republic on the move').

Whereas François Hollande had managed to secure 28.6 per cent of the votes in the first round of the presidential election in 2012, Benoît Hamon, the PS candidate in 2017, and despite the support of the Greens, obtained only 6.4 per cent of the votes, the second worst result for a Socialist candidate since 1969. François Fillon, the candidate of the Republicans in 2017, with 20 per cent of the votes, lost 7.2 percentage points compared with the score obtained by Nicolas Sarkozy in 2012. The combined score of the Socialist and the Republicans in 2017 at the presidential election amounted to only 26.4 per cent of the votes in 2017, compared with 55.8 per cent in 2012. The debacle was almost as bad for the Socialist Party in the legislative

Table 3.1 Comparison of the votes for the candidates by party in the first round of the presidential election, 2012–17

Party of the presidential candidate	2012	2017	Evolution
NPA (New Anticapitalist Party)	1.1	1.1	=
LO (Worker's struggle)	0.5	0.6	+0.1
Left Front/France insoumise (Untamed France)	11.1	19.6	+8.5
Europe Ecology – The Greens	2.3	–	
Socialist Party*	28.6	6.4	**–24.5***
Democratic Movement	9.1	–	
*En Marche!***	–	24	**+14.9****
UMP/Republicans	27.2	20	–7.2
Debout la France (France arise)	1.8	4.7	+2.9
National Front	17.9	21.4	+3.5
Others	0.4	2.2	+18
Total	*100*	*100*	

Source: Ministry of the Interior. *The Greens supported Benoît Hamon, the candidate of the Socialist Party. The change between 2012 and 2017 is calculated with the sum of the score of the Greens and the Socialist Party in 2012. **The Democratic Movement supported Emmanuel Macron (En Marche!) in 2017. The evolution is calculated with the sum of the respective scores of the Democratic Movement and En Marche! between 2012 and 2017.

Table 3.2 Evolution of the votes by party at the first round of the legislative elections, 2012–17

Party	2012		2017		Evolution (votes)
	Votes	Seats	Votes	Seats	
Far Left	1	0	0.8	0	−0.2
French Communist Party			2.7	10	+2.7
France insoumise (former Left Front)*	6.9	10	11	17	+4.1
Europe Ecology – The Greens	5.5	17	4.3	1	−1.2
Socialist Party	29.4	280	7.4	30	**−22**
Miscellaneous Left	3.4	22	1.6	12	−1.8
Radical Party of the Left	1.7	12	0.5	3	−1.2
Regionalists	0.6	2	0.9	5	+0.3
Democratic Movement	1.8	2	4.1	42	+2.3
En Marche!	–		28.2	308	**+28.2**
Republicans (former UMP)	27.1	194	15.8	112	−11.3
Various centrists**	2.8	14	3	18	+0.2
Radical Party	1.2	6			−1.2
Miscellaneous Right	3.5	15	2.8	6	−0.7
National Front	13.6	2	13.2	8	−0.4
Others	1.5	1	3.7	5	+2.2
Total	100	577	100	577	

Source: Ministry of the Interior. *In 2012, the French Communist Party presented candidates together with the Left Party in the Left Front. **The label 'various centrists' groups the New Centre and the Centrist alliance in 2012, and the UDI (Union of the Independent Democrats) in 2017.

elections, in which, in the first round, it lost 22 percentage points compared with 2012 (from 29.4 per cent of the votes to 7.4 per cent). The PS managed to keep only 30 seats out of the 280 it had in 2012.

All parties allied with the Socialists in government between 2012 and 2017 experienced losses in the legislative election (Europe-Ecology the Greens, Radical Party of the Left). The Republicans experienced an 11.3 per cent loss (from 27.1 per cent of the votes in 2012 to 15.8 per cent) and obtained its worse score in the history of the Fifth Republic.

La République en Marche, allied with the Democratic Movement, benefited from the losses of the two main governing parties and obtained 308 seats and 28.3 per cent of the votes in the first round. This result is particularly noteworthy for a political movement that had never stood for a legislative election in the past and that presented mostly unknown candidates in the election against very experienced politicians, even though the movement managed to rally some former Socialists and Republicans. Among the most notable defeats, several former Socialist ministers did not even manage to get through to the second round (including Benoît Hamon, François Lamy, Aurélie Filipetti or Matthias Fekl); several others lost in the second round (Jean-Jacques Urvoas, Myriam El-Khomri and Najat Vallaud-Belkacem). These legislative elections confirm the institutional 'honeymoon effect' following French presidential elections that leads to the reinforcement of the political camp of the winning president (Dupoirier and Sauger 2010; Evans and Ivaldi 2017).

Two political actors situated at the far end of the political spectrum compared with the traditional governing parties confirmed their already historical results of 2012. Marine Le Pen improved her presidential election score of 2012 by 3.5 per cent, managing to send the National Front into the second round of the presidential election for the first time since 2002 and securing the best score ever obtained for a FN candidate in the presidential election; 21.3 per cent. Jean-Luc Mélenchon (*France insoumise*) obtained 19.6 per cent of the votes in 2017, 8.5 per cent more than in 2012 when he already made a significant breakthrough. At the legislative elections, both the National Front and *France insoumise* obtained much more limited electoral results than in the presidential election. The National Front obtained roughly the same score as in 2012 with 13.2 per cent of the votes in the first round in 2017 but gained eight seats (two seats in 2012). *France insoumise* (not allied with the Communists as in the 2012 election) secured around 11 per cent of the votes in the first round (6.9 per cent for the Left Front in 2012) and gained 17 seats.

The electoral defeat of the previously dominant political actors of the Fifth Republic confirms trends already at work in 2012. However, for the first time, the previous duopoly of the Socialist Party and the Republicans over the presidency and the majority in parliament was completely dismantled.

Dividing lines among French voters in 2017

French voters in 2017 were particularly angry: angry at the incumbent president François Hollande in particular, and angry at their political elites in general. They were also strongly divided over cultural issues such as immigration, and over issues related to the management of the economy (specifically, the perceived consequences of globalization, European, integration and economic deregulation).

Just as they did in 2012, French voters expressed particularly harsh judgements on the action of the incumbent president. François Hollande was the first ever president of the Fifth Republic to decline to stand for re-election. His catastrophic popularity ratings largely explain this decision.

Hollande started with an approval rate of 55 per cent, the lowest in the history of the Fifth Republic, and finished his term with a 14 per cent approval rating only weeks before the 2017 elections (Evans and Ivaldi 2018). This drop was even more severe than Nicolas Sarkozy's, who experienced a very sharp decline of popularity during his single term. The French election study (Gougou and Sauger, 2017) organized straight after the second round of the presidential election in 2017 shows that only 0.5 per cent of the respondents were 'very satisfied' with Hollande's actions, and 18.8 per cent 'satisfied'. More than a third of the respondents (36.3 per cent) were 'not satisfied at all'. According to Evans and Ivaldi, these ratings can be explained by the 'disconnect between the performative and essentially rhetorical acts of the presidential campaign, on the one hand, and the reality of hard policies, on the other hand' (2018, p. 21). The disappointment concerned in particular his management of the economy: in 2017, only 16 per cent of the French people considered that the economy had improved during his term, whereas 52 per cent considered it had got worse. The election of Hollande in 2012 was, moreover, largely a form of punishment of the incumbents, Sarkozy and the Republicans, for their handling of the global economic crisis, and their lack of efforts to limit social inequalities (Grossman and Sauger, 2014; Sauger and Raillard, 2014; Lewis-Beck and Nadeau, 2015). But the inability of the new executive voted in in 2012 to bring back growth and to reduce unemployment and social inequalities soon appeared obvious to many citizens, explaining in turn largely the fall of its popularity (Sineau and Cautrès, 2013). More generally, Grossman and Sauger have shown how the centrality of the presidential election in France crystallizes excessive expectations that are destined to be shattered very rapidly, feeding the distrust towards French political institutions and their representatives (Grossman and Sauger, 2017). Such trends have been reinforced since the constitutional reform of 2000, when the mandate of the president was reduced from seven to five years. Shortly after this reform was approved by referendum in September 2000, in 2001, there was a reform of the electoral calendar to place the presidential elections immediately before the legislative elections.

French citizens have always distrusted their political representatives, but this disdain was particularly prominent in the 2017 elections. Historically, since 1990, France is one of the West European countries in which citizens least trust their political parties and politicians (Bedock, 2017, p. 15). A yearly poll conducted yearly since 2009 (*Baromètre de la confiance politique*, CEVIPOF) confirmed this growing trend: in 2017, fewer than 10 per cent of French citizens trusted political parties; 69 per cent did not trust the left or the right to govern the country; 82.5 per cent considered that politicians did not care about ordinary citizens; and 70 per cent were dissatisfied with the way democracy works in France (CEVIPOF, 2017). The French Election Study of 2017 (see Table 3.3) also showed how widespread negative opinions about politicians were during the presidential campaign.

Table 3.3 French opinions about politicians in 2017

	Agree
The majority of politicians do not care about people like us	69%
The majority of politicians are trustworthy	22%
The politicians are the main problem in France	47%
The majority of politicians are only interested in the rich and the powerful	62%
Corruption such as bribe-taking is widespread/quite widespread among politicians	85%

Source: French Electoral Study 2017

Only 22 per cent considered politicians as trustworthy, almost half of them agreed with the idea they were the main problem in France, and 85 per cent considered that corruption was a widespread phenomenon. By way of comparison, 38 per cent of French people thought that 'politicians [were] quite corrupt' in 1977, 55 per cent in 1990 and 60 per cent in 2006 (Chiche et al., 2010, p. 74).

Political attitudes during the 2017 political campaign were also marked by the salience of cultural issues related to immigration and terrorism (Evans and Ivaldi, 2018). Gougou and Persico demonstrate that, in 2017, the most important dividing line for the French electorate separated anti-immigration and authoritarian individuals from individuals in favour of immigration and culturally liberal (Gougou and Persico, 2017). The importance of these issues for both parties and voters confirms the 'hexagonal tension' identified by Tiberj more than a decade ago (2008), related to the growing importance of immigration in the political attitudes and behaviour of French voters. A survey conducted by the CISE (Italian Centre for Electoral Studies) in April 2017 on the perceptions of policy issues by French people showed that a vast majority of the French electorate (between 70 and 79 per cent) supported policy objectives such as the limitation of the number of refugees, the ban of the Islamic veil in public space, the limitation of immigration and the restriction of welfare for immigrants (Emanuele, De Sio, and Michel 2017). In that survey, 91 per cent considered that the fight against terrorism was a priority (the same proportion as those prioritizing action to bring down unemployment), making it the joint main concern of the electorate. Evidence based on cross-national rolling surveys has also shown that the terrorist attacks in France in 2015 and 2016 shifted part of the public opinion towards the right on security issues, particularly among left-wing sympathizers (Brouard, Vasilopoulos, and Foucault, 2018). The French Electoral Survey of 2017, moreover, confirms this polarization of the French electorate on cultural issues (Table 3.4). There is an opposition between, on the one

Table 3.4 Opinions about immigration among voters for the four main candidates in the 2017 presidential election

% who agree	Mélenchon voters	Macron voters	Fillon voters	Le Pen voters	All respondents
Immigrants are generally good for France's economy	**61%**	55%	38%	11%	43%
Immigrants are a source of cultural enrichment	**79%**	77%	55%	21%	60%
Immigrants come for social benefits	29%	33%	58%	**81%**	48%
There are too many immigrants in France	34%	38%	62%	**93%**	56%

Source: French Electoral Study 2017

hand, far-left and centrist voters who hold quite positive views about immigration; and on the other, right and far-right voters who overwhelmingly see immigration as a cultural and financial burden. Le Pen voters are particularly distinctive even in comparison with supporters of François Fillon, showing that the strong opposition to immigration remains a very distinctive trait of FN voters (See Table 3.4).

To put these trends in historical perspective, the tolerance of French people towards other groups and immigrants rose from 2012 and continued to rise during the whole term of François Hollande, after a sharp decline when Nicolas Sarkozy was in power, as evidenced by the longitudinal index of tolerance of Tiberj (Chapter 9). However, in 2016 it started to decrease again. What remains is the fact that these issues have been strongly politicized and polarizing in France for more than two decades (Castelli Gattinara and Morales, 2017).

On socio-economic issues, the main divide in 2017 was between neoliberal, Europhile and pro-globalization opinions on the one hand, and pro-state and anti-globalization opinions on the other (Gougou and Persico, 2017). As underlined by several authors and unlike previous campaigns, Europe and most specifically socio-economic questions at the European level were quite heavily politicized during the 2017 campaign. Indeed, 'Europe' now constitutes a cleavage in its own right in the French electorate (Schön-Quinlivan 2017; see also Chapter 12). In the French Electoral Study of 2017 (Gougou and Sauger, 2017), around half of the respondents were in favour of economic policies run by the state and considered that globalization harmed the functioning of democracy in France. A large majority of French people (63 per cent) agreed on the negative effects of globalization on France's economy. Table 3.5 shows that supporters of Mélenchon to some

Table 3.5 Opinions about the economy and globalization among voters for the four main candidates in the presidential election in 2017

% who agree	Mélenchon voters	Macron voters	Fillon voters	Le Pen voters	All respondents
Customs barriers and economic protectionism should be restored in France	36%	26%	37%	**91%**	48%
Globalization prevents democracy from working as well as it should in France	45%	25%	30%	**69%**	44%
In order to face economic issues, it would be better to have state control rather than freedom for firms	**61%**	29%	17%	42%	41%
Economic consequences of globalization are extremely negative for France	65%	47%	49%	**83%**	63%
Being part of the European Union is a good thing	62%	**86%**	79%	26%	60%

Source: French Electoral Study 2017

extent, and especially those of Le Pen, were much more critical of the effects of globalization on French economy and democracy than those who voted for Fillon and Macron. Le Pen voters were overwhelmingly supportive of economic protectionism through customs barriers, unlike other voters who were more divided on this point. Mélenchon's voters – and, to some extent, Le Pen's – were much more prone than those who supported Fillon and Macron to support state interventionism in the economy. Mélenchon voters were also much less Europhile than those who picked Macron or Fillon, but much more so than the voters of Le Pen of whom 74 per cent considered that belonging to the EU was a 'bad thing'.

To summarize, those who voted for Mélenchon differentiated themselves from the rest of the respondents because of their support for state control of the economy. On the rest of the items, they were quite close to the average respondent. The voters of Macron were particularly Europhile, and much less critical of globalization and its effects than the average respondent. Fillon voters were the most liberal economically, and were, like the supporters of Macron, more supportive of the EU and less critical than the average voter of the consequences of globalization. Finally, Le Pen's supporters stand out as particularly distinctive: 9 out of 10 supported protectionism, they were extremely critical of the effects of globalization on the French economy and democracy, and they were particularly Eurosceptic.

This brief portrait of the French electorate in 2017 confirms that the traditional left–right cleavage that had structured French political space before that year could not, in 2017, fully explain the main political attitudes of the various groups of voters. The reinforcement of the anti-globalization/Euroscepticism cleavage, taken together with more 'traditional' issues such as immigration and the economy, blurred the dividing lines.

The changing French party system between 2007 and 2017: from *tripartition* to tripartism

The results of the 2017 election, despite the clear elements of change it involved, did not happen out of the blue. There are, in fact, several elements of continuity with recent electoral cycles, and evidence that this reshuffling of the French electoral space was already well under way at least a decade before 2017.

Like many other democracies, France has, since the 1980s, experienced the appearance of cleavages linked with globalization and European integration, and with the politicization of immigration, and of the environment (Bornschier and Lachat, 2009). This led to the emergence of a strong far-right party, the National Front, and to a growing importance of immigration and law and order issues in the political debate (Tiberj, 2012). As a consequence, between the end of the 1980s and the end of the 2010s, France was characterized by the *tripartition* (three-way split) of the electoral space (Grunberg and Schweisguth, 1997, 2003) with one left-wing block dominated by the Socialist Party, a moderate liberal right-wing block dominated by the Republicans and a far-right block dominated by the National Front. The three blocks were largely impermeable, each with clearly distinctive policies on socio-economic and cultural issues, and distinct, differentiated electorates. Political parties operated on the basis of *front républicain* (Republican front, or *barrage*), meaning that governing parties would systematically support any adversary of the National Front in the event that it got to the second round. However, by the time of the election to the presidency of Nicolas Sarkozy in 2007, this system of *tripartition* started to break apart. The invisible, moral barrier between the electorate of the National Front and that of the UMP (Union for a Popular Movement, currently called the Republicans) became increasingly porous. This was because of the positions held by President Sarkozy on law and order, and immigration; indeed, he deployed a rhetoric formerly 'owned' by the National Front (Gougou and Labouret, 2013). This strategy explicitly aimed to win over FN voters and explains why the 2007 elections constituted a 'breaking point' for the French electoral order (Martin, 2007). Sarkozy's strategy had two immediate consequences in the 2007 presidential election: first, reducing Jean-Marie Le Pen's score to 10.4 per cent; and second, the new strategy of the centre-right with François Bayrou who obtained 18.6 per cent of the votes. The latter launched the Democratic Movement (*MoDem*) in the aftermath of the 2007 election and put an end to the previous strategy of alliance with the then UMP. In the longer run, elections in France became increasingly 'overshadowed by the threat of the radical right' (Evans and Ivaldi, 2018), with a continuous growth in support for the National Front between 2010 and 2017.

In 2012, the French electoral order cracked further still, this time on the left, with the surge of the *Front de gauche* (Left Front). This electoral alliance was composed of the Left Party and the French Communist Party. It was created in 2008 and supported a clear break from what they described as the neoliberal and moderate economic policies implemented by both parties of government (the Socialist Party and the UMP). The Left Front obtained 11.1 per cent of the votes in the 2012 presidential election. The reshaping of the far-left in France between 2012 and 2017 then took the form of the rise of the political movement of Jean-Luc Mélenchon, la *France insoumise* (Untamed France). This movement progressively took its distance from its former Communist ally with which Jean-Luc Mélenchon had always had complicated and contentious relationships. The aim of LFI was to build a political force with the potential to become the dominant actor of the left, with an anti-austerity and Eurosceptic political agenda. LFI clearly sought to differentiate itself from the Socialist Party.

In the 2012 presidential election, the National Front obtained its best score at the time with 17.9 per cent. Even though the swing from right to left with the election of Hollande may have given the illusion of the return of the 1984 electoral order to some, the 2012 election confirmed that the right and the far right now shared the 'same core ethnocentrist and conservative electorate' (Gougou and Martin, 2013, p. 142). Even though Bayrou only secured 9.1 per cent of the votes in the 2012 presidential election, the electoral potential for a strong centrist and Europhile alternative in the next electoral sequence was, with the benefit of hindsight, confirmed.

The emergence of a 'new electoral order' was evidenced by the results of the intermediary elections between 2012 and 2017 and by a new situation, not of *tripartition*, but of tripartism. As explained by Martin (2015), tripartition refers to the division of the *electorate* between three blocs (left, parliamentary right and far right), whereas tripartism refers to the structure of the French *party system*. From 2012 onwards, there were three electoral forces (PS-LR-FN), each in a position to qualify for the second round of the presidential election. Only two of them were able to win in the second round despite their relative weakness compared with the FN (PS, and LR) thanks to the two-round electoral system which is more favourable to parties that are able to build alliances in view of the second round, which is not the case of the FN (Sauger, 2007). During the municipal elections in 2014, the FN secured 1,544 municipal councillors and 11 municipalities. It then secured the first position in the European elections of 2014 with 24.9 per cent of the votes, and again in the European elections of 2019 with 23.3 per cent of the votes. The departmental and regional elections of 2015 were marked by a severe electoral defeat of the Socialists, a large victory for the Republicans in terms of seats but not in terms of votes; and also a strong surge of the National Front that usually did not fare so well in local elections (25.2 per cent of the votes in the departmental elections, 27.7 per cent in the regional elections). As always, the National Front, despite its historical results during the first round of the 2015 elections, was severely penalized in the second round. This is the consequence of the electoral system and of its inability to gather a majority of the votes in the second round, as vote transfers occur between government parties mostly (Ehrhard, 2016; Sauger, 2007), but also of the Republican front preventing alliances with the National Front, as described above. What was striking compared with usual second-order elections in France is the inability of the Republicans to strongly capitalize on the unpopularity of the left government (Martin, 2016), unlike what had happened in the previous electoral cycle (2007–12) in which the PS made electoral gains at the expense of LR (Evans and Ivaldi, 2018).

To summarize, several elements were in place well before the 2017 election: the waning of the governmental left challenged by a radical left alternative, the relative difficulty of the Republicans in benefitting from the weaknesses of the Socialists and the strengthening of the National Front. This growing polarization of the French system and the challenge to government parties should not hinder the fact that, as underlined by Evans and Ivaldi, only 'one year prior to the 2017 race, the French political system appeared irrevocably locked into a situation of alternation between left and right' (2018, p. 28). With the exception of the 2007 election and the performance of François Bayrou, no centrist electoral force advocating for an electoral strategy outside of the two main traditional governing parties had managed to build a credible alternative over the long term. Most observers foresaw that the 2017 presidential and legislative elections would end just like the intermediary elections occurring between 2012 and 2017, that is to say with an alternation in favour of the Republicans because of the weakening of the Socialist Party, and the inability of the National Front to win in the second round. The ability of Emmanuel Macron to overthrow the existing system must, we argue, be therefore imputed to contingent events occurring before and during the campaign.

The 2017 campaign: primaries and corruption scandals as catalysing events for Macron's success

The 2017 presidential campaign was certainly one of the most eventful that ever took place in France (Evans and Ivaldi, 2018). Firstly, the two main government parties – but also the Greens – chose to use open primaries to select their candidates, leading to the victory of unexpected challengers (respectively, François Fillon and Benoît Hamon) from the poles of their respective camps. Secondly, the courts played an unprecedented part in this campaign, by indicting the frontrunner, François Fillon, and summoning the main radical candidate, Marine Le Pen, a month before the election, to appear in front of a judge over allegations of misusing European Union funds.

The Republicans organized their primaries in November 2016 ('primary of the right and of the centre') and opened it to any voter accepting to sign a declaration endorsing 'the values of the Republicans' and paying a small fee. The Socialist Party and other small allies organized the 'primary of the Great Popular Alliance' in January 2017 on the same lines. The open primaries pose a fundamental challenge to the logic of the French presidential election: the successful presidential candidate must always be able to gather support not only within her own political family during the first round, but also outside of it during the second. What was made obvious during the two open primaries is that this particular mode of candidate selection, due to the characteristics of the 'selectorate' (i.e. party sympathizers who paid a small fee to participate in the primaries), favours outsider candidates rather than the favourite and moderate ones. Put forward by Bueno de Mesquita et al., the selectorate can be defined as the body of people responsible for the selection of a candidate or a leader for an election (Bueno de Mesquita et al., 2005). In this regard, the primaries were instrumental for Macron's victory because they led to the selection of candidates holding more extreme ideological positions than the optimal presidential candidate, opening a vast electoral space for a centrist candidate such as Macron (Evans and Ivaldi, 2018). Indeed, the voters who chose to participate in these electoral contests were sociologically very distinctive from the median French voter: richer, older, higher on the social ladder and more likely to hold a diploma, in the case of the participants in the primaries of the right and the centre (Braconnier, 2017), whereas this phenomenon was somehow less marked for the Socialists. In this regard, the open primaries could be compared to a form of limited or 'census suffrage' (Gouard et al., 2017, p. 1128). Also of note is the very high level of politicization of those who voted at the primaries, who are distinctly more politicized and feel much more politically competent than the average voter (Gouard et al., 2017). As underlined by Mény (2017), the open primaries did not only fail to unite the troops within the parties before the campaign as expected by the headquarters of the two parties: they actually exacerbated intra-party tensions by leading to the selection of ideologically 'radical' challengers.

The primaries of the right and of the centre attracted 4.4 million voters, twice as many as the primary held by the Socialist Party in December 2005, and a third more than the PS primary of 2012. Nicolas Sarkozy was eliminated in the first round, and the moderate front-runner candidate Alain Juppé came second, far behind François Fillon. The latter, indeed, managed to secure first place in the first round (44 per cent of the votes) and won with a very comfortable margin the second round (66.5 per cent of the votes). This unexpected victory of François Fillon in the primary has been attributed to two elements: his use of a Christian rhetoric valuing an *ethos* of honesty, discretion, hard work and selflessness (Lebaron, 2017); as opposed to Nicolas Sarkozy and his pro-business, neoliberal and very conservative political platform suiting the core electorate of the Republicans, as opposed to Alain Juppé.

On the left, on 1 December 2016, François Hollande announced his decision not to run again. During the subsequent primaries, held in January 2017, Manuel Valls, Hollande's prime minister between 2014 and 2016, represented the liberal wing of the Socialist party, and was opposed by two main contenders: Arnaud Montebourg and Benoît Hamon. Both men were so-called *frondeurs*: they belonged to the minority of the Socialist Party who had strongly criticized François Hollande's economic policies during his presidential term. Mirroring the primary of the right, the 'moderate' candidate on the left lost: Benoît Hamon won the primary against Valls with 58 per cent of the votes in the second round. As underlined by Mény,

> "By the last week of January, the script of the presidential race seemed to be already fully written: Fillon was a strong candidate of a centre-right that over the past five years had taken over most of the local, provincial and regional governments and recovered its grip on the second chamber, the Senate; (...). [O]n the other side, Hamon was a weak candidate whose programme was contested and criticized in its own camp" (2017, p. 271).

This scenario failed to materialize because of the scandal that befell François Fillon in late January 2017. Over the course of the primaries of the Republicans in August 2016, François Fillon had launched an attack on Nicolas Sarkozy, one of his main opponents as seen above, and who was embroiled in many political scandals. Fillon had argued: '*Qui imagine le général de Gaulle mis en examen*? ('Who would imagine General de Gaulle being indicted'?). As already mentioned, the integrity and moral rectitude claimed by François Fillon was one of his main assets in the presidential race. But the campaign took a new turn when the *Canard enchaîné*, a satirical weekly newspaper featuring investigative journalism, on 25 January 2017, revealed that Pénélope Fillon (Fillon's wife) had allegedly received several thousands of euros for a fictitious job as a parliamentary assistant to her husband between 1997 and 2012. The 'Penelopegate' story then dominated the French media for several weeks. It was followed by numerous unforeseen developments, making the situation of François Fillon ever more untenable. Successive revelations in the *Canard enchaîné* showed that his children had also been paid to work for him in parliament for around 50,000 euros between 2005 and 2007. Other newspapers provided evidence of sumptuous gifts including watches and suits, thus further destroying the image of the sober, Christian François Fillon. He was officially indicted on the 14 of March 2017 by the *parquet national financier* (the national financial prosecutor) for misuse of public funds (Evans and Ivaldi, 2018a).

Despite a promise made on 26 of January 2018 on France's prime-time TV news channel TF1 to resign if he were to be indicted, Fillon kept on with his campaign until the end. This was despite several attempts to replace him by Alain Juppé; and numerous defections within the candidate's team, including among his closest lieutenants. Penelopegate was concomitant with the steep decline of Fillon's popularity, and the rise of Macron. Whereas in November 2016, in the aftermath of the primary, Fillon had around 28 per cent of voting intentions, this figure dropped to 20 per cent in late January and stabilized at around 18 per cent for the remainder of the campaign. Conversely, whereas Macron had attracted around 14 per cent of the vote intentions in November 2016, this figure reached 20 per cent in late January 2016 and quickly stabilized at around 25 per cent after that date.[1]

By the end of the campaign, Macron had also benefitted from the indictment of Marine Le Pen, who was embroiled in several scandals. The National Front has always used anti-corruption rhetoric to castigate corrupt political elites. However, Marine Le Pen was summoned by judges in Nanterre over accusations of a breach of trust in the European Parliament on 3 March 2017 for having diverted funds intended for parliamentary assistants to pay people working for the party. She decided to block the investigation by refusing to answer to the justice until after the end of the parliamentary campaign, and was only officially indicted on 1 July 2017. This came at a time during which the National Front was involved in several other scandals including irregularities with the funding of the 2012 presidential campaign, and assistants in the Nord-Pas de Calais region used to work for the party, amongst others (Le Monde, 2017). Although Le Pen tried to divert attention from the 'plot' against her and her party, these scandals did affect her: her voting intentions went down from around 25 per cent in March 2017, to around 21 per cent for the remainder of the campaign.

Future perspectives for the French party system

Macron's victory was certainly not a foregone conclusion, nor was it an inexplicable surprise. It was an 'election by default' because of the gap between supply and demand: what the parties were offering, in comparison with the demands of the voters (Rouban, 2018). Macron managed to occupy a vast electoral space created by the decline of the two traditional governing parties, and by the polarization of the French electorate that was increasingly divided around issues linked to globalization, immigration and Europe, as seen above. The precursors of 2017 were already to be found at least ten years before Macron's election, in particular after the strategic decision made by Sarkozy to go after Le Pen's voters. The increasing porosity of the electorates of the right and the far right, followed by the gradual demise of the Socialist Party and the emergence of a strong far-left contender (Mélenchon and LFI) created a strong opportunity for a centrist, market-friendly and Europhile candidate in 2017 to win the election. Over the course of the campaign, the designation of two ideologically polarizing candidates by both the Republicans and the Socialists further widened the political space available to Emmanuel Macron. In the end, the corruption scandals that

---

1   Source: *Enquête électorale française 2017*, CEVIPOF-Le Monde, IPSOS-Sopra Steria

damaged Fillon and Le Pen constituted the decisive trigger for Macron's election, by decisively weakening François Fillon who had been the favourite to win. The question that remains at the time of writing (2020) is of course the following: was 2017 a blip, or the founding year of a new electoral order in France?

We have seen above that there are three possible scenarios to be considered: the return to the former status quo with a bipolarized political life and a strong National Front (now the National Rally), the quadripartition of the French political space into four blocs and the emergence of a three-pole party system with a strong centre.

The first hypothesis seems very unlikely, at least at the national level. Despite the ability of the Republicans, and, to a lesser extent, of the Socialist Party to win in many cities in the 2020 municipal election, the grip of LREM and of the National Rally at the national level has been confirmed after 2017 in the European elections in 2019. The national and the local French party systems appear increasingly distinctive. At the national level, the Socialist Party, now headed by Olivier Faure, remains extremely weak and quite unclear with regard to its position *vis-à-vis* other parties. Benoît Hamon jumped ship to create a new political movement called '*Génération.s*' The results of the European elections of 2019 showed that the French left is more divided and fragmented than ever. The Socialist Party, allied with other small parties gathered a mere 6.2 per cent of the votes. *France insoumise* lost many votes compared with the presidential elections and only gathered 6.3 per cent of the votes, whereas *Génération.s* obtained 3.3 per cent. The Greens, traditionally in the left bloc, obtained 13.5 per cent of the votes and managed to successfully challenge the former leadership of the Socialist Party in French metropolises in the 2020 municipal election, such as Marseille, Bordeaux, or Lyon. In December 2017 the Republicans elected a new leader, Laurent Wauquiez, who then resigned after the very bad results of his party during the European elections, as the Republicans only won 8.5 per cent of the votes, replaced by Christian Jacob in 2019. The party is still torn by a gap between a more 'progressive' right and a 'conservative' one (Bernard, 2018). This led to the departure of several important political personalities such as Xavier Bertrand or Alain Juppé. The National Rally confirmed that it is the main contender of *En Marche!* at the national level, and secured the first position in the European elections of 2019 with 23.3 per cent of the votes (22.4 per cent for *En Marche!*).

The second hypothesis is that of a *quadripartition* of the French political space with LFI, PCF, *Génération.s* and possibly the Socialist Party and the Greens drifting on the left, LREM as a moderate left party, LR as a moderate right party and RN on the far right. This would imply that the more moderate wing of LR prevails and continues to refuse to work with the far right, and that *En Marche!* occupies what was previously the position of the Socialist Party and the centre. Again, this seems quite unlikely: after three years in power, Macron and his majority have implemented pro-business policies and lean much more to the right than to the left in the eyes of French voters. An inquiry conducted one year after Macron came to office by the CEVIPOF and Ipsos show that 76 per cent of the respondents consider that Macron's policies benefit the more privileged, and position him on average at 6.7 on a 0–10 left–right scale (www.ipsos.com/fr-fr/grande-enquete-bilan-dun-de-presidence-demmanuel-macron). In other words, if anything, Macron and LREM tend to be replacing the centre-right rather than positioning themselves as moderate left. This leads us to the third hypothesis.

Some authors such as Robert Elgie underline the 'return of the eternal *marais*', i.e. a political life dominated by the centre (2018). The '*marais*' (swamp) refers to a (derogatory) concept coined by Maurice Duverger, who argued that France, between 1789 and 1958, had been governed by the centre over 80 per cent of the time (1964), including in 'centre' representatives of the so-called moderate left and the moderate right. Whereas French political life has been characterized since the 1980s by a strong bipolarization, with swings between left and right in government, and the existence of a strong far-right camp, the 2017 elections seem to suggest that the centre, understood in this context as a mix between LREM, *MoDem* and 'moderate' right and left defectors, is well placed to play a very central role in the new French electoral space. Gougou and Persico suggested in 2017 that we may witness in the future the emergence of a new *tripartition* with a far-left pole composed of LFI, the PCF, *Génération.s*, EELV and what remains of the Socialist Party; a far-right pole composed of the National Front, LR and other potential allies; and a centrist pole around LREM and defectors from the moderate left and the moderate right (Gougou and Persico, 2017). This, however, would imply that these parties are willing to coalesce or to form durable electoral alliances, a condition that is far from being fulfilled.

For the moment, there are many contradictory signals from the headquarters of the different political parties when it comes to the future alliances, making the recomposition of the electoral blocs particularly difficult to predict and the 'borders' of the three blocs porous and instable. The municipal elections of Spring 2020 have shown the ability of the Republicans to resist at the local level – in particular in medium-sized cities - and have suggested that the Greens may claim the leadership of (part of) the left in the following local and national elections. The extremely disappointing results of LREM, including in cities in which the movement had obtained very impressive results in 2017 confirm its lack of local anchorage and the difficulty to replicate at the local level the context that led to the victory of Macron and *En Marche!* in 2017. Finally, the National Rally failed to win major cities except for Perpignan, confirming its well-known difficulties to translate votes into seats both at the national and local level.

In the end, the French electoral landscape in 2020 resembles to some extent a form of the 'polarized pluralism' described by Giovanni Sartori (1976), characterized by two bilaterally opposed (and internally divided) camps that cannot unite and have little perspective of governing in the near future on either the left or on the right, and a strong centrist pole with ill-defined borders in a system characterized by fragmentation and ideological polarization.

4 ALL CHANGE? PARTISAN REALIGNMENT AND PARLIAMENTARY REFORM UNDER EMMANUEL MACRON

Rainbow Murray

The presidential and parliamentary elections of 2017 could be viewed as what Evans and Norris (1999) term 'critical elections', both in terms of their transformative effect and their relationship to broader political change. In this chapter, I explore two fundamental ways in which these elections were both the cause and consequence of more fundamental changes to the French political system. First, the election saw the definitive end of traditional bipolar (left–right) competition within France, with both the mainstream left and the mainstream right falling into the cracks between the centre and the extremes (see too Bedock, Chapter 3 in this volume). Second, the election triggered a drastic change in political personnel, with most of the political class being evicted and replaced with novices. I examine both sets of changes in more depth, contextualizing them within the broader landscape of French politics, considering how such fundamental changes came about, and debating their long-term implications for French politics.

For many years, France was described as a 'quadrille bipolaire' (Cole, 1990; Andersen and Evans, 2003; Grunberg and Haegel, 2007), with two main parties on the left competing with two main parties on the right. On the left, the Communists initially garnered some 25 per cent of the vote, bolstered by their contribution to the Resistance during the Second World War. The prolonged absence of the left from government reduced the pressure on the Communists to conform to the constraints of governing. Meanwhile, various iterations of centre-right and Gaullist (right-wing) parties governed together more or less willingly for the first two decades of the Fifth Republic. Things began to change thereafter, with the growing strength of the Socialist Party (PS) coinciding with the steady decline of the Communists and the emergence of smaller left-wing parties such as the

Greens and Radicals. Meanwhile, the 1980s also saw the emergence of the National Front (FN; now the RN; see Crépon and Lebourg, Chapter 5), a far-right party which increasingly encroached on the electorates of the mainstream parties. While the electoral system prevented the FN from making significant gains in the National Assembly (AN), the surprise qualification of their leader, Jean-Marie Le Pen, to the second round of the presidential elections in 2002 sent shockwaves throughout the French party system. One consequence was that the centre-right UDF party was effectively cannibalized by the larger Gaullist party to create the UMP, a catch-all party on the right. This led to a new period of relative stability, which no longer took the form of a 'quadrille' but was arguably still bipolar, with the UMP on the right competing against the Socialists and their allies on the left, while the FN presented a nuisance but not a serious threat to the main parties of government.

The centrists fared relatively well in presidential elections thanks to their charismatic leader, François Bayrou, but had only a marginal presence in parliament. As with the 'quadrille bipolaire', this new party system took the form of centripetal competition, whereby two major blocks on either side of the centre competed with each other to capture the floating voters located in the ideological space between the two parties. This tendency towards competition on the centre ground led Marine Le Pen (daughter of Jean-Marie, and leader of the FN since 2011) to come up with the scathing nickname of 'UMPS', a portmanteau indicating the ideological convergence of the two main parties. Despite this critique, both parties offered distinctive policy platforms and programmes.

In 2017, things shifted dramatically. For reasons discussed below, the UMP – renamed *Les Républicains* (LR) in 2015 – lurched to the right. Meanwhile, the PS lurched to the left. Both parties now found themselves placed some distance from the median voter, and rather close to their rivals at the extremes of the political spectrum. They found themselves competing for votes and ideas with the FN on the far right, and the resurgent *France insoumise* (FI) on the far-left. For the many voters with more centrist leanings, a vacuum emerged which was filled very effectively by Emmanuel Macron and his newly created centrist party, *En Marche!* (latterly *La République en Marche*, LRM). The consequence was a new five-party system comprising a strong centre, strong parties at both ends of the political spectrum and marginalized parties of the mainstream left and right who found themselves outflanked on both sides. This very much resembles Sartori's (1976, p. 311) model of multipolar, centrifugal competition, whereby the centre is now not just a contested space but a pole, with voters adhering to the centre rather than just floating within it from one side to the other. The axes of competition shift from the traditional centripetal left–right dynamic, to a centrifugal contest between the centre ground and the two poles at each extreme of the political spectrum.

The first half of this chapter explores these changes to the party system in more depth. It begins with an account of how the two mainstream parties each managed to drift away from the centre ground, and then considers how Emmanuel Macron exploited this opportunity to create a new major political force. I discuss whether these changes are a temporary blip, or a longer-term trend that will result in a permanent reshaping of the contours of partisan competition within France.

The second half of this chapter goes on to consider the repercussions of a dramatic change in political personnel following the exodus of the political old guard and the arrival of many neophytes. The changes in the composition of parliament come alongside an ambitious programme of parliamentary reform that seeks to change some of France's core institutions in quite significant ways, including changes to the electoral system, reducing the size of parliament, introducing term limits and lowering the threshold for calling a referendum. If enacted, the cumulative effect of these changes would be to reduce the power of parliament, arguably to the benefit of the executive.

The chapter will conclude by reflecting on whether these changes really are fundamental or just incremental steps on shifting sands. I also consider the extent to which all these changes are a result of the upsurge of populism across the globe, and ask why France has, once again, been exceptional in its response to this phenomenon.

Partisan realignment

There are a few common factors that prompted both the PS and LR to drift away from the centre at around the same time, even though the underpinning logic within each party was quite separate. Part of the problem lay in a general malaise within French politics, situated within a broader backlash against mainstream politics that was triggered by the global recession that marked the decade leading up to the 2017 elections, and the hardship that it entailed. As with other countries, this was evidenced in growing support for more radical parties. At the same time, both parties struggled with internal divisions; they tried in vain to reconcile the more electorally minded elements, whose instincts were moderate and whose policies targeted the floating voter, and the more radical elements who wanted to steer their parties away from the centre and into firmer right or left territory. The motivations for leaving the centre were often ideological in nature, even if they were sometimes presented as a means of making the party more competitive against the threat of the far right and (to a lesser extent) the far left. Last but not least, these strategic and ideological divides had ample opportunity to rise to the surface due to unsatisfactory leadership in both parties and the ill-fated use of primaries as an attempt to resolve the problem.

What's left of the left?

While the left in France have held power less often than the right, and have suffered for many years from internal divisions, their position in 2012 was surprisingly strong: they held the presidency, both chambers of parliament, and the majority of regional and local offices to boot (Sawicki, 2013). Indeed, the right complained bitterly about an excessive concentration of power in the hands of a single party, the PS (a phenomenon that had not troubled them in the slightest when they were the party holding all the cards). For the Socialists to have gone from supremacy to wilderness in just five years is quite a feat of failure.

A big part of the problem was François Hollande's difficult presidency. His main appeal in the 2012 election was his contrast to Nicolas Sarkozy, the unpopular incumbent president whom Hollande defeated. Sarkozy was dynamic, impulsive, fast-paced, abrasive; Hollande was none of those things. While Hollande had excelled in backroom politics as first secretary of his party, his lack of charisma, poor leadership skills and indecision quickly poisoned his presidency. His relationships, both personal and political, were handled badly, and he was frequently embarrassed by errors of judgement (see Drake and Cole, Chapter 2 in this volume).

The most damaging of all, however, was his political programme, which he failed to sell to a sceptical public. His socially liberal policies, such as legalizing gay marriage and trying to introduce gender-sensitive training in schools, created significant disquiet among France's conservative right, and mobilized social conservatives against his government, with a resultant strengthening of their presence within LR (see Raison du Cleuziou, Chapter 6 in this volume). At the same time, his response to repeated terrorist attacks, including a prolonged state of emergency and an attempt to strip terror suspects of the French part of dual citizenship, provoked unease from social liberals. Meanwhile, Hollande's economic policies were inconsistent and unsuccessful (see Milner, Chapter 10 in this volume). Initial attempts to reduce France's deficit by introducing very high taxes on top earners only led to the flight of numerous high-wealth individuals. As the presidency progressed and the unemployment rate continued to go up rather than down, Hollande's economic policies became increasingly liberal, but whereas social liberalism is associated with left-wing values, economic liberalism was perceived by many on the left as right wing and as a betrayal of socialism and the promises made in the election. Growing disquiet within the party was hardened by the presence of senior members of the government who were unabashedly centrist or even right-leaning in their thinking. These included the prime minister from 2014, Manuel Valls, whose subsequent political career has placed him on the centre to centre right; and Emmanuel Macron, who made clear that he was not a member of the PS and did not adhere to Socialist values. These appointments, while intended to broaden the party's appeal in a country that votes to the right more often than to the left, served further to alienate the left of the party. Towards the end of his presidency, faced with a rebel faction within his own party, Hollande needed to rely on a loophole allowing him to bypass parliament in order to get his most contentious economic policies through, such as making it easier to hire and fire people.

Despite all his efforts, Hollande failed to deliver on his most high-profile promise of bringing down unemployment, and with his popularity ratings lower than the unemployment figures, he realized he could not credibly stand for re-election. This decision was reinforced by the release of a book by two journalists, revealing many of the president's indiscretions and casting a very negative light on Hollande's suitability for high office (Davet and Lhomme, 2016). However, it was not only Hollande's own prospects of re-election that had been poisoned by his presidency. Many of the key figures of the PS had either quit in disgust or become tarnished by association. A lacklustre contest to be the party's candidate resulted in the nomination of Benoît Hamon, one of the Socialist rebels who sat firmly on the party's left and had little appeal to floating voters.

Meanwhile, many of those on the left were turning instead towards the harder-left FI, led by Jean-Luc Mélenchon, a charismatic and outspoken leader with far more presence than Hamon. At the same time, Macron's candidacy for the 2017 presidential election garnered support from those who did not support a lurch to the left, including Valls, whose own bid to defeat Hamon in the primary had been unsuccessful. Consequently, Hamon's candidacy attracted the support only of the remaining die-hard core of PS voters. When FI did better than the PS in the presidential election (Hamon obtained a devastatingly low 6.3 per cent), the once mighty PS found itself in ruins, squeezed into irrelevance by more dynamic and popular parties to its immediate left and right on the political spectrum.

A further disaster awaited in the legislative elections, where the party lost all but 30 of its seats – a spectacular collapse given that it had previously had an absolute majority in parliament. The loss of revenue triggered by this political freefall obliged the party to sell its symbolic headquarters in Paris, relegating the party to a semi-literal as well as political wilderness from which it has, at the time of writing in 2020, been unable to return. In the 2019 European elections, the party fared even worse than in the 2017 presidential elections, plummeting to less than 6.2 per cent of the vote (see Drake and Meunier, Chapter 12 below). While it is hard to imagine a party with such a strong grass-roots foundation collapsing completely, there is no sign as yet of a light at the end of the tunnel in which the PS has found itself.

What's wrong with the right?

If things were already not rosy with the Socialists by 2017, and were about to get worse, as seen above, they were far from thriving for the Republicans either. On the contrary: the 2010s were a tumultuous decade that saw the party increasingly cede the centre ground to its rivals, at the cost of power. As with the PS, this problem was exacerbated by poor leadership and an inability to hold/occupy a distinctive space on the ideological spectrum.

Problems began to emerge during the presidency of Sarkozy (2007–12). Aside from the president's divisive personality, the party faced a bigger ideological challenge as it found the far right encroaching on its turf. While the FN seldom out-polled LR, it did have a significant nuisance factor, in the sense that it could create 'triangulaires' whereby the second round of a parliamentary election went from a two-horse race (left–right) to a three-horse race (left–right–far right) with the risk that the FN would syphon votes away from LR and allow the PS to win. There was some evidence of this in 2012. The FN also remained an ominous threat in presidential elections, with the risk that the FN candidate would qualify at the expense of one of the mainstream candidates – a risk first realized in 2002, and then repeated in 2017. Hence, while the FN did not meet the first of Sartori's criteria for relevance ('coalition potential'), it did meet the second criterion ('blackmail potential', namely the ability to influence the direction of competition), prompting LR to compete in an increasingly centrifugal rather than centripetal way (Sartori, 1976, p. 108). In other words, LR shifted their ideology to the right in a bid to compete with the far right.

There are numerous reasons why such a strategy has not to date been successful. The first is straightforward: by deserting the centre ground, they have ceded the turf where the majority of voters are located, and have alienated many floating voters as well as many of their own moderates. It is very difficult to win an election under such conditions. The second, related, problem is that they have paved the way for a more moderate party to replace them as a credible party of government, as I will consider in more detail in the next section. The third issue is that aping the policies of the far right almost never serves to win back lost voters. Instead of maintaining a 'cordon sanitaire' and discrediting the views of the FN, LR have legitimized the FN's discourse by incorporating their rhetoric on immigration into mainstream politics. People who might previously have viewed the FN as too extreme have now been desensitized to such arguments, bolstering the FN's credibility. Rather than returning to the LR party fold, FN voters have been reassured that their preference for the far right is socially acceptable. As a consequence, the RN vote has held steady, while the LR vote has continued to decline.

It would be premature, however, to conclude that the FN are the source of all of LR's woes. The party has been crippled by its own internal divisions and a succession of problematic leaders who have failed to win over the public. In addition, various scandals have rocked the party, drawing question marks over its integrity and its competence to govern.

The party's woes can, in some respects, be traced back to Jacques Chirac, who was at risk of losing in 2002 to Lionel Jospin until the surprise elimination of the latter assured Chirac of re-election. However, problems became more acute under Sarkozy. His brash, 'bling-bling' image did not sit well with the traditional conservative electorate of LR, and his increasingly radical discourse on immigration alienated moderates within the party (Haegel, 2013). A critical turning point came in the second round of the 2012 election, when François Bayrou, who had polled 9 per cent in the first round, broke his party's traditional alliance with the right and instead offered his support to Hollande, citing Sarkozy's use of far-right rhetoric as his reason.

This cemented the schism between centrists and LR that had commenced in 2002, when most of the centrist UDF party had been absorbed into the UMP umbrella, leaving the remaining centrists out on a limb. The UMP had been founded in 2002 by uniting the Gaullist RPR party with various other parties on the right under an umbrella party, ostensibly designed to support Chirac's bid for re-election against the threat of Jean-Marie Le Pen. Those who did not align themselves with the UMP were threatened with having a UMP candidate run against them. Only a small band, renamed *Mouvement Démocrat (MoDem)*, resisted, with their leader Bayrou putting in respectable performances in the 2007 and 2012 presidential elections but then winning only a handful of seats in parliament.

Sarkozy's defeat left a leadership vacuum at the head of the party, and the leadership contest that followed was deeply divisive. François Fillon, who had served as prime minister for the whole of Sarkozy's presidency, lost very narrowly to Jean-François Copé, and refused to accept the result. Both candidates accused their rival of foul play. While Copé managed to assert himself as victor, the underlying rivalries continued to simmer under the surface. The party then faced a series of scandals relating back to the financing of Sarkozy's presidential bid. Copé himself became embroiled in the 'Bygmalion' scandal, facing accusations of inflating invoices in order to bankroll a friend's business. This, combined with poor results in the 2014 European elections, brought down Copé's leadership. Following an interim leadership while a new contest was organized, the party once again chose Sarkozy as its leader. His 'retirement' from politics in 2012 was short-lived, and it was soon apparent that Sarkozy aspired not only to lead his party but also to be its candidate again in the 2017 presidential election. Wary that the party leader would be seen as the de facto candidate, and himself aspiring to the presidency, veteran rival Alain Juppé agreed not to run against Sarkozy for the leadership in 2014 only on condition that Sarkozy agree to organize primaries for the presidential nomination.

In the event, the primary was disastrous. The clashes of ideology and personality simmering close to the surface of the party were allowed to boil over in full view of the public. The primary was seen as a head-to-head between Sarkozy, on the right of the party, and Juppé, a more moderate conservative with less appeal amongst the party faithful but more appeal to the broader electorate. However, the unexpected victor was in fact Fillon, spurred on by the religious right who had mobilized against issues such as gay marriage. Fillon's candidacy proved devastating for the party; his ability to mobilize the base was not matched by an ability to connect with the electorate, with his conservative values jarring against the more modern approach of Emmanuel Macron. The killer blow came when a scandal blew up regarding using public money to pay Fillon's wife to do jobs that did not exist. While Fillon insisted upon his innocence and refused to stand down, his ratings plummeted and he did not recover sufficiently to make it into the second round of the presidential election, although the race was very close, as seen in Bedock's Chapter 3 in this volume. Numerous elements within the party struggled to conceal their contempt for their own candidate.

LR remained in this weak position at the time of the legislative elections, with Macron being very effective in syphoning off the moderates within the party, as detailed below. Having lost its left flank, the party veered yet further to the right, choosing the staunchly right-wing Laurent Wauquiez as its next leader. The hard lines taken by Wauquiez won over neither his party nor the electorate, and following a catastrophic performance at the European elections in 2019, where LR obtained a historic low of 8.5 per cent of the vote, Wauquiez became the latest leader of LR to stand down. He was replaced by Christian Jacob, former leader of the UMP/LR parliamentary group in the National Assembly, after another internal contest in October 2019. Just like the PS, LR has found itself squeezed by the parties to its left and right, unable to maintain its status as the catch-all party of the centre right.

The rise of the centre

There are many reasons why Emmanuel Macron rose to prominence in 2017, and here is not the place to discuss most of them (see Drake and Cole, Chapter 2 in this volume, also Cole, 2019; Pedder, 2018). What is important here is that Macron's rise was aided by the changing configuration of the party system. With the PS shifting to the left and LR shifting simultaneously to the right, there was an unusual opportunity to capture a much wider centre ground than usual. Previous centrists had been pushed down by the bipolar nature of the party system, with alliances on the left and on the right presenting the only credible governing forces. However, Macron seized upon the opportunity to capitalize on the many disillusioned moderates in both mainstream parties who no longer felt able to represent, or vote for, a party that had deserted the centre ground.

Macron's success in creating a dominant party in the political centre can be attributed, alongside his personal qualities, to three main explanations. The first is the opportunity created by the almost simultaneous collapse of the left and right, detailed above, whereby both parties were deeply internally divided and represented by presidential candidates who were rejected by the public. The second is the nature of the French semi-presidential system. The third is Macron's skilful reading of the political climate and his ability to play the cards he was dealt to his best advantage. Let us consider the second and third explanations in more depth.

The nature of the semi-presidential system is significant because Macron succeeded first and foremost as an individual. His presidential bid was based on his own profile and charisma, backed by a nascent party whose name even bore his own initials. It was not until after his victory in the presidential election that his party began to look like a credible party of government. Many candidates for parliament were selected only in the wake of the presidential election. Why does all this matter? In a parliamentary system, it would have been much harder for Macron to establish his party so quickly as a prospective governing force. To become a prime minister in a parliamentary system he first would have needed to lead his party to victory in a parliamentary election, where the appeal of the leader is only one factor in play among many others. Instead, he benefited from the sequencing of the presidential and parliamentary election cycles, effectively rendering the parliamentary elections a second-order election where the electorate provides their president with a governing majority. It is inconceivable that LRM could have won an absolute majority of seats without the imperative to align the legislature and the executive, borne out of frustration with previous periods of cohabitation whereby the president did not have a majority in government. Just as this would not have occurred within a parliamentary system, so it would not occur in a presidential system, where there is greater emphasis on the separation of powers, and it is more common to have a divided legislature and executive. But in France, when both major parties failed to deliver an electable candidate, the door was opened for a strong centrist candidate to sweep in and take over the country.

The nature of the semi-presidential system is indeed important for understanding why France has seen the successful emergence of a centrist party while in other countries they have tried and failed; a comparative perspective, in other words, helps us contextualize Macron's win. For example, in the UK, a similar problem yielded a very different outcome. The centre-left Labour Party moved significantly to the left under the leadership of Jeremy Corbyn, while the Conservative Party moved significantly to the right under the influence of its Eurosceptic (latterly, more specifically pro-Brexit) wing. Centrists from both sides attempted to join forces and create a more centrist movement, but to no avail; without the unique opportunity presented by presidential elections, it is too hard to break the traditional partisan divide. In Germany, the inability of both the left and the right to form a governing majority used to result in alliances with the centre, allowing the latter to punch above its weight, but in recent years we have more often seen 'grand coalitions' between the left and the right, with both parties remaining in play despite their declining seat share. In the US, even in the wake of a very radical populist president, Donald Trump, the party system has to date retained its traditional bipolar bipartism.

Alongside this structural explanation for Macron's success, we must also recognize the successful tactics that he has adopted to establish and maintain his position of power (see too Bedock, Chapter 3, for her discussion of contingent and structural factors in 2017). From the outset he was effective at drawing in discontented figures from other parties, and offered positions of responsibility to allies from both sides. This served to strip both PS and LR of their moderate wings, thus reinforcing their shift away from the centre and from the median voter. Macron also managed to get the existing centrists to support him, offering François Bayrou a prominent position in his cabinet in exchange for support in the presidential election. Yet the alliance of equals imagined by *MoDem* proved to be nothing of the sort, with the latter party being subsumed by LRM and its leader falling from grace and exiting the cabinet only a few months into Macron's presidency. Macron won a parliamentary majority without needing to rely on *MoDem*'s deputies. Everyone from the moderate left to the moderate right became absorbed into Macron's brand under the label 'Macron compatible', giving him total ownership of the centre ground.

Yet Macron has not positioned himself directly in the centre, and this is also an indicator of a skilful tactician. While remaining moderate, Macron has leaned more to the right of centre, with the nomination of Édouard Philippe, formerly of LR, as his prime minister as a clear statement of intent. His decision to bat more often to the right than the left makes good sense for three reasons. First, it has enabled Macron to place clear water between his own government and his role in the preceding (deeply unpopular) Socialist government. Second, the French electorate vote more often to the right than the left, so Macron is maximizing his appeal to the median voter. Third, while both the PS and LR were severely weakened after the 2017 election, the PS was in a more vulnerable position, with fewer seats in parliament and the recent legacy of five disastrous years in power. Macron judged that he could safely leave the PS to die on its own sword, with its voters forced to choose between the hard left (who are not widely viewed as a credible party of government) and LRM. Conversely, LR was more of a force to be reckoned with, not least because of its strong presence in the French Senate and its more substantial presence in parliament. Siphoning off key players from LR and offering its moderate voters a centre-right political programme has been very effective in keeping LR in check. By encroaching quite thoroughly on their more electable terrain, Macron has thwarted attempts at a comeback by LR and trapped them in the political desert. Philippe's replacement as prime minister in July 2020 with Jean Castex, another former LR politician, is a continuation of this strategy.

That is not to say that Macron's centre-right positioning has come without a price. He has struggled to shake off the label of '*président des riches*', reflecting both his own personal history as a former banker and his policies, which have been seen to favour the wealthy at the expense of the working classes. (See Chapter 11 for more discussion of the popular backlash against Macron and the perception that he is out of touch with working people.) But his success in the 2019 European elections, where LRM obtained more votes than LR, the PS and FI put together, demonstrates that he has consolidated his position as a major governing force in the centre of French politics.

Last but not least, Macron's approach to the *Rassemblement National* (RN, formerly the FN) is congruent with the realignment of the French party system into a multipolar, centrifugal system. Unlike LR, whose attempts to cosy up to the far right were part of what drove some of their members towards LRM, Macron has placed himself in clear opposition to RN. At present, they are the strongest alternative political force in France, in the sense that they came top of the polls in the European elections and were the only other party to qualify for the second round of the presidential election. But they do not pose any real threat to Macron, as they cannot rally enough support to win a presidential election or a parliamentary majority. In the plausible scenario that Macron again finds himself head to head with Le Pen in the 2022 presidential election, his oppositional stance towards them increases his ability to rally the rest of the electorate around him and ensure his own victory. Hence, we now have two major poles in French politics – the centre and the far right – with the far left being a third, smaller pole. Each of these poles stands in opposition to the other two. Meanwhile, the PS and the LR now lie in the diminished space between two poles, trying unsuccessfully to compete with both sides. Instead of centripetal competition between the left and right, there is now centrifugal competition between the centre and the political extremes.

In the conclusion below, I consider the extent to which these changes to the party system are a temporary consequence of the 2017 election, or a more long-term realignment. First, let us turn to the second major change in French politics: the composition of parliament.

Parliamentary reform

Part of Emmanuel Macron's presidential campaign became a centre point of his inaugural 'State of the Union' speech, namely the promise to reform France's political institutions. The delivery of such a speech, an annual occurrence at Versailles before both chambers of parliament, is itself an innovation, inspired by the US. The proposals varied from relatively modest to potentially quite radical. They were inspired, in part, by the deal struck before the first round of the presidential election with François Bayrou, whereby Macron agreed to take on Bayrou's agenda of reforming and cleaning up politics. They fit well with Macron's image as a relative outsider to politics, standing above party politics and seeking to change the way that things are done. The reforms, outlined below, include tackling clientelism, changing the electoral system for parliamentary elections, introducing term limits, reducing the number of seats in both chambers of parliament, facilitating the use of referenda and abolishing the Court of Justice.

A stand against clientelism

Unlike all of the other measures discussed below, one of Macron's reforms was introduced directly at the start of the parliamentary term. It involved scrapping the 'parliamentary reserve': a sum of 130,000 euros allocated to each deputy to spend on supporting projects within their constituency. The obvious problem with these funds was that they were perceived as a potential source of corruption, as the deputy could use the funds to support their own pet projects or as a form of 'pork' aimed at boosting their prospects of re-election. Hence, scrapping this money was seen as a way of increasing transparency and removing the temptation of clientelism. However, there has since been pressure within constituencies to find other ways to raise funds for projects, so deputies are now involved in practices such as encouraging sponsorship from local businesses and promoting crowd-funding. These measures are more transparent and inclusive than the previous funding scheme, but have still attracted some criticism due to the decisions made by deputies about whom to approach for funding, and for what purpose.

A more proportional electoral system

France's current electoral system for legislative elections consists of single-member districts and is conducted over two rounds, with candidates needing to exceed a threshold (12.5 per cent of registered voters) in order to qualify for the second round, at which point a plurality of votes is required to win. As with any majoritarian electoral system, this creates distortion between votes cast and seats obtained, with larger parties benefiting at the expense of smaller parties such as the FN/RN, *MoDem* and the Greens. The impact on the FN was highlighted very clearly in the 1980s: in 1986, the electoral system was changed to one of proportional representation by the PS in the hope of mitigating the scale of their electoral defeat. In this election the FN obtained 35 seats, their best ever result (although modest in comparison with what they would obtain in contemporary times based on their vote share in recent elections). The RPR-UDF, upon winning the election (that took them into cohabitation with President Mitterrand), immediately reversed the changes to the electoral system, and the FN lost all but one of its seats in the 1988 election, despite obtaining the same vote share (9.8 per cent) as in 1986.

Macron's proposals were more modest than the changes introduced in 1986. He proposed a mixed electoral system, with most seats elected in the traditional way, topped up by 15 per cent of seats elected via proportional representation to reduce disparities between vote share and seat share. This figure was subsequently revised upwards to 20 per cent, although it still fell short of the 30 per cent demanded by François Bayrou (Lemarié and Mutelet, 2018). Parties would still need to exceed a threshold of 5 per cent of votes cast in order to be eligible for the seats distributed by proportional representation. If implemented, these measures, while relatively limited in their scope, would make it harder for any party to obtain an absolute majority of seats in parliament, while enabling the RN to have a seat share more in line with its vote share.

Term limits

Another of Macron's proposals was to cap at three the number of successive terms that a deputy could serve. In principle, this looked like a very democratic move. It would prevent the same people from holding onto parliamentary seats for decades at a time, ensuring political renewal and the entry of new people with different ideas and perspectives. It would potentially increase diversity within parliament, as one of the major barriers for women and other under-represented groups is the repeated re-election of incumbents within winnable seats. It would also stop parliamentary politics from being a life-long career, promoting instead the inclusion of people drawn from beyond the political world who have other experiences and qualifications to offer.

Yet, on closer inspection, this reform is not as democratizing as it at first appears. By limiting deputies to three terms, the reform prevents the accumulation of experience, knowledge and institutional memory. My own previous interviews with deputies reveal that it often takes at least one full parliamentary term to get to know all the hidden rules and workings of parliament, and longer still to rise through the ranks to positions of seniority. If people are evicted from parliament as soon as they have mastered the rules of the game and reached a point of being able to exert influence, parliament ends up being an assembly of novices. One consequence of this is that it potentially gives an upper hand to the executive, as there will be fewer senior deputies in place to challenge the government. Another is that, while ostensibly favouring renewal and inclusion of people from outside the world of politics, the proposal actually risks conferring even bigger advantages on political insiders. Those who have worked within politics prior to becoming deputies – such as parliamentary aides – have a significant head-start upon entering parliament, and are able to hit the ground running. This advantage over their contemporaries slowly washes out as their fellow parliamentarians become more experienced, but if terms are limited then political outsiders will have little opportunity to catch up, leaving the insiders to rule the roost.

Reducing the number of seats in both chambers of parliament

Another of the proposals was to reduce the number of seats by 25 per cent, taking the National Assembly from 577 to 433 seats, and the Senate from 348 to 261. The original proposed reduction of 30 per cent was even more dramatic. The rationale for this reform was to concentrate resources in fewer hands, thereby increasing the means at the disposal of parliamentarians. However, France already has one of the highest ratios of constituents to deputies of any European country (Breteau and Sénécat, 2018). One potential consequence would be to increase the burden of casework within the constituency, with the corresponding effect of reducing the amount of time that deputies would be able to devote to their parliamentary work. Another would be to allow parliamentarians to expand their team of hired staff in order to manage their workload better, with the consequence that a greater proportion of parliamentary work would be undertaken by non-elected officials.

Power to the people?

One of the proposed institutional reforms would make it easier to call a referendum, by expanding the range of issues that can be voted upon by referendum, and reducing the level of support required from 20 per cent to 10 per cent of deputies, and from 4.7 million to 1 million voters. Again, this proposal is intuitively appealing. It would allow for a higher degree of participatory democracy, giving the public more say on certain flagship issues without having to wait until the next election. It might ease some of the recent unrest caused by legislation on certain social issues, such as gay marriage, and would take the heat off a government responsible for passing such legislation. However, plebiscitary democracy also has significant drawbacks. In a country that already suffers from election fatigue due to multiple levels of elected office, some of which are elected over two rounds, the extended use of referenda risks reducing rather than increasing civil engagement. Referenda are also reductionist in nature, often presenting a dichotomous choice on complex policies of which the public might have quite limited knowledge. And no one launching a referendum can assume safely that they will obtain their desired outcome. One important lesson that France might learn from the fallout of the UK's referendum on Brexit is to 'be careful what you wish for'.

Much ado about nothing?

The reforms to France's institutions were given a high profile in the early months of Macron's presidency. They were briefly revived in August 2019, when they were presented to the Council of Ministers. However, they have not yet gone before parliament, and there are no immediate plans to do so. The reason is simple: the Senate, where Macron does not have a majority, are opposed to the reforms, and constitutional reform cannot pass without the Senate's approval. Senators, unsurprisingly, are not keen on reforms which reduce their numbers and limit the duration of their parliamentary careers. Rather than having a showdown with the Senate, Macron has allowed the reforms to be kicked into the long grass, hoping that he might one day get the numbers in the Senate to push the reforms through. But the composition of the Senate renews slowly, with only half of senators up for re-election at a time, and there is no guarantee that Macron will obtain a majority at the senatorial elections in 2020 (the last to be held during his current term as president). For all the talk about reform, it is therefore quite possible that the French legislative elections of 2022 will be contested with the same number of seats and the same electoral system as in previous years.

A revolution in the composition of parliament?

The second major element of change to the French parliament comes in the form of a dramatic change of personnel. The 2017 legislative election witnessed the most significant political renewal of the Fifth Republic. No fewer than 75 per cent of deputies elected were new entrants to the National Assembly (AN), compared with 37.8 per cent in 2012 and 25.3 per cent in 2007. The cause of this huge wave of renewal was the partisan realignment outlined in the first part of this chapter, whereby many Republican and most Socialist deputies were swept out of power, while Macron's newly formed LRM party took 312 seats (out of 577). Only 28 of these deputies were incumbents who had defected to LRM after previously winning office on a different party ticket; the remainder were new arrivals, and many had no prior political experience at all. This was a radical change for the AN, which had previously been composed of experienced politicians: a mixture of long-serving deputies, professional politicians (mainly former parliamentary assistants), former ministers, former civil servants, and people with substantial local political experience (with many deputies falling into several of these categories). By contrast, many of the new arrivals were drawn from civil society, and were seen as representing a 'new politics'.

This radical change presents many interesting questions. Who were the new entrants, how different were they to their predecessors, and how representative were they of France more broadly? How did they adapt to life as a deputy, and what changes resulted from this sudden change of personnel? Did they view politics differently from the 'old guard'? Were they able to introduce a fresh approach, or did their inexperience leave them trailing behind their more senior colleagues? Some of these questions are yet to be answered, but an initial analysis is provided below.

In terms of the profile of the new entrants, in some respects they do indeed better reflect the diversity of France. LRM boasts 48 per cent women amongst its deputies, a far higher proportion than the other parties, which explains how parliament as a whole went from 73 per cent men in 2012 to 61 per cent men in 2017. Previous research (Murray, 2008) has demonstrated that male incumbency is a major obstacle to gender parity, and LRM, with very few incumbents among their candidates, took advantage of the perfect opportunity to feminize parliament. Their deputies are also more diverse in terms of their ethnic and age profiles, with 35 ethnic minority deputies compared with 10 in 2012 (which itself was a record, in a parliament that historically has elected very few non-White deputies from mainland France). The average age of LRM deputies is 46, compared with 55 in the previous parliament, and included several deputies in their early to mid-twenties. In all these respects, this new cohort of deputies has taken major strides in making parliament more diverse and inclusive.

There are caveats, however. The long-standing lack of representation of France's working classes continues in the current parliament, with LRM's deputies being more highly educated than the population at large and drawn disproportionately from high-status professions (Le Foll, 2017). More than half of them held managerial roles, sometimes at quite a senior level within major corporations. Others headed their own business or were members of the professions. Very few came from low-paid, low-status or casual employment. Furthermore, not all of the new entrants were total political novices. Many had been active in other parties previously, including holding previous elected office at the national or local level, or working as a political aide. In fact, a study by *Le Monde* concluded that 182 of LRM's deputies had held prior elected office, and barely a third of LRM's new deputies were genuine political novices (Vaudano and Breteau, 2017). Nonetheless, the overall picture is one of an unprecedent number of political neophytes drawn from a broader spectrum of French society.

Did these newcomers to parliament have a different way of doing politics? An initial response would be affirmative. Many new deputies came to politics from the world of business, attracted by Macron's 'start-up' approach to LRM, and keen to introduce greater efficiency into politics. Like many citizens with little knowledge of parliament, they did not understand why the chamber of parliament was usually so sparsely populated, and adopted a culture of presenteeism, with a minimum of a third of their ranks in the chamber at any time. This presenteeism was also facilitated by a desire to focus more on the national rather than local dimension of being a deputy; recent reforms to prevent deputies from combining national office with major local office meant that most deputies were focused solely on their parliamentary role. Constituency work was seen as of secondary importance to legislative roles, with local matters seen as the prerogative of local office-holders. Hence, unlike their predecessors (who traditionally spent Tuesday–Thursday in Paris and the remainder of the week in the constituency), LRM deputies would be in Paris from Monday morning to Friday evening.

An additional consequence of the desire for efficiency, coupled with an emphasis on party loyalty, was that deputies initially voted for the government's legislation with a minimum of revision or fuss. Numerous bills whizzed through parliament in its first few months, with LRM deputies dutifully approving everything at the appropriate junctures. Meanwhile, the 'old guard' – especially the incumbent deputies who had joined ranks with LRM – were not so much revered for their experience, as marginalized due to their association with a way of doing things from which the new arrivals were so keen to distance themselves.

Perhaps inevitably, this new way of doing things did not last. Morale plummeted among LRM deputies as they began to feel like they were nothing more than a rubber stamp for Macron's proposals. Given the high socio-professional status of many of the new entrants, they were used to exercising power and influence, and felt very disillusioned when they discovered that their new roles entailed more work and more constraints, in exchange for less pay than they were used to and less impact than they had expected. They felt that the considerable expertise and skill sets that they were bringing to their new roles were not being put to good use. The strain of trying to be present in all places at all times, and to perform well on all fronts, quickly led to burn-out. Some considered leaving (Lemarié, 2017). Others realized that things had to change. And change they did.

Starting in early 2018, an ongoing process of adaptation began, with deputies gradually acquiring a better idea of what the role entailed and how to thrive within their new positions. Some changes were relatively subtle; for example, deputies realized that some of the trappings of the job that had previously seemed like unnecessary indulgences, such as the use of taxis or chauffeurs, were actually necessary given the many demands on their time (Rescan 2018). Other changes were more significant. Deputies began to become more assertive within their party, most notably through a growing willingness to amend legislation. LRM's attempts to rein in and control deputies' every activity within parliament have consequently fallen by the wayside; instead, deputies are competing to do well in league tables demonstrating to constituents how pro-active each deputy has been. As a consequence, amendments to legislation have risen from a handful to hundreds or even thousands per bill, making the process slower, more complicated and less likely to produce the government's desired outcome. Deputies have also become a little more willing to speak out in defence of their actions, rather than hiding from the media for fear of going off message.

Deputies have also begun to understand how to prioritize different aspects of their workload, with the consequence that attendance in the chamber of parliament has begun to fall back to its previous levels. What outsiders to politics interpret as laziness or absenteeism is actually a reflection of the multiple demands on a deputy's time and their inability to be in all places at once. As deputies realized that they could often exert greater influence through attending committees, meeting with ministers or lobbying within the party than they could through sitting for hours in the chamber, waiting to vote, their choices and behaviour became more aligned with their predecessors. A gradual realization dawned on them that not everything about the 'old politics' was wrong.

Similarly, the initial disdain for constituency work began to evaporate as LRM began to realize the critical role that deputies play in creating a local party base. Without a strong party structure established in each locality,

LRM has had to build up a party from nothing, developing their members and activists, preparing candidates for local and regional elections, and shoring up their national candidates' support base. None of this can be achieved if their only elected officials – their deputies – showed no interest in their own constituencies. So, just like their predecessors, LRM deputies are now becoming more deeply immersed in their constituencies, to the point that some are now considering running for local office, even though this will necessitate resigning from their parliamentary seats (Rescan 2019a).

Hence, by half-way through their first term as deputies, LRM's newcomers had gone through a baptism of fire, learning on their feet, figuring everything out the hard way, and finally discovering that some of the rules of the game of politics simply cannot be changed. As they continue to mature and to settle into their roles, they may yet find innovative ways to make their mark on parliament, but their initial attempts to revolutionize political practice demonstrated more naivety than *savoir faire*. Their inexperience caused them to make some mis-steps and to be dominated by the government. The coming years will show whether, as more seasoned politicians, they can finally come into their own.

Conclusion: *plus ça change, plus c'est la même chose*?

This chapter begins with the question 'all change?'. At a first glance, the political landscape was radically different in the wake of the 2017 elections. The party system had realigned, new parties had emerged while the previous stalwarts of French politics languished by the wayside, and the composition of parliament has changed almost beyond recognition. Further major reforms have been promised that would shake things up even further. Yet one of the main themes of this chapter is that these changes are neither as sudden nor as dramatic as they might at first appear.

The changes to the party system are the culmination of a longer-term process of change. The collapse of the PS was rather sudden and spectacular, but the rise of the RN has been a long time coming, and its growing influence on the behaviour and discourse of LR is also not a new phenomenon. The most significant change has been the emergence of a major new political force located in the centre ground, and the corresponding shift to a multipolar, centrifugal party system. It remains to be seen whether this shift is temporary or long-lasting. At present, neither the PS nor LR has recovered sufficiently to present an electoral threat to Macron, who has consolidated his position at the centre – in all senses – of French politics. Even if LRM's dominance begins to wane, it is hard to envisage a return to the traditional left–right stand-off that has for so long dominated politics in France and elsewhere. The rise of populism, the far right, and new social movements such as Green parties is causing an international wave of partisan re-alignment, although the peculiarities of the French semi-presidential system have allowed the emergence of a strong centrist party where this has not been possible in other political systems.

As for the changes to parliament, they are perhaps not as dramatic as they at first appeared. Parliament is certainly more diverse, and by achieving close to gender parity from the outset, LRM are well placed to maintain a gender-balanced cohort of deputies. In other respects, the promise of major change has somewhat fizzled out. Most of the institutional reforms promised by Macron have been blocked by the Senate and have dropped down the political agenda; their likely effects would have been to strengthen the executive and weaken the legislature, which is something that an increasingly confident AN is also more likely to resist. Likewise, the arrival of political novices into parliament produced a fairly temporary change in working patterns, followed by a return to the practices of previous cohorts once the new generation discovered what it actually took to be a deputy. LRM deputies are spending more time in their constituencies and less time in the chamber, making more revisions to legislation and showing reduced willingness to toe the party line come what may. In other words, *plus ça change, plus c'est la même chose, après tout.*

5 2007–17. FROM FATHER TO DAUGHTER: SHIFTS AND CONSTANTS IN THE LE PEN STRATEGY

Sylvain Crépon and Nicolas Lebourg

Marine Le Pen was elected president of the National Front (FN) in a vote by party members on 11 January 2011, at the age of 43. Her then 83-year-old father, Jean-Marie Le Pen, had just stepped down after 39 years at the head of the party. The results were officially announced at the 14th FN congress in Tours, where many party activists and all members of the party's two governing bodies, the Political Bureau and the Central Committee, had gathered for the occasion. The operation was a first: the former president had never sought a vote of confidence from party members to legitimize his presidency. With 67.65 per cent of the vote, the new president had claimed a resounding victory over her opponent Bruno Gollnisch (60 years old), Jean-Marie Le Pen's former right-hand man and the movement's second highest-ranking official. While Gollnisch had run a campaign that held firmly to the ideological positions of the FN's former leader, to the point of legitimizing his anti-Semitic and racist diatribes, Marine Le Pen strove to distinguish herself not only from her opponent's positions, but also from her father's nationalist legacy. To this end, she talked publicly about some of their disagreements – the German army's abuses during WWII, for example, which her father had always downplayed but which she claimed to condemn – saying in passing that once, a quarrel on the subject had led to a temporary break between them (Chombeau, 2006, pp. 299–305).

When asked about anti-Semitism just after her election as party leader, she said that what happened in the Nazi extermination camps during WWII was 'the height of barbarism', adding that she felt 'no affiliation with what the German army once was' (Le Pen, 2011), distancing herself from her

(Translated from the French by Jessica Edwards)

father, who in 1987 had described the Holocaust as 'a minor detail'. During the party leadership campaign, she made herself out as a champion of republican values – critical to legitimacy in the French political arena – in a bid to woo those voters who were receptive to some of her party's central ideas, particularly on immigration, while claiming to be shocked by her father's variously racist, sexist or homophobic remarks. The aim, clearly, was to break the electoral glass ceiling that had so far prevented her party from winning convincing victories.

This shift did not begin with the leadership campaign in 2010–11, but in 2006, when Le Pen senior chose Marine to lead his campaign for the 2007 presidential elections. From this central position, she was able to roll out her own strategy, which focused on putting a republican, secular and universalist spin on the nationalist ideology in order to drag her party out of the political margins. Marine Le Pen nonetheless had to deal with her father's extremist remarks, as he continued to promote a frame of reference heavily influenced by the nationalism of Charles Maurras, the leading theorist of the French extreme right and its anti-Semitic and xenophobic foundations in the first half of the twentieth century. But once she became the sole leader of the FN in January 2011, Marine Le Pen had free rein to refocus the party strategy as she saw fit, a task she set to brazenly, at the cost of a new break with her father, whom she had no qualms in ousting from the party to prevent him undermining her game plan.

But did this discursive, and therefore strategic, break mean a fundamental change in party ideology? Had the FN, renamed the *Rassemblement National* (RN) in 2018, definitively broken away from the extreme right-wing nationalism that had characterized it until then? This chapter analyses the gradual renewal of the FN over the course of Marine Le Pen's political career. First we focus on the precursors of the reconfiguration she initiated following her father's crushing defeat in the second round of the presidential election against Jacques Chirac in 2002. We then, second, retrace the 2007 campaign and the addition of the republican theme to Le Pen senior's signature historical nationalism. Third, we discuss how this strategy was consolidated during the 2012 presidential campaign, the first real political test for the brand-new FN president who was now her party's candidate. We look, fourth, at the about-turn on societal issues through which Marine Le Pen appeared to break with the reactionary legacy of her political family. In the fifth section, we focus on the 2017 French presidential campaign, exploring ideological and programmatic shifts, particularly, sixth, at the economic and social level, and the electoral gains that can be linked to them. In the end, we will see that, despite real changes, and far from constituting an ideological upheaval, this renewal perpetuates an essentializing, exclusionary, nationalist rationale hinging on national identity.

The post-2002 period, or the precursors of a strategic shift

No one expected Jean-Marie Le Pen to qualify for the second round of the 2002 presidential elections, not even his own party. So when the media announced after the first round on 21 April that incumbent president Jacques Chirac would be facing the leader of the FN, the surprise was absolute. At the time, the National Front was emerging from an internal crisis that may well have threatened the party's existence. The years 1998 and 1999 had seen a feud between Jean-Marie Le Pen and the party's number two official, Bruno Mégret. Mégret openly contested the fact that the party president, who had become temporarily ineligible following his indictment for assaulting a Socialist candidate during the 1997 parliamentary campaign, was proposing that his wife stand instead of him in the next elections. This internal dispute led to a split of the FN, with Mégret eventually creating his own political party, the National Republican Movement (*Mouvement national républicain* or MNR), and taking nearly half of the FN's activists and leaders with him.

In the end, Le Pen was declared eligible, but it was an enfeebled National Front that campaigned in 2002. Yet despite a lack of financial and human resources, the party managed to get its leader into the second round of the most important of French elections. It was the National Front's first convincing electoral victory. The party had, briefly, disrupted the traditional left–right contest that had structured most of the presidential and legislative elections under the Fifth Republic, kicking off for the first time a crisis in the French political party system. Although the traditional right–left divide subsequently restored itself a few weeks later in the parliamentary elections held after the re-election of Jacques Chirac, thus apparently signalling a return to normal (Martin and Salomon, 2004), this election was a trauma for most of the actors of the traditional political parties. While euphoric at first, Le Pen and the main FN leaders quickly succumbed to disbelief, then despondency. In the two weeks between the first and second rounds of those presidential elections, France experienced the largest demonstrations since the Liberation. Hundreds of thousands of French citizens (more than a million at the height of the mobilization) marched in protest against what they dubbed the FN's extremist, xenophobic ideology. Faced with the scale of the protests, a large part of the leadership of the FN realized that Jean-Marie Le Pen would never become President of the Republic, at least not as long as he revelled in making the kind of openly racist and anti-Semitic remarks that earned him widespread public disdain (Crépon, 2012). In the second round, the FN leader won less than 20 per cent of the vote – the worst showing of any candidate in the second round of a presidential election under the Fifth Republic.

The youngest of the three Le Pen daughters, Marine, was dismayed by this pitiful performance and decided to form a team called *Générations Le Pen* to investigate its causes, and decide how best to address them. The members of this informal group scoured the electoral sociology research, including studies by the *Centre d'étude de la vie politique française* (CEVIPOF), the main electoral sociology laboratory at the *Institut d'Etudes Politiques de Paris*, which showed that, depending on the elections, between 40 and 60 per cent of FN voters did not want Jean-Marie Le Pen to become President of the Republic. And this for two main reasons: first, voters did not believe he had the skills to serve in the highest office and, second, they felt he would in fact threaten democracy (Perrineau, 2002, pp. 212–13). Hence the paradoxical question: how do you win a major election when your own voters do not want to see you elected? The *Générations Le Pen* team concluded that the FN must commit to a strategy that would show it was a party capable of governing and did not pose a real threat to democratic values. 'Normalization' and *'dédiabolisation'* ('de-demonization', a term the FN had already been using for some time) became the watchwords of this strategy. The next presidential election would give them the opportunity to put their strategic groundwork to use.

The 2007 campaign: emergence of the republican theme

In 2007, Jean-Marie Le Pen launched his presidential campaign with confidence. He told everyone from friends to journalists to expect a repeat performance of 21 April 2002, if not better. It was at this point that Marine began to make her break from under Le Pen. Her father entrusted her with the strategic management of his election campaign, an official recognition of her ascent in the FN apparatus. Despite having to deal with an unintelligible organizational chart (Bruno Gollnisch was in charge of 'operational management', Jean-Claude Martinez was 'special advisor for strategic foresight' and Louis Aliot 'coordinator' of the drive to get the necessary 500 signatures from elected officials that any candidate needs to obtain to run for president) she managed unmistakably to make her mark on the campaign. One way in which she sought to show her party in a new light was to put a republican spin on the topics her father addressed – references to the French Revolution and the Republic – to allow the party to culturally conform, and thus, potentially, to finally win the elections.

The 'Valmy speech', which the FN leader gave on 20 September 2006 at the symbolic site of the revolutionary armies' decisive victory over the Prussian army in 1792, was Marine Le Pen's strategic masterstroke. In this speech, Marine Le Pen reached out to 'French people of foreign origin' while extolling republican values. 'French people of foreign origin, I invite you too to join us, you whom we have so successfully assimilated in the past (...). I call on you to share our values. As long as you respect our customs and laws, as long as you aspire only to get ahead in this country through hard work, we are willing, as we have always been in the past, to accept you into the national and republican *creuset*. In conclusion, the 2007 presidential candidate praised 'the Republic, as our Constitution defines it: secular, democratic and social'.

As the proud heir to the French far-right tradition, Jean-Marie Le Pen had until then habitually criticized the ideological foundations of the French Revolution and the Republic – particularly human rights, with their univer-salist assumptions that, in his opinion, threatened the preservation of French identity. The FN leader had always presented himself as the sworn enemy of 'immigration waves', which he considered 'impossible to assimilate', and he had railed against unfair competition from immigrants depressing the labour market, as he saw it. So the Valmy speech came as a surprise to the entire political community, including the far-right camp itself. The tactic hit the mark, and the media began to take an interest in the young 'heiress' who was setting a new tone for the old FN tunes. It was also in 2006 that the FN communications team designed a poster showing a young woman of colour (variously interpreted as mixed race or North African) with a stern expres-sion making a thumbs-down sign, next to a slogan criticizing the ineffective-ness of social policies on both the left and right: 'Nationality, assimilation, social mobility and *laïcité*, Left/Right, they've ruined it all. Le Pen for President 2007'. Until then, the FN was forever condemning the young descendants of immigrants living in poor suburbs for their so-called violence and refusal to assimilate. The poster ran counter to that position and appeared to address these populations directly, with an eye to the upcoming elections. Thus, the FN official speech used for the first time the concept of *laïcité*, which in 1905 had established the strict separation between the State and the Church and that the French extreme right had so far fought, and through which the presence of Muslims in France has been questioned during the last three decades.

In 2007, Marine Le Pen nonetheless had to contend with her father's extreme-right style which was palpable throughout the party's programme for the presidential election. As with every election programme since 1988, it was preceded by an introductory statement from the candidate featuring typically far-right semantics. For instance, Jean-Marie Le Pen characterized his programme as a stand against the 'totalitarian yoke with a democratic mask', which is how he implicitly referred to liberal democracy. He framed the nationalist struggle within the history of the twentieth century, from the fight against communism to the wars for decolonization, in a lyrical style redolent of Charles Maurras. The aim was the 'liberation of France', a coun-try with an 'age-old civilization', where the nation and its borders are 'as essential to life as the planks of a boat: a bulwark against the threatening waves and a hull that contains all the passengers' hopes'. The preamble to the programme stressed two key measures in particular: identity and the protec-tion of the unborn child. 'The French have an exceptional age-old civiliza-tion,' it reads. 'They must retain its benefits. Consequently, French nationality must be acquired, for the most part, through parentage. Naturalization will be allowed if the foreigner who seeks it is worthy. France cannot take in all the world's poor and needy. France will therefore, with the help of the countries concerned, organize the return of immigrants to their countries of origin in conditions that respect their dignity. Innocent human life, from its inception to its natural end, will be protected and the family given pride of place' (*Elections présidentielles 2007, Programme du Front national*, p. 2). The 2007 programme pledged to repeal abortion laws and the Civil Solidarity Pact (PACS), to enshrine the 'right to life' in the Constitution, and to put in place the principle of 'national preference' which had structured most of the FN discourse since the 1980s. Marine Le Pen would have to wait until she was finally in the running to take over from her father as party president to bring her strategy fully into play.

The 2012 presidential elections: the republican strategy in full swing

Once she became an official candidate for her father's succession as head of the National Front in 2011, Marine Le Pen was able to unleash the full force of her strategy to reconfigure the FN platform and discourse. To do so, she shrewdly employed two complementary tactics: first, steering the party towards the republican norm so as to attract voters still hesitant to support the FN; and second, continuing to play the populist and Islamophobia card as a means to set the party apart from the rest of the political field and reassure its base. While this dual objective had structured the FN strategy since the movement was founded (Dézé, 2012), it became particularly pronounced from 2010 to 2011 onwards. The FN's new icon had already begun to deploy this dual discourse much more assertively during her internal campaign against Bruno Gollnisch for the party presidency.

The populist movements emerging in Western Europe provided her with a ready source of inspiration, particularly Geert Wilders' PVV (*Partij voor de Vrijheid*, Party for Freedom) in the Netherlands and Oscar Freysinger's UDC (Swiss People's Party or Democratic Union of the Centre) in Switzerland. This new style of populism had conceptualized an original form of xenophobia combining a rejection of Muslim immigrants with both the defence of liberal values (women's rights, LGBTQ rights and gender diversity), and the principles of secularism and freedom of religion which, allegedly, Muslims refuse due to Islam's fundamentalist dimension (Camus and Lebourg, 2015). Wilders even claimed to stand up for the Dutch Jewish community against the supposed hostility directed towards them from people of North African descent. Marine Le Pen used this frame of reference to present herself as an advocate of a certain type of social progressivism (defence of gays for example), and thereby modernize her party's image. But such normalization should not be understood as deradicalization. In fact, the process was not new. Neo-fascist and racialist elements had been strategically putting up a republican, social, non-reactionary front since the 1980s, keeping under wraps anything that might link them to the losers of World War II.

On 10 December 2010 in Lyon, while campaigning for the FN presidency, Marine Le Pen declared: 'I'm hearing more and more accounts about the fact that there are some neighbourhoods where you wouldn't want to be a woman, a homosexual, a Jew, or even French or white'. Thus she rehashed the old 'anti-white racism' theme that her party had used since the 1990s, and presented herself at the same time as the best defence against the supposed anti-Semitism of people of North African origin. In fact, opposition to Islam in the name of social progressivism and secularization was the core of the new argument put forward by Marine Le Pen's National Front. The party would now focus on opposing '*communautarisme*', a term which, unlike its English cousin 'multiculturalism', is systematically used in a pejorative sense; '*communautarisme*' is castigated as a threat to republican universalism. The reason it is constructed as a threat is to delegitimize policies for the recognition of minorities, which many political party members in France, whether right wing or left wing, see as a prelude to the fragmentation of society.

In this way, the new-look FN weighed into a debate that had until then been waged between different segments of the left and met with hostility from the right as a whole, opposed to multicultural policies in the name of preserving national identity. Presenting herself as the true defender of republican universalism against its alleged main enemy – political Islam and those who seek its official recognition in the public arena – Marine Le Pen broke down what had previously been fairly clear borders between nationalism and universalist republican values. Elisabeth Badinter, a major figure of feminism in France with close ties to the Socialist Party, unwillingly contributed to justifying this new FN strategy when she complained in September 2011 that 'apart from Marine Le Pen, there was no one left to defend the policy of *laïcité*' (interview in the magazine *Le Monde des religions*, 28 September 2011).

Jean-Marie Le Pen spoke of secularism only sparingly and often used an anti-republican frame of reference in his speeches, no doubt due to the tactical alliance he had maintained with certain fundamentalist Catholic circles since 1984. In contrast, his daughter now aimed to present her party as one of the most secular in French politics. To avoid appearing to discriminate against a specific religion, namely Islam, she told *Le Monde* in September 2012 that she would amend the Constitution with the statement, 'the Republic recognizes no community' (interview in the *Le Monde*, 21 September 2012) using the term to mean ethnic and sexual minorities as well as religious communities. Nonetheless, in the same interview, she said she wanted to prohibit the wearing of the Islamic headscarf and the kippah in the public space, understood in the broad sense to include 'shops, public transport and the street' (in a heated debate the burqa was banned in France in 2011). Such a measure would have been a break with the foundations of the 1905 law that only prohibits civil servants from wearing religious symbols, and only within public institutions.

Despite her push for 'de-demonization', Marine Le Pen proved herself unafraid of making inflammatory remarks to rally her party's base, or to grab attention from the media, who saw – and see her – as a bankable political commodity (Dézé, 2015). In Le Pen's speech in Lyon on 10 December 2010, she compared Muslims praying in three Parisian streets on Friday afternoons, due to a lack of room in the nearby mosques, to an 'occupying army'. The future FN president elaborated, 'I'm sorry, but for those who really like to talk about the Second World War, if we're talking about occupation, let's talk about this. Because this is clearly an occupation of territory!' Eerily, this statement echoed a comment of her father's in an interview in January 2005 with *Rivarol*, a far-right weekly magazine bent on clearing Marshal Pétain's name. 'In France at least', he is quoted as saying, 'the German occupation wasn't particularly inhumane, even if there were some blunders, which is inevitable in a country of 550,000 square kilometres' (*Rivarol*, 7 January 2005). The interview caused a scandal, and Marine Le Pen was held to account for her father's comments several times when she was running to replace him. By drawing a parallel between the Muslim presence in France and an occupying army, she deflected the criticism of the FN's position regarding WWII (the party had many collaborationist members when it was founded) onto a population that it ostracizes. As such, the comments were symbolic of the discursive reconfiguration under way within the FN.

'Sexual nationalism' as a legitimization strategy

At the National Front's traditional May Day celebration in 2011, Marine Le Pen told an enthusiastic crowd, 'Whether you're male or female, heterosexual or homosexual, Christian, Jewish, Muslim or a non-believer, you are above all French!' The newly elected president of the National Front thus confirmed the discursive shift she had officially promoted in her party since the campaign for the primaries. In addition to endorsing republican values by implying that the acquisition of French nationality does not depend on a specific origin, she explicitly distanced herself from the sexism and homophobia that had until then characterized her political family by arguing that women and especially homosexuals have their rightful place in the community of citizens. Here again, Marine Le Pen was heavily influenced by the social liberalism of Geert Wilders. The Dutchman made the defence of homosexuals one of the *leitmotifs* of his anti-Islam stance, as in his opinion, homophobia is mainly the preserve of Muslim populations. Marine Le Pen implied the same thing in her speech on 10 December 2010 in Lyon, when she claimed that women and homosexuals are stigmatized, if not assaulted, in certain areas with a high concentration of people of immigrant origin – that is, North African and therefore Muslim people whose 'archaic' culture is incapable of adapting to modern mores (see Dudink, 2013 for a good analysis). Despite this conventional Islamophobia, the new FN president earned the wrath of the far right's ultra-conservative circles, who could not bear to see her defend people they considered deviant in terms of the order of natural law (Crépon, 2015). Moreover, she did not explicitly speak out against abortion, maintaining even during her father's presidential campaign in 2002 that she did not wish to repeal the 1975 Veil Act that legalized voluntary abortion in France. The FN programme for the 2002 presidential elections, entitled *For a French Future*, had proclaimed: 'Abortion, involving a third party, the unborn child, cannot be considered legitimate; the Nation, meanwhile, must provide for its own continuity over time. The abortion laws go against the Common Good of our country and will be repealed.' When asked about this during the 2002 campaign, Jean-Marie Le Pen's daughter answered frankly: 'Can you see us bringing women who have had abortions before the courts?' (Bastié, 2016).

This is another point on which the FN president differed sharply from her father. Le Pen senior was in the habit of saying that women's role was to procreate in order to regenerate the national population, hence his fierce opposition to abortion and to policies promoting gender equality. The FN's platform in the 1990s advocated that mothers be encouraged to return to the home so that they could 'devote themselves full-time to their children's education' (Front national, 1990). The FN leader also cultivated 'manly' values in his speeches, praising misogyny, homophobia and the use of physical force in politics in turn. Since its beginnings in the nineteenth century, nationalism has been combined with the masculinist stance that consists in painting foreign enemies as effeminate in order to belittle them (Mosse, 1997, pp. 69–71). In the early twentieth century, European anti-Semitic literature also used to portray Jews as effeminate as proof of their deviance, thereby justifying their exclusion from the national community (Mosse, 1985). Although he was himself in contact with homosexuals (Beauregard and Lebourg, 2012), Jean-Marie Le Pen was quick to indulge in homophobic insults. For example, he compared homosexuals to 'capons' before a gathering of hunters (speech given on 20 February 2007) and asserted that homosexuality, 'if it develops, leads us to the world's extinction' (interview on the TV programme *L'heure de vérité* on *Antenne 2*, 13 February 1984).

Things changed with Marine Le Pen's arrival at the head of the National Front. In the early 2010s, when she was still only a candidate to succeed her father, some far-right media outlets were reluctant to see a divorced woman who lives in a blended family without having remarried become the president of the main French nationalist party, and attempted to discredit her by outing several high-ranking FN officials as gay (Crépon, 2015, p. 201). Far from harming her image, the revelations instead served her rebranding efforts. The new face of French nationalism claimed to be a victim of the conservative clan of the far-right movement, while striving to represent a modern nationalism in tune with a certain social progressivism. The strategy quickly paid off at the ballot box: Marine Le Pen managed to win as many votes from women as men in the 2012 presidential elections. In the first round of the 2012 presidential election, the gap between male and female voters narrowed to 1.5 points, down from 3 points in 2007, 7 points in 1995 and 6 points in 1988 with Jean-Marie Le Pen as candidate (Mayer, 2015, p. 315; Amengay et al., 2017). In doing so, Marine Le Pen disrupted the 'radical right gender gap' (Givens, 2004) that until then had seen far-right parties struggle to attract women voters (Mayer, 2015). Marine Le Pen's personality, and the fact that she was (and is) a working, divorced woman, undoubtedly made some women less reluctant to vote for a party embodied until then by a man who readily cultivated sexism, indeed misogyny. As such, her criticism of the male chauvinism of young North Africans managed to strike a chord with some women voters who were loath to vote for her father.

The 2012 presidential election – Marine Le Pen's first shot at the highest office in the land – was a fairly successful trial run. With 17.9 per cent of the vote, she admittedly remained far behind the two candidates who qualified for the second round, incumbent president Nicolas Sarkozy (27.18 per cent) and the socialist candidate François Hollande (28.63 per cent). But her third place, well ahead of the left-wing candidate Jean-Luc Mélenchon (11.1 per cent) and, more importantly, well ahead of her father's 10.44 per cent in 2007, vindicated her strategy. By winning over a young, popular and more female electorate with her efforts at republican legitimization, and above all by luring Sarkozy into engaging with her party's themes – national identity, security, a rejection of globalization and the defence of disadvantaged categories – she kept herself at the centre of the debate. Her party grew stronger throughout François Hollande's five-year presidential term, including in the various mid-term elections. In the 2014 European elections, for instance, the National Front came far ahead of the other parties with 24.86 per cent and sent 24 of its members to the European Parliament (the conservative right-wing party *Union pour un movement populaire* – UMP – came second with 20.81 per cent). Party leaders could now claim that the FN had become the 'leading party in France' and that it was once again in a position to offer attractive rewards to those who joined it. Getting to the second round of the 2017 presidential election was becoming an increasingly plausible scenario. While the 'de-demonization' strategy now seemed to have worked, the party still had to win the battle for credibility by showing that it had what it takes to run the country. So while the leadership doubled down on the strategy of republican legitimacy and social progressivism, it also endeavoured to appear a responsible, managerial party and win over those sceptical of its competence to govern. Under François Hollande, the FN experienced unprecedented scores in the four mid-term elections between 2012 and 2017; and in a poll carried out in 2015, 22 per cent of respondents thought that the FN proposed 'effective solutions' against 13 per cent for the Socialist Party (Odoxa, 2015).

The 2017 presidential election: a programme that steered clear of doctrine

The FN's 2017 programme, called 'In the name of the people', translated concrete aspirations into 144 measures over seven chapters, each on a specific theme: A Free France; A Secure France; A Prosperous France; A Just France; A Proud France; A Powerful France; A Sustainable France. There was no longer any mention of the nation's history or past, and the lyrical wording had been abandoned. The aim as announced in the introductory sentence of the preamble was to 'restore order over a period of five years'. To reassure her potential voters, she took great care to make it clear that, for her, it was not a question of establishing a new regime, but of holding elected office. She emphasized the point by specifying: 'My project, as you will see, consists of a real revolution in proximity'. The goal was no longer to embody the collective venture of a far-right nationalist party, but of applying the theme of 'proximity' to the social, economic and democratic spheres. The term 'proximity' is repeated three times in the FN president's preamble and seven times in total in the whole programme, and denoted an intention both to become more pragmatic, and to get closer to people, two aspects so far absent from former programmes. Of course, the need to liberate France was still there. So were the organicist references, and the opposition between patriots on the one hand and the 'globalists' and 'Europeanists' working on the other to knowingly dissolve the French national identity; but while this worrying view of the world persisted, the edge had been taken off it.

Marine Le Pen's text in the preamble to her programme was adapted to today's electorate. At just one page long with a narrow lexical register, it required no prior knowledge or ideological references to understand. The programme itself no longer dealt with doctrine. The style was direct. Each concrete, concise and numbered measure was introduced by a verb in the infinitive. The third measure states, for example: 'Ensure all French people are represented through proportional representation in all elections'. The programme dispensed with philosophical argument and went straight to the proposals, which made it no less ideologically coherent.

In 2017, the family was no longer the primary reference, and biological organicism was replaced with a legal vocabulary that brought *souverainisme* to the fore (this word, imported from Quebec, is used by French right-wing and left-wing political parties alike in the sense of defending national status against international institutions and transnational economic or cultural phenomena). What is called for now to liberate France is sovereignty – full monetary, legislative, territorial and economic sovereignty. Support for 'a pro-natalist policy' (measure 52), which did not now entail the prohibition of abortion, was linked to a social policy agenda rather than to a biological clash castigating the upsurge in migration and the nation's decline as it was 2007. Thus the granting of non-means-tested family benefits to the higher socioeconomic categories is presented as a 'universal' measure. As for the thorny issue of same-sex marriage – introduced in 2013 despite massive protests from conservatives (in which Marine Le Pen refused to take part) – it is addressed in the programme between raising the index point for civil service pay and pensions and assistance for people with disabilities. The proposal appeared to be a shrewd compromise between several perspectives: repeal of the 2013 Taubira Act (which introduced same-sex marriage, named after the minister who introduced it) but without retroactive effect (same-sex married couples remain married), in favour of a return to the Civil Solidarity Pact in an improved form (measure 87). From now on, thus, societal policy, which used to prevail, became part of social policy.

The central issue was no longer the demographic clash between nationals and immigrants, but recovering national and popular sovereignty, with an emphasis on the use of referendums, the adoption of proportional representation (which favours parties without allies) and the notion of proximity. These are all principles that the FN had long advocated, with Jean-Marie Le Pen campaigning on the idea of a Sixth Republic in the 1988 presidential election and on a referendum-based republic in 2002. The 2017 programme also reiterated a promise to facilitate enrolment in private schools, but rather than being based on pro-natalist ideas or religious identity, it came under the theme 'Make France once again a country of freedom'. Clearly, the full *souverainisme* that this programme pushed for was the convergence of Dutch-inspired populism and a more traditional national populism. The objective was to distance the party from far-right regimes and instead propose far-right governance within a democratic framework (Reungoat, 2015).

The security issue was also given a republican gloss. Rather than referring to 'ethnic gangs' as in 2007, the 2017 programme claimed to 'target the 5,000 leaders of delinquent and criminal gangs identified by the Ministry of the Interior'. In fact, the Interior Ministry's report of 19 January 2012 on gang violence put the number of criminal gangs at 313. In both 2007 and a decade later, in 2017, however, the issue of immigration was closely linked to security. Both programmes called for foreigners convicted of a criminal offence to be automatically deported, without any mention of the legal difficulties involved in setting up such a measure in a constitutional state. While in 2007 it was a question of deporting illegal immigrants, banning immigration altogether, or even 'reversing migration flows', the 2017 proposal was to reduce net legal migration to 10,000 annually.

Moreover, both programmes called for the abolition of the *jus soli* principle, which currently allows any child born in France to foreign parents to obtain French nationality at age 18 if he or she makes the request, in favour of *jus sanguinus*, making the acquisition of nationality much more restrictive. As for dual nationality, which the National Front has always opposed on the basis that nationality cannot be divided, it would now only be abolished for non-European foreigners. Above all, in the aftermath of the attacks in Paris on 13 November 2015 and Nice on 14 July 1996, which killed 130 and 86 people respectively, the issue of the fight against Islamism became more central than ever. The platform for the 2017 presidential election recommended that all foreigners flagged with a 'fiche S' for suspected Islamist sympathies be deported. The 'Fichier S' – 's' for 'state security' – is a register of individuals under police surveillance for various reasons (banditry, tax evasion etc.). The register has no fewer than ten categories, but includes many individuals suspected of involvement with Islamist terrorism. The National Front therefore maintained its core nationalist principles, but in a form that avoided contradicting French institutions too emphatically.

2017: economic and redistributive policy

According to Cas Mudde, the programmes of far-right populist parties rarely go into economic issues in much depth, since their primary obsession rests with preserving national identity (Mudde, 2007). While the National Front is no exception, there has been an appreciable shift since 2012. The party's programme for the presidential elections that year, which was stripped of any ideological preamble, addressed economic policy in much more detail than before. This shift reflected the need to keep within the same coalition those of its supporters who like the party's welfare chauvinism, and also to appear credible to the well-to-do: in 2015, 19 per cent of voters living in households with 6,000 euros or more per month were considering voting FN, against 36 per cent of those whose monthly income was less than 1,250 euros (Perrineau, 2016).

As Ivaldi observed, socio-economic issues accounted for 37 per cent of the 2012 programme (which is still 10 points below the average for the other political parties), compared with 16 per cent in the late 1990s, while over the same period there was a decrease in 'cultural' themes centred on identity (Ivaldi, 2015, pp. 166–7). Nonetheless, economic and social issues were still heavily linked to the question of national identity, given the intention to implement measures of 'national preference' and 'economic patriotism'. In 2017, Marine Le Pen simply reverted to recommendations made in the 1990s by Bruno Mégret, whose stated objective was to turn the FN from a protest party into a party capable of governing (Ivaldi, 1995, p. 167).

Economic and social issues had a similar degree of importance in the 2017 FN programme as that of 2012. This time the programme projected a certain pragmatism in these areas, without abandoning the nationalist principles that serve to distinguish the party from the rest of the political field. 'National priority', once the cornerstone of the social agenda, was now only one of several measures of 'economic patriotism'. Its objectives were also less ambitious. Whereas the book that first introduced the policy (whose author, Jean-Yves Le Gallou, soon became one of the movement's main leaders) proposed that companies could choose to hire only French nationals or could lay off foreign employees first (Le Gallou, 1985), the 2017 programme more 'modestly' advocates giving French nationals priority for social housing and instituting an additional tax for hiring foreign workers (measure 38).

It should be noted that such measures are not nearly as discriminatory as the legislation of 1932 and 1935 that resulted in 345,000 foreigners leaving France in 1936 (Singer-Kerel, 1989). The fact remains that Part V, entitled 'A Proud France', called for the famous 'national priority' to be included in the Constitution, which would entail far more far-reaching consequences than the aforementioned tax on hiring foreign workers. Since this principle is contrary to constitutional principles, applying it would require much more radical changes to the Constitution than a simple amendment.

The principle of national priority corresponds to what historian Roger Griffin describes as an 'ethnocratic perversion of liberalism' (Griffin, 2000), and must not be confused with progressive redistributive social policies rooted in universalist principles (although this could well be part of the FN strategy). The principle of protectionism present throughout the programme was therefore a way of reconciling the organicist conception of the nation with the need, as the FN saw it, to secure managerial and pragmatic legitimacy. Free trade agreements were rejected outright; public food procurement at the national or local levels must rely exclusively on French companies. Another stated intention was to 'develop short food supply chains, by reorganizing the industry'. Here the FN took up the ethno-localist issue introduced by the radical far-right identitarian movement, many of whose activists have joined the FN (François, 2012). 'Localism' has since become a recurrent theme in the FN's communications, particularly during the pre-campaign phase of the 2019 European elections; and the greening of the party at that contest was also of note.

In continuity with previous programmes, the 2017 programme favoured small and medium-sized enterprises (SMEs) and tradespeople with 'common sense' measures: reserving a share of public procurement for SMEs, simplifying administrative procedures, improving social security for workers who do not benefit from the advantages of the wage-earners' social security scheme. Beyond the economic aspects, here the National Front addressed the socio-professional categories whose votes regularly swing between the right and the far right. In 2017, 46 per cent of self-employed people (shopkeepers, tradespeople, small business owners) voted for the FN candidate. The FN targeted them with talk of a legitimate hierarchy in which the self-employed, who see themselves as the losers in the welfare state, would no longer be sandwiched between the 'oligarchy' of 'globalized' capitalism with its obscene profits above, and the immigrants who supposedly get all the social benefits below.

For all that, Marine Le Pen advocated a hefty social policy agenda. The trend towards a greater social thrust began in the 1990s, with campaign posters claiming *Le social, c'est le Front national!* (which loosely translates as 'The National Front means social protection'), and has been steadily building since (Ivadli, 2015, p. 172). Thus the 2017 FN programme featured specific social measures and, even more than in 2012, called for extensive state interventionism. It advocated the repeal of the El Khomri Act (which was instrumental in liberalizing the labour market under President François Hollande), raising pensions and setting retirement at the age of 60, facilitating donations, reducing interest rates on loans and overdrafts for both households and businesses, and so on. It did not go so far as to raise the minimum wage, a measure liable to satisfy private-sector employees on a modest income – the core of the FN's electoral clientele – but to displease small-business owners at the same time.

In any case, this discourse responds to the anxieties of the working class, an electorate with little education, mainly confined to low-status jobs, living in poor peri-urban areas and haunted by the fear of losing what little they have managed to accumulate through hard work and sacrifice (Mayer, 2015). Workers who vote for the FN/RN sit very much on the right of the political spectrum (Gougou and Mayer, 2013). In the 2019 European elections the FN won 40 per cent of the working-class vote. In her speeches, Marine Le Pen cleverly echoed those who feel left behind by globalization – the people she calls 'invisible' – telling them that with her they will get their revenge and strike fear into the Paris and Brussels establishments who understand nothing about their daily lives. Her nationalist agenda based on closing borders, stopping or even reversing immigration and establishing 'national priority' for access to employment or social benefits was thus designed to appear as a set of common-sense solutions to a politically disenchanted popular electorate who no longer believe in the solutions of traditional parties – a phenomenon seen in many European countries since the 1990s (Bornschier and Kriesi, 2012).

Conclusions

Since her political emergence within the National Front in 2006, Marine Le Pen has managed to reorient the party line significantly, in terms of policy as well as strategy. The fact that this reorientation took place around Marine Le Pen and for her benefit suggests that it may not last long when the time comes for her to be replaced. The party's name change at the last convention in March 2018 symbolized in itself the culmination of this process of leadership change and political reorientation. Marine Le Pen's statement following her party's success in the 2019 European elections, when it came out on top with 23.3 per cent of the vote, says it all: 'The Front national was Jean-Marie Le Pen's party. The Rassemblement National is mine' (interview with the magazine L'obs, no. 2847, 30 May 2019). In the space of 13 years, she has succeeded in making a (first) name for herself which is in itself a political brand, to the point that some have spoken of 'Marinism' instead of 'Lepenism' ('Le 'marinisme'? Du neuf avec du vieux', L'Obs, 1 May 2015). Nevertheless, the full sovereignism with which she attempted to legitimize the party's nationalism in 2017 caused a great deal of confusion among the FN's own voters, and between the first and second rounds of the presidential election, she more or less abandoned the idea of leaving the Eurozone. That version of

'Frexit' had been envisaged by her former right-hand man Florian Philippot; he subsequently left the party a few months after the presidential election, and the idea was abandoned during the campaign for the European elections in spring 2019. The two party lists that did advocate 'Frexit' (Florian Philippot's Patriots and François Asselineau's *Union populaire républicaine*) together garnered less than 2 per cent of the vote. It was, moreover, on this very point of confusion (departure or not from the Eurozone?) that Marine Le Pen had so publically floundered in the television debate against Emmanuel Macron in May 2017 between the two rounds of presidential voting, leading some right-wing media to promote her even more conservative niece Marion Maréchal.

Marine Le Pen has not had it all her own way. The RN leadership has to deal with internal conflicts that have arisen over what some see as an overly accommodating view towards immigrant assimilation. The famous 2006 poster showing a young mixed-race woman denouncing the inanity of assimilation policies (see above) certainly helped the FN attract the attention of an electorate traditionally reluctant to vote for it. But it also angered some officials who felt that it blurred the identity-based message that allows the party to stand out from the rest of the political field.

In short, the 2017 campaign, and even more so the campaign for the 2019 European elections, aimed at avoiding the twin traps of radicality on the one hand, and banality on the other. The successes of the *Rassemblement National* have led other parties, mainly on the right, to take up its favourite themes. The identity- and security-focused agenda has thus become unavoidable in political debate in France, as in many other European countries (Arzheimer, 2009), with the result of further strengthening the legitimacy and base of the far-right party (Arzheimer and Carter, 2006). It now appears clear that, while the progress of Jean-Marie Le Pen's National Front depended on his extremes, Marine Le Pen's *Rassemblement National* can rely on the extremes of others.

6 THE CATHOLICS STRIKE BACK? CONSERVATIVE CATHOLICS AND THE RESHAPING OF THE FRENCH RIGHT

Yann Raison du Cleuziou

The influence of French conservative Catholicism on the evolution of the political parties of the French right is a new and paradoxical development. At the beginning of the 2000s, historian René Rémond observed that Catholics had become the target of a new form of latent Antichristianism, which manifested itself in harassment and taunting (Rémond, 2000). Sociologist Danièle Hervieu-Léger spoke of the 'end of a world': The Catholic faith, she wrote, had lost all authority in contemporary French culture (2003). The symbolism of their omnipresent religious heritage had become indecipherable for the majority of French people. Not one of the major parties on the left or the right in France mobilized in 2005 to ensure that the preamble of the proposed EU 'European Constitution' referred to the 'Judeo-Christian heritage', as requested by Pope John Paul II (the Constitution never came into force). The French presidential campaign fought in 2007 by Philippe de Villiers, whose sovereignist and anti-Islamic programme also included the protection of the family and of a life led in accordance with the social doctrine of the Church, drew only a handful of votes: 2.23 per cent of the voters. More than ten years later, however, in 2017, as Catholic religious practice continued its decline, political figures on the left and the right were making reference to 'France's Christian roots' in their speeches. Catholicism today has regained a symbolic authority in French politics, possibly as a result of its recognition as a national heritage; or because of the influence that Catholic conservative activists have gained over political parties.

This chapter will first describe the special status of this religious minority that retains the privileges of its past power. Second, it will explain the transformation of the social movement against same-sex marriage into an influential political lobby. Third and last, the chapter will show how the electoral appropriation of Catholics became a very controversial issue during the presidential election of 2017, between the right and the far right in particular, but also regarding *La République en Marche*. As its title suggests, the chapter is focused mainly on the role played by conservative Catholics in the reshaping of the French right, culminating in the 2017 presidential election campaign. Beyond this specific focus on organizational party politics, moreover, the chapter contributes to a revived discussion on the changing nature of France's relationship with the Catholic religion and values.

A religious minority that retains the political and symbolic resources of its past majority status

On 16 April 2019, the emotion provoked by the fire of Notre Dame Cathedral in Paris was a timely shortcut to think about the very special status of Catholicism in French society. Even though religious practice is in decline, Catholicism remains a common heritage for both believers and unbelievers. The war of the two Frances, the Catholic and the republican, is no longer relevant even if tensions persist with the most conservative and militant fringe of Catholics. In this context, Catholicism has become a source of meaning available to political actors regardless of any allegiance to the Church. Paradoxically, the decline of the faith itself allows a growing appropriation of Catholicism as a cultural heritage and possibly as a symbolic resource for politics.

A Catholic church of France in sociological and political decline

Who are France's Catholics? There are a number of different answers to this question. Within the French population (aged 18+), the number of French who describe themselves as Catholic oscillates between 44 per cent and 54 per cent according to surveys (see Pèrez-Agote, 2012; Bréchon, 2019). One indicator of their degree of integration into the Catholic Church is considered to be the frequency with which they attend mass. A number of different rhythms of practice coexist in this respect: only 2 per cent of French people attend mass once a week; 2.5 per cent attend at least once a month; 2.5 per cent attend on a more irregular basis, for occasions connected with movements of which they are members; 11 per cent attend only for large seasonal festivals; and 36 per cent never attend, with the exception of family occasions (baptisms, weddings and funerals) (Raison du Cleuziou, 2018). The majority of surveys estimate the number of practising Catholics at around 4.5 per cent. By contrast, around 15 per cent of French people declare that they have made specific commitments in the name of their faith. This notion is a highly elastic one, and ranges from catechism to being a scout, from belonging to a parent–teacher association to participating in a liturgical group (Raison du Cleuziou, 2018). Catholic activism is therefore not directly linked to worship practices. Whatever the indicator used, quantitatively Catholicism has been in clear decline since the 1960s, experiencing a genuine 'collapse', in the words of historian Guillaume Cuchet (2018).

Parallel to this statistical decline, Catholics have given up thinking of themselves as a counter-power against the Republic. Since the 1960s, France's Catholic bishops have refrained from instructing their flock on how to vote. This has been due just as much to full recognition of the autonomy of the temporal order as it has been to the internal plurality of Catholicism. It thus potentially makes any intervention a rift-causing factor that contradicts the calling to preserve the unity of faith between Christians, and between the dioceses and Rome. Although some priests used the authority of their position to influence the political engagement of Catholics during the 1970s and subsequently, this practice has remained marginal outside of certain traditionalist or progressive minorities. In general, bishops have intervened immediately to preclude extremist manipulations and refocus on the legitimate exercise of the vote. Since the 1980s, it is only against voting for the National Front (FN, since 2018 renamed the National Rally or *Rassemblement national*, RN), judged to be xenophobic, that bishops have considered it legitimate to intervene. In this way, they paradoxically affirmed the recognition of democratic deliberation and of the 'freedom of choice' which has been left to Catholics (Donegani, 1993). The bishops promote civic engagement as the free participation of individuals in political life, reminding Catholics of the principles that should guide their consciences without going so far as to tell them how to mark their ballot papers.

Over the course of the twentieth century, the Catholics deteriorated from a group 'for itself' to a group 'in itself'; namely, a hierarchically ordered strategy for the exercise of influence has been replaced by individual and secular behaviour (Deloye, 2006). The Catholic factor in the vote remains structurally significant, but in the form of a legacy of the past. In electoral sociology, voting among practising Catholics for the mainstream right-wing parties is a deep-set tendency which has been observed at each election since the 1970s (Michelat and Simon, 1977; Dargent and Michelat, 2015; Tiberj, 2017). In the presidential elections of 2007 and 2012, regularly practising Catholics voted for the parliamentary right (the *Union pour une Majorité Populaire* (UMP)) in proportions well above the national average from the first round onward: Nicolas Sarkozy most likely received 49 per cent and then 45 per cent of their vote respectively (Dargent and Michelat, 2012). In light of this inertia in Catholic voting, would the 2017 presidential election show any sign of change? The surveys from the first round revealed no surprises. François Fillon, candidate of *Les Républicains* (successor of the *UMP*), received 44 per cent of the vote among regular practising Catholics. The 2017 election thereby confirmed once again the highly predictable character of the Catholic vote.

Catholicism's return to the centre of politics is not, therefore, the consequence of an evolution in the episcopate or in the Catholic electorate. It is instead the result simultaneously of an instrumentalization of the Catholic culture in the political arena, and of the mobilization of a certain number of lay Catholics in order to defend family values.

A Catholicism favoured by the republican order

The French Republic recognizes freedom of worship by affirming the neutrality of the state with respect to religions. Often subject to controversy and dispute, the Law of 1905, which defines the religious neutrality of the State and guarantees the exercise of individual liberties, is first and foremost a law guaranteeing freedoms: it does not set out to preclude religious belief in private spaces, and on the contrary protects their expression in public spaces. In spite of this secularism, however, the Catholic Church retains privileges which place it above other religions in the Republic (Poulat, 2003). It is for this reason that tens of thousands of Catholic churches have been maintained by the State since 1905 without this being perceived as in receipt of indirect subsidies. In 1905, the churches were in effect nationalized, and their upkeep made the responsibility of the State or municipality. Furthermore, as General de Gaulle used to say: 'The Republic is secular; France is Christian'. The Law of 1905 separated the apparatus of Church and State but did not call the Christian way of life into question: public holidays belong to the Catholic calendar of celebrations, and public canteens serve fish on Fridays, often enough without this being a source of controversy, or no more so than the Easter eggs decorated in classrooms, or Christmas trees. As these practices have become cultural rather than religious, their character has shifted them outside the scope of the rules on secularism and thereby legitimized their perpetuation within the Republic. Catholicism benefits in this way from a very significant form of positive discrimination – particularly in comparison with the stigmatization to which Muslim cultural practices can be subjected.

Philippe Portier has shown that reference to France's religious matrix has been growing in significance since the beginnings of the Fifth Republic (Portier, 2013). General de Gaulle publicly celebrated France as the project of God himself. François Mitterrand welcomed John Paul II at Lourdes with an acknowledgement of France's indebtedness to the Church. A few years later, he launched the commemoration of the Baptism of Clovis. The beginning of the twenty-first century was marked by a strengthening of this discourse.

Nicolas Sarkozy, President of the Republic between 2007 and 2012, was a driving force behind this. At an address delivered at the Lateran Palace in December 2007, he defended Catholicism's contribution to French society and to the Republic. He began by recognizing the value of France's Catholic heritage and asserting the necessity of its perpetuation for the preservation of national unity. He then asserted the importance of the hope provided by religion for civic-mindedness, which he declared to otherwise be at the risk of disappearing. His conclusion to that particular speech has been the subject of widespread commentary; he claimed that: 'in the transmission of values and the instilling of the difference between good and evil, the teacher will never be able to replace the priest or pastor, even if it is important that they come close to doing so, because they will always lack the radicalism of a life sacrificed and the charisma of a commitment borne by hope' (Sarkozy, 2007). This stance signals an evolution in the interpretation of secularism, from indifference to an appreciation of the social contribution of the religion (Portier, 2016).

François Hollande, president from 2012 to 2017, broke with this line seeking the symbolic convergence between Catholic order and republican order. But he had to face a powerful social movement led by Catholics in opposition to his legalization of same-sex marriage. His successor, Emmanuel Macron, returned to a more conciliatory position to rally Catholics as much as possible. In April 2018, invited by the bishops to the *Collège des Bernardins*, Emmanuel Macron declared that he wanted to 'restore the link between the Church and the State'. In a tone recalling the speech made by Nicolas Sarkozy at the Lateran Palace, he stated that 'France has been strengthened by the commitment of Catholics'. Finally, he expressed hope that 'the Catholic sap' will continue 'to make our nation live' (Macron, 2018).

This speech joins the words of intellectuals such as Pierre Manent or Marcel Gauchet who, with different arguments, consider that Catholicism is an indispensable resource for the maintenance of civism and the commons that make the republican order viable. The variation of Emmanuel Macron on the theme of 'roots' is an illustration of a very French 'secular Catholicism'. For example, Emmanuel Macron, as President of the Republic, can declare that the reconstruction of Notre-Dame 'is our destiny' without raising indignation. The fire of the cathedral of Paris showed that, if Catholicism is only a marginal source of personal identity, its cultural and patrimonial forms remain legitimate for the expression of collective emotion and national unity. Catholicism, as the Church retracts, becomes a cultural heritage available as a political resource.

'Christian roots': a politically instrumentalizable, secularized Catholicism

This secularization of Catholicism can also be observed through the growing mobilization of 'Christian roots' in the rhetoric of French nationalist and populist leaders (Raison du Cleuziou, 2019). The reference to Catholicism as France's historical religion is used to justify the characterization of the Muslim way of life as foreign (Roy, 2019). In this context, Catholicism as a heritage resource for the assertion of national identity has returned to the centre of political debate. In October 2015, Robert Ménard, Mayor of Béziers, who politically is close to the National Front, declared his intention to prohibit the opening of new 'kebab' restaurants, in the name of France's 'Judeo-Christian tradition'. In June 2016, Mayor of Tourcoing Gérald Darmanin called for a ban on the construction of minarets in France to be inscribed in the French Town Planning Code, on the grounds that: 'We are not an Islamist territory, but a country with Christian roots' (Darmanin, 2016).

In addition, certain members of parliament on the right have attempted to revise the Constitution to include mention of the Catholic character of French culture. In 2016, Christian Democratic Party MP Jean-Frédéric Poisson proposed an amendment to a bill for a revision of the Constitution on the deprivation of nationality. His objective was to revise article 1 of the Constitution to state that France has 'Christian roots'. MP Valérie Boyer proposed a similar amendment. In 2018, this idea returned to the agenda thanks to MP Eric Ciotti. They did not succeed. The aim of these initiatives was to confer a 'heritage' character upon Catholicism so that its practices can be subsidized by the State. Following this logic, a number of right-wing elected officials fought so that the town halls could exhibit nativity scenes at Christmas time. Paradoxically, elected representatives acting in the name of the Republic are providing Catholicism with the sort of symbolic authority capable of reversing the sociological decline of religious practice and preserving the Church in its dominant position as the religion of the French.

The beginning of the twenty-first century has been marked by the emergence of a new national narrative. Christian roots have taken on a political function similar to that of the image of the Gauls in the republican culture of the nineteenth century (Borne, 2014). This image enabled the assertion of a national unity that predated the deeds of the kings, and the glorification of a spirit of independence in the face of German imperialist pretensions inherited from Rome. These Christian roots make it possible to assert that France finds its unity in a Christian heritage that is the inheritance of both believers and non-believers: the sons of Clovis and the sons of the Enlightenment. France is not a spiritual desert vulnerable to Muslim conquest, the argument goes, but a civilization to which the latter owe respect and submissiveness. This political mobilization of Catholicism as a symbolic resource of a nationalist or populist struggle can be observed in other European countries (Brubakers, 2017). It is not a 'return of religion' but rather a secularization of religion as a cultural frontier in the service of a nation-building policy (Marzouki, 2016).

A social movement against the secularization of family values

The secularization of French society contributed to change the way Catholics thought of themselves. On the one hand, from the first bioethical laws adopted in 1994, they understood that Catholic morality was becoming marginal, particularly on sexual issues. The conservative Catholic activists tried to renew their mode of action in order to restore legitimacy to their convictions. Their main agenda was to oppose the desacralization of the traditional family model. On the other hand, the composition of the church is transformed by the decline in the number of believers: conservative families have become increasingly important as they have succeeded in transmitting faith, more than the others. Through these transformations of its base, the Church has tended to take a conservative turn.

During the 1990s, the affirmation of the gay movement was closely observed and feared within the French Catholic Church because it represents a frontal attack on both the family order and the difference between the sexes that Pope John Paul II put at the heart of his preaching. Interpreted as the manifestation *par excellence* of the deconstruction of the natural order by modern individualism, the homosexual is perceived as the enemy and homosexuals thought of as victims in need of enlightenment (Raison du Cleuziou, 2019). In 1999, the first stage in the legal recognition of homosexual couples had already caused a significant mobilization among France's Catholics (see Chapter 7 in this volume for further discussion). The ecclesiastical authorities formed strategic alliances to support their opposition to homosexuals: with right-wing political elites, intellectuals, legal experts and psychoanalysts in particular. Finally, and furtively, they also reached out to Jewish, Protestant and Muslim communities in a common front to oppose homosexuality (Béraud and Portier, 2015). In addition and since the beginning of the 2000s, the Catholic Church has been producing a counter-discourse on gender that has been widely broadcast. This 'anti-gender campaign' has had a European dimension (Kuhar and Paternotte, 2017). Once again, in 2012, it was amongst the Catholics that the opposition to the same-sex marriage organized itself, although it extended beyond their circle.

La Manif pour tous: a secular group steered by Catholics

The defeat by François Hollande of Nicolas Sarkozy in the presidential election of May 2012, followed by failure in the legislative elections, marked the beginning of a new series of events in the political history of the Catholics in France. On 30 June 2012, the day of the tenth annual Gay Pride celebrations, Laurence Rossignol, the French Minister for Families, announced in Paris that the campaign promise made by François Hollande to make civil marriages available to same-sex couples would be kept. The draft bill was to be steered by Justice Minister Christiane Taubira. At masses held on 15 August of that year, the bishops issued an official prayer which implicitly condemned this extension of marriage to same-sex couples.

Subsequently however, the lay mobilization was to structure itself independently of the bishops and priests of the Church. It did so primarily on the basis of conservative Catholic organizations, such as associations for the protection of the family and pro-life movements. Their coalition was to give birth to a specific structure: *La Manif pour tous* (LMPT). One particular Catholic sensibility was the key to this mobilization: the observants (Raison du Cleuziou, 2015). This is a Catholicism based on family networks and which constitutes a relatively homogeneous group. It is a bourgeoisie whose capital is essentially one of heritage: the certainty of embodying true Catholicism and of being the guarantors of authentic French identity. An integrated group, in the sense of Anthony Oberschall (1973), the observants see themselves as a minority upholding universal values and aspiring to restore the Church of France, which they consider 'half-hearted', and more broadly French society, which they view as 'decadent'.

Mobilization against the Taubira draft bill did not attract only Catholics, nor did it draw all Catholics into the cause. Many parishes were profoundly divided by LMPT (Raison du Cleuziou, 2018). Finally, many Catholics, including those on the right, have other priorities in politics than the definition of legitimate marriage and parentage.

Between 2012 and 2016, this mobilization took the form of eight major demonstrations. Although street protests are not entirely foreign to the Catholic right, the scale and frequency of these actions were unprecedented (Tartakowsky, 2014). LMPT chose to give a secular character to the demonstrations, as well as to their arguments. This choice was not incompatible with the discourse of the ecclesiastic authorities, who employed primarily anthropological arguments founded on 'natural morals' rather than on evangelical revelation. This secular choice also reflected a will to 'appeal to the people' and to gain the legitimacy that democracy confers upon the majority. The organizers of LMPT also chose to stage the demonstrations in the form of festive parades inspired by the Gay Pride marches. The slogans avoided any form of homosexual stigmatization and prioritized the protection of children's right to have 'a mum and a dad'. These strategic choices were not shared by a minority of Catholics close to the fundamentalist networks that are the heirs to the schismatic bishop Marcel Lefebvre who refused to recognize the legitimacy of the Second Vatican Council, or by certain minor nationalist groups. Behind the fundamentalist *Civitas* lobby, these demonstrated separately and on different dates and denounced homosexuality as a sin.

The LMPT coalition was eventually to split over the goals of the struggle, but it remained active on a large scale until 2013. LMPT succeeded in rallying people by setting aside the organizational, territorial, social and religious splits that divide the Catholics. The two spokespersons Tugdual Derville and Frigide Barjot (real name Virginie Tellenne) were an illustration of this with their extremely different styles. The first is a Catholic pro-life activist, whereas the second is a parody artist who has made a return to Catholicism in 'born again' evangelist style. The left-wing Catholics of the '*Poissons Roses*' supported the LMPT coalition, as did activists from an old royalist movement such as *Action Française*. The mobilization also reached beyond Catholicism, finding support among certain Muslim, Protestant and Jewish organizations, albeit without this inspiring significant mobilization within these groups. The demonstration of January 2013 was the most successful, with 340,000 participants according to the police.

In March 2013, faced with the steadfastness of the government, the coalition split over the action it should adopt. Inspired by the Arab Spring uprisings, Béatrice Bourges, President of the *Collectif pour l'Enfant*, split away from the position of LMPT and attempted to merge the family cause with other forms of anti-government contestation. She called on her activists to revolt, seeking backing from far-right activists in search of confrontation with the police. This radicalization deprived LMPT of part of its moderate support on the left and within other religions. The *'Jour de Colère'* (Day of Anger) demonstration, organized on 26 January 2014, was the short-lived outcome of this merger of anti-government contestation targeted by the 'French Spring'. The protest was marred by anti-Semitism which served to discredit all the groups involved.

At the heart of LMPT, another split was to take place in May 2013 during voting on the draft bill. Frigide Barjot adopted a strategy of negotiation with the government and proposed a compromise: the creation of a civil pact offering homosexuals societal recognition of their conjugal status without bringing about a change to the legal framework surrounding parentage or adoption. This position resulted in her expulsion from the leadership of LMPT, where she was replaced by Ludovine de la Rochère, a conservative Catholic activist. Frigide Barjot then founded *L'Avenir Pour Tous*, with the aim of revising the Taubira Law into a civil partnership. Despite the bill being passed, LMPT under the leadership of Ludovine de la Rochère decided to continue its actions until, she hoped, it was repealed. The fight, justified as conscientious objection in the name of children's rights, consequently shrunk to an activist base made up of Catholic conservatives. A certain number of minor activist enterprises born on the margins of the mobilizations, including *Les Veilleurs*, *Les Gavroches*, *Les Sentinelles*, *Les Hommen* and *Les Antigones*, chose autonomy, and attempted to institutionalize themselves while continuing to participate intermittently in LMPT activities (Della Sudda and Avanza, 2017).

Certain activist members of LMPT favoured an intellectual approach to continuing the struggle. In September 2015, as part of the activity of *Les Veilleurs*, Gaultier Bès, Paul Piccarreta and Eugénie Bastié launched the *Limite* journal. They sought to overcome the left–right divide by claiming to be both pro-degrowth environmentalists, and Christians. References to Jacques Ellul, George Orwell and Georges Bernanos supported a radical denunciation of market capitalism and the artificialization of lives that accompanies it. Other intellectuals opined that the threat posed by migration outweighed the environmental issue. They asserted the right of a people to perpetuate its culture and denounced the inaction of the State in the face of France's Islamification. They came together in the monthly *L'Incorrect*, created in September 2017 by writer Jacques de Guillebon with the support of financier Charles Beigbeder and Laurent Meeschaert. These different initiatives taken together have contributed to a revival of conservative and, in general, dissenting thought in France (Raison du Cleuziou, 2019).

A strategy of electoral lobbying

After the parliamentary approval of the Taubira Law in May 2013, and in order to keep up the mobilization and lay the ground for a political shift in its favour, the LMPT group attempted to broaden its range of activities by forming an electoral lobby (Raison du Cleuziou, 2019). Their first foray into the electoral arena was in the primaries organized in May and June 2013 by the UMP to select a candidate for Paris City Hall. In order to encourage their activists to make the move 'from the pavement to the polls', the movement published a leaflet on each candidate specifying their position on the Taubira Law. In November 2013, the approach was extended to all municipal elections. Ludovine de la Rochère unveiled a municipal charter which candidates hoping for LMPT support had to ratify in public. The representatives were thus subjected to a tactic forcing them to clarify their position with respect to family policy. By March 2014, around 1,300 candidates had signed the municipal election charter. This strategy was refined with each new election. In order to support its electoral brokerage offer, LMPT commissioned surveys before and after each election to demonstrate the importance of family concerns among voters. This operation benefited from the legitimacy lent to it by experts. Patrick Buisson, former strategic advisor to President Nicolas Sarkozy, provided support in the media for the idea that the future of the parties of the right depended on their alignment with the expectations of the conservative electorate.

A strategy of party restructuration: the case of *Sens Commun*

Independently of LMPT, other Catholic activists sought to remedy the causes of the failure that is for them the Taubira law. The *Sens Commun* political party was created in November 2013. This initiative was taken by several LMPT activists who were involved in the UMP but were getting no support from the party. They decided to reinvest in their party by creating a balance of power that was more favourable to their agenda, focused on family policy. Their strategy was to form, by means of *Sens Commun*, an internal lobby group within the UMP in order to influence the manifesto and win elected representatives. In exchange for activist support, they wanted to negotiate a commitment from the UMP's leadership to repeal the Taubira Law. They chose a secular approach in order to bring together all those French people of the view that the conservative fight could not be confined to the protection of the family, and that the fight must instead be extended to an overall plan for society. In December 2013, Jean-François Copé, then president of the UMP, accepted a partnership between his party and *Sens Commun*. His leadership was being challenged, and he hoped in this way to find new activists to support it. The young movement established a system of double membership and situated itself clearly within the UMP in order to create a balance of power that was favourable to its political agenda.

It received a very positive reception from those UMP parliamentarians who had committed to strong support for LMPT.

Sens Commun achieved rapid success as the reshaping of the parliamentary right favoured its strategy. In the context of the succession of Jean-François Copé, *Sens Commun* positioned itself with a manifesto based on 'the right that we want' and organized a hearing of the main candidates for UMP leadership during a dramatic meeting on 14 November 2014. This occasion brought the young movement its first significant media coverage. In May 2015, on the initiative of Nicolas Sarkozy, the transformation of the UMP into *Les Républicains* (LR) enabled them to achieve an additional stage of institutionalization. Three senior members of *Sens Commun* were appointed to LR's organizational structure. Furthermore, the results of the departmental and regional elections of March and December 2015 respectively, which saw the right return, enabled the young movement to obtain some 20 local representatives. The *Sens Commun* team thus benefitted from a favourable organizational situation and got places on the leadership team of the UMP. Due to its success, in other words, *Sens Commun* became an effective interface for mobilizing practising Catholics in the political parties. *Sens Commun* was also courted by other parties that sought to capture the Catholic electorate from LR. Both the FN and Dupont Aignan's *Debout la République* proposed an alliance with *Sens Commun*, an eventuality rejected by the young party. In October 2016, a structure with a similar stance was created in the National Front: *Cercle Fraternité*. It promoted the protection of the family within the FN and claimed to be close to the conservative line defended by Marion Maréchal-Le Pen.

Belief in the existence of an unexploited conservative cleavage in the electorate led some to conceive of the creation of a new party. This was the ambition of the '*Droite-hors-les-murs*' (the right outside the walls). This informal collective, bringing together former minister Charles Millon, financier Charles Beigbeder, mayor Robert Ménard, writer Jacques de Guillebon and even the former face of political conservatism Philippe de Villiers, sought the emergence of a populist conservative party, following the line of Patrick Buisson, and capable of forming a bridge between the FN and LR. On 18 and 19 May 2016 in Béziers, Robert Ménard launched the '*Oz ta droite*' collective in an attempt to occupy this political space. Several manifesto proposals corresponded directly to LMPT demands, including the non-retroactive repeal of the Taubira Law or the banning of surrogacy. These various initiatives demonstrated the determination of mobilized Catholics to weigh on the 2017 presidential election campaign, which is now considered.

Conservative Catholics and the 2017 presidential and legislative elections

From the first demonstrations against the Taubira draft bill during autumn 2012, the elected representatives of the opposition had to position themselves in relation to the LMPT movement. The exercise was a delicate one as, by taking part in protests, they risked being instrumentalized by a social movement they did not control. If they did not, however, their capacity to embody the opposition would be called into question. Until the vote on the bill in May 2013, the majority of UMP leaders were willing enough to accept being placed at the head of protests. Not all were, however: former Prime Minister François Fillon, for example, never once marched or expressed his support for the movement. Once the bill had been approved, participation became a more delicate matter, because it obliged professional politicians to commit to repealing the law in the event of a shift in support. This caused certain representatives to keep their distance. LMPT, however, deployed a strategy of intense lobbying in order to force them to commit to repealing the Taubira Law. It is in this way that LMPT became an important factor in the restructuring of the French right. This appeared strongly between the primaries organized by the main right-wing parties in November 2016 and the presidential election of April and May 2017.

The 2016 primary of the right and the centre, and the confrontation between candidates to represent the LMPT

For the 2017 presidential elections, LMPT repeated its electoral brokering strategy with a small number of variations. The context for this was highly favourable, due to the primaries of the right and centre planned for November 2016. This innovative consultation mechanically lent weight to the Catholic electorate known to make up part of *Les Républicains'* voters (Gouard, 2017). In June 2016, LMPT used two polls to frame the issue of the upcoming election. These showed among other things that nearly two-thirds of voters in the primaries wanted to see the Taubira Law revised by the new president. In September 2016, a report with 40 proposals for a new family policy was distributed by LMPT. This report framed the proposed transaction thus: candidates had to agree to these proposals if they wanted to benefit from the support of the 'pro-family' group. The report could be used by voters as a check box to determine their choice. In order to finalize the brokerage by setting a deadline, 16 October 2016, a demonstration was announced in Paris. This was a technique to elicit a declaration, giving candidates the opportunity to express their support by joining the protest, or by delivering a speech at the podium. By choosing to refrain, they were potentially depriving themselves of electoral visibility and perhaps leaving the benefits to their rivals.

Within the UMP, the position of *Sens Commun* as the representative of conservative Catholicism was not unquestioned. The Christian Democratic Party, created by Christine Boutin and allied to the UMP since its creation, claimed to be the most faithful to LMPT's battle. In September 2015, its president Jean-Frédéric Poisson announced his candidature in the primaries of the right and centre. He clearly positioned himself as the candidate embodying the aspirations of LMPT. However, the majority of candidates in the primary attempted to obtain the favour of the Catholics or 'pro-family' group as a well-identified segment of the LR electorate. Alain Juppé appeared at Lourdes for mass on 15 August. François Fillon confessed his faith in a book. The majority of candidates presented themselves as Catholics in the interviews that they provided to weekly magazine *Famille Chrétienne*. The primary thus found itself 'Catholicized'.

On 1 September, *Sens Commun* publicly communicated its support for François Fillon. Its goal of achieving power implied agreeing to work with a candidate without sharing the entirety of their beliefs, on the basis of a compromise. Among conservative Catholics, the choice of François Fillon rather than Jean-Frédéric Poisson sparked an enduring debate. Contrary to Jean-Frédéric Poisson, the positions of François Fillon on the Taubira Law indeed appeared somewhat tepid. Following a good start to his campaign in the primaries, Jean-Frédéric Poisson went on to rally the support of a number of important figures in *Droite-hors-les-murs*, including Charles Beigbeder and Robert Ménard. Even within the FN, Marion Maréchal-Le Pen supported him. They believed they had found the candidate who would break through and create a movement uniting the conservative right-wingers to whom they were appealing. Jean-Frédéric Poisson accepted this support. He clearly positioned himself as the candidate of *Droite-hors-les-murs* in declaring himself open to alliances with the *Front national*.

François Fillon: candidate of the conservative Catholics?

The results from the first round of the centre and right primaries temporarily put an end to the fight between those claiming to represent conservative Catholicism. With 44.08 per cent of the vote (1,890,266 votes), the success of François Fillon reflected considerable mobilization. The supporters of Jean-Frédéric Poisson had no choice but to admit defeat, Poisson having received only 1.45 per cent of the vote (62,346 votes). Even though he had scored highly in Versailles and exceeded 10 per cent in some regional areas, his popularity had remained confined to these areas. Within the LMPT web, the triumph of François Fillon also represented the victory of *Sens Commun* over other attempts to mobilize conservative Catholics.

With the success of François Fillon secured, the LMPT coalition regrouped and eliminated the strategic divergences which had divided it only a day before. All came together to retrospectively interpret the success of François Fillon as the consequence of the electoral contract struck between the Catholics/pro-family groups and the candidate. This framing of the election as a transaction was confirmed by many articles in the press. In an interview given to *Le Monde* on 21 November 2016, Emmanuel Macron described the former Prime Minister as the leader of 'true economic and social conservatism' and attributed a significant 'role' to LMPT in this evolution (Pietralunga 2016). Alain Juppé, who likewise had made it through to the second round of the primary, attacked François Fillon over the ambiguity of his stance on abortion. Although Fillon reaffirmed his dedication to this 'fundamental right', many of his supporters nuanced these remarks, adding that it should remain an exception. For the centre right and the left, the 'conservative Catholic' label was used strategically to discredit François Fillon. On the contrary, however, this tactic succeeded in boosting Fillon's credit among LMPT activists. The very considerable victory of François Fillon in the second round of the right and centre primaries, with 66.49 per cent of the vote (2,919,874), was interpreted in media coverage as a return of Catholicism to politics.

The unexpected outcome of the primary contributed to the assumption that *Sens Commun* was the 'secret army' behind François Fillon's success. The movement became omnipresent in the press. Many media groups honoured it with their headlines and lent credibility to the idea of its hidden power. However, the beginning of the presidential campaign was characterized primarily by a return to party concerns. François Fillon and his campaign director Patrick Stefanini shared the key concern of distributing responsibilities to all the LR *notables*, and especially to those who had supported other candidates during the primaries.

As a result, *Sens Commun* was marginalized in the campaign team. Yet it undertook to serve François Fillon with unreserved loyalty in order to rise to power with him. Its involvement in François Fillon's campaign apparatus in effect maintained the latter's position as a presidential candidate who was able to satisfy some of the Catholics' expectations. In the event of victory, some compensation for the small party could be expected. On account of its support for Fillon, *Sens Commun* was attacked by those who did not consider François Fillon to be the best candidate for the Catholics. The National Front MP Marion Maréchal-Le Pen attempted to mobilize Catholic voters in support of her aunt Marine Le Pen. In November 2016, the MP's position in favour of ending the reimbursement of abortion by social security was a clear signal to the electorate. By comparison, the positioning of François Fillon could only appear lukewarm in the eyes of the observant.

On 25 January 2017, *Le Canard enchaîné* revealed alleged payments made to Pénélope Fillon as a parliamentary assistant to her husband, and then to his successor Marc Joulaud. The president of *Sens Commun*, Christophe Billan, denounced a conspiracy against the candidate. This appeared obvious to him in light of the leniency shown by the media to Emmanuel Macron, compromised, according to him, by grave conflicts of interest. He defended the candidate due to the importance of his programme for France as he, Billan, saw it. Thus, the qualities of the programme were substituted for the personal qualities of the candidate put forward during the primary. Frigide Barjot launched a petition in support of François Fillon in order to restore the aura that she had lost in May 2013 with her expulsion from LMPT. Since then she had worked constantly to restore her authority as a mediator between the political class and the Catholics. Her petition gathered more than 30,000 signatures.

On 1 March, François Fillon announced that he had been indicted by the National Financial Prosecutor's Office. The following day, his Paris home was searched. Defections in his team multiplied. On 3 March, Patrick Stefanini, his campaign director, stood down, leaving the campaign team in total disarray. A dozen *Sens Commun* activists came to replace the party activists, primarily in minor tasks such as answering phone calls. Within the LR, many MPs wanted François Fillon to withdraw his candidacy in order to make way for Alain Juppé, the candidate who had come second in the primaries. François Fillon decided instead on a large rally to bring together his supporters at the *Place du Trocadéro* on 6 March. *Sens Commun* was involved in the organization of the event, and its activists occupied an important place within it. The rally was a success, with about 30,000 to 50,000 participants, and renewed the legitimacy of the candidate.

The supporters of Alain Juppé attempted to counter the obstinacy of candidate Fillon by denouncing the radicalization of his supporters. They highlighted the growing influence of *Sens Commun*. Fillon's strategy appeared to lend credibility to this interpretation. On 17 March, he gave an interview to *Famille chrétienne* in which he committed to abolishing the offence of obstructing abortion. On 28 March, he received Ludovine de la Rochère at his campaign headquarters. He stepped up the signals sent to the Catholic electorate. On Easter Weekend, he appeared at the sanctuary of Paray-le-Monial before participating in the Easter Vigil of a Coptic community. On 16 April, he declared that he might include members of *Sens Commun* in the government, which the left denounced as reactionary. The elected representatives of the centre right feared being marginalized within the mainstream right to the benefit of the conservative Catholic right. They attacked the archaism of *Sens Commun* in the media.

The failure of François Fillon in the first round of the presidential election caused a shock within right-wing Catholicism. The centre right attributed responsibility for the defeat to *Sens Commun*. Three-quarters of practising Catholics always vote in favour of the mainstream right-wing candidate in the second round of the presidential election. The circumstances made this doubly ominous: since the primaries, this electorate had been (wrongly) identified with extreme conservatism and Marine Le Pen was in the second round. Having been deprived of its candidate, was there not a risk that the Catholic right might ally itself with the National Front?

The second round: a possible turning of the Catholic vote towards the *Front National*?

The definition of the legitimate Catholic vote once again became a disputed issue in the second round of the 2017 presidential election. Emmanuel Macron came out in favour of extending medically assisted procreation.

Ludovine de La Rochère called to vote against him without coming out in favour of the National Front candidate. As shown by Jérôme Fourquet, the radicalization of part of her base hardly left her a choice (Fourquet, 2018). Frigide Barjot called to vote blank. *Sens Commun* and the *Parti Chrétien Démocrate* adopted a 'neither–nor' line and left their voters free to make their choice. The quarrels over strategy in the primaries, suspended by the success of François Fillon began once again.

That was not all, however, because the tensions of the second round had mobilized those Catholics who up to that point had kept their distance from the electoral lobbying operation conducted in the name of the 'Catholic vote' by LMPT and other movements like *Sens Commun* or *Droite-hors-les-murs*. The Bishops' Conference of France intervened with a text inviting Christians to show discernment. Their *communiqué* simply gave a reminder of the evangelical obligation to welcome strangers, which could be read as a condemnation of Marine Le Pen. However, they also denounced the harmful effects of liberalism, whether it be on the economy, society or bioethics, which could also be read as a reluctance to endorse Emmanuel Macron. Many Catholics criticized the ambiguity of this position that they feared could legitimize the vote in favour of the far right. A number of Catholic intellectuals opposed LMPT in an attempt to bring Catholic voters back to Emmanuel Macron. Macron appeared to them to be the presidential candidate most compatible with the evangelical values with which they associate themselves.

In the second round of the presidential elections, the IFOP survey for *Pèlerin* of 7 May 2017 showed that Emmanuel Macron was chosen by 71 per cent of regular practising Catholics. Marine Le Pen drew only 29 per cent of votes among them, which was her best score among this electorate and confirmed the significant progress of the FN vote already observed amongst Catholics in the regional elections of 2015. Nevertheless, this vote remained below national averages and did not invalidate the finding that the majority of practising Catholics were still reluctant to vote for the FN. The FN vote was only above the national average among non-practising Catholics. The results of the 2017 presidential election suggest, therefore, that the FN was becoming normalized among French Catholics.

Conclusion

In France, despite the continued decline in the number of practising Catholics, Catholicism has once again become a significant political resource for the right. Faced with the rising profile of Islam, the reference to France's Catholic history is enabling elected representatives on the right to draw a symbolic border keeping French Muslims in a position of subordination and deviance. For their part, conservative Catholic activists, disappointed by the weakness of right-wing parties' ethical positions, have mobilized to defend their convictions by themselves, particularly against making marriage available to same-sex couples. They have discovered their capacity to mobilize and decided to use this in order to influence the right-wing parties. But the forms taken by this politicization have divided Catholic activists. Should they engage in politics or attempt to transform society at its foundations? Reinvest in established parties or create new ones? Be morally intransigent or make reasonable accommodations? Act by claiming their Catholic identity or more discreetly, try to embody the values of the Gospel?

The failed candidature of François Fillon and the instrumentalization of *Sens Commun* by centrist and left-wing currents of the LR demonstrated the complexity of these tactical issues. The right remains divided between those who believe that a conservative Catholic shift is necessary for its reconstruction, and those who believe that this option can only end in failure.

7 OLD THINKING ABOUT NEW FAMILIES: REPRODUCTIVE AND SEXUAL POLITICS IN A TECHNOLOGICAL AGE

Bruno Perreau

During his 2012 presidential campaign, François Hollande declared he would open up assisted procreation to single women and lesbian couples should he be elected. Indeed, France used to restrict medically assisted procreation – *procréation médicalement assistée* – to heterosexual couples. However, Hollande's first government decided not to include medically assisted procreation in the bill of law on gay marriage and adoption scheduled to be discussed before the French parliament in the fall of 2012. The reason put forward was strategic: medically assisted procreation would complicate the debates and would be better discussed together with other bioethical issues. After several months of street protests against the law on 'marriage for all' (see Chapter 6), the government decided to postpone any further discussion on medically assisted procreation and eventually abandoned the reform altogether.

In 2017, during his own presidential campaign, Emmanuel Macron made a point of taking the opposite view. Coming from a new generation, he asserted that he would work on reforming assisted procreation as soon as 2017. A few months after his election, Emmanuel Macron stepped back: he explained that he wanted an 'appeased debate' and that 'consensus' had to be built before presenting any official bill (*L'Express*, 2017). On 18 March 2019, during a debate organized at the Élysée Palace with more than 65 intellectuals, he confirmed that things needed to be thought over first (*France Culture*, 2019), thus postponing the parliamentary discussion (*Le Monde*, 2019). LGBT organizations protested. The State Secretary for Equality between Women and Men, Marlène Schiappa, explained that the law would be on the Parliamentary agenda before summer 2019 (*Le Parisien*, 2019). Debates started in the National Assembly in September 2019, and the Senate discussed the text in January 2020. Right-wing senators introduced an

---

(Translated from the French by Patsy Baudoin)

amendment that allowed for the reimbursement of expenses related to medically assisted procreation only for heterosexual couples. The National Assembly withdrew this amendment from the final text, which was adopted on 31 July 2020. The scope of the law was, however, more restrictive than expected. The National Assembly opened assisted procreation to single women and lesbian couples, but banned egg donation within lesbian couples, except in cases of infertility. Trans people were deliberately left out of the reform: they were not allowed access to assisted procreation. The sexual mutilation of intersex children was not explicitly prohibited by the law. Last but not least, the government introduced an amendment to oppose the automatic recognition of legal parenthood in the case of surrogacy carried out abroad (article 4bis; Assemblée Nationale, 2020). The non-biological parent must adopt his or her own child, and parents must be married.

Why such similarities between François Hollande and Emmanuel Macron? The main explanation might be an institutional one: the practice of institutional accretion (whereby elected representatives create new councils and committees in order to externalize decision-making or consultative processes) has emerged as the routine response to controversial social policy issues under successive governments (Thelen, 2003). Neoliberal governance (by which the socialist party abides since 1983) perceives antagonistic views only as a source of institutional instability (Mouffe, 2005). As a consequence, programmatic choices tend to be hidden – or euphemized – when a social question is doomed to be too contentious. Another explanation might point to professional trajectory. François Hollande and Emmanuel Macron were educated in the same elite schools (*Sciences Po* and *École Nationale d'Administration*). Emmanuel Macron was appointed Deputy Secretary General of the Élysée by François Hollande in 2012 and became his Minister of Economy, Industry and Digital Affaires in 2014. It is perhaps not surprising that they share the same procedural approach when it comes to tackling disputed societal issues; neither Hollande nor Macron took a clear stance on reproductive technologies before their election, with regard to equality (between families) or freedom (to choose how one becomes a parent) or both.

The continuity between Hollande's and Macron's presidency has shaped current debates on bioethics. On 5 June 2018, France's advisory council on bioethics, the *Comité Consultatif National d'Éthique* (CCNE), published its summary report drawn from the Estates General on Bioethics. The report documented citizens' discussions and experts' assessments that were gathered over nearly six months throughout France about new medical techniques (transplants, stem cells, genomic medicine etc.), euthanasia and artificial intelligence as well as medically assisted procreation and the recognition of families resulting from their use (*Comité Consultatif National d'Éthique*, 2018). The report laid out the parliamentary work that would lead to the revising of bioethics laws by the end of the year. The previous bioethics law of 7 July 2011, had provided for its own revision within seven years. President of the CCNE Jean-François Delfraissy recently applauded this new 'health democracy', considering that the Estates General on Bioethics enabled a renewal of democracy through citizen participation (*YouTube*, 6 June 2018). But things are less obvious when we take a closer look. First, there is the question of the representativeness of these assessments. For the most part, participants were professionals (solicited by the local health networks who organized the discussions) and activists who, with more resources (training, networks, financial support), intervened a lot during the public meetings and commented in droves on the Estates General's website. Thus, the opponents of the Taubira law of 17 May 2013, the law that opened up marriage and joint adoption to homosexual couples, were particularly mobilized, arguing against allowing lesbian couples and single women access to medically assisted procreation and against the legalization of surrogacy as well as sometimes even in favour of repealing the Taubira law itself (*États généraux de la bioéthique*, 2018).

Second, approaching new forms of conjugal and family life solely on the basis of medical technological developments considerably restricts the scope of possible reform. The medical casting frames the collective discussion, whereas it is precisely this framework that should be questioned. This work is all the more needed as France is undergoing a major transformation of its family way of life, well beyond issues of assisted reproduction: for ten years, the number of civil union contracts (*Pacte civil de solidarité or PaCS*) has been close to that of marriage, around 200,000 a year (INSEE, 2018a); among new marriages, 3 per cent are same-sex marriages (Decharme, 2018). Today, nearly 60 per cent of children are born out of wedlock, a figure that has doubled in 30 years (INSEE, 2018b).

First, I plan on locating the attendant bioethical discussions of 2018 in the broader context of the sexual, reproductive and conjugal policies established in France since the mid-1960s. I will explain how, starting in the 1980s, sacralizing the fertile body as the nation's treasure has not only led to restricting the use of reproductive technologies but has also fostered the emergence of reactionary rhetoric that is hostile to the recognition of sexual minorities. This has resulted in a muted recognition of homosexual couples and the exclusion of other reforms such as medically assisted procreation and surrogacy. I will review the various discursive registers that have been mobilized (social risk, human ecology, symbolic order) and demonstrate that Emmanuel Macron's presidency accentuates this phenomenon of paradoxical recognition by inscribing it in a rhetoric of moral equivalence between opponents and advocates of same-sex parenting and transparenting. In the end, I will offer a critical analysis of the very notion of bioethics, which I propose to substitute with a technopolitical approach, whose general philosophy I will elaborate.

The body, a nation's treasure

Laws regarding sexuality and parenting as well as family law have changed considerably since the mid-1960s. The baby boom generation reached adulthood and ushered in a new relationship to work, domesticity and sexuality. Although political speeches at the time continued to focus on the birth rate (Mossuz-Lavau, 2012, p. 45) – with General de Gaulle even pleading for a France with 100 million inhabitants – a certain pragmatism tended to prevail among parliamentarians. The increased rate of women's participation in the workforce responded to the national need for economic expansion. Contraception was required for reasons of public health, including limiting the use of abortion. Legal professional backgrounds and more broadly a legalistic culture characterized the make-up of the elected assemblies: it was a time when, according to Dean Jean Carbonnier, the 'legal legislator' reigned (quoted by Vauchez, 2009, p. 114). Owing to their training, these parliamentarians knew that parentage is a fiction, that is to say, a convention sealed by law, whether or not it is based on reproduction. Reforms multiplied that separated parenting and family life from procreation. They were strengthened in the 1970s by the establishment of more liberally orientated public policies under the leadership of France's new President Valery Giscard d'Estaing. The many reforms that emerged included matrimonial regimes allowing married women to have their own bank account (13 July 1965); contraceptive pills (19 December 1967); the adoption law (11 July 1966); the establishment of parental authority to replace paternal power (4 June 1970); the equal treatment of legitimate children born in the context of marriage and natural children born outside of wedlock (3 January 1972); the majority at 18 years of age (7 July 1974); the legalization of abortion (17 January 1975); divorce by mutual consent (11 July 1975); and, at the initiative of the newly elected Socialist majority, equalizing the age of consent for sex between heterosexuals and homosexuals (4 August 1982).

In the 1980s, a new cycle began and there were fresh discussions about new reproductive technologies. In France, the first child conceived by in vitro fertilization, a 'test tube baby', was born in 1982. There was a demand for the new reproductive technologies. A commercial system for surrogate parentship was created in 1983 under the name of the National Association of Artificial Insemination by surrogacy (*Association nationale de l'insémination artificielle par substitution*). A gynaecologist from Marseille, Sacha Geller, became the head of another organization, *Alma mater*, which advocated paying surrogate mothers and for their right to abandon giving up the child. To counter these demands, the Socialist government established the CCNE. Comprising representatives from the medical professions, the main religions as well as lawyers, philosophers and journalists, the CCNE undertook an initial expert assessment; their main conclusion was that reproductive assistance should be limited to cases of medical infertility. In its wake, other reports proposed limiting parentage to two parents of different sexes

(Braibant, 1988; Lenoir, Sturlèse, 1991; Bioulac, 1992). On the basis of the CCNE's expert assessment, Édouard Balladur's Gaullist government passed three bioethics laws promulgated on 1 and 29 July 1994. These marked a turning point: for the first time, heterosexuality became a condition for parentage, medically assisted procreation being reserved for heterosexual couples, whether married or living together for more than two years. Surrogacy was forbidden for everyone in the name of the unavailability of the human body. The mechanism that built the fertile body into a model became diffused into the whole area of family policies. And so, social workers who issued approvals for adoption required adoption candidates to be in a heterosexual relationship or, if they were single, to be planning a heterosexual relationship (Perreau, 2014, pp. 104–6). They must be able to impart to the child the importance of reproduction and the difference between the sexes. The courts have often validated this interpretation, which represented a complete departure from an earlier law of 1966 (Borrillo and Pitois, 1998, p. 150). This position, which conceives of social organization as based on biological function, represents what jurist Daniel Borrillo has called 'neo-biologism' (Borrillo, 2014, p. 309). In 2005, the CCNE explained that, 'the purposely asexual word homosexuality makes it possible to deny the difference between the sexes as being insignificant. What is at stake here are the paternal function and the maternal function and their complementarity for a constructive and edifying relationship of parenting/parentage' (*Comité Consultatif National d'Éthique*, 2005, pp. 25–6). Following the term renewal of some of its members (many of whom are appointed by the government), the CCNE finally acknowledged on 15 June 2017 that being opposed to medically assisted procreation for all women is untenable in a context of the right to move and reside freely within the EU (*Comité Consultatif National d'Éthique*, 2017). The CCNE therefore proposed to open it up to single women and lesbian couples but wished to restrict reimbursement for the procedure to heterosexual couples. Thus there would be medically assisted procreation based on necessity and medically assisted procreation based on comfort, which therefore would not be reimbursable. The biological must maintain primacy. The CCNE was, furthermore, in favour of 'the elaboration of an international convention for the prohibition of surrogacy' (*Comité Consultatif National d'Éthique*, 2017, p. 40).

France's long-standing position *vis-à-vis* medically assisted procreation and surrogacy did not stand the test of Europeanization. As in the case of medically assisted procreation, the freezing of oocytes or sperm before sex reassignment is permitted in neighbouring countries such as Italy, Spain and Belgium (children born of artificial insemination in Belgium are nicknamed 'Thalys babies' in reference to the high speed train linking Paris and Brussels). In the matter of surrogacy, Christiane Taubira had already signed, on 25 January 2013, an authorization to issue certificates of French nationality to children born abroad by surrogacy, if at least one parent is French (Ministry of Justice, 2013). In the Mennesson v. France and Labassee v. France cases

(European Court of Human Rights, 2014), the European Court of Human Rights went further because it considered that not recognizing in France a parentage established by surrogacy (in this case in the United States) conflicts with article 8 of its convention because it violates a child's right to privacy. The European Court of Human Rights condemned France once again in two cases: one concerning a single applicant (Foulon v. France) and another concerning an applicant for civil union (PaCSé) with a man (Bouvet v. France) (European Court of Human Rights, 2016). Attacked by the Lawyers for Childhood (*Juristes pour l'enfance*), a group close to the *Manif pour tous*, the main opposition movement to same-sex marriage, the Taubira authorization was validated by the Council of State (*Conseil d'État*, 2014). In a judgment of 3 July 2015, the Court of Cassation (which had refused the transcription of parentage in the Mennesson and Labassee cases) now considered the transcription of the civil status of a child born to a surrogate abroad, one of whose parents is a French national, to be compliant with French law and the European Convention on Human Rights (*Cour de cassation*, 2015).

In August 2019, the Council of State considered that the refusal to issue French nationality to a child born of surrogacy was illegal (*Conseil d'État*, 2019). In October 2019, the Court of Cassation declared that, in the Mennesson case, the recognition of both parents was in the best interests of the children (*Cour de cassation*, 2019a). The Court confirmed, in December 2019, that its jurisprudence applied to same-sex couples, married or not (*Cour de cassation*, 2019b). However, the executive branch has typically resisted such a change. Socialist Manuel Valls, prime minister 2014–16, intervened publicly to remind everyone that 'surrogacy remains absolutely prohibited in France' (quoted by Pascual, 2015).

The new law on bioethics adopted in July 2020 now requires that, in the event of surrogacy abroad, the non-biological parent adopts his own child in order to be recognized as such in France. This is a significant step back from the jurisprudence of the Court of Cassation, especially since adoption is not open to unmarried couples. This was the situation of lesbian couples having recourse to medically assisted procreation abroad before this bioethics law of July 2020 (*Cour de cassation*, 2014). France's position is therefore very uneven: on the one hand, it prohibits surrogacy, but on the other, it recognizes the children's French nationality and, in an integrated European system, must henceforth transcribe their civil status.

Biologism and majority universalism

If France today defends a certain idea of nature, it is because it considers that the idea is good for the whole of humanity. This was the substance of President Jacques Chirac's arguments when he took a stand on 29 April 1997 against reproductive cloning, a few months after the announcement of the cloning of Dolly the sheep in Scotland. In response to the CCNE report he had received on the subject, he said: 'While cloning is clearly prohibited in France, the essential problem is that it be banned everywhere in the world' (Chirac, 1997). The universalist logic affirmed there is directly in line with that of the French Revolution, with its abstract and conquering principles. This universalist logic was, however, built on the exclusion of women and minorities. Only the Revolution's White man could embody universalism. This is why it served to justify the colonial project: in addition to territorial expansion and its stakes of economic and cultural domination, it was the superiority of the Western male body that the colonial enterprise sought to assert. Cast away to the side of primitive masculinity, the native man was to be domesticated by white and civilized masculinity, and indigenous women overpowered willingly or by force (rapes, forced unveilings etc.). In a recent book, historian Todd Shepard has shown how decolonization has displaced these representations, particularly within the student and revolutionary movements of the 1970s, fascinated as they were by the idea of a wounded Western masculinity (Shepard, 2018). It is thus possible to wonder whether the bioethical expertise that emerged in the early 1980s was not an attempt to symbolically repair this fallen Western body by engaging in a new, universalist project. This is why questions of bioethics deserve to be thought of as part of a broader reflection on the body, identity and belonging. It is no mere coincidence that the first disputes around the Islamic veil started in the late 1980s just when France was celebrating the bicentenary of its Revolution and faced xenophobic speeches from far-right and right-wing conservatives. During a rally on 19 June 1991, Jacques Chirac referred to the parasitic, proliferating, and dirty immigrants' body, and opposed it to a national model of family life: '[…] the French worker […] who works with his wife […] and who sees on his landing a crammed family, a father, his three or four wives and twenty or more kids, who earns 50,000 francs in social benefits, without of course working! If you add to that the noise and the smell, well the French worker on the landing, he goes crazy' (YouTube, 2006).

The treatment of medically assisted procreation and surrogate parentship shows that the universalism France displays only materializes within the restricted framework of majority norms, a framework that the law can periodically extend. In France, these majority norms are those of the fertile parental couple. This is what the sociologist Marcela Iacub called 'l'empire du ventre' (the 'empire of the womb') (Iacub, 2004). It is as if the biological, not the parental project, created the parent. It occasionally happens that child welfare services remove children from their foster families when behaviours become too affectionate and may seem to make a claim over the biological family. Thus, in a judgment of 7 July 2010, the Court of Appeals of Amiens had to reverse the decision a child welfare service made and return children to their foster family. Foster placements always occur because of serious events experienced by children (sexual abuse, violence, psychiatric disorders etc.), and the interest of the children would warrant not inflicting new trauma on them in the name of the supremacy of biological facts. Today the 'empire of the womb' threatens the framework for delivering a child anonymously. Article 326 of the Civil Code allows a woman to give birth without revealing her identity. Having no parentage at birth, the child is placed up for adoption. In the Philippe Peter case, however, the Court of Cassation reversed the adoption because the paternity of a child born under such anonymity was recognized (*Cour de cassation*, 2006). The court thus put into question the very logic of giving birth anonymously (the recognition of the biological father breaking the de facto secret of the identity of the biological mother).

Full adoptions are also more and more frequently called into question. Full adoption consists in replacing biological parentage by adoptive parentage, thereby erasing the biological parents from the child's civil status (when they are known). However, as long as full adoption was restricted to heterosexual couples, adoptive parents could act as if they were the child's biological parents. The approval procedure must itself last nine months. Child welfare services and public and private agencies that mediate between parents and children also accept that parents ask to adopt children who are similar to them, including in the case of international adoption. Appearances could therefore be saved. But with the opening up of full adoption to same-sex couples, pretending is no longer possible. Therefore, for many, full adoption becomes a threat to the biological order and must stop (Perreau, 2014, p. 38): in January 2018, then president of *les Républicains*, Laurent Wauquiez, opposed all full adoptions in favour of simple adoption in all cases (which adds the two parentages, whereby the adopted child has a biological and an adoptive parent). His intervention was enthusiastically welcomed by the *Manif pour tous* (*Manif pour tous*, 2018), whose first spokesperson, Frigide Barjot, had already previously favoured simple adoption as the easier way to deny full adoption to gay couples (Écoiffier, 2013). Full adoption had already been considerably reduced in the last fifteen years. In 2016, 2,802 children were adopted in full adoption, compared with 3,694 in 2007, 4,244 in 2001 and 4,537 in 1990 (INSEE, 2018b). This situation emerged from a drop in the number of international adoptions (685 international adoptions in 2017 as against 1,569 in 2012 and 4,136 in 2005) and from social welfare policies for children. These policies make it more difficult to adopt children, preferring instead to place children in foster families and hoping to return them to their biological families, even when this is in vain and leads to children spending most of their young years in foster care. The full adoption system, however, perfectly addresses many situations: abandoned children with no known origin or removed from their families because of abuse, etc. The system was specifically designed so that children are not torn between two parentages and feel that they fully belong to their adoptive family. The law of 11 July 1966, which resettled the right of adoption, followed the Novak case, the case of a child tossed from one family to another at the discretion of judicial decisions over nearly ten years (Perreau, 2014, p. 5). Full adoption is thus complementary to simple adoption, which layers the biological and adoptive family, essentially meeting the needs of intra-family adoptions, that is to say, most often, the adoption of a spouse's children of the age of majority after remarriage. In 2016, there were 7,072 simple adoptions as against 9,412 in 2007, 6,455 in 2001 and 4,087 in 1990 (Insee, 2018b). The 2014 Théry-Leroyer report, requested by Dominique Bertinotti, Minister of the Family, to explore the 'new protections, new securities, and new rights for children' sought to make simple adoption easier compared with full adoption for child placement cases (Théry and Leroyer, 2014, pp. 107–11).

A paradoxical recognition of homosexual couples

This biological logic goes even further. Even when, after years of fighting by LGBT activists, the law recognized sexual minorities (PaCS, marriage for all, joint adoption open to same-sex couples), legislators have consistently been careful not to undermine the biological model. The idea of a civil union contract for homosexual couples took off in 1989 after a Court of Cassation decision refused to recognize homosexual cohabitation (*Cour de cassation*, 1989). It was therefore necessary to find other solutions for the security of gay couples, many of whom faced health and inheritance problems at the heart of the AIDS epidemic. LGBT associations, including Aides (one of the main anti-HIV organizations in France that was founded by Daniel Defert after the death of his companion, philosopher Michel Foucault), proposed several versions of civil union contracts. After the unexpected dissolution of the National Assembly in 1997, new legislative elections were held. The Socialist Party had to draft a program quickly and therefore adopted various proposals from civil society, including that of the civil union contract. Once elected, things were different. The prime minister, Lionel Jospin, preferred to let several members of his parliamentary majority present a bill on the PaCS in order not to assume direct responsibility for it. Similarly, the government wanted to be sure that the PaCS had no effect on parentage. Minister of Justice Elisabeth Guigou was therefore responsible for reducing the scope of the text and, to do this, relied on sociologist Irène Théry's analyses; the latter was hostile to PaCS and spoke of it undermining the symbolic order and destroying social bonds. The sociologist indeed claimed that the PaCs would lead to 'unisexual parentage' and that it was therefore necessary to resist it in order to 'preserve culture' and not reduce the other sex to a mere 'provider of life' (Théry, 1997, p. 26). On 9 October 1998, there were not enough Socialist representatives in the National Assembly to vote in favour of PaCS. For only the second time under the Fifth Republic, the majority was a minority in number. A second version of the law had to be put forward. This one was the subject of lengthy debates in the National Assembly and in the Senate, where the right, buttressed by its first real success since the legislative elections, led a campaign of parliamentary obstruction. The law was finally promulgated on 15 November 1999. It offered all couples a civil contract signed before a district court (*tribunal d'instance*) and without effect on parentage, leaving thousands of children without double parentage.

This story picked up again when, after a session of the seminar on the 'sociology of homosexuality' held at the *École des Hautes Études en Sciences Sociales* (School of Advanced Studies in Social Sciences) in 2004, Françoise Gaspard, Didier Eribon, Daniel Borrillo and Caroline Mécary published a call to the mayors of France: an invitation to celebrate gay marriages. On 5 June 2004, Noël Mamère, Ecologist Mayor of Bègles, did so and provoked a huge debate. The Socialist Party condemned the move, considered disrespectful of the law. The idea the initiators of the petition had was precisely to raise jurisprudence to the level of the European Court of Human Rights, since the parliamentary path was politically closed (Eribon, 2004, pp. 59–81). Cornered by its left wing and overtaken by the adoption of same-sex marriage by other European Socialist parties, especially in Belgium and Spain, the French Socialist Party ended up backing marriage reform, but only if that meant not opening up adoption to same-sex couples. Although she had long been hostile to the opening up of marriage and joint adoption to homosexual couples, Ségolène Royal included this double demand in her presidential campaign of 2007. In 2013, she declared in fact never to have been in favour of it ('Gay Marriage …', 2013). During the 2012 presidential campaign, François Hollande for his part supported the opening up of medically assisted procreation to single women and lesbian couples, but he backpedalled in 2013, deciding to rely on the opinion of the CCNE, which has always strongly opposed it. Emmanuel Macron did the same in 2017, declaring his support but preferring to wait for the CCNE's opinion. The CCNE report was issued in June 2018 and, as seen above, supported for the first time the extension of assisted procreation to lesbian couples.

The 2013 Taubira law itself maintained biases against gay couples so as not to disturb the biological norm. Several homosexual organizations proposed replacing the words 'father' and 'mother' with the word 'parent' in the Civil Code. This possibility was not only ruled out in parliamentary debates, but a difference in treatment was even introduced between heterosexual married couples and married same-sex couples. For the former, the presumption of paternity is automatic: a child born in the context of a marriage is the husband's child, a possible contestation of paternity notwithstanding. For the latter, the biological parent's spouse must adopt the child, a process that takes several months. If the biological parent dies in the meantime, the child is orphaned. The creation of a presumption of kinship would have prevented such discrimination. But the challenge for legislators was to not dissociate the primary connection between supposed fertility and parentage. The history of the broadening of gay rights is therefore a history of denials and embarrassments around the role of biology. This is manifest even in the implementation of public policies: although joint adoption has now been opened up to same-sex couples through marriage, many child welfare services prioritize applications for adoption according to their deviation from the biological standard. I have shown, following a large survey of child welfare services before the Taubira law was adopted, that this was a common practice toward single people (Perreau, 2014, pp. 117–21). The implementation of the law confirms this. Considered 'atypical' in relation to the biological norm, gay couples wishing to adopt are only supported in their efforts (Moreau, 2018) if they turn to children also judged to be deviating from the norm (physically or mentally disabled, sick etc.). Thus, a mechanism is set up whereby biology justifies the social order and where this justification is itself naturalized in the name of the 'typical' majority norm. This mechanism further erases the whole constructed aspect of parentage and limits the recognition of new ways of life.

When the system falters all the same, under the pressure of European law, and of the demands by organizations and critical intellectuals, some experts – the same ones in 1998 as in 2018, Jean-Pierre Winter, Claire Neirinck or Sylviane Agacinski for example – play the role of gatekeepers (Zucker-Rouvillois, 1999). Their discourse, structured around the notion of social risk, provides them with symbolic dividends in the media. It cements platitudes about adoptive families and assisted procreation: the death of the symbolic father, the instrumentalization of women's bodies, child trafficking etc. Reactionary Catholic movements mobilized in 2012 and 2013 against the Taubira law merely took over these already well-established elements of language.

The new language of family policies

The social risk discourse gradually became part of family policy during the 1990s. Several factors favoured this phenomenon. The first was the position of social workers who, buried in administrative hierarchies, tend to dramatize their challenges in order to preserve their area of competence (this is particularly the case of *assistantes sociales*, who face a rising liberal management of their services and more and more frequent competition from external stakeholders who are better endowed with professional and social capital – physicians, psychiatrists, psychologists – and are, by definition, more mobile; Serre, 2009, pp. 150–1). The second factor is the dissemination of a whole literature on self-performance via psychology and life counselling magazines. The concept of parenthood (which refers back to the 'proper' way of parenting), first born in the wake of psychoanalyst Therese Benedek (Benedek, 1959), became a very popular catchall concept: '*la parentalité*' (Perreau, 2014, pp. 90–6). Finally, the third factor is that of the economic crisis and mass unemployment that led successive governments to try to better organize aid and support for the most vulnerable people, which requires building public policies as anticipation tools or even predicting individual behaviours. The family becomes a safe haven and parents true 'partners' in social policies (Verjus and Boisson, 2005, p. 462). With what is virtually a public service mission, these partners are highly supervised: raising a child is raising a 'child of the fatherland' (as the French national anthem states) who will ensure the future of the country, as if families were all foster families for the State.

The rhetoric of risk is also gaining momentum because it echoes the one developed in the 1990s around the environment, after several health scandals such as the asbestos scandal (Henry, 2007). In 2012 when the law that opened up marriage to same-sex couples, and thus joint adoption too, was proposed, a group of Catholic activists established the *Manif pour tous*. Other movements quickly followed, such as *le Printemps francais, les Hommen, les Antigones, les Veilleurs* etc. Using very varied techniques to intervene in the public sphere (especially demonstrations, street vigils and lightning actions to disrupt a cultural or sports event), they all relied on the discourse the Vatican shaped after the 1995 Beijing Conference on Women's Rights. Many states indeed supported gender as a new public policy category, a more effective one because it was more flexible in terms of social protections, pay equity and the fight against violence and discrimination. The Vatican saw in it a danger for the strict division between man and woman, male and female, father and mother, a division essential to its theology and in worship, organized around the principle of the non-mixing of the sexes. The Vatican then set up several councils charged with observing the uses of the notion of gender in the world, both in public policy and in university research (Paternotte, 2015). Very soon these committees referenced 'gender theory' as a set of works originating in the United States that deconstruct gender. In particular, they targeted queer theory and philosopher Judith Butler, author of the well-known *Gender Trouble* (Perreau, 2016, pp. 56–9). The Vatican offered an alternative approach to 'gender theory', namely 'human ecology' – about protecting the traditional family the same way nature itself should be protected.

On the *Manif pour tous*' placards and posters, the Minister of Justice Christiane Taubira was shown sawing down trees, which is to say simultaneously destroying the family tree and nature itself (Perreau, 2016, pp. 60–1). Tugdual Derville, one of the organization's spokespersons, was still explaining in May 2018 that we must 'respect the ecology of women' (YouTube, 2018). The ecological argument is clever: it makes it possible to intervene in the public sphere without using theological arguments, an approach that would have been ineffective in a country that claims to be secular. In addition, by playing on anti-Americanism (the supposed paragon of artificial culture, where individualism and commerce are presumed to reign supreme and enable all abuses in assisted reproduction), the *Manif pour tous* claimed to be on the side of patriotism and anti-capitalism as well as against cultural imperialism and unbridled globalization. Judith Butler has often been attacked online and at conferences as intellectual, lesbian, American and Jewish; she embodies the internationalized minority group ready to destroy the nation. The idea of a minority conspiracy is very old (Perreau, 2016, pp. 147–57) and feeds on denouncing foreigners. The enemy of the interior is the objective ally of the outside enemy. Christiane Taubira, who is of Guyanese origin, was often caricatured as a monkey or Godzilla at the time of the marriage-for-all discussions (Perreau, 2016, pp. 62–3). For its opponents, queer monstrosity is embodied in the monstrosity of the racialized body because their nature is a wild, untamed nature. The model of human ecology by contrast fantasizes nature as civilized and harmonious; its fertile heterosexual couple, with its sexuality limited to the goals of procreation, is the model. The opening up of marriage to gay couples could therefore bring down not only the biological model of childbirth (since 2016, the *Manif pour tous* has been fighting against 'medically assisted procreation without a father') but also the idea of sexual temperance (marriage today requires not only fidelity but also a sexual consumption that is neither too great, nor too weak, and in forms that the law has ceaselessly defined) (Borrillo, 2018, pp. 45–54).

The discourse of risk bears another consequence, that of seeking to overthrow the power relations between the majority and the minority. The danger is the acting minorities, who are presumably secretly controlling the government in the face of a silent and dominated majority. To support this thesis, reactionary activists have not hesitated to take up the goal of diversity. They claim a voice as if they were themselves a minority. In October 2016, the *Manif pour tous* called for 'demonstrating as you are', featuring people with disabilities, seniors and even gay couples (to the extent that they oppose marriage for all). The *Veilleurs* (a movement that, to protest the Taubira law, organized prayers and public vigils to meditate on the family and the meaning of life) regularly quoted Gandhi, Martin Luther King or Albert Camus. Éric Lemaître, a Protestant activist with the *Veilleurs* at Reims, explained: 'I do not have a social gospel on one side and a moral gospel on the other! (…) The new slaves are those individuals who go to the end of their unlimited desires. Who are prisoners of themselves.(…) That's why we quoted Martin Luther King and that's why we also sing the Negro Spiritual *Let my people go*' (quoted by Lindell, 2014, p. 39). Reactionary movements are no longer content to claim the status of silent majority. They conceive of themselves also as oppressed minorities and thus seek to credit the thesis of moral equivalence between their struggles and those of sexual minorities. This is why they use the term 'gender theory': to speak of 'theory' (and sometimes 'ideology') allows them to establish a camp-against-camp opposition to the supporters of equal rights. Power relations are thus erased in the name of the principle of contradiction. Emmanuel Macron is emblematic of this movement: during his presidential campaign, he said about Philippe de Villiers (a former minister and a fervent Catholic known for his anti-abortion positions) and Éric Zemmour (an anti-feminist journalist and TV columnist and a supporter of the France-is-in-decline set of arguments): 'these are people with whom I talk. One of the fundamental mistakes of the last five years has been to neglect a part of the country that has good reason to live in sad resentment and passion. This is what happened because of marriage-for-all; we humiliated that France' (Garcin, 2017). Emmanuel Macron is not just appealing to reactionary voices. He considers that they have 'good reasons' to oppose the equal treatment of citizens. For those who suffer from discrimination, this discourse of moral equivalence is the first of many oppressions, since it denies the specificity of their situation.

Finally, risk and moral equivalence form a Gordian knot with a third type of discourse, that of the symbolic order, whose principal representative during the PaCS discussion was sociologist Irène Théry. In a direct line with Emmanuel Mounier's philosophy of personalist Christianity (founder of the journal *Esprit* which routinely publishes Irène Théry's articles), the symbolic order refers to the idea that the destiny of the individual is to accept his determinisms far from the fantasy of any liberal narcissistic power or the communist idea of surpassing oneself in the collective. Personalism had a great influence on the 'second left' movement, which tried to modernize the Socialist Party in the 1970s (Robcis, 2013, pp. 213–61). This philosophy left a long-lasting mark on the new generation of the Socialist Party (Martine Aubry, François Hollande, Ségolène Royal, Dominique Strauss-Kahn, Jean Glavany etc.), which constituted most of the Jospin government from 1997 to 2002. For Irène Théry, PaCS was the embodiment of the rejection of the difference between the sexes which, inherited from nature, must order social organization. Having lost the PaCS battle, Irène Théry had to maintain her credibility as an expert: she therefore lined up with PaCS and the opening up of marriage, adoption and assisted procreation to same-sex couples, but only if sexual difference was reinvested into the ways of establishing parentage: she argued that information about the procreating couple (sperm donor, surrogate mother, egg donor etc.) systematically appears so that a gay couple could not be said to be procreating as such. This was the same argument that the *Manif pour tous* developed, even if the movement drew opposite conclusions, namely the refusal of marriage and joint adoption. Discussions around the symbolic order also shifted to the question of gender. On 12 July 2016, trans people witnessed a demedicalization of the changing of their civil status (it is no longer necessary to present a medical professional's certification to change one's civil status) through a parliamentary amendment that required, nevertheless, that a judge assess their request beforehand. The determination of gender must therefore remain at the discretion of the State, as the individual cannot claim to determine his gender freely. In 2007, Irène Théry explained that '(…) some solutions proposed by transgender identities sometimes give the impression of refining [identity logic] more and more desperately, in the hope of eventually dissolving it in its own logic: each individual would be a class all on his own' (Théry, 2007, p. 255). This fear of people's self-determination leads to a catastrophic discourse that other philosophical currents have echoed. The journal *Débat*, directed by Marcel Gauchet, expressed the same worried point of view about 'egotistical individualism' (Théry,

2016): in 2014 the journal published a special issue in which children of gay families were compared to 'transgenic corn' (Berger, 2014, p. 145) and gay marriage to a 'perverse mechanism' (Heinich 2014, p. 128). Although very violent, these positions circulate quite freely in the context of French republicanism, which, for its fear of communities coming to compete with the Nation, is also wary of the emergence of vernacular cultures (Perreau, 2014, pp. 112–16).

Technologies of the self

Over the last three decades, the emergence and spread of new reproductive technologies have dramatically changed people's perceptions of their gender, sex, health and so on. This is a profound epistemological change that has aroused many reactions and still does: a new type of relationship to oneself is emerging, based on the idea of controlling one's body, of self-care and also of performance. Patients are becoming more active in choosing among the medical protocols that are offered to them. Unmarried and coupled women's organizations are fighting for medical assistance in procreation. Transgender activists have already obtained that their change of civil status does not require any medical certification. These few examples illustrate not only the emergence of new uses of technology (*teknè*) but also of a set of discourses (*logos*) that strive to rethink the relationships between body, technique, identity and belonging. These are what we can call, in line with Michel Foucault, 'technologies of self' (Foucault, 1988). They open up new relational possibilities but also raise a concern, namely of the commercialization of the body.

To respond to this concern, France has embarked on an enterprise of sacralizing the body as a place of self-truth. The CCNE has long explained that technology was only intended to repair the body, that is to say, to restore it to a supposed 'natural order'. This way of thinking led to prohibiting surrogacy and, until 2020, restricting medically assisted procreation to cases of medical infertility in heterosexual couples. It also explains why France is slow to recognize the possibility of choosing the end of life. This philosophy has had a considerable impact on the way the social bond is conceived in France. If the biological is thought of as a place of truth, how then is it possible to be a hospitable country to migrants, who do not readily have a biological link to the nation? (Boudou, 2018) How not to consider adoptive families as ersatz biological families? How to recognize lifestyles that are not determined by biology, such as friendships or neighbourhood ties, which are so precious to older people? How to apprehend interventions on the body, now widespread, which are not intended to repair but improve it (aesthetic care, dietary supplements, hormones etc.)?

The resistance to new technologies of the self can be explained by the way the State was constructed. In France, the State historically preceded the Nation: it was first organized around civil law with the adoption of the Civil

Code in 1804. Since then, whenever the authority of the State is called into question, family rights are called in to the rescue. The creation of the CCNE in 1983 can thus be understood as a quest for meaning in the context of the end of decolonization, of the worsening of the economic crisis and of the rise of the extreme right. When coming to power in 1981, the Socialist Party, which had long been hostile to the institutions of the Fifth Republic, had to pledge its loyalty to the State. Sacralizing the fertile body in the name of French humanist heritage was a ready-made means of doing so.

In conclusion, however, I would like to put forward another hypothesis. If new technologies of the self are feared, it is because they bring to light the artificial ways the entire body politic is organized. It requires a great deal of artifice to lead to reproductive coitus: romantic stories inculcated from childhood to facilitate romantic dating; asymmetrical gender role constructions using clothing, grammar, social status; seduction techniques (dinner, outings, declarations etc.); financial and material support of the birth rate by both national and local institutions, etc. In other words, where we perceive sex, sexuality and family life as obvious, they are already the products of a whole set of technologies (Preciado, 2014).

Is it not time to take a look at this reality? Paul Preciado added: 'With certain radical changes in view, the political management of body technologies that produce sex and sexuality can be seen to progressively become the business of the new millennium' (Preciado, 2008, p. 105). To accept our technological condition is also to accept the very fragility of life, not to sanctify it but to give ourselves the means to better withstand the effects of power exercised thereupon. These are the struggles that patient organizations lead against big pharmaceutical groups, as in the case of the Levothyrox scandal (Houdayer, 2018) or Act Up's mobilizations (Broqua, 2006). These are the struggles of transgender people (Foerster, 2012). These are the mobilizations against the misuse of personal data in a surveillance society (Harcourt, 2015). It is also the criticism put forth against neoliberal policies that crush the bodies of workers, employees and the unemployed, when, conversely, the dominant classes manage to protect themselves from their effects (Louis, 2018). France has been clinging for several decades to the 'bioethical' management of bodies, reproduction and families. It is now time to place users, patients, multinational families and minorities at the centre of the making of laws. The technopolitical era has already begun.

8 TERRITORIAL GOVERNANCE IN FRANCE: BETWEEN RECENTRALIZATION AND DIFFERENTIATION

Alistair Cole and Romain Pasquier

Introduction

When formally introduced in 1982, decentralization was declared to be the 'grand affair' of the first Mitterrand presidency. Ever since then, decentralization in France has been pulled in somewhat different directions by the instruments of central steering, by processes of local and regional capacity building and by a very imperfect process of territorial differentiation and identity construction (Cole, 2006). Adapting a phrase used to refer to Welsh devolution, decentralization is a process, not an event, but a process with no agreed end point or starting analysis. It has been the object of many political and institutional battles over recent decades. The main cleavage is that between the traditionalists (*anciens*) and the modernists (*modernes*); the former favour the territorial status quo (centred on preserving the rights of the 35,000 or so communes and the 101 departments), while the latter support the alternative pole represented by the intercommunal authorities (*Etablissements publics de coopération intercommunale* – EPCI) and the regions. On each occasion, the powerful local government associations have joined the battle: the Association of Mayors of France and the Association of Departments of France tend to favour the status quo, while the Assembly of Regions of France (ARF), and *France Urbaine* (representing France's cities and urban areas) generally argue in favour of a major reform of the complex territorial structure. Finally, there are powerful institutional veto players, most notably the Senate, the second chamber, which is the main chamber ruling local government relations and which has a veto on most matters of local and regional government, including constitutional change.

This mix of territorial differentiation and state steering has also given rise to two main academic approaches, each seeking to explain the role of local actors in public policy and central–local relations. In the first instance, Pasquier et al. (2013) define the notion of 'territorial governance' as 'the totality of those situations of non-ordered and non-hierarchical cooperation which contribute to the construction, the management, or the representations of a territory, in particular with respect to its institutional and economic environment'. This approach emphasizes territorial differentiation and recomposition at the local and regional level (Kernalegenn and Pasquier, 2018). A second approach insists on the fact that the territorialization of public policy and of the logics of governance must not lead the analyst to underplay the role of the State, which has invented new forms of central steering (Epstein, 2005, 2015; Le Galès and Vezinat, 2014). If the State has physically reduced its presence in the territories, it has devised new forms of central regulation – such as calls for projects, performance indicators, quality labels, prizes and policy evaluation – that allow it to strengthen its overall steering and to govern at a distance (Béal et al., 2015). These approaches are complementary, rather than competitive, insofar as they both attempt to describe and analyse the new types of interaction between state and territorial actors in France. They represent the twin faces of an incremental process of state reform and decentralization that has mobilized a myriad of energies over the past two decades.

This chapter compares and contrasts the two main trends of the long past decade. The first section overviews and presents the French model of local and regional government and discusses in general terms the development of local and regional councils in the course of the past long decade (2007–20). The second section pinpoints the inconsistencies of the Hollande period (2012–17); in this section, we report the findings of a major survey of local and regional authorities implemented by the authors from 2016 to 2018, with a view to elucidating contemporary debates. Section 3 interprets Macron's balanced approach (*en même temps*) to local and regional government, one in which central impulsion is counterbalanced by a recognition of the right to difference, more explicit than that of previous French Presidents. The chapter concludes by a reflection on the twin faces of state reform and territorial capacity.

The French model of local and regional government between institutions and policies

We now provide a brief overview of the institutions of France's complex system of local and regional government, before, second, identifying several wicked challenges that have confronted French governors over the past two decades.

As of January 2019, France counted 34,970 communes, 1,264 public corporations with tax-raising powers, 101 departmental councils and 18 regional councils. The existence of so many small communes (accounting for 40 per cent of all such local government units in the entire EU) has come to symbolize the extreme fragmentation and duplication of the French local government system (though their number has been reduced in the past few years through mergers). The French model is one whereby four levels of subnational authority (communes, *intercommunalités*, departments and regions) cooperate and compete to deliver public services (Table 8.1).

Table 8.1 France's local and regional authorities

Type	Number	Functions
Communes	34,970	Varying services, including planning permission, building permits, building and maintenance of primary schools, waste disposal, some welfare services
Tax-raising intercommunal corporations (EPCI), including metropolitan councils, urban communities, city-wide communities and communities of communes	1,258	Permanent organizations in charge of intercommunal services such as firefighting, waste disposal, transport, economic development, some housing, structure plans
Departmental councils	101	Social affairs, some secondary education (*collèges*), road building and maintenance
Regional councils (mainland France, Corsica and overseas)	18	Economic development, transport, infrastructure, state–region plans, some secondary education (*lycées*), training
Special statute authorities	5	The Corsican territorial authority has enhanced regulatory powers. The Lyon Metropole exercises the functions of the Rhône Department on its territory. Martinique and Guyane have special statutes, as does the Department of Mayotte.

Source: Direction Générale des Collectivités Locales (2019) Les Chiffres-clés des collectivités locales, Paris: Interior Ministry, p. 8.

The core features of the system established in the 1982–83 decentralization reforms are somewhat ambivalent. One core principle of the model is that of the *blocs de compétences*, viz. the attribution of specific functions to different levels of local and regional government. In theory, this quasi-federal approach is coherent and logical: issues of proximity are, in theory, the policy province of the communes; welfare functions are largely reserved for the departmental councils; and economic development, transport and strategic planning are the responsibility of the regions, the latter acting in cooperation with the French State and the European Union. The approach bears some resonance of the EU doctrine of subsidiarity, whereby decision-making should be taken at the lowest possible level.

The principle of a neatly organized distribution of functions has not withstood the reality of public policy making in France's localities and regions, however, where policy problems spill across levels. If local authorities are in principle specialized in their functions, concentrating on particular areas of public policy, in reality they each intervene across the spectrum of public policy. Until the 2015 NOTRE law (*LOI no. 2015-991 du 7 août 2015 portant nouvelle organisation territoriale de la République*), each could claim a 'general administrative competency' that allowed them to intervene in any issue of territorial interest. These fine legal distinctions have preoccupied public lawyers (Marcou, 2006), while political scientists have emphasized the limited nature of French decentralization, which conceives of the role of local and regional authorities in terms of policy implementation. Certainly, they have very few legislative or regulatory capacities by comparison with counterparts in Germany, Spain, Italy, Belgium or the devolved nations of the UK (Cole, 2006; Pasquier, 2016).

At the level of institutions, controversies have centred around whether any reform of the *millefeuille territorial* is possible. The basic structures have proved very resistant to change. The reasons for this blockage are in part institutional. Senatorial opposition presents a powerful obstacle to any far-reaching reform. They are also in part professional, insofar as the well-entrenched local government associations have resisted reform. On the other hand, substantial reforms have taken place over the past long decade, and these form the heart of the chapter. These have included more central control over the financial autonomy of local authorities under the impact of economic crisis (especially since 2007); the creation in 2014 of the 15 or so Metropolitan Councils (*métropoles*) in France's largest cities; a reform of the map of the regions (operational in 2015) and a proposed constitutional amendment to enshrine territorial differentiation. All in all, these reforms represent responses to broader policy challenges.

Broader policy challenges

Any account of institutions in terms of stasis would make little sense in the context of far-reaching broader changes that have challenged French governors to reform local government (and local government to reform itself). Two broad trends set the stage for a more detailed analysis of political action in the past decade. These relate, first, to economic globalization – and the related process of metropolitanization – which have proved to be a major challenge for French territorial organization. Second, they refer to the impact of the 2007–8 economic crisis on France's localities and regions.

The first of these dimensions relates to the changing context within which French local government functions. New economic and demographic trends emerged at the turn of the twenty-first century, with economic growth centred around the dynamic metropolitan zones, while small towns and rural areas stagnated. Overall, geographical inequalities increased, so much so that the theme of the 'territorial fracture' has been a mobilizing one (Pasquier, 2018). The image of the State as the guarantor of territorial justice has been profoundly challenged. Far from its traditional role as the driver of national and spatial planning, and the guarantor of social and economic modernization, the State has been directly accused of favouring metropolitan cities, for example during the Yellow Vests protests of Autumn 2018 (see Chapter 11 for a discussion of these protests).

Territorial systems are subject to growing tensions between zones in expansion, and those in decline and decay (Pasquier and Perron, 2008). The management of these tensions between winning and losing territories represents a major challenge of public policy and can aggravate relations between central government and the local and regional authorities. In France, in relation to the developments outlined above, new trends have emerged with the concentration of growth around the large cities, which has aggravated existing territorial inequalities and tensions (Veltz, 2008). During the 1990s and 2000s, the phenomenon of metropolitanization produced a shift in favour of dynamic city regions, such as Lyon, Bordeaux and Nantes. Around one-half of demographic growth in France was produced in 11 cities between 1990 and 1999: Paris, Toulouse, Lyon, Montpellier, Nantes, Marseille, Rennes, Bordeaux, Strasbourg, Nice and Toulon.

These new tensions have provoked a debate over the question of social territorial justice. In the post-war period, the French welfare state was partially constructed on the idea of spatial planning (*aménagement du territoire*). According to this perspective, which was an important frame for public policy during the post-war decades, the role of the central state is to remedy the spatial inequalities produced by social modernization and economic globalization (Pasquier, 2016a). The policies undertaken by the Hollande presidency illustrated these tensions between liberating the most dynamic areas and ensuring a proactive spatial planning policy. On the one hand, in 2014 the Ayrault government created the General Commissariat for Territorial Equality (CGET) which was given responsibility for formulating and implementing a policy designed to ensure fair and equal territorial treatment in a context of economic crisis. On the other hand, the 2014 MAPTAM law was specifically designed to vest the metropolitan areas with the means to deliver economic growth.

The second wicked challenge is that of managing financial penury. The past long decade (2007–19) has been one of sustained economic crisis and financial constraint. The first impact of the economic crisis of 2007–08 was to set in motion a process of enhanced central controls over local and regional authorities. The subject of local public expenditure has received substantial academic attention (for example Le Lidec, 2012). From 2004 to 2008, several commissions reflected on the subject and various reports were published

(Camdessus, 2004; Pébereau, 2006; Richard, 2006; Attali, 2008). All emphasized the costs of France's territorial system and its negative effects on the competitiveness of companies and public finance accounts. The initial driver for this recentralization lay squarely with the national government, in the form of the Fillon government's centralization of the levy of the business tax (*taxe professionnelle*) in 2010, the rate of which had previously been determined by the local authorities themselves. The business tax on firms was replaced by a new fiscal basket, known as the Territorial Economic Contribution (*cotisation économique territorial* – CET), which uses criteria determined by central government (based on a mixed calculation of ground rent and the total value of the firm). This move was justified by the need to control local public expenditure and ensure a more even distribution of taxation resources between local authorities.

The longer-term pressures on central–local relations were constant: how to control public expenditure, monitor public authorities and limit their propensity to employ agents. But the significance of these constraints was greatly increased by the economic crisis of 2008 and the responses of the EU and national governments to this crisis. The financial crisis of 2008, and the obligations it generated, provided a new opportunity structure for supporters of a reform of France's territorial structures (Cole et al., 2016). Successive governments of left and right have used this context to announce 'structural reforms', to borrow the language of the European Commission and the OECD (OECD, 2014), and to rein in public expenditure. These domestic pressures were reinforced by the introduction of new budgetary instruments and controls at the EU level – discussed in detail in Cole et al. (2015) – that had a direct spillover effect into the administration of local and regional authorities.

The economic crisis of 2007–08 produced new forms of tension between Paris and Brussels. Since the crisis of 2008, French governments have been regularly called to account by the European Commission, in order to reduce a budgetary deficit that from 2008 to 2017 exceeded the criteria outlined in the Stability and Growth Pact for countries in the Eurozone. As a counterpart for the extra time agreed by the European Commission for the French government to bring down their deficits to the 3 per cent European threshold, successive French governments themselves introduced tighter budgetary control policies, increasingly strict since 2012–13. The worsening of the budgetary situation in France in 2012–13 forced the government to implement an unprecedented programme of budgetary reduction, under the pressure of the European Commission.

This mix of external and internal constraints has exercised a permanent pressure on French public finances and eroded local fiscal autonomy. Since 2010 there has been a reduction in the proportion of locally levied taxes in local and regional government finance. Local taxes have been replaced by central transfers, or by mechanisms allocating local authorities a proportion of national taxes (the case of the *départements* and VAT) over which they have no control whatsoever. The new model is much less advantageous for local authorities, and for the regional and departmental councils, which together witnessed their locally raised resources diminishing to 10–25 per cent of their total revenue. Prior to 2010, local and regional authorities had raised around 40 per cent of their revenue, with the figure reaching 50 per cent for the departments (Pasquier, 2012, p. 182).

Over the past long decade (2007–19), there have thus been important developments in the model of local government and central–local relations in France. After a series of reforms begun under the presidency of Nicolas Sarkozy (in 2009–10), President Hollande undertook, in 2014–15, a territorial reform which purported to control public finances and to rationalize and simplify the complex structures of local and regional governments, details of which are considered below.

Reforming local government and territorial administration: the Hollande presidency's half-hearted rationalization

The lost long decade was characterized by inconsistent and rather contradictory public policies, which failed to overhaul the institutions. In this section, we analyse the inconsistent and contradictory policy stances of the Hollande administration (2012–17).

Positioning himself against his predecessor Sarkozy, President Hollande announced the abolition of the territorial councillor and the advent of a new territorial reform, to be steered by the Minister of Decentralization, Marilyse Lebranchu, from the autumn of 2012 onwards. This new reform soon became bogged down in negotiations with the local government associations; it was also made fragile by the weakness of the government's political majority and the urgent budgetary situation. In Autumn 2013, Prime Minister Jean-Marc Ayrault decided to split the announced reform into several smaller projects which, in practice, tended to contradict each other. Accordingly the 2014 law known as MAPTAM (*LOI n° 2014-58 du 27 janvier 2014 de modernisation de l'action publique territoriale et d'affirmation des métropoles*), the first major reform, re-established the general administrative competency clause that had been suppressed in the 2010 law; this allows local and regional authorities to develop policies in relation to any area deemed to be in the general interest. The MAPTAM law also conferred a new legal status on the French metropolitan councils in the large cities, close in practice to the provisions of the Law of 6 December 2010 voted under President Sarkozy, but with a more extensive impact. The rationale of MAPTAM was to position French cities in the international context of competition aggravated by economic globalization. Thus, the government was caught between a national vision of spatial planning and the need to promote local and urban liberties in order to respond to the pressures of international competition. National elites have typically hesitated between these two visions (strengthening local liberties versus enhancing national regulation), but they have proved incapable of finding the right balance between the two.

After President Hollande's election, there was a deterioration of public finances, coupled with a growing pressure from the European Union for the second Eurozone economy to engage in structural reform. In January 2014, Hollande announced the creation of a competitiveness pact (*pacte de responsabilité*) designed to lower business taxes and charges in order to relaunch the competitiveness of the French economy. This lowering of charges on businesses of around 30 billion euros was financed in part by substantial budgetary savings. For the first time since the decentralization laws of 1982–83, local and regional authorities suffered a cut in finances over the four-year period of 2015–17, their budgets being reduced by 3 billion euros in 2014 and a total of 11 billion over the next three years (2015–17). This financial constraint provided a useful means of pressure for the central government seeking to reform the fragmented structure of French local government.

The coherence of these efforts was undermined by electoral reversals. In March 2014, the presidential majority suffered a major defeat at the municipal elections; this was followed shortly afterwards by the nomination of a new prime minister, Manuel Valls, who was much less close to the local government associations. Valls announced a new direction for local government, centred on a specialization of the departmental and regional authorities, the reduction in the number of regions in mainland France and the hollowing out or even abolition of the departmental councils, with 2020 as the time frame for this to be implemented. Faced with the hostility of his governmental majority, however, as well as that of the Senate, Valls soon abandoned the project of abolishing the departmental councils. In September 2014, the Socialists lost their majority in the Senate, effectively making it impossible to change the constitution or abolish anything. Nor was depriving these councils of their competencies any longer on the cards. During the parliamentary debates in spring 2015, the government even abandoned the idea of transferring the responsibility for roads or lower secondary education from the departments to the regions.

The second major law of the Hollande presidency was originally designed to strengthen the regions and produce more clarity in relation to who does what in France's complex pattern of sub-national governance. Enacted on 7 August 2015, the NOTRE law, as mentioned above, certainly strengthened the role of the regions, but this was limited to four main areas: the management of EU structural funds, school transport (inter-urban transfers), economic development and spatial planning. In the latter two fields, the regions thenceforth were responsible for formulating five-year plans that, in theory at least, have to be respected by all other local authorities. They are recognized as having a leadership role in the field of territorial economic development and planning. The above discussion emphasizes, however, that structural reforms are difficult, even when the economic context appears to be favourable to thoroughgoing reform. Departmental and communal interests represent a formidable obstacle to the fundamental reform of French decentralization.

The third major reform of the Hollande presidency was the reform of the regional map in the summer of 2014. The then government argued for the creation of 'large regions', in order that they be better equipped to respond to the challenges of economic globalization and the competition between cities and regions within Europe. French regions are now slightly larger than their German counterparts, their average surface covering 25,000 km² against 22,300 km for the German *lander*, though the latter have higher concentrations of population (an average of 5.1 million inhabitants against 2.9 million for the French regions). But they do not have the same legal constitutional or financial capacities to develop their territories. In 2014–15, the Valls government opted for a minimum functionalist reform of the regions, which modified the scale of regional public policy, but without genuinely addressing the question of the capacity to act, or of the new relationship to be developed between the central state and the new regions. In the law of 16 June 2015, a new map of the regions was produced, reducing their number from 26 to 18 (of which 12 in mainland France, along with Corsica and 5 overseas regions). Several regions remained unchanged: Bretagne, Centre-Val-de-Loire, Corse, Pays-de-Loire, Île-de-France and Provence-Alpes-Côte-d'Azur (PACA). All the other regions were merged to create larger entities.

The redrawing of the regional map was justified in terms of size (the optimum size to succeed in a competitive European and world environment) and economy (economies of scale, avoiding duplication, rationalizing back-office functions). In one interview carried out as part of our trust and transparency project (see below), a PS deputy in the Ardèche Department summed up the prevailing sentiment about the reform of the territorial map: 'this was a political decision, motivated by a – contested – belief that size would allow economies of scale, as well as arming French regions with the necessary size to compete at the European level'. Size itself is misleading: the new Hauts-de-France region (the merged region of Nord/Pas-de-Calais and Picardy) has a population superior to that of Denmark and a landmass equivalent to that of Belgium, yet it has minor regulatory and no legislative powers and a limited budget. Arguments based on size were more prominent than those of restoring historical regions or minority nations, as in the case of the UK (Scotland and Wales) and Spain (Catalonia, the Basque Country and Galicia).

The authors were involved in a major cross-national project on trust and transparency in multi-level governance; as part of this project, a nationwide survey (YouGov, n. 3003) was carried out into attitudes to the French regions in general and the reform of the territorial map in particular (Cole and Pasquier, 2017). We also conducted semi-structured interviews with around

40 actors in two French regions, Bretagne and Auvergne-Rhône-Alpes, centred in part on evaluations of reforms during the Hollande presidency. The results of the survey have been extensively debated elsewhere; the most striking headline findings lay in the deep degree of mistrust of all political institutions (Cole et al., 2018). The survey demonstrated quite clearly an accountability deficit in this pattern of multi-level governance. Though deeply ambivalent or hostile to all institutions, when surveyed, French citizens showed greater trust in two levels of government over the proposed alternatives: the city (for most routine matters of public policy) and the national government (for welfare provision, equality of treatment and national planning). Support for the intermediary levels of sub-national government (13 regions and 96 departments) was sector and place specific but provided a thin form of legitimization. The key absence was the European Union, barely identified at all as a significant actor even in fields where it manifestly performs a core role. In the context of ongoing crisis of trust, citizens look to urban and national levels of government to provide protection.

The second dimension of the survey and interviews was to cast doubt on the transparency of the reform of the regional map; there were no local referendums, and there was no genuine involvement of key stakeholders. The result was arbitrary and uneven; redrawing the regional map owed more to expediency and political pressures than to a closely argued plan (which explains why historical Bretagne, defended by Defence Minister Jean-Yves Le Drian, successfully resisted attempts at merger, while Alsace did not). All those interviewed in Auvergne-Rhône Alpes agreed that the opportunity costs of an institutional merger were substantial (concerning the terms and conditions of workers and the merging of administrative units from the former Rhône-Alpes and Auvergne regions). While there might be institutional gains, these were offset at the time of interviews by the 'disruptive' consequences of merger (in the expression of one interviewee). Finally, measures of trust in France's regions varied according to place. Where there is some sympathy for the region, this is most evident in the case of the traditional region (Bretagne) than in the merged regions of Auvergne-Rhône-Alpes (a fusion of two regions) or in the geographically vast New Aquitaine (a merger of three previously existing regions).

The results of the trust and transparency project anticipated the full-scale rejection of existing elites that carried Macron to power in 2017.

Emmanuel Macron: between central steering and the temptation of territorial differentiation

Presidents Nicolas Sarkozy and François Hollande both used the arguments of financial constraint and the need to control public expenditure as a means of undertaking territorial reforms. In contrast, it is far more difficult to ascertain an underlying logic or a consistent approach towards territorial restructuring in the Macron presidency. Emmanuel Macron acknowledged the difficulty of reforming the structures of sub-national government and administration. Was this hesitation caused by tactical precaution? Or was it the result of bureaucratic obstacles? Or simply, a relative lack of interest in *les territoires*? Two examples now discussed suggest that President Macron sought – *en même temps* – to strengthen the instruments of state monitoring of local authorities while simultaneously liberating their creative potential.

There is plenty of evidence to support a central steering hypothesis. Emmanuel Macron had served as the Assistant General-Secretary of President Hollande's presidential staff (from 2012 to 2014) and as Minister for the Economy from 2014 to 2016. In this latter capacity, Macron was closely associated with the pursuit of a tough policy of control of local public finances. Once elected, president Macron remained true to form. He announced the abolition of the main local tax – the *taxe d'habitation* – by 2020 and an overall reduction of 13 billion euros of local government expenditure over the course of the presidency. This control of local government expenditure had, by 2019, been implemented by a system of financial contracts, in the main defined by the central State, and accounting for 80 per cent of total local government expenditure. The larger local authorities were invited to sign these contracts with the State. There are very strong incentives for local authorities to sign these contracts: the government announced that non-signatories would face steeper fines if they failed to meet their legal obligations. In the end, some 322 authorities signed contracts with the State, whereby they agreed to limit their expenditure increase to 1.2 per cent per annum, in return for stable financial transfers over the five-year period. By September 2018, 70 per cent of the larger local authorities had entered into a contract with the State, with 93 authorities refusing to sign. Those signing included 121 mayors (83 per cent of the target population), along with an even higher proportion of the presidents of the relevant intercommunal public corporations (known as urban communities and agglomerations). On the other hand, only 43 presidents of general councils (44 per cent of the total) and 9 presidents of regional councils (53 per cent of the total) agreed to the new contracts.

The beginnings of the Macron presidency were frantic, in this as in other areas. The new president's top-down governing style made itself felt in the field of central–local relations, so much so that local and regional councillors voiced their fears for the future of local freedoms. There was some reason for local discontent: local authorities were alienated by the proposed abolition of the main local tax levied by the *commune* (the residency tax, or *taxe d'habitation*); by the threats to abolish the property ownership tax (*la taxe foncière*), also levied by the *communes*; and the Finance Ministry exercised an ever tighter control over local government expenditure. Macron has continued and deepened an ongoing process of financial centralization. The traditionally co-operative relations between the local government associations and central government broke down under the government led by Édouard

Philippe, in reaction to tighter central controls. The Macron phenomenon appeared to these local and regional governmental interests as a form of new-look Jacobinism: a young, liberal, but frankly centripetal force.

The use of centrally determined contracts was one signal that strengthened the central steering interpretation. Another was the return of the prefects (the central State's representatives) into the local sphere, as the prefects negotiated the contracts on behalf of the French State during the summer of 2018. In response, Macron has faced stiff opposition from the local government organizations. In July 2018, the main local government associations – the Association of Mayors of France (AMF), the Assembly of Departments of France (ADF) and the Association of Regions of France (ARF) – jointly decided to boycott the 3rd National Territorial Conference, a new initiative created by Macron to engage a dialogue between the State and the main local and regional authorities. This move was followed by the adoption of the 'Marseille Appeal for local liberties', at the ARF's conference on 26 September 2018, a document signed by 1,200 local politicians (including the most important mayors and presidents of the departmental and regional councils). In this call, the local politicians challenged the prime minister, reminding him that 'we are not operators of the State, but democratically elected local politicians'.

On the other hand, interpreting Macron is not straightforward; his balanced approach (*en même temps*) has produced an interesting synthesis, whereby central impulsion is counterbalanced by a recognition of the right to difference, more explicit than that of previous French Presidents. In his speech to the first national conference of the territories, on 17 July 2017, Emmanuel Macron asserted: 'I firmly believe that, in the great majority of cases, the territories know what is the best form of organization to meet their needs. We need to build this Girondin pact, which, without breaking national unity, will give our territories the means to act in a spirit of shared responsibility'. One year later, in a speech at Quimper in Bretagne, on 23 June 2018, Macron stated that he was favourable to a 'decentralization of projects and a form of territorial differentiation that can build on local projects and develop form of solidarity between places'. He called in particular to make the 'Bretagne region a laboratory of this decentralized project-based approach'. In this speech, Macron implied that the flexible adaptation to the challenges of globalization required a move to a form of enlarged right to difference, where local and regional authorities are given more regulatory powers, especially at the regional level. To what extent was Macron reacting to the fact that the regions had been asking for more powers in the field of water, culture and the environment since the turn of the century? Some discussion of the tradition of resisting legal difference is essential in order to understand this dimension.

The Jacobin/republican narrative has traditionally been hostile to the idea of territorial diversity. The construction of modern France was based on the affirmation of a powerful central authority against territorial specificities and differences. The republican narrative has continued to shape decentrali-zation, caught between a belief in local liberties and local public policy-making – but within the context of a powerful and pervasive central State which, unlike in a number of other European states, has preserved the essence of national-level law-making and regulatory powers.

France's silent revolution has consisted in a steady erosion of the bases of republican uniformity, notwithstanding the routine speeches celebrating ter-ritorial equality and general republican principles. There has been the devel-opment of a form of statute-specific territorial governance: not only in historical 'national regions' such as Corsica, but also in leading metropolises (the Lyon model). The decentralization reforms of 2003–04 (usually known as Act 2, coming after Act 1 of 1982–83) represented a real break in terms of relations between metropolitan France and the overseas territories, depart-ments and regions. The constitutional revision of 28 March 2003 provided the basis for each major overseas authority to adopt a form of devolved rule that contained territory-specific provisions.

This logic of territorial differentiation has specifically applied to Corsica, whose regulatory powers have increased incrementally over the past 15 years. The French Constitutional Council made several key judgements in the early 1990s, at least some of which paved the way for a more enhanced form of territorial autonomy for Corsica. In 1991, the Constitutional Council refused to validate the proposed law that referred to the 'Corsican people', arguing that this was contrary to the republican principle of indivisibility. But the Council did confirm that the Corsican territorial authority has a hybrid form of existence, somewhere between a mainland French region and a more autonomous overseas devolved territory. The prime minister, as for-mal head of government, must consult the Corsican Territorial Authority (CTC) 'on any proposed laws or decrees that have a specified Corsican dimension'. The victory of the Corsican nationalist forces in 2015, and again in 2017, might have an impact in the longer term. The creation of the new unified territorial authority on 1 January 2018, along with the pragmatic stances adopted by Gilles Simeoni, the President of the Corsican Executive, leaves open the possibility of a gradual transformation of relationships between central government and a new generation of Corsican politicians (Roux, 2017).

This trend towards territorial differentiation has not been limited to regions or overseas territories that are isolated geographically, or with specific histories. The Île-de-France region, for example, has greater powers at its disposal than the other French regions in matters of transport, environment and the provision of collective services. The key law in this respect is that of the MAPTAM (see above), voted in January 2014, which established the metropolitan city authorities in general and provided for a specific statute for the City of Lyon. The 'capital of the Gauls' combines the functions of the inter-communal authority (public corporation – *établissement public*) with that of the department; the new Lyon metropolitan council resulted from a merger between the Lyon City and the Rhône Department. It has its own special legal character, which sets it apart from the other metropolitan councils announced in the MAPTAM (or created shortly thereafter).

Macron's territorial policy must be interpreted in the context of these broader evolutions. The modernizing president has embraced the theme of experimentation and diversity. There has been movement, for example, in the case of the merger of the two Alsace departments and the creation of a new territorial authority for Alsace (within the much-decried Grand Est region). Or in Corsica, as seen above, where the Philippe government agreed to a strengthened Corsican authority, without ceding to the demands of the nationalist–autonomist coalition in power in Corte. The most substantial move in the direction of more territorial differentiation, however, lies in the proposed constitutional reform which would embed a 'right to difference' within the Constitution itself. The right to 'experiment' already exists. However, it is defined in the 1958 Constitution, as reformed in 2003, in a rather restrictive manner: one level of local or regional authority can bid to run a particular service on an experimental basis for a period of up to 5 years (article 37.1). But then the decision must be taken to transfer this service to all similar public authorities (for example, regions in the case of the ports), or else to abandon the experiment. This clause is a right to generalization, rather than to experimentation. In the proposed (and at the time of writing postponed) constitutional reform, article 15 of the Constitution asserts that 'certain local and regional authorities might be able to exercise a limited number of competencies that do not need to be extended to all authorities in the category'. The proposed amendment also permits local authorities to opt-out of certain laws or regulations, where there is a legal basis to do so. Rather paradoxically, the State has instigated and supported moves to more territorial differentiation, as it has seen the political and economic gains to be had from allowing local and regional authorities to engage in experiments and adopt territorially specific public policies.

We finish this chapter with a brief commentary on the result of the 2020 municipal elections. The first round took place on 15 March 2020 in highly unusual circumstances, at the onset of the Covid-19 crisis. The first round was marked by the solid performance of LR (e.g. Toulouse), PS (Paris, Rennes, Nantes, Lille) and RN incumbents (e.g. Henin-Beaumont), the failure of LREM candidates to break through in Paris and Marseille and deep divisions in Lyon (where LREM was split). Overall, 30,000 mayors of the smallest communes were elected or re-elected on the first round, consistent with established practice. For once, however, the commentary on election night was not centred on the results of the first round. The executive became mired in controversy over whether this first round should have gone ahead, given that premier Philippe had announced a national emergency the previous evening.

The second round was eventually held on 28 June 2020, largely overshadowed by the Covid-19 crisis. The heavy trends of the first round were confirmed: the highest abstention rate of any municipal election in the Fifth Republic (58.4 per cent); the poor performance of the presidential party, with fragile roots in the country at large; the resistance of Socialists in their last bastions (Paris, Lille, Rennes, Nantes); the solid performance of LR in its bastions (Toulouse, Tourcoing); the capture by the RN of Perpignan, its first leading city of over 100,000 inhabitants since the FN won Toulon in 1995. Above all, the contest witnessed the victory of a handful of Green mayors, elected at the head of broad left-wing coalitions in leading French cities such as Lyon, Bordeaux, Strasbourg and Marseille. Somewhat paradoxically, the best 'presidential' performance was that of Édouard Philippe, then Prime Minister, re-elected as mayor in the Norman city of Le Havre, who resigned shortly after as premier, to be replaced by Jean Castex.

As in the other fields considered in this book, the Covid-19 crisis has had important implications for central–local relations and modes of territorial governance. In its own way, Covid-19 provides an insight into the inconsistencies of Macron's approach to decentralization. In the first instance, Macron asserted the need for central steering. Days into the crisis and questioned about the superior performance of neighbouring (federal) Germany, Macron explicitly asserted that France is not a federal state, hence all parts of the territory should be treated in the same manner. The French President initially rejected any idea of territorially distinct responses to the Covid-19 crisis – and went as far as to sanction local and regional authorities that had attempted to obtain masks or other equipment on their own behalf. Then, faced with the evidence that the pandemic was spreading much faster in certain parts of the country (the Paris region, eastern and northern France) than others (the west, south-west and south-east) Macron changed track and arbitrated in favour of allowing local prefects to develop localized responses (such as details of the conditions for quitting lockdown) in liaison with mayors (Floc'h, 2020). This position confirmed the trends discussed above whereby President Macron favoured strengthening the prefect, the State's representative in the 96 main departments, as the response to issues of local and regional importance. However, the main dysfunctions occurred within the State, especially in the tense relations between the prefectures and the regional health agencies (*agences régionaux de santé* – ARS) (Dupré, Jaxel-Truer and Laurent, 2020), while the regional councils demonstrated expertise in terms of economic prognosis and contributed important resources to the main fund to compensate firms for their enforced closure (Béatrice, 2020). The government's ambivalent response instinctively looked to the State as the arbiter of the public good and mistrusted local and regional authorities. In one major development, however, Macron was forced to acknowledge the value of the mayors and the municipal councils, thereby resurrecting the mayor–prefect 'couple' that had been so important in the pre-decentralization period (Roger, 2020a, 2020b).

Future perspectives

French Presidents come and go, but the structural dilemmas of French local and regional government remain as constants. What we labelled as the twin faces of State reform and territorial capacity are apparent within each presidency, as well as between them. A movement of financial recentralization has gathered pace, whether under governments of the right (Sarkozy) and left (Hollande) alike, a movement continued under Macron. On the other hand, each president attempted to grasp the potentially liberating capacity of local reform.

The most obvious interpretation is that of a prolonged attempt to strengthen central steering.

In this chapter, we have argued that France has experienced a form of neo-Jacobinism (referring to the centralizing tradition of the French Revolution) over the past long decade. It has witnessed a recentralization of local government finance, a structural reform of local and regional councils and a reform of the territorial organization of the State. These developments have taken place against the backdrop of powerful external constraints, by which we refer to the mix of legal and budgetary norms and top-down institutional pressures which partially shape the operation of local and regional authorities and policy communities (Pasquier, 2016b). Regions and metropolises are at the heart of these processes, since they are affected by local, national, European and even global policy dynamics. Under Macron, the main reaction thus far has been that of financial recentralization and closer political control. His suspicion of local and regional authorities was apparent during the Covid-19 pandemic.

The other dimension – territorial capacity and the right to difference – also came to the fore under a Janus-faced Macron, who declared himself ready to adopt the gamble of more territorial right to difference. His motivations might well have been instrumental. To survive politically, Macron needs to build his own political base in the country at large and appeal to supporters in regions such as Bretagne or metropolises such as Lyon. The inconclusive results of the 2020 municipal elections were scarcely encouraging in this respect. Adapting France's system of local and regional government to contemporary challenges sits well with the broader Macron project of modernizing France by challenging the role of intermediary forces, as local and regional authorities are sometimes framed in the Macron lexicon. Having said this, there is a world of difference between abstract aspirations of centralized efficiency and modernization and the real world of local and regional communities that proved so important as a focus point for citizens during the Covid-19 crisis.

9 RACIAL PREJUDICE IN MULTICULTURAL FRANCE

Nonna Mayer and Vincent Tiberj

This chapter explores the evolution of prejudice in France over the last 30 years, with a focus on anti-Semitism and Islamophobia. The data comes from the annual Barometers on racism of the National Consultative Commission for Human Rights (CNCDH – *Commission Nationale Consultative des Droits de l'Homme*) which we analyse at length every year, with Guy Michelat and Tommaso Vitale, for the Commission's annual report to the prime minister (Mayer et al., 2019). The Barometer on racism for 2019 (Mayer et al., 2020) was published too late to form the basis of this chapter's analysis, but its data confirms exactly the same trends as the Barometer for 2018.

Building on the studies of prejudice and its transformations since World War II (Pelinka et al., 2015), the first part shows the slow decline of prejudice in France. The second part highlights what anti-minority prejudices have in common, as part of a more general ethnocentric–authoritarian vision of society. The third part explores the transformations of prejudice, shifting from blatant to softer, more subtle forms of expression, and from biological to symbolic boundaries; it will be focused on antisemitism and islamophobia. A concluding section compares these French trends with their American and European counterparts and proposes further paths of research.

The slow rise of tolerance

A commonly received idea is that racism in general, and anti-Semitism in particular, are on the rise in France, kindled by the electoral dynamic of the populist radical right following the 2008 Great Recession, the 2015–16 terrorist attacks in Paris and Nice and an unprecedented influx of refugees. In the fall of 2018, the French Prime Minister Édouard Philippe solemnly denounced the rise of anti-Semitic and racist aggressions in France, and proposed to strengthen the triennial National Plan against Racism and Antisemitism that, since 2012, has been the responsibility of the Interministerial Delegation to Fight Racism, Antisemitism and LGBT hate

(DILCRAH – *Délégation Interministérielle à la Lutte Contre le Racisme, l'Antisémitisme et la Haine anti-LGBT*). Together with the enduring electoral appeal of Marine Le Pen, these incidents would be the proof that France is less and less tolerant toward its minorities. However, if one looks at opinions, instead of acts, and takes a long-term perspective, we see that, far from declining, tolerance has increased.

In order to provide an overview of opinions towards minorities, a general indicator was constructed, the Longitudinal Tolerance Index (Box 9.1).

Box 9.1 The construction of the Longitudinal Tolerance Index (LTI)

Vincent Tiberj created the index in 2008, according to the method set out by the American political scientist James Stimson. This index aims to measure the evolution over time of public opinion towards minorities. Rather than depending on one single question, a method likely to suffer from measurement biases or errors from one year to another, the index aggregates 69 series of questions denoting prejudice towards ethnic and/or religious minorities and asked at least three times in the National Consultative Commission for Human Rights (CNCDH (*Commission Nationale Consultative des Droits de l'Homme*) Barometer. The CNCDH Barometer has now run from 1990 to 2018, and 43 of the questions that compose it were asked at least 10 times.

Year by year, each of the series of questions is ascribed a value, which is the ratio of tolerant answers to the sum of tolerant and intolerant answers. Once these values have been computed for all 69 series, a statistical procedure 'summarizes' the information that they contain, leading to a synthetic indicator where scores are comparable from one year to another. The overall tolerance score can theoretically vary between 0, if the people questioned never gave a tolerant response, to 100 if they systematically gave a tolerant response. Thus, a higher score on the index for a given year indicates a progression of tolerance in French public opinion, whilst a decrease indicates a surge of intolerance. A second advantage of this method is that the results are much more reliable than if they were based on a single question, or even a group of questions. For instance if 56 per cent of the sample ($N = 1,000$) think Roma form a group apart in the French society, there will be 95 chances out of 100 that the correct proportion varies between 59.2 per cent and 52.8 per cent, with a margin of error of +/– 3.2 per cent. However, for the overall index, the margin of error will drop to +/– 1.6 per cent, for the same confidence interval of 95 per cent. One can also develop specific indexes by minority when there are enough relevant questions. At this stage, the data allow for the construction of a LTI for the Jewish, Muslim, Maghrebian, Black and Roma minorities.

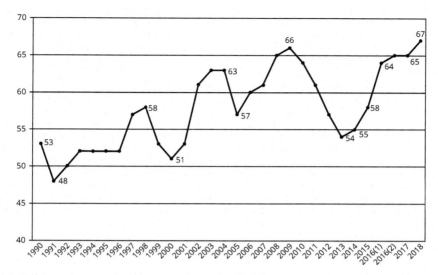

Figure 9.1 The Longitudinal Tolerance Index (LTI)

Source: Author's calculation based on the CNCDH Barometer. The unit of the Y axis is the score on the LTI.

The first lesson to draw from the index (Figure 9.1) is the evolution of French society towards a better acceptance of the 'other', in sharp contrast to the commonly received impression of an increasingly racist and anti-Semitic France. Anti-Semitism in particular made the headlines in 2019 after the verbal aggression of the philosopher Alain Finkielkraut in the midst of a Yellow Vests demonstration, coming after the painting of swastikas on photos of Simone Veil, and the tearing out of trees planted in memory of Ilan Halimi (a young man kidnapped and killed because he was a Jew and 'Jews have money'). However, the level of the LTI rose from 54 in 1990 to 66 in 2009 and 67 in 2018, its absolute record over the period, an increase of 11.5 points. The evolution is not linear – there are ups and downs, steps forward and back – but the overall trend over the last 30 years is the rise of tolerance.

In the long run, the two main explanatory factors of this increase in tolerance are rising levels of education and generational renewal. Both are developments that contribute to the diffusion of anti-racist norms in the population as a whole, and more generally to the diffusion of permissive, post-materialist values (Inglehart, 1990). In 1968, only 8 per cent of the French population passed the '*bac*' (*baccalaureate*), the examination that marks the end of high school (around age 18) and gives access to university, and 45 per cent had no formal educational qualification at all. In 2006, in contrast, 37 per cent of the population had at least the baccalaureate, 22 per cent had a university degree and the percentage without any formal qualification at all had dropped to 21 per cent. Indeed, the connection between education and tolerance is one of the most stable results over time and across countries.

In terms of generational renewal, among those who voted in 2017, 59 per cent were not old enough to do so in 1981 and a quarter were not even born then. The impact of this turnover on racism is spectacular: each new generation is more tolerant than the previous one (Stimson, Tiberj and Thiébault, 2009). In 1999, the score on the tolerance index rose from 45 out of 100 for the cohorts born between 1940 and 1955, to 53.5 for those born after 1967. In 2018, in comparison, the value of the index varied between 61 for the oldest cohort and 69 for the most recent ones. Getting old does not necessarily mean becoming more bigoted, as is often assumed. Respondents born between 1940 and 1955 were between 44 and 59 years old in 1999. Twenty years later, they were aged between 64 and 79, but far from becoming intolerant, they had become *more* tolerant. Clearly, anti-racist norms (i.e. the general rejection of racism and biological races in Europe after WWII) have been gradually spreading through French society over the last 20 years.

However, the process is not straightforward. The LTI shows a number of peaks (1998, 2003–04, 2009, 2018), often followed by abrupt falls, such as between 1998 and 2000 (–7 points) or between 2009 and 2013 (–12 points) (Figure 9.1). These variations reflect the combined influence of long- and short-term factors. Xenophobia and racism are often seen as stable attitudes, inherited from early childhood during the crucial years of primary socialization, and that are reinforced over time (Adorno et al., 1950; Allport, 1954; Tajfel, 1978; Inglehart, 1990). The variations of the tolerance index show the limits of this conception. Indeed, the reactions of individuals to 'others' are sensitive to context and current events. Stanley Feldman and Karen Stenner have shown how conditions of 'normative threat' can activate authoritarian predispositions and translate them into words, if not acts. A good example is the sudden drop in the index in 2005, after three weeks of urban violence following the death of two young boys, Zyed Benna and Bouna Traoré, who had hidden in an electric substation while trying to escape from the police. The ethnic and religious framing of the events by the media and the political class, putting forward the 'Islamization of the suburbs', the 'criminalization' of these populations and a clash of cultures, largely accounts for the rise of fear and anti-migrant and/or anti-Muslim sentiment that developed at that time (Davet and Lhomme, 2018; Lagrange, 2006; Sala Pala, 2006; Kokoreff, 2008). The impact of contextual factors is even stronger when opinions are not consistent. Paul Kellstedt (2003), following John Zaller, emphasizes the ambivalence of our attitudes towards 'others'. The same individual can simultaneously be disposed towards tolerance *and* intolerance; the prevalence of one over the other will depend on the environment and the information the person receives (political debates, recent events).

Another line of explanation for these short-term fluctuations is the so-called thermostatic theory of public opinion (Wlezien, 1995). Public opinion, after a while, can react against the policies implemented by the government on a given issue, here immigration or asylum rights. For instance, this has been proven with the support for redistribution policies in the USA (Stimson, 2004) and in Canada or the UK (Soroka and Wlezien, 2010). This may explain the variations of our index during the periods 1996–2001 and 2002–08 for instance. In mid-1996, France saw mediatized occupations and expulsions of immigrants from the Saint Ambroise and Saint Bernard churches in Paris, and accordingly, the issue of the 'sans papiers' (undocumented migrants) emerged in the political arena. The repressive legislation passed at the time by the conservative government of Alain Juppé (i.e. the Debré Law on immigration voted on April 24, 1997) fuelled a wave of petitions and demonstrations protesting against this policy (Siméant, 1998), and moved public opinion in favour of immigrants and foreigners: the index gained 6 points between 1996 and 1998.

In the same way, the 'step backwards' can be read as a reaction against the regularization of the 'sans papiers' implemented by the Socialist government which came to power in 1997, headed by Lionel Jospin. One can also note that the six highest scores on the index in the 2000s occurred under a right-wing government, which during the period 2007–09 was characterized by tougher migratory policies and the launch of the so-called great debate on French 'national identity' (Hajjat, 2012). However, other movements on the index depend on events that are not necessarily political. Thus, the peak of tolerance observed in 1998 can be seen as an effect of the football World Cup won by a multicultural French team and so dubbed as a 'Black–Blanc–Beur' victory. In contrast, the lasting and sharp decline in tolerance observed between 2009 and 2013 (–12 points) results from a mix of economic and political factors. The effect of the 2008 recession, the first of this magnitude for 30 years, was not immediately obvious. It appeared only when the crisis worsened, bringing about factory closures, increased unemployment (from 7.5 per cent in early 2008, to 10.3 per cent at the end of 2012), worries about sovereign debt in European states, budget cuts and increases in taxes. All these factors exacerbated the rejection of immigrants taken as scapegoats. However, other factors played a role too, such as the vote of the law on same-sex marriage promoted by Justice Minister Christiane Taubira, a Black woman, public enemy number one of the most conservative Catholics (Raison du Cleuziou, 2019), or the debates around the question of giving the right to vote to long-term resident foreigners.

Equally striking, but more surprising, is the sharp rise of tolerance (4 points in 2 years on the index) observed after the terrorist attacks of 2015–16 and its continuous rise ever since, although at a slower pace. This goes against a well-rooted belief that Islamist terrorism feeds xenophobia. Looking at the impact of all the terrorist attacks that took place during the period covered (the Paris bombing of 1995, the Washington and New York attacks of 2001, the Madrid and London bombings of 2004 and 2005), we see a different story. After 1995 and 2001 the tolerance index remained stable, and after the 2004–05 and the 2015–16 episodes it rose. There is no mechanical connection between terrorist attacks and changes in public opinion. We argue instead that it depends on how the events are presented and framed. For example, the 9/11 attacks were framed very differently in the USA and in Europe (Truc, 2016). The dominant analysis in the US media referred to a 'new Pearl Harbor', fuelling patriotic attitudes in the American public. European media focused more on the human drama, touching a cord in the public. The predominant interpretation of the French 2015–16 attacks, with the exception of the far right, did not put the Muslim community under scrutiny, or question its loyalty. This is also the case of the 'We are Charlie' demonstrations of 11 January. The CNCDH survey conducted in February 2015 sheds light on the profile and motivations of the marchers, showing that clearly the 'Charlies in the streets' were not demonstrating against Muslims nor voicing any xenophobic messages (Mayer and Tiberj, 2017). Among the demonstrators, young people, educated, urban, left wing, open to immigration and culturally progressive were over-represented.

The LTI, as discussed above, gives the average annual level of tolerance. Nevertheless, averages can be misleading. To check this, we compared levels of tolerance towards specific minorities. We will see in the next section that opinions about minorities can come together and proceed from a general tendency to disregard out-groups.

What prejudices have in common

The CNCDH Barometer includes enough questions to construct a specific index for five minorities and check if the same factors explain their variations. These minorities are Blacks, Jews, Maghrebians, Muslims and Roma. There are specific questions in the survey for each group. For example, do Jews/ Muslims/Blacks/Maghrebians form a group separate from the rest of society, a group open to others or not a group at all? Of course, many Jews come from Maghreb and a growing number of Muslims in France are Black, but we are working on public perceptions, not on the exact composition of these groups.

These minority LTIs (Figure 9.2a, b) show a clear hierarchy of prejudice. At one end the Roma are steadily the most rejected group by far, with an index varying between 19 and 35 over the period, 32 points below the average on the global LTI (on Romaphobia, see McGarry, 2017). A majority of respondents still believe in old stereotypes, describing Roma as nomads who exploit children, live on theft and trafficking, and do not want to integrate. This is a particularly striking result when one knows the cultural and social heterogeneity of the Roma population (Olivera, 2010). Conversely, the two most accepted groups are Jews and Blacks, with a score of respectively 79 and 78 in 2018, some 11 points above the average ILT (Figure 9.2a). At the beginning of the period, in 1990, Blacks were far more accepted than Jews, with an LTI score 20 points above theirs. But their score went down between 1997 and 2005, while conversely the scores of the Jewish minority shot up. The turning point for the latter is the beginning of the Second Intifada in 2000. The spectacular surge of anti-Semitic actions at that time, and the violence it brought about (Figure 9.3), seems to have had the opposite effect on public opinion, which firmly condemned the violence and showed compassion for the victims.

a

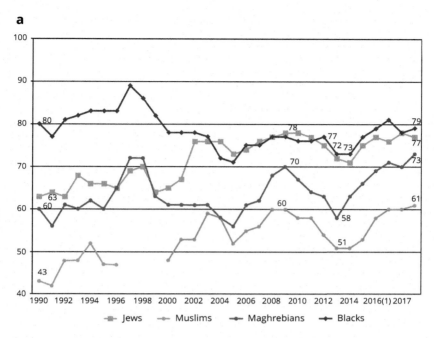

b

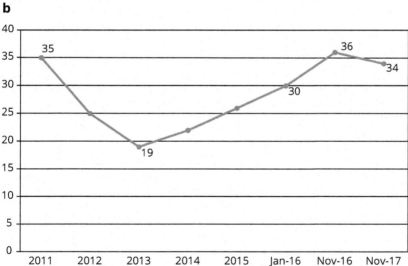

Figure 9.2 (a) Longitudinal Tolerance Index by minority (b) Longitudinal Tolerance Index for Roma

Source: author's calculation based on the CNCDH Barometer.

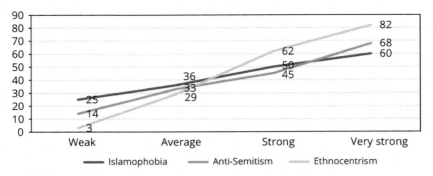

Figure 9.3 Prejudice towards Jews and Islam by level of authoritarianism

CNCDH Barometer, November 2018. Entries are percentages.

In comparison, Maghrebians, coming from the three former French colonies in North Africa, have a more negative image, and Muslims the worst of all. Although their index improved over the period in total, by 12 points for the former and 17 points for the latter, they lag way behind Jews and Blacks (73 for Maghrebians and 61 for Muslims, versus 77 and 79). In the galaxy of prejudice, Maghrebians and Muslims have taken a growing importance, in parallel with the debates about immigration and diversity, communitarianism, fundamentalism, and the alleged incompatibility of Islam with French republican values.

Yet, in spite of this hierarchy, opinions towards all minorities are tightly correlated; they are part of a coherent 'ethnocentric' attitude (Adorno et al., 1950) which consists in looking at the world through the lens of one's own culture, valuing the group to which one belongs (in-group) and its norms, and rejecting the others (out-groups) and their way of life. In the CNCDH Barometer survey, by way of example, respondents who have a negative image of Jews tend to also have a negative image of Muslims, of immigrants, of foreigners in general. To analyse the relationship between the different prejudices towards minorities we use another tool, attitudinal scales. We look for patterns of answers, selecting those that are part of a same negative attitude towards Jews for instance (anti-Semitism), or Muslims (Islamophobia), or groups in general (ethnocentrism). Correlations between the three prejudices are each positive and range between 0.22 (Islamophobia and anti-Semitism) and 0.50 (ethnocentrism and Islamophobia). As also shown by Adorno and his colleagues some 60 years ago, ethnocentrism goes together with an authoritarian–hierarchical vision of society. It assigns an inferior place to other groups, not only ethnic minorities but groups with different norms (sexual minorities, feminists, homeless). Other authors, in line with Gordon Allport's work (Allport, 1954), use the term 'group-focused enmity' (Zick, Wolf et al., 2008; Zick, Küpper et al., 2011). They show in the same way that all types of prejudice are connected and linked to an unequal vision of society. The scores of respondents on our ethnocentrism scale are tightly correlated with their score on an index of authoritarianism, which includes questions about the acceptance of homosexuality, the death penalty and courts' decisions. The same goes for prejudice towards specific minorities measured by scores on a scale of anti-Semitism and a scale of aversion to Islam or Islamophobia (Figure 9.3). As one moves from respondents with low to high scores of authoritarianism, the proportion of them with high scores on the scale of Islamophobia increases by 35 percentage points, on the anti-Semitism scale by 54 percentage points and on the ethnocentrism scale by 79 percentage points.

Last one must check if the same factors explain the different types of prejudice. A logistic regression model allows us to test the specific impact of each variable ceteris paribus, once the effects of all others have been controlled for. The selected variables are gender, age, education, subjective economic position, political orientation, cosmopolitanism, origin and religion. We would expect the elderly and the least educated to be more prejudiced, less exposed to democratic norms and less open to other cultures. A right-wing orientation usually goes hand in hand with a more authoritarian and hierarchical view of society, favouring ethnocentrism. A feeling of economic decline (living less well than before) classically feeds resentment toward minorities, who are deemed responsible for hardship, as does parochialism – being isolated from the rest of the world – measured on an index of cosmopolitanism combining frequency of travel and residence abroad. The absence of immigrant background (measured by number of non-French parents or grandparents), and belonging to the mainstream Catholic religion, would also, we expect, favour prejudice against minorities.

Four variables have a significant impact on all three scales, all things being equal: political orientation, subjective economic situation, origin and religion. Political orientation is the major predictor by far (Table 9.1). The more right wing a person is, the higher their chance to be ethnocentric, anti-Semitic or Islamophobic, the highest scores being found at the extreme right and among the supporters of the *Rassemblement National*. Then comes a deteriorating economic situation, belonging to the Catholic religion (as opposed to a minority religion) or no religion at all, and having an exclusively French background. Gender has no effect whatsoever, and the other variables play differently for each type of prejudice. Education has only a strong impact on the level of ethnocentrism, coming just after political orientation. Moreover, the effects of education and political orientation reinforce each other. The predicted probability of having high scores on the ethnocentrism scale goes from 13 per cent among far-left respondents with 2 years or more of university education to 87 per cent among the far-right ones without even the baccalaureate (Figure 9.4). However, the impact of political orientation is greater: even non-educated left-wingers are far less prejudiced than very educated right-wingers (35 per cent versus 75 per cent).

Table 9.1 Predictors of high scores of ethnocentrism, anti-Semitism and Islamophobia in 2018

Logistic regression	Ethnocentrism	Islamophobia	Anti-Semitism
Left–right scale	***	**	***
Economic insecurity	***	***	*
Origin	*	*	***
Religion	***	**	*
Cosmopolitanism	**	*	–
Education	***	–	–
Age	–	–	**
Gender	–	–	–
R^2 Nagelkerke	*0.41*	*0.12*	*0.16*

Sig. *P < 0.05; **P < 0.010; ***P < 0.001. Asterisks refer to the most significant modality of each variable. Source: CNCDH Barometer, November 2018.

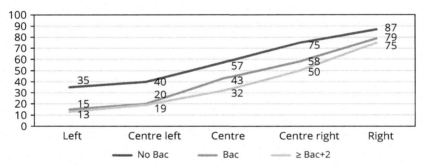

Figure 9.4 Predicted probabilities of ethnocentrism by level of education and political orientation

Source: CNCDH Barometer, November 2018. Entries are percentages.

Yet one finds no significant relation between education and Islamophobia or anti-Semitism. Some of the respondents who reject Islam's religious practices are driven by their supportive attitudes towards women or gays; and some of those who reject Jews by their condemnation of Israel's policies in the Middle East, rather than by ignorance or a global rejection of the 'other' (vide infra, Section 2). As for cosmopolitan attitudes, they attenuate ethnocentrism and aversion to Islam, but not anti-Semitism. As for age, it only has an impact on anti-Semitism, the older generations appearing far more prejudiced against Jews than the younger. Overall, the statistical coefficient summing up the explanatory power of the variables included in the model is much higher for ethnocentrism than for anti-Semitism and Islamophobia (the respective R^2 values are 0.40, 0.16 and

0.12). The fact that the ways of expressing prejudice have changed, blurring the border between what is and is not racism or anti-Semitism, is a possible line of explanation.

The transformation of prejudice

In the previous section, we have shown that prejudice against minorities is slowly declining, particularly among younger, educated and left-wing respondents. In spite of the evidence though, several authors question this decline, arguing that racism is still there, but wearing new clothes. Since World War II and the extermination of 6 million Jews, anti-racism has become the norm in Western democracies and prejudiced opinions towards minorities are more difficult to hold; they are expressed less openly, less obtrusively. From this perspective, the 'other' is no longer rejected as biologically or morally inferior, but as different, according to his or her values and culture. This argumentation could be racism in disguise, a racism described as 'symbolic' (Kinder and Sears, 1981; Mc Conahay, 1981), 'subtle' (Pettigrew and Meertens, 1995), 'differentialist' (Taguieff, 1985) or 'aversive' (Dovidio et al., 2016). We would expect to see this 'new' racism develop more particularly among young, educated, left-wing individuals, a priori the least likely to be prejudiced, and who do not consider themselves racist. In the United States, the debate has focused on anti-Black prejudice, in France, on anti-Jew and anti-Muslim prejudice.

The new anti-Semitism?

Jews are the oldest established minority in France, from the time of Roman Gaul (Hadas Lebel, 2015). The French Revolution gave them full citizenship. During WWII, a quarter of the 325,000 Jews living in France were deported, with the help of the French police; only 2,566 returned. A new dynamic started after the independence of Algeria, in 1962, with the return of French settlers from Algeria, including an important Sephardic Jewish community. Today France has the largest Jewish minority in Europe, estimated at nearly half a million (Della Pergola, 2016, p. 7).

Pierre-André Taguieff (2002, 2004) was the first to describe in France the emergence of a 'new' anti-Semitism developing among leftists and Muslims. He called it the 'new Judeophobia', arguing that its targets are not Semites (which would include Arabs) but Jews. This prejudice hides the old anti-Jewish prejudice behind the criticism of Israel and Zionism and the defence of the rights of Palestinians, uniting leftists and Islamist activists in the defence of a common cause. This idea of a 'new anti-Semitism' has attracted a large following, raising the spectre of a 'red (for leftist)–green (for Islamists)– brown (for fascists) alliance' and an 'anti-Semitism of the suburbs'. In April 2018, a 'Manifesto against the new anti-Semitism' published in *Le Parisien* directly accused the Muslim community of this 'new Judeophobia', denouncing a 'quiet ethnic cleansing' in certain neighbourhoods, accusing public authorities of laxness for 'electoral reasons', because 'the Muslim vote is ten times bigger than the Jewish vote'. The manifesto was written by Philippe Val, former editor of satirical weekly French newspaper *Charlie Hebdo*, and backed by major politicians (Nicolas Sarkozy, Manuel Valls, Jean-Pierre Raffarin, Bertrand Delanoë), high-profile public intellectuals (Elisabeth Badinter, Jean-Claude Casanova, Alain Finkielkraut) and academics (Dominique Schnapper, Benjamin Stora, Pierre-André Taguieff). The fact that anti-Semitic acts, as reported by the police, rose in a spectacular fashion after the start of the Second Intifada, and flared up at each operation of the Israeli army in the occupied territories (Figure 9.5), gives support to the idea of a new anti-Semitism driven by hatred of Israel and Zionism.

Yet the dynamics of acts on the one hand, and attitudes and behaviour on the other, are different (Ajzen and Fishbein, 2005). While police statistics show a rise in often-violent anti-Semitic acts since 2000 (Figure 9.5), the Longitudinal Tolerance Index shows a growing acceptance of Jews (Figure 9.2a). To understand the paradox, one must take a closer look at the survey questions about Jews on the one hand, and the image of Israel and the Israeli–Palestinian conflict on the other. Undeniably, the image of French Jews has evolved positively since WWII and the most blatant anti-Semitic stereotypes have faded. In 1946, two years after the liberation of the concentration camps, 54 per cent of the French people questioned by IFOP still considered that Jews were 'above all a race' [these references to the post-war surveys are from Mayer (1993 and 2004), Roux (2006) and Bensimon and Verdès-Leroux (1970)]. In comparison, by 2018, fewer than 9 per cent believed that some races are superior to others. Also in 1946, fewer than one-third considered French Jews to be 'as French as any other French', compared with 89 per cent today. In 1966, one year after the end of the Oecumenical

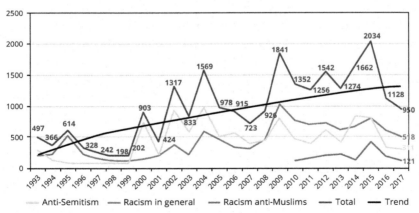

Figure 9.5 Trends of racist, anti-Semitic and anti-Muslim acts

Source: Ministry of the Interior, 2018.

Council of Vatican II that absolved the Jews of deicide (being responsible for the death of God's son, Jesus), 27 per cent of the French population were still not willing to admit that 'Jews are not responsible for the death of the Christ' (Bensimon and Verdès-Leroux, 1970, p. 82), whereas now this fraction is negligible. In 2000, 52 per cent of the sample considered that a person publicly calling somebody a 'dirty Jew' should be sentenced by the court; in 2018 the figure was 86 per cent. As for negationist opinions over the years, these have been regularly declining. Only 17 per cent considered that one talks too much about the extermination of Jews during World War II in the 2018 barometer, the same proportion as in the 2000 barometer.

Compared with other minorities, the image of Jews is also by far the most positive. For instance, the proportion that considers Muslims to be as French as any other French people is 10 points below the number for Jews, and 26 below the number for Roma. The Jewish religion has a negative image for 19 per cent of the sample, but for the Muslim religion, the figure is 30 per cent. Jews are seen as 'a group apart' by 23 per cent of the French population, but Muslims by 36 per cent and Roma by 66 per cent. These differences explain why the tolerance index for Jews is higher than for other minorities.

Nevertheless, two very ancient stereotypes resist. One associates Jews with money ('Jews have a special relationship with money'), a reputation going back to the Middle Age when lending money was forbidden to Catholics. The second associates them with power and influence ('Jews have too much power in France today'), in line with the Protocols of the Learned Elders of Zion, a document forged by the Russian secret police to disseminate the myth of a Jewish conspiracy (Taguieff, 1992). The rate of agreement with these stereotypes fluctuates according to the context, rising every time there is the feeling that Jews form a privileged minority, and that there are double standards, and then falling back. For instance, the average proportion of respondents who believe that Jews have excessive power is around 20 per cent. But the figure almost doubled in 1999–2000 when Jews who had been victims of spoliations during the War got financial reparations. It shot up again in 2014, first when the anti-Semitic show of the humourist Dieudonné was banned, in January of that year; and then during the summer when pro-Palestinian demonstrations against the Israeli army's intervention in Gaza (Protective Edge) were banned. That very year, the approval of the stereotype about money reached a record level of 62.5 per cent; by 2018 it was down to 38 per cent.

A point to note here is that anti-Semitism, like all forms of prejudice, has always been in constant evolution. For instance, the creation of the State of Israel in 1948 changed the image of Jews around the world. In the 1930s, they were seen as eternal wanderers and stateless. After 1948 they were suspected of 'dual loyalty'. In the 2018 barometer, 36 per cent of the sample considered that 'Israel matters more for them than France'. Two questions cover more specifically the 'new Judeophobia' dimension. A list of words is proposed, including 'Israel', asking if it evokes something positive, negative or neither positive nor negative. Another question asks about responsibilities for the continuation of the Israeli–Palestinian conflict (the Israelis, the Palestinians, both). After the Six-Day War of 1967 the image of Israel considerably deteriorated in French public opinion (IFOP Collectors, 2014), and it systematically evokes more negative than positive feelings (34 per cent negative versus 24 per cent positive in 2018), with a peak of negative opinions at the two ends of the political spectrum (47 per cent on the far left, 38 per cent on the far right). Israelis are much more often than Palestinians held responsible for the conflict (15.5 per cent against 1.5 per cent, with a record level of 29 per cent on the far left). However, in both cases, the most noticeable result is the refusal to take sides: 42 per cent do not answer the question about the image of Israel or choose the answer 'neither positive nor negative', while 83 per cent do not answer the question about the continuation of the conflict, or consider both sides responsible. Politics in the Middle East may well arouse passion, and regularly trigger anti-Semitic acts, but when it comes to opinions, the issue appears peripheral. The old stereotypes, especially those about power and money, predominate.

A principal component analysis on these 10 questions reveals three distinctive factors structuring the opinions: 'old anti-Semitism', 'anti-Israelism', and 'anti-Judaism' (Table 9.2). The first factor is structured by the old

Table 9.2 Principal component analysis on the questions about Jews and Israel

	Components		
	1	**2**	**3**
Jews have too much power in France	**0.753**	−0.165	−0.085
Jews have a specific relationship with money	**0.690**	−0.325	−0.157
For French Jews, Israel is more important than France	**0.586**	−0.026	−0.351
French Jews are not as French as any other French	**0.584**	−0.207	0.375
Jews forms a group apart in society	**0.531**	0.118	0.009
Negative or very negative opinion of 'Israel'	0.354	**0.631**	0.207
In France we talk too much about the extermination of Jews during WWII	0.330	0.348	−0.379
Negative or very negative opinion of the 'Jewish religion'	0.189	0.550	**0.526**
No need to harshly sanction public insults such as 'dirty Jew'	0.192	−0.059	**0.519**
Israelis share the largest responsibility in the continuation of the conflict	−0.014	**0.644**	−0.395

Source: CNCDH Barometer. November 2018. Cumulated explained variance: 49 per cent (first factor 23 per cent, second 14 per cent, third 12 per cent).

stereotypes about Jews, their alleged power, relationship with money, 'communitarianism' and 'dual loyalty'. The second is structured by a negative opinion of Israel and a rejection of these traditional stereotypes about Jews. The third is structured by a negative opinion of the Jewish religion and tolerance towards anti-Semitic insults.

These results clearly therefore contradict the 'new Judeophobia' thesis. One can be critical of Israel and its policies without being prejudiced against Jews. And the profile of the respondents aligned on these three factors is also at odds with Taguieff's theory. The 'old' anti-Semitism is more common among the older cohorts, with a low level of education, located on the right or far right of the left–right scale. They appear intolerant of not only Jews but also other minorities, with high scores on all our scales of prejudice. In contrast, 'anti-Israelism' is present mostly among middle-aged French, educated to at least the *baccalaureate*, close to the left and radical left, and clearly not racist, with low scores on all our scales of prejudice including anti-Semitism.

Regarding, finally, a specific Muslim anti-Semitism, ad hoc studies are needed, owing to the small number of declared Muslims in a standard survey, around 6 per cent of any sample. The relationship to politics of immigrant-born French survey (RAPFI: *Rapport au Politique des Français Issus de l'Immigration*), conducted in 2005, is one of the rare studies of a national representative sample of 1,000 French citizens of Maghrebian, African or Turkish origin, 62 per cent of whom were Muslims (Brouard and Tiberj, 2005, 2015). They indeed appear more inclined to approve anti-Semitic stereotypes. For instance, 39 per cent (against 19 per cent in a mirror survey representative of the French population at large) believed Jews have too much power in France, and the most likely to endorse it were the most religious, with a conservative approach towards Islam. Yet a majority of the Muslim respondents rejected the stereotype.

The new Islamophobia?

France also has the largest Muslim population in Europe after Germany, estimated at a little over 4 million according to the Trajectories and Origins (TEO) survey data (Simon and Tiberj, 2013). It forms the second religious group in France after the Catholics. Islam has been at the heart of French public debate since the first 'Islamic "headscarf affair"' in 1989, when young Muslim schoolgirls refused to take off their scarf in the classroom, challenging the French fundamental principle of secularism (*laïcité*) (Benhabib, 2008). A long conflict ensued, and led to the law of 2004 that prohibits the wearing of ostentatious signs of religious affiliation in public schools, and to the law banning the burqa in 2010. Controversies continue. The rise of Islamic fundamentalism and the multiplication of terror attacks (Toulouse in 2012; Paris and Saint Denis in 2015; Nice in 2016) have bred suspicion and increased pressure on French Muslims, who are regularly summoned to distance themselves from terrorists (which Muslim authorities did repeatedly as shown by Geisser et al., 2017). Moreover, with each terrorist attack, anti-Muslim acts increase (Figure 9.5). For instance, in 2015, 429 acts and threats were declared to the police, a 223 per cent increase in one year. Yet opinions, although much less positive about Muslims than Jews, have slowly become more tolerant, in spite of these attacks. As we saw above in the case of anti-Semitism, the paradox could be explained by the emergence of new 'symbolic' or 'subtle' forms of 'Islamophobia' prejudice that are more difficult to detect, because they can be hidden behind the defence of republican values such as secularism and women's rights.

The term 'Islamophobia' has a long history that one cannot develop here (Hajjat and Mohammed, 2013). The Runnymede Trust's report on 'Islamophobia: its features and dangers' of 1997 coined the term in the UK; it came later to France. Vincent Geisser was the first to use it in his book about 'The new islamophobia' (2003). In a symmetry with Taguieff's 'new Judeophobia', discussed above, Geisser portrayed critics of the Muslim religion as disguising blatant anti-Muslim and, more generally, anti-immigrant, sentiments. Although the term 'Islamophobia' is now commonly used in social science research to describe prejudice against Islam (the religion) and Muslims (who practise Islam) (Asal, 2014), it has remained controversial in the French public debate. Many left-wing intellectuals, usually more tolerant, refuse to use the word, claiming it makes it impossible to criticize the Muslim religion without being called racist. Such is the case, for example, of the journalist Caroline Fourest, a historical figure of *Charlie Hebdo*, who systematically (and wrongly) presents Islamophobia as a concept crafted by the Iranian mullahs to support their political project (Asal, 2014).

One must therefore untangle actual prejudice against Muslims from what is genuine, value-based criticism of a religion. The CNCDH Barometers include two types of questions directly related to Islam and Muslims. Some are the same for all minorities (are they as French as any other, do they form a group apart in society, does Islam evoke something positive or negative?). Others are specific to the Muslim religion, asking if the respect for the following rituals and practices (headscarf, burqa, prayers, Ramadan fast, food taboos etc.) can be a problem when living in French society. The LTIs by minority (Figure 9.2a) show that Muslims are systematically less well accepted than Jews, throughout the whole period. But since 9/11 and the headscarf affair, which put Islam at the heart of the political debate, Muslims are much more rejected than Maghrebians or Arabs, although the majority of the latter are in fact Muslims. There is clearly more to it than the legacy of the 'colonial fracture' (Lemaire et al., 2005): Islam itself is rejected as such.

To what extent are these 'Islamophobic' opinions disconnected from plain ethnocentrism, or prejudice against the 'other'? Figure 9.6 provides an answer. The data come from the January 2016 CNCDH Barometer, conducted after the 2015 terror attacks, but we find the same results for the following years. The curves, resulting from four logistic regression

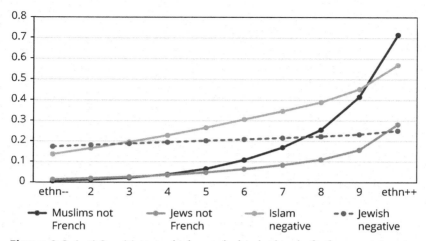

Figure 9.6 Anti-Semitism and Islamophobia by level of ethnocentrism

Source: CNCDH Barometer. November 2016.

models, represent the predicted probabilities of giving a negative answer to two questions about the 'Frenchness' of Muslims and Jews and to two questions about the image of their respective religion. The independent variable is the score on a scale of ethnocentrism, based on a set of questions addressing generic prejudice, not mentioning any particular group. Respondents are ordered in deciles, from the most tolerant (decile 1) to the most intolerant (decile 10).

We note the following: First, the more ethnocentric the respondent, the more likely he or she is to have a negative opinion of both groups and of Islam, and to a lesser extent, the Jewish religion. Islamophobia and anti-Semitism follow the same pattern: 71 per cent of the most ethnocentric respondents (decile 10) are likely to question the Frenchness of Muslim citizens, and 59 per cent to have a negative feeling toward Islam, whereas among the least prejudiced, the chances are 1 per cent and 14 per cent respectively. Second, even the least prejudiced (deciles 1 and 2) have a more negative image of religions (Judaism and Islam) than of their followers (Jews and Muslims). This is a result in line with the French secular tradition, in a country where 'religion' as such evokes something positive for only 39 per cent of the sample, and even less (34 per cent) among left wingers. Last, the most ethnocentric hardly reject Jews and the Jewish religion more than the non-ethnocentric: Muslims and Islam are by far their main concern.

Figure 9.7 shows the acceptance of various Muslim rituals and practices by degree of ethnocentrism. For each one, respondents were asked whether it could be a 'problem for living in French society' or not. One practice is still massively rejected, whatever the level of ethnocentrism: the burqa, officially banned since the 2010 law prohibiting 'concealment of the face in public space' (Law no. 2010–1192, 11 October 2010). The headscarf, which started

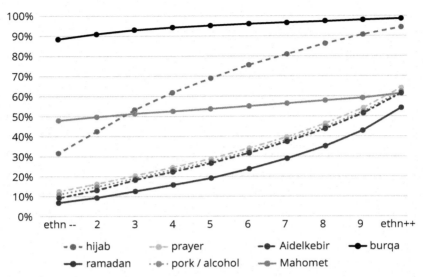

Figure 9.7 Islamic practices are a problem for living in French society

Source: CNCDH Barometer. November 2018. Entries concern the predicted probability of finding Islamic practices problematic for living in French society.

the debate about the place of Islam in France (see above), is still a divisive issue. It is massively rejected by the most prejudiced (deciles 7–10); the most tolerant are themselves divided, torn between the acceptance of diversity and the principle of neutrality in the public space. Even in the first decile, with the lowest scores of ethnocentrism, 25 per cent see it as a problem. And a minority of even the most tolerant find problematic the banning of images of the Prophet, at the root of the *Charlie Hebdo* attack. Here too, respondents are torn between conflicting values: respect for other religious beliefs on the one hand and freedom of expression, including the right to blasphemy, on the other. But all other practices are massively approved (praying, fasting for Ramadan, not eating pork or drinking alcohol, sacrificing a sheep for Eid). At the other end of the spectrum, the most prejudiced respondents tend to reject all these practices, including the most private such as not drinking alcohol, or praying. They reject Islam as a whole, considering it alien to French society.

To sum up, negative attitudes toward Muslims and Islam, as towards Jews, are part of a more general ethnocentric vision of society. In that sense, Islamophobia is a prejudice like any other, and the most intolerant respondents reject the Muslim religion as well as its followers. There are also tolerant respondents who reject some of these practices for good reasons, as they see it. For example, they see the veil as a symbol of women's oppression or as a

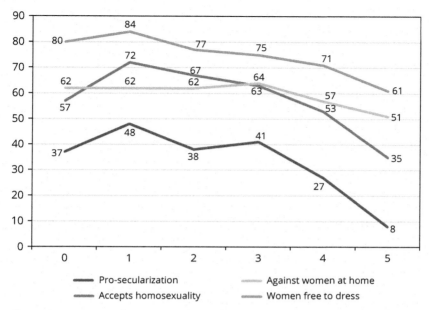

Figure 9.8 Image of women, gays and secularism by aversion to Islam

Source: CNCDH Barometer. November 2018.

breach in the principle of secularism. Lastly, there are respondents who are not particularly attached to women's rights, freedoms of expression or secularism, but who put their defence forward as a way to voice their resentment toward Muslims in an acceptable way. Cross-tabulating attitudes towards women, gays and secularism by scores on a scale of aversion to Islam (Figure 9.8) helps disentangling the respondents' motivations (Mayer et al., 2018). There is a negative correlation between aversion to Islam and a secular–liberal vision of society. The most inclined to defend feminism, LGBT rights and secularism are those with the lowest scores on the scale of aversion to Islam.

Conclusion: the French case in perspective

Surveys have their limitations. The answers depend on the data collection mode (face-to-face or online), the framing of the questions, how they are understood, the context in which they are asked, and so on. And each country has its idiosyncrasies. However, when one compares France with the USA or other European countries, the trends are quite similar. In the American context, with the legacy of slavery, the colour line is central. The most recent surveys on the perceptions of Blacks by Whites show, as in France, a gradual improvement, and a decline in the most blatant expressions of racism (Krysan and Moberg, 2016). In Europe, the European Social Survey (ESS) of 2014–15 had a specific section on attitudes towards migrants and minorities (Heath et al., 2016 and 2019). Compared with the 2002 survey, they show that in all 21 countries surveyed but 2 (Austria and Czech Republic), agreement with the idea that 'one's country was made a better place to live as a result of migration' had increased. As in France, some minorities are more accepted than others, and the hierarchy is the same. Asked whether one should allow many, some, a few or none of different sorts of migrants, Roma are by far the most rejected, followed by Muslim people, while Jews are the most accepted (banned by respectively one third, one quarter and 10 per cent of the sample). The factors explaining these attitudes are the same: education and generational turnover. Moreover, the gap between the proportion of tolerant answers among the young, educated, on the one hand, versus the old, uneducated, on the other, is growing, reaching a record figure in France (over 50 per cent). The Macron presidency is ambiguous regarding diversity. The president has tried to sidestep the debate (for example by postponing a major speech about his conception of *laïcité*), while at the same time he has followed a restrictive approach toward refugees and has kept positioning himself as the best defender of the Republic against the *Rassemblement National*. In this regard, he could lose on both sides, alienating both tolerant and intolerant voters.

10 SOCIO-ECONOMIC POLICY AND GOVERNANCE: THE DIFFICULT AND CONTESTED POLITICS OF REFORM

Susan Milner

The watchword of Emmanuel Macron's presidential campaign was reform. His presidency began immediately with a series of 'big bang' decrees reforming France's labour legislation, which, the new president argued, was necessary to open up the economy. Labour law enshrined in the *Code du Travail* was, he pronounced, 'obsolete and unsuited' to the contemporary world of work (Macron, 2018). Far-reaching reform of labour law formed part of a wider programme of deregulation, complemented by tax reductions and overhaul of the social security system, in order to reduce public debt and encourage business investment.

For several decades, France has been considered a 'problem' country in relation to its ability to carry out reforms in the context of globalized capitalism. Although a broad consensus existed about the need for reform, the country has been sharply divided about how to reform and with what outcome. Thus, President Sarkozy was elected on a platform of far-reaching reform in 2017 but ended his term of office with most of his promises unfulfilled and his initiatives incomplete: a presidency characterized by missed opportunities for change, or *'la rupture manquée'* (Milner, 2013; Smith, 2013). Systemic reform of labour law, although a long-standing demand of French business, was resisted by trade unions, which had shown capacity to mobilize large numbers and organize strike movements, despite numerical weakness as measured by membership figures. The scope of the 2017 reform and the speed of its enactment are therefore all the more remarkable. However, although Emmanuel Macron had campaigned on the theme of the need for a clean break with the policies of the Hollande presidency, he had benefitted from the headwind of reform created after 2014 (Milner, 2017).

The 2017 reform and its accompanying programme of changes to social security therefore need to be assessed in light of the more incremental reforms introduced under the previous presidency. Moreover, they need to take account of a gradual process of liberalization begun some years before the Hollande presidency and continued under governments of both left and right (Vail, 2017).

This chapter begins with an account of the changes to French labour law which have taken place since 2012, in order to assess the extent of reform after 2017. As will be shown, incremental reform was adopted under the Hollande presidency in response to France's distinctive problem of rising unemployment, particularly youth unemployment. This approach, previously pursued under governments of both right and left although with important differences, resulted in patterns of 'dualization' which have characterized socio-economic reform in continental European welfare states (Emmenegger et al., 2012); that is, the relative job security and protection of standards of working conditions for the 'core' workforce were mostly retained, whilst newer labour market entrants tended to be employed on short-term contracts and more 'atypical' work schedules with shorter guaranteed hours. The OECD has long highlighted this feature of the French labour market, recommending instead more flexible employment contracts and better training for labour market entrants to make it more inclusive (see e.g. OECD, 2017). The European Union, too, has consistently advocated a programme of labour market deregulation, reduction of social security costs and the tax take, and investment in youth training schemes (EU, 2017). The Macron reform programme offers the prospect of more thorough-going change which is likely to result in closer alignment with the prevailing EU model of fiscal discipline and perhaps the Anglo Saxon model of socio-economic regulation, although in the short and medium term domestic practices of regulation may limit the extent of real change, particularly in larger companies.

As well as labour law, two other aspects of reform are examined in the following two sections. Section two contextualizes and outlines President Macron's programme for reform of France's distinctive welfare system. The driver for these changes is primarily debt reduction, which President Sarkozy had promised but failed to deliver, and President Hollande had begun to undertake in the latter period of his presidency. Together these current and planned reforms, alongside labour law reform, indicate much more radical systemic change than was enacted under the two previous presidencies, because they threaten the traditional power base of trade unions in the public sector and begin to dismantle the distinctive governance features introduced in the 1970s. The third section of the chapter focuses on 'social partnership', which has been a characteristic mode of reform, but which successive presidents have sought to reshape. Although President Macron continues to consult trade unions and business, his reform processes are directed by the executive, and indeed in order to enact reform he has willingly confronted resistance from trade unions.

In conclusion, the implications of the mode and scope of reform are considered with reference to the extent to which they successfully navigate the possibilities for resistance which bedevilled previous presidencies. Trade unions' failure to halt labour law reform under François Hollande made it easier for the new president to enact change, with a strong parliamentary majority and a weak and divided political opposition. However, the unexpected *gilets jaunes* movement (see Chapter 11) highlighted the weaknesses of the Macron presidential style and showed the limits of top-down reform in France. In 2019, the movement caused the executive to pause its reform programme, marking the end of the reformist first half of the Macron presidency and ushering in a more uncertain second half. The hiatus demonstrates the difficulty of reforming without also increasing state expenditure to cushion the impact of change, in a system where the middle classes stand to lose from reform as well as lower-income groups, and where there is a tradition of successful mobilization against welfare cuts (see Bonoli and Palier, 2000).

Labour law reform: the Holy Grail of reform at last?

France has long been seen as having strong employment regulation through labour law (rather than, for example, through collective bargaining). This feature fits the broader historical institutional pattern characterizing France, of a strong State and weak social actors such as trade unions. Consequently, those wishing to deregulate the French economy focused on labour law. According to the OECD's strictness of legislation index, which measures how strongly employment contracts are regulated, France has relatively strict employment legislation, and its score increased slightly between 2003 and 2013; that is, legislation became a little more protective, whereas it decreased in many other countries (OECD, 2018a). Those wishing to reform French labour law aimed to increase numerical flexibility by making it easier to hire on temporary contracts and especially by making it easier to make people redundant. As mass redundancies became a political issue, however, campaigning politicians found it easier to find ways of creating temporary contracts alongside open-ended employment (Emmenegger, 2014), whilst tightening redundancy protection.

Policy-makers continued to experiment with new forms of short-term contracts whilst seeking to tie them to specific business projects and to pledges on job creation and employee training, and simultaneously using taxation to dissuade employers from relying on them (Lepage-Saucier et al., 2013). Governments, beginning with the left in the 1980s, also sought to encourage more flexibility for employers through decentralization of collective bargaining. In other words, labour legislation was hollowed out but retained as an overarching regulatory framework. As a result of the reluctance to carry out more thorough-going deregulation, it was claimed by some economists, by business lobbyists and by politicians on the right that France's labour legislation discouraged businesses from recruiting for fear of not being able to shed labour in hard times (see Romei, 2017).

Temporary employment grew significantly in the French labour market after 1980. At 16.9 per cent of total employment, the proportion of temporary employment in France is higher than the EU and OECD averages (OECD, 2018b). Young people entering the labour market are predominantly employed on temporary (fixed-term) contracts: 58 per cent of employed young people aged between 15 and 24 in 2017. Yet despite the limited flexibility provided by labour market dualization, in the form of temporary contracts, the unemployment rate continued to grow, and increasing numbers of people were locked out of the labour market, particularly young people seeking to enter it. Unemployment rose from 9.8 per cent of the active population in 2012 to 10.1 per cent in 2016, and youth unemployment from 24.4 per cent to 24.6 per cent (although as discussed further below, both rates began to fall after 2016) (Insee, 2019). We note that youth unemployment figures need to be treated with caution because they are a proportion of all those aged 15–24 in the active population, that is, excluding young people in education or training. If students are included in the calculation, the figure falls from 20.8 per cent in 2018 to 7.8 per cent. This distinction is important in comparing across countries because the student population varies in size.

These figures help to explain why President Macron justified his labour law reform on the grounds not just of tackling unemployment but also of opening up the labour market to outsiders (those not currently in employment, particularly young labour market entrants). The labour code, he argued, discouraged employers from taking on employees on open-ended contracts due to high costs of firing. His reform project built on the preparatory and legislative work undertaken under the previous executive.

Under François Hollande's presidency, labour law came onto the political agenda after the change of government after January 2014 when Manuel Valls took over as prime minister, and brought in Emmanuel Macron as finance minister. A report by economist Gilbert Cette (later one of the leading economists publicly to support Emmanuel Macron in the 2017 presidential campaign) and lawyer Jacques Barthélémy for the thinktank Terra Nova, which had been a key support for François Hollande in 2012, advocated a complete overhaul of labour law, with a new architecture based on the principle that the state should define only the fundaments of employment regulation and that collective bargaining should take precedence over law. The report's authors acknowledged that such a reversal of the relationship between law and bargaining could only occur if the bargaining parties, particularly trade unions, were strengthened and could be seen to represent a majority of the employees covered in any agreement. However, they suggested that in that case virtually all areas of employment could be regulated by collective agreement, including minimum wages (Barthélémy and Cette, 2015). Also in 2015, in a report commissioned by Manuel Valls, lawyers Robert Badinter and Antoine Lyon-Caen outlined their own version of a new architecture of labour law, taking care to identify areas where the State still needed to establish foundational principles, not least in order to comply with EU legislation (Badinter and Lyon-Caen, 2015). The basic principle was the same: in order to tackle youth unemployment, a more flexible way of regulating employment at the level of individual companies was needed, within the constraints of fundamental law and the basic guarantees offered by sectoral bargaining.

Finally, the government commissioned a report on the ways in which collective bargaining could complement or replace law. The report by Jean-Denis Combrexelle, president of the Economic and Social Committee, argued that sectoral bargaining needed to be simplified and rationalized, that an annual programme of bargaining should be agreed in advance, and that local-level bargaining should be the main locus of regulation, on the basis of a clear representative majority and of core principles defined by law (Combrexelle, 2015; see also Venturi, 2015). In the longer term (four years down the line), the Combrexelle report recommended, a wider overhaul of the regulatory architecture should take place, once the bargaining structure and parties had been prepared and strengthened. The government set up a social partner dialogue to examine the longer-term process of rewriting the labour code. Employers' organizations meanwhile renewed their push for numerical flexibility, advocating the concept of 'agile' contracts, as in an open letter to President Hollande 2016 (see Prissette, 2016), because it allowed them to focus on the aspects of labour law they most wanted to reform or eliminate. In particular, they wanted to reduce the number of tribunal cases alleging wrongful individual or collective dismissal, by rewriting labour law to extend the scope of justifiable redundancy.

In line with the Combrexelle report, the government set to work straight away to establish the proposed reordering of legal norms in the areas of working time, working conditions, employment and wages. In February 2016, *Le Parisien* newspaper leaked a draft bill which confirmed the trade unions' fears about the inversion of norms, whereby company agreements could and should take precedence over sectoral agreements and even the law. After a petition against the law, which secured over a million signatures, the unions together with youth associations organized a series of days of mass protest in March, as the government presented a revised version of the text. An early concession was the removal of planned caps on employment tribunal payments (later restored in one of Macron's decrees). The fourth day of protests culminated in the beginning of the *Nuits Debout* movement when young people occupied the *Place de la République* in Paris in an echo of the Spanish *Indignados* or the UK/US Occupy movements (see Béroud, 2018a).

The government met with youth leaders in an attempt to defuse the growing protest movement, and offered new funded measures to support active labour market policies for young people. Faced with a hardening of protest on the streets, the government finally resorted to pushing the bill, known as the El Khomri law after the social affairs minister who presented it, through parliament under the 'guillotine procedure' (Article 49.3). A rebellion by Socialist Party MPs failed to gather enough support. Street protests had by now escalated and been met with sometimes violent opposition by the police, and resistance to the law entered a critical phase in May when petrol supplies were blockaded and an all-out rail strike was declared. The government held firm, helped by the imminent summer holidays, and the law was finally adopted on 9 August 2016.

In its attempts to get the bill through parliament, the government had made some concessions in the final text on the basic principle of inversion of legal norms, emphasizing instead the broadening of the bargaining agenda, but they used working time to establish a precedent, to show how local flexibility could work in practice to adapt higher-level standards. The El Khomri law reiterated the basic legal principle of the 35-hour week, established by the Aubry laws in 1999–2000, and the maximum legal time of 48 hours per week in line with EU law, but it stipulated that scheduling of work in excess of the legal norms could be decided either by a sectoral or by a company-level agreement. The threshold for payment of overtime and the fixing of the overtime wage rate could be set by local-level bargaining, or in the absence of company-level bargaining, by a sectoral agreement. Thus, on the key question of the relationship between 'normal' working hours and the point at which they could be considered and paid at overtime rates, the company level became the reference point (*Journal Officiel*, 2016). The same principle applied to decisions on payment of public holidays and various forms of individual leave. The El Khomri law also included the 'majority' rule which meant that collective agreements at company level need to be signed by organizations representing over 50 per cent of the workforce (previously at least 30 per cent). More controversially, it opened up the possibility that, if the 50 per cent threshold could not be reached, companies could consult employees directly by electronic 'referendum'.

Although the initial impact of the El Khomri law was delayed by legal challenges, meaning that it never effectively came into force, as it was quickly supplanted by President Macron's 2017 decrees, it nevertheless prepared the way for the Macron decrees substantively (by establishing the principle of the new architecture of norms and applying it even in a formally cautious way to working time); epistemically by creating the expert justification for reform; and also institutionally in terms of the precedent set by the political process (the 'guillotine') used by President Hollande's government to get the El Khomri bill through in the face of parliamentary opposition. The Macron reform thus built on the earlier initiative in five complementary decrees, which were presented together on 31 August, signed by the president on 22

September, and finally ratified by parliament on 30 December 2017, to come into force in January 2018.

The Macron decrees covered three main areas. The first concerns collective bargaining. The reform defined the respective competences of sectoral and company-level bargaining and set out the legal requirements for each. Sectoral bargaining is now annually obligatory on minimum wages and pay scales (which should include consideration of gender equality), and basic rules on the use of fixed-term and open-ended contracts, including probationary periods; every three years on gender equality measures, skills, training and workforce planning, and support for disabled workers; and every five years on pay scales (and on working time if a third or more of jobs in the sector are part-time). Company-level agreements cannot be less favourable to employees in these areas; however, the company level prevails in other areas (such as for example bonuses, or working time scheduling). Companies with 50 or more employees must bargain annually on wages; every three years on pay scales, on support for disabled workers, and on gender equality. A penalty of up to 1 per cent of the total wage bill remains applicable for non-compliance with the bargaining requirement on gender equality. Large companies with over 300 employees must also bargain every three years on skills and workforce planning. In all cases, the bargaining timetable must be agreed in advance for a period of four years. Company agreements can be signed by elected workforce representatives in the absence of trade union delegates, and where there are no elected bodies, individual employees can be nominated by trade union federations to bargain on their behalf, in which case any agreement must be approved by a majority of the workforce.

The second area of reform concerns the creation of a new structure for workplace representation, sweeping away the existing complex multi-tier model (works delegates, works committees and health and safety committees) and replacing it with a single body. Previous incremental reforms under governments of right and left had allowed the formation of a single body in medium-sized companies, on a voluntary basis. The new social and economic committee is now obligatory in all companies with 11 or more employees, taking over all the responsibilities of the former bodies. As well as representing the workforce individually and collectively, the committee has a social function and also an economic role, particularly in larger companies where it has legal rights to information. In line with the new rules on collective bargaining outlined above, it can participate in bargaining, rather like the German model where increasingly collective agreements are signed by works councils at company level rather than by sectoral union federations. Its members are elected for a period of four years, and the principle of trade union preference (trade union lists have priority in a two-round process) is retained. The electoral lists must be gender-equal, and seats are attributed on the basis of gender parity.

The third area of innovation relates to laws on employment contracts and redundancy. The new measures on collective bargaining allow for sectoral agreements on the use of short-term contracts, which can be renewed, and 'project' contracts. The definition of collective redundancies for economic reasons is expanded to make it easier for companies which are profitable to justify plant closures or labour shedding at specific sites. The idea is that in larger companies, in line with decrees on collective bargaining, workforce planning should be the subject of negotiation which could allow employers to shift responsibility for decisions on redundancy away from the State and the law to company-level processes. The new social and economic committee is expected to play a bigger role in managing such processes.

Overall, substantial parts of the existing labour code were rewritten in the 2017 Macron decrees so that the shift from law to collective bargaining recommended in the earlier high-level reports and by many other experts has been brought into effect. Moreover, the primacy of local-level bargaining in some areas of pay such as bonuses and profit-sharing, working time (including overtime pay) and conditions was asserted as an integral part of the new employment regulation structure. The sector retains an important role in setting minimum standards, assuming that the local bargaining processes follow the format expected by the decrees. By setting out the legal requirements more clearly, allowing defined areas of local discretion, and making it easier to set up workplace representative structures, the executive argued that its purpose was to establish a 'virtuous' pattern of bargained flexibility and pragmatic dialogue (Pénicaud, 2017).

However, a number of concerns have been expressed about the impact of the changes. A series of opinion polls in autumn 2017 and spring 2018 showed French public opinion divided on the reform, with some suggesting a majority (52 per cent of those surveyed) supported the move but others indicating as many as 58 per cent opposed it. In particular, respondents approved of the new 'project' contract but feared new rules on redundancies. A survey of HR managers conducted by Louis Harris in April 2018 indicated broad support in companies for the reforms, particularly the new representation structure and the simplification of redundancy rules, but only a minority thought it would have a significant impact on their company and fewer than a third anticipated initiatives in the next few months (mainly on negotiating in the absence of union delegates, and setting up a new CSE) (Levy et al., 2018).

A further survey of business professionals, commissioned by the government's advisory group *France Stratégie* which has the task of evaluating the reform, showed a low level of awareness, especially among smaller companies, and indicated that their overriding perception of the reform was that it made it easier to fire employees (CSA, 2018). *France Stratégie*'s evaluation group's preliminary report therefore focused on fears that businesses would not engage in wholesale bargaining but would take advantage of the ability to fire workers more easily (*France Stratégie*, 2018). The ability to decide redundancies through a company agreement seems to have been the main short-term change introduced by the Macron labour law decrees. In this the reform reinforced a process opened up in 2008, by making it harder for individuals to claim unfair dismissal. To date there is little evidence that the reform has strengthened workplace dialogue; however the effects are expected to take some time, as the deadline for the new merged workplace representation structure was the end of 2019.

Social security reform: bringing France into line?

As noted above, labour law reform formed only the first part of a planned overhaul of France's 'social model', also including social security. Social security reform has proved challenging for France's leaders as there is strong public support for social protection, and trade unions have often been able to mount effective resistance to planned changes. France's welfare model is distinctive in its institutional form, its funding and its outcomes. Spending is high, accounting for 46 per cent of public spending in 2016 (Ferras, 2017), and although the tax take is also high, it is insufficient to cover expenditure (OECD, 2018c). At the same time, the welfare state is relatively successful in reducing poverty and inequality (compared for instance with other OECD countries), but it also leaves some important gaps in coverage. Squaring all the different objectives of socio-economic policy, that is, simultaneously reducing expenditure and the tax take without exacerbating inequality, is therefore a difficult balancing act. All three aspects (funding, expenditure and governance) are inter-related.

Under the Fifth French Republic, a distinctive bipartite and tripartite governance structure (managed by employers' organizations and trade unions to different degrees depending on the fund, and steered by the State) was developed to manage a funding model based on payroll contributions for health, pensions and unemployment benefits as well as family benefits and vocational training, which together make up over two-thirds of expenditure on social protection. This welfare model thus rests on a tension between universalism (benefits for all regardless of employment status, funded by direct taxation and administered by the State) and employment-based rights and responsibilities funded by payroll contributions and managed by social partners as well as government (Damon, 2017), which became particularly acute during a time of low economic growth, low wages and persistent unemployment.

From the 1990s, the employers' lobby, notably *Medef* (*Mouvement des Entreprises de France*, the main employers' association, representing larger companies in particular), campaigned for a decrease in payroll contributions, and sought to use their place within the governance structure to achieve it. This objective chimed not just with the centre right's preference for lower taxes and lower State expenditure, but also with a significant body of centre-left thinking which highlighted the disproportionate burden placed on low-to-middle-income salaries (compared with progressive income tax as a means of welfare funding, for example). Meanwhile, parliament has repeatedly sought a bigger role in welfare management in order to curb the growth of expenditure (Ferras, 2017). The thrust of such moves has been to establish the principle of stronger state planning of expenditure, with parliamentary oversight of budget planning since 1995 (Palier, 2005). Consequently, social security deficits have decreased significantly since 2010, and were on course to break even during the Macron presidency, before the pandemic struck. Successive reforms, whilst seeking to curb expenditure (particularly for pensions), have also resulted in a shift away from payroll contributions, which accounted for 77 per cent of funding in 1959 to 61 per cent in 2015, towards general taxation, which gives a greater role to the state in managing the funds (Ferras, 2017, p. 72). Nevertheless, several influential think-tanks as well as high-level parliamentary and government commissions drew attention to the weaknesses of the welfare governance structure in the run-up to the 2017 elections, related to the twin aims of reducing spending overall and moving away from employment-based benefits to universalistic funding and expenditure (see in particular Germain, 2016).

With the change of executive in 2017, reform began on health, pensions and unemployment funds. Reform largely took the form of tightening conditions of eligibility for benefits in order to reduce expenditure, whilst at the same time deploying a discourse of universalism which consisted in practice of removing 'special' benefits for some groups of employees, and opening access to benefits to those previously excluded by conditions attached to payroll contributions (such as the self-employed). In all three cases, unions resisted the reforms but had little success in their attempts until mobilization in December 2019 against planned changes to pensions.

One of the key pledges in Emmanuel Macron's 2017 presidential campaign concerned reform of unemployment benefits to tighten conditions of eligibility, whilst also giving access to benefits for self-employed people, allowing employees to access benefits after resigning from their job in order to stimulate voluntary mobility, and extending eligibility for long-term unemployed. The government invited trade unions and employers' associations to negotiate on these proposals. The resulting agreement of 22 February 2018 on access to benefits after resignation did not meet the government's expectations, as it continued to tie eligibility to payroll contributions. The government published its own proposals for reform in June 2018, which were enacted by decree in July 2019. The two decrees were based on three main changes: first, making it more difficult for those on very short-term contracts to claim unemployment benefit; second, setting a cap of 30 per cent of earnings for those in the top income bracket, after six months of claiming; and third, extending benefits to those who resign (after five years' service, compared with the seven stipulated in the social partner agreement). Trade unions denounced the 'cynical' move to reduce the number of unemployed people by removing their benefits, whilst experts criticized the initiative as 'extraordinarily punitive', a term adopted by a *Le Monde* editorial (*Le Monde*, 2019; see also Méda, 2019).

A second area of social security reform concerned health expenditure. In line with his manifesto pledges, Emmanuel Macron's government switched most of the funding for health spending to the incomes-based *Contribution Sociale Généralisée*, doing away with employee contributions and phasing out employer contributions. As noted above, this change in funding corresponds to EU policy recommendations. It signalled a change of approach which would lead to proposals for systemic change in the mode of delivery. Although his campaign suggested that social partners should themselves come up with reform proposals, in practice he chose a more top-down approach, with the presentation to parliament in early 2019 of proposals to rationalize hospitals by specialization and create local health groupings, in line with recommendations of the high commission (*Haut Conseil pour l'avenir de l'assurance maladie*). More drastic reforms such as those proposed by the centre-right candidate François Fillon in 2017, to ration reimbursement of medical fees, are not (yet) on the table, but may still reappear in the longer term, particularly if funding is linked to local health administration. However, the capacity of health-sector professionals and their unions to resist reform has been increased by the revival of public-sector protest in 2019, as seen in a long-running strike of (relatively weakly unionized) hospital emergency services staff throughout the year, to call attention to staff shortages (see Chabas, 2019).

The opportunity to force a change of policy direction was most clearly seen in the case of pensions reform. In his 2018 speech to parliamentarians at Versailles, President Macron announced a merger of the different occupational pension funds in 2019 (completing Nicolas Sarkozy's unfinished reform), as part of the wider reform promised in early 2018 aimed at establishing a 'universal' system where everyone would be entitled to the same level of pension regardless of the type of contribution scheme, based on a points-based calculation (see COR, 2018). The exact details of the reform were not announced at the outset, as a high-level commission was set up to steer wider social partner negotiations and a public consultation. Although his presidential manifesto pledged to retain the current 'pay-as-you-go' system whereby today's pensions are funded by today's contributions, many commentators predicted that a comprehensive pensions reform would inevitably usher in a bigger space for private pension funds, since the avowed aim is to cut costs to the State whilst also reducing employer contributions (see Harribey and Marty, 2018). On the other hand, some analysts argue that the consultation was left open enough for a consensual outcome (Rain, 2018). However, consensus proved difficult because some public-sector employees with existing occupational funds (entitling them for example to payouts based partly on final salary) were likely to lose out with a shift to universal benefits. As with the health insurance reform, experts began to question the fairness of the planned changes, and even economists close to the president openly criticized the content of the government's proposals (Aghion et al., 2019).

The *gilets jaunes* movement radically changed the social climate in France and enabled unions to reframe and repoliticize pensions reform. Whereas the government had sought to justify reform on grounds of universalism, that is, eliminating more favourable pension schemes for a small number of public-sector workers and aligning their pensions with those of other employees, opposition to the planned changes focused on the need for strong public services and support for public servants, and it mobilized support for the 'pay-as-you-go' system on grounds that it fosters intergenerational solidarity. These themes had resonated strongly in the *gilets jaunes* movement. Moreover, by pitting perceptions of presidential elitism against 'the people', the *gilets jaunes* movement had undermined the government's universalistic discourse (Lespinet-Morel, 2019). As a result, unions were more united against pensions reform than they had been under the Sarkozy presidency, and able to capitalize on strong public support. The days of action in early December 2019 attracted more support across the country than any previous demonstrations since those in the winter of 1995 which toppled the government of Alain Juppé. With more demonstrations and one-day strikes planned, the resignation of the chair of the pensions reform commission Jean-Paul Delevoye on 16 December threw the process into chaos.

In an interview with *Time* magazine in September 2019, President Macron acknowledged the deep resentment caused by his reforms but argued that he had to continue 'to the end of the road' in order to achieve results (Walt, 2019). This meant that he needed to listen to people more and help them to understand the purpose of reform, he said, but he intended to carry on with planned changes, including to pensions. Despite the scale of opposition to pension reform, the president and government chose to continue to try to face down the protests. Even if this strategy pays off, however, the escalation of conflict over pensions suggests that the remainder of the Macron presidency will be clouded by unrest and social division.

Reforming outside the institutions of social dialogue

The unexpected spread and popularity of the *gilets jaunes* movement also highlighted a characteristic of the Macron presidency which constitutes a potential political weakness, namely the preference for determined top-down reform over the institutions and practices of social consensus. The government continued to consult social partners, that is organized business associations and trade unions, but did not hesitate to override their agreed positions, as shown above in the case of social security policy changes. President Macron's impatience with the process of social dialogue echoed that of his predecessors, including François Hollande who in his memoirs spoke of the obstructive tactics of some unions particularly the *Confédération Générale du Travail* (*CGT*) (Hollande, 2019, p. 258).

Early in his presidency, Emmanuel Macron had shown a willingness to confront unions head-on with his reform of the publicly owned rail transport company SNCF, which he had adopted by decree, with a subsequent parliamentary discussion and vote. The decree, he argued, had 'saved the service from certain bankruptcy' through 'an unprecedented reform' (Macron, 2018). The change of status from public establishment to SA (corporation), which leaves it for now in public ownership but limits the extent of debt it can incur, did not result in privatization but opens the way for future such changes, in particular by allowing competition from other providers on regional and national networks from 2019 to 2020. The reform also removed the special status (job security) enjoyed by rail employees, for future recruits. Predictably, this sparked a large-scale strike movement on the railways, starting in March 2018, in the hope of influencing the parliamentary debates. Public opinion, which had previously often supported rail strikes despite the negative impact on travellers and commuters, was more divided this time, and the strikers failed to shift a majority in favour of reform. By April the strikes had abated somewhat, but they resumed in May, to fall back again in June. In pushing the reform through early in his presidency, Emmanuel Macron's government had won a decisive battle in the broader programme of change, successfully reframing the reform project as targeting pragmatic, modernizing goals (Rozès, 2018). It certainly reflected a weakening of French trade unions' capacity to mobilize around a common counter-project (Béroud et al., 2018).

The government's determination to push through reforms even in the face of opposition placed the more radical unions in a difficult position. In this respect the El Khomri law undertaken in the last phase of the Hollande presidency made reform easier for his successor, because the failure of the left opposition weakened the prospects of successful mobilization to the Macron reform of labour law. However, a significant change since 2017 is that the reform programme also left 'reformist' unions, which had previously been courted by governments, with little influence over the pace and content of policy change (Béroud, 2018b). In an era of economic liberalism, trade unions' influence over public policy has become ever more limited (Béroud and Pernot, 2018, pp. 266–7).

By side-lining trade unions and social dialogue processes in this way, the executive has arguably undermined the basis for labour law reform. The overhaul of labour law was justified by the need to move towards a more consensual style of governance, with state regulation replaced by decentralized bargaining. It is unlikely to succeed without supportive actions to shore up the institutions and actors involved. The thrust of reforms to date has been to make it more difficult to strike and to encourage instead collective bargaining, and indeed the 'radical' CGT is now almost as likely to sign workplace agreements as the 'reformist' CFDT (Romans, 2018). Yet significant gaps remain in bargaining coverage and in workplace representation, in all but the largest firms. Thus the political choice to shift from law to bargaining in the context of weak unions, as in France, is likely to lead to further disempowerment of unions as regulatory actors, to increased employer power and to labour market deregulation.

In terms of policy, the erosion of trade unions' capacity to mobilize their 'veto power' to halt or slow reform undoubtedly helped President Macron to speed up his reform agenda. However, it also weakened their 'weather vane' function which signals to policy-makers how far their reforms are socially acceptable to voters (see Milner, 1999). This helps to explain why protest in France has taken on newer, more protean forms of organization and why it took the executive by surprise. Although in many ways the *gilets jaunes* movement indicates the weakness of intermediary bodies such as trade unions, it has also allowed a united trade union front to reposition itself as a vehicle for social justice claims.

Conclusion

This overview, undertaken just over half-way through the Macron presidency, has highlighted the extent of reform and its potential impact, not necessarily on the basis of the size or importance of each initiative taken separately, but considered together as a broader, coherent reform project which also tackles the institutions of governance. Since 2017, reforms have focused on reducing state regulation of employment and giving more flexibility to businesses to regulate labour, and on shifting the management of social security funds from social partners to the State and shifting funding from payroll contributions to general taxation. Over and above the objective of reducing public debt, in line with France's obligations under Eurozone management, the reform programme is driven by a vision of France as a 'competition state' (Cerny, 1997; Genschel and Seelkopf, 2014), with reforms justified by a discourse of globalization, priority given to lowering taxes on business, and state investment channelled into skills, innovation and productivity. In a country where previously reform has been seen as difficult due to the stickiness of institutions and the power resources of veto actors such as trade unions, policy intervention has been led by executive power vested in a charismatic leader able to command an absolute parliamentary majority and determined to side-line trade unions' veto powers. But this did not happen overnight: the ground had been laid by decades of incremental reform and gradual liberalization, and previous initiatives and experiences which have had the effect of weakening effective opposition both in and outside parliament.

The reform project is therefore likely to result in systemic change over the longer period. However, in the short term, path dependency and the existence of political constraints, despite executive power, mean that reforms may be more modest in scope than their executors intended. In the second half of his presidency, Emmanuel Macron and his government have seen their scope for action constrained by growing social unrest and strong criticism from experts and other policy stakeholders, including some who previously supported his programme. Public opinion has grown mistrustful of the presidential style and programme, which are both vulnerable to charges of elitism. Already the executive has shown signs of faltering in some aspects of its reform plans, preferring to postpone promised changes in the face of criticism or perceived lack of support, as the early optimism of the Macron victory has given way to a gloomier public assessment of his programme (see Courtois, 2018). Pension reform could yet force a more radical change of approach. Finally, the reform programme is highly dependent on renewed economic growth, which the Macron presidency initially kickstarted through an appeal to business confidence, building on the tax credits initiative introduced under his predecessor. However, the economic benefits were taking longer to materialize, even before the Covid-19 pandemic struck, and social inequalities continued to rise. The impact of the pandemic will be a sharp rise in unemployment, and long-term damage to the economy, against which the Macron reforms look powerless.

11 THE YELLOW VESTS MOVEMENT: CAUSES, CONSEQUENCES AND SIGNIFICANCE

Emilie Tran

Ignited by rising fuel prices and high costs of living, the Yellow Vests (*Gilets jaunes*) movement (YVM) is a grassroots protest that started online in France in May 2018, and transformed into nation-wide mass demonstrations in November 2018, with striking scenes of violence that made the news headlines worldwide. A year later, the mobilization had lost momentum and yet still endured. This chapter reviews the causes, consequences and significance of the movement that shook the Macron administration, and led the president to change his stance and tune, ushering in an unprecedented consultation exercise with the population at large, the Great National Debate (*Le Grand débat national*). Having portrayed himself as the 'master of the clocks' who sets his own schedule, Emmanuel Macron had to admit to the necessity of changing, at least his method of government, if not the overall direction of his politics. The shift constituted the start of the 'second act' of his five-year term.

In what follows, the first section reviews the causes of the movement. Behind the immediate triggering factors lie several underlying, systemic motives: first, 50 years of urban development policies which have ultimately resulted in a territorial divide; second, a widening wealth gap which aggravates the territorial divide; third, diverging values depending on socio-economic status and across territories; and fourth, political defiance towards the elite, if not distrust of the whole political system. The second section reviews the costs in terms of economic impact and human casualties. The third section discusses the political outcome of the Yellow Vests movement, from the Great National Debate (GND) to the incapacity of the Yellow Vests to translate itself into an institutionalized political force. Finally, we will conclude on the significance of the Yellow Vests movement by comparing it with other grassroots movements in France's history, and other seemingly leaderless horizontally organized movements of the twenty-first century elsewhere in the world.

The causes

Triggering factors: rising fuel prices and an ecotax

Ever since the first oil crisis in 1973, fuel prices have been on the rise globally, which is translated into the price paid by motorists at the pumps. In France, government policies, irrespective of party affiliation, have made oil one of the most heavily taxed goods, but since 2016, successive French governments undertook to remove the advantage it had been giving to diesel over gasoline for years. While diesel accounted for less than 5 per cent of the car fleet in France in 1980, this rose to 30 per cent a decade later, and to 70 per cent by the early 2010s (*Comité des Constructeurs Français d'Automobiles*, 2012, 2019), due to a succession of factors. The oil shocks of 1970 made access to fuels more uncertain, so it was necessary to optimize consumption, which was possible with diesel engines. Furthermore, as climate change has become an international issue, France sought to neutralize greenhouse gases, considered to be the cause of global warming, and therefore encouraged diesel engines that emit less carbon dioxide than gasoline vehicles, by deciding to tax diesel less. As the wind turned in favour of diesel, French automobile manufacturers also focused their research on improving diesel vehicles (Raymond, 2013). The French were increasingly seduced by diesel cars that are more expensive to buy, but less expensive to run thanks to the more favourable tax policy on diesel. With 21 million diesel vehicles representing 68 per cent of its fleet of passenger cars in 2019, France is the country with by far the most diesel vehicles in Europe. The rate of ownership of diesel vehicles is much higher in rural and peri-urban areas than elsewhere. Half of the households living less than 10 kilometres from the closest city centre in France own a diesel vehicle, but the ratio climbs by almost 20 points as soon as one lives at 10 kilometres or further from the city centre (68 per cent), to reach up to 77 per cent among people living more than 60 kilometres from a large metropolis (Ifop and Fondation Jean Jaurès, 2017).

However, the balance of scientific evidence has pointed out the harmful impact of fine-particle pollution on health and environment, and various studies agreed that diesel engines pollute more than gasoline-powered vehicles. As a result, a number of French cities have pledged to ban diesel cars: by 2024 for Paris, 2025 for Strasbourg and 2030 for Grenoble. Another incentive to phase out diesel vehicles consists of decreasing the price gap per litre between diesel and gasoline by taxing diesel more, a policy that was brutally accentuated in 2018, in order to bring gasoline and diesel to the same price by 2021. In October 2018, the price of diesel was actually higher than that of gasoline at one fifth of France's gas stations. Indeed, from 2010 to 2018 the price of unleaded petrol 95 increased by 20.9 per cent, but diesel by 42 per cent. By comparison, over that same 8-year span, the minimum wage increased by only 10.8 per cent. This price adjustment represented a major drawback for motorists who would join the Yellow Vests movement: having

Table 11.1 Climate–energy contribution as tabled in the Finance Laws

2014 Finance Law		2018 Finance Law	
2015	€14.5/t CO_2	2019	€55/t CO_2
2016	€22/t CO_2	2020	€65.4/t CO_2
2017	€30.5/t CO_2	2021	€75.8/t CO_2
2018	€44.6/t CO_2	2022	€86.2/t CO_2

Source: Ministère de la Transition écologique et solidaire, 2017 and 2019.

been given incentives by government policy and car makers to prefer diesel vehicles over the years, they now found themselves on the wrong side of history, being blamed for polluting the environment and made to pay the price for it. However, this tax increase – the ecological or carbon tax – impacts all motorists, not only owners of diesel engines. Ever since the French parliament adopted the climate–energy contribution in the 2014 Finance Law, and the 2015 Law on Energy Transition and Green Growth, the price for one tonne of carbon dioxide (t CO_2) emitted has been increasing abruptly (Table 11.1).

Given the drop in oil prices – a 72.5 per cent drop in the average price per barrel between July 2014 and January 2016 – the increase in the carbon tax had been, until the end of 2017, relatively painless for the majority of motorists. In 2018, the carbon tax generated annual revenues approaching €10 billion, and the 2018 Finance Law – Emmanuel Macron's first five-year finance bill – programmed further rises of the carbon tax, to €55/t CO_2 in 2019, and this hike constituted the spark that became the Yellow Vests movement.

In spring 2018, when a full fuel tank cost suburban resident, Priscilia Ludosky, 70 euros instead of the 45 euros she had used to pay not so long ago at the same gas stations, the 30-year-old woman launched on 29 May 2018 a detailed fuel-price petition on Change.org (Change.org, 2018), asking the authorities to lower taxes on fuel. Without knowing it Ludosky, who was a motorist commuter like any other, laid the foundation of what would become the Yellow Vests movement. In October of the same year, another woman, 50-year-old Jacline Mouraud, posted a soon-to-be viral Facebook video (at www.youtube.com/watch?v=06pOTxTvnBU) to protest against the rise of the carbon tax to €55/t CO_2 in January 2019, as the Macron administration had planned to finance climate protection (see Table 11.1 above). A 30-year-old truck driver, Eric Drouet, for his part, created a Facebook page entitled '*blocage national contre la hausse du carburant*' (national blockade against the increase of fuel price), calling for a national blockade to be held on November 17. Ghislain Coutard, a mechanic in his mid-30s from the south of France, also posted a video on Facebook asking people who opposed the tax increase on fuel to display ostentatiously inside their car their high-visibility vest that since 2008, all motorists are required to carry by law. Intelligence services identified eight people in total, five men and three women, aged between 27 and 35 years old, all from the Île-de-France region, and without any militant past, who relayed similar calls on Facebook, garnering 43,000 pledges of participation, and accounting for 1,500 actions across metropolitan France. By mid-November 2018, when mass demonstrations began, Ludosky's petition had itself gathered 845,000 signatures. According to the Ministry of the Interior, on 17 November, the first Saturday – subsequently referred to as Act I of the Yellow Vests mobilization – accounted for 287,710 participants in 2,034 locations (Audureau, 2019). Every Saturday thereafter, calls to gather in the big French cities were followed by 300,000 people on average in November 2018, and 100,000 on average in December 2018. The movement mobilized around roundabouts, symbols of automobile mobility and the post-war transformation of road infrastructures. Indeed, France counts almost 65,000 roundabouts, twice as many as the number of its *communes*.

The hundreds of thousands of people who took part in the Saturday mobilizations indicate that the Yellow Vests was and still is a leaderless, horizontal social movement for economic justice, stemming from the middle and working classes living in rural and peri-urban areas, who rely on their passenger cars to commute, and who felt that they were the ones shouldering a disproportionate burden for the cost of ecological transition.

Systemic causes

Opinion polls (Institut Montaigne and Elabe, 2019) and research (Fourquet and Manternach, 2018; Algan et al., 2019) have revealed that the Yellow Vests movement brings together diverse profiles, French people of all political stripes and all ages, throughout France. They mainly live in small towns, suburban (*périphéries*) or rural areas. Either they work but their income is low or volatile (self-employed, farmers), or they are retirees with modest incomes. Women are well represented: single mothers, part-time workers and recipients of small pensions. Initially launched to protest against the rise in fuel prices, as discussed above, the movement had by the end of November 2018 aggregated no fewer than 42 demands that the Yellow Vests' spokespersons sent, in late November and early December, to media outlets and legislators, asking the latter to translate their various demands into pieces of legislation. Their requests for reforms now extended to include housing, the tax system and public finances, employment, wages and pensions, immigration, healthcare, transportation and education: ultimately, public policy governance overall. The diversity of the movement's proposals indeed shows that the Yellow Vests perceived themselves to be the losers of changes leading to social downward mobility.

The first such transformation is economic liberalization and technological developments that have been detrimental to low or unqualified socio-professional categories in developed countries, including France. Workers and employees have generally suffered from globalization: deindustrialization makes them compete with low-cost labour from all over the world, which has served to increase their economic and social insecurity. French farmers also face fierce competition in the global market. Globalization, tertiarization and the digitization of the economy have contributed to outclass these categories. The precariousness of the working classes extends to the intermediate strata of the society, as evidenced by the deterioration of living conditions in the suburban residential areas designed in the 1960s for the middle classes, which relates to the second systemic factor, that is, territorial transformation.

For decades, urban planning policy has depopulated French villages as well as small and mid-sized towns to create American-style suburban neighbourhoods of single-family detached homes, along with large retail areas for shopping, and where the car is the ultimate means of transportation. The social categories embodied by the Yellow Vests can no longer afford housing in larger cities, nor do they have access, as a consequence, to the public services concentrated there. Adding to such social disintegration, they are shunned for living in what is referred to as the 'ugly France' (*la France moche*), ever since *Telerama* magazine coined that now-iconic expression (de Jarcy and Remy, 2010). As shown by demographer Hervé le Bras's map of the Yellow Vests, the November 17 mobilization was particularly strong in the most rural departments (*départements*) comprising a 'diagonal line of emptiness' (*le diagonale du vide*) that runs from the French Ardennes in the northeast to the Pyrenees in the south-west (Riché, 2018). Whereas the middle class has grown insecure (Guilly and Noyers, 2004), the upper layers of society are overrepresented in the main metropolises (Le Bras, 2014) that concentrate growth and wealth. In these economic powerhouses, everything is designed according to the needs of this affluent population. Indeed, it is argued that the French social divide (*fractures françaises*) (Guilly, 2010) is now polarized between, on the one hand, the 'ghettoization from above'; and on the other, the 'France from below' (*la France d'en bas*), or 'peripheral France' (*la France périphérique*) (Guilly, 2014), which is ignored by the political and cultural sphere.

The third transformation behind the Yellow Vests movement is of a cultural nature. The Yellow Vests lack the postgraduate degrees and the global outlook that would give them access to stable well-paid jobs in the vibrant environment of the big cities. They are at odds with the dominant values of cultural liberalism conveyed by the urban elites, who look down upon anyone considered to be misogynist, xenophobic, closed-minded, protectionist, nationalist, or as Benjamin Griveaux, the then spokesman of Édouard Philippe's government (2017–19) summed it up: 'the guys who smoke fags and who ride diesel cars. That's not the twenty-first century France we want'. The Yellow Vests revealed another divide in the French society, between those who want to move away from fossil-fuelled cars and favour everything organic in their lives, and those who fail to make ends meet at the end of the month. In January 2018, as soon as the government announced the plan to reduce the maximum speed on secondary roads from 90 km/h to 80 km/h (*Securité routière*, 2018), this measure provoked a strong rejection from motorists who felt it infantilized them (Hamelin, 2018), and it rapidly became one of the topics that was most talked about (AutoPlus, 2018). Various groups and associations such as 40 Million Motorists and the French Federation of Angry Bikers initiated mobilizations that led to more than 250 actions across metropolitan France during the months preceding the entry into force of this measure on 1 July 2018. This mobilization against the 80 km/h limit was a forerunner of the exasperation of drivers who would speak more assertively a few months later in the Yellow Vests movement. When it comes to grocery shopping, individuals with only primary and secondary school education are price conscious and favour promotional offers, whereas graduates and postgraduates give greater importance to the mode of production and quality products (Anses, 2017). Since not all the French can afford to switch to electric modes of mobility and organic food, the defence of ecology and food consumption patterns have become a new tool of social distinction.

For the Yellow Vests, the above evolutions and shifting values have marginalized them socio-economically, geographically and culturally, making them the 'fluorescent markers' of the French profound social divide (Fourquet and Manternach, 2018). The deep and lasting sense of malaise and dissatisfaction with their lives and future prospects affect their well-being, it is argued (Perona, 2018), and they are said to form the 'unhappy France' (*la France malheureuse*) (Perona, 2019). As a consequence, the Yellow Vests feel they are no longer represented by any political party, and that their preferences do not influence policy-making, and all the more so after Terra Nova (2011), a think tank that used to be close to the Socialist Party and now close to President Macron, issued a report recommending the left-wing party to forego the working class in order to appeal to the 'France of tomorrow' (*la France de demain*): a new left-wing electorate comprising graduates, the youth, minorities and women, and the poor neighbourhoods who share a progressive outlook. Abandoned thus by the traditional left, the 'unhappy' and 'peripheral' France from 'below' has taken refuge either in abstention or in protest votes for Marine Le Pen's National Rally.

The costs

Economic impact

In July 2019 in the National Assembly, a group of deputies from the presidential party LREM, issued a report on the economic, social and budgetary costs of the blockades, violence and damage arising from the Yellow Vests movement. The report argued that the YVM had had a negative macroeconomic impact in the fourth quarter of 2018, and that the microeconomic impact would be felt beyond 2019, although it would be difficult to measure accurately (*Assemblée nationale*, 2019). As early as 10 December 2018, after four consecutive Saturdays of demonstrations, Bruno Le Maire, the Minister of the Economy and Finance, said on the radio (RTL, 2018) that the Yellow Vests rallies and ensuing closed shops, burned cars, damaged street furniture, looting and blockages, would cost 0.1 per cent of GDP growth in the last quarter of 2018, a figure later increased to 0.2 per cent by the French National Institute for Statistics and Economic Research (Insee, 2018, p. 48). Le Maire had deplored the fact that the blockages had had a 'severe impact' on sales: many shops were looted, notably in Bordeaux and Paris, leading some big-name stores in shopping districts such as the Champs-Elysées and the Grands Boulevards in Paris to close, amidst fears of acts of vandalism and significant decreases in customers' attendance on the weekends of major rallies. Retailers estimated their loss in revenue at 460 million euros within the first three weeks of the movement (Garnier, 2018). In a hearing conducted by the Senate at the end of March 2019, Le Maire estimated that the economic cost, as Yellow Vests rallies continued, would total 4.5 billion euros, spread over 2018 and 2019, an impact that he considered 'severe' (Renaud-Garabedian, 2019, p. 18). The Senate report published in mid-July (Renaud-Garabedian, 2019) argued that, although 0.1 per cent of growth to the French economy in the last quarter of 2018 was a relatively low figure compared with overall national wealth, the impact of the violence perpetrated on the sidelines of the Yellow Vests demonstrations since 17 November 2018 was nevertheless underestimated, and would continue to be felt in the second half of 2019, despite the slowdown of the Yellow Vests rallies. For the period from 17 November 2018 to 31 May 2019, insurance companies paid out 217 million euros to victims of acts of vandalism across France (Renaud-Garabedian, 2019), of which 90 million euros to Parisians (Jérôme et al., 2019). More than half of those receiving insurance compensations were merchants, artisans and service providers who were the most affected by the Saturday rallies. Shopkeepers and artisans in city centres reported an average loss of 30 per cent of their turnover. Shopping malls reported around 2 billion-euro losses, and the hotel industry 850 million. However, the parliamentary report warned that there would be a number of indirect outcomes such as the drying up of cash reserves of companies that would result in difficulties in paying social contributions and taxes, as well as delays or defaults of payment to suppliers. The consequence would be an increased risk of insolvencies and job losses. Employment contract terminations and bankruptcies were expected to appear in the second half of 2019, along with an increased number of ensuing legal proceedings, including liquidations.

Besides insurance companies, the State itself was also paying a high price. Local authorities paid out 30 million euros in total, including 7.6 million for Toulouse and 12.6 million for Paris, for the repair or replacement of street furniture on 24 November and 1 December. In addition, the extra mobilization of law enforcement forces cost 46 million euros – 30 million for the police and 16 million for the *gendarmerie* – in addition to the 500 million euros for the repair or replacement of the 3,200 speed radars damaged or destroyed since the beginning of the Yellow Vest movement, according to the Minister of Interior Christophe Castaner in August 2019 (*Vie Publique*, 2019; *Ouest France*, 2019). The repairs after the damage to the Arc de Triomphe alone cost 1.2 million euros (Le Monde and AFP, 2019).

The striking scenes of violence that made the news headlines worldwide also weighed on the tourism sector in December 2018 and throughout the first quarter of 2019, with a drop of 4.8 per cent in hotel attendance by foreign visitors. At the time of writing (in December 2019), it remains to be seen whether the difficult social climate of the Yellow Vests movement, coupled with the protests and strikes in response to the proposed reform of France's pension system in late 2019, may also have an impact on the decisions of foreign investors and France's economic attractiveness, which will be measured more concretely by 2020 and 2021.

Under the pressure of the Yellow Vests movement, the Macron administration enacted a set of emergency economic and social measures in December 2018 and April 2019. These consisted of the cancellation or deferral of certain taxes and social contributions, a gesture which amounted to 17 billion euros of tax giveaway to households most in need, of which 10 billion had been announced in December 2018, while the rest unfolded throughout 2019 and 2020 (Alemagna, 2019). In order to remedy the decay and, in some cases, complete shutdown of public services, which the Yellow Vests had been denouncing, Emmanuel Macron revealed the creation of *Maisons France Services*, a one-stop administrative service in the areas that lack them most: 300 were to open in January 2020, and 2,000 by 2022 (Gouvernement. fr, 2019). However, according to a group of right-wing and centre-right senators who contributed to the above-mentioned parliamentary report, these measures were either devices that already existed, or unsuited to the economic reality of the business sector; they complained that these measures looked like 'bandages on a wooden leg' (Renaud-Garabedian, 2019, p.10). However, according to Éric Heyer and Xavier Timbeau, respectively from Sciences Po and the French Observatory of Economic Conditions, these emergency measures, and especially the 10 billion euros offered by the government in December 2018 to respond to the crisis, not only helped support the French people's purchasing power, but also funded economic growth. In fact, France, which had been predicted to fare better than any other country of the Eurozone in 2019 (OFCE, 2019, p. 13), did actually fulfil the previsions (Insee, 2020; *Ministère de l'Économie et des Finances*, 2019).

Human casualties

As the Yellow Vests protests moved into metropolitan areas, clashes between the police and demonstrators became more violent. Radical and violence-prone Yellow Vests, as well as Black Blocs, at times overwhelmed and high-jacked rallies in acts of looting and destruction, notably in Bordeaux, Toulouse and Paris. In the capital, the sacking of the Arc de Triomphe on 1 December 2018, the burning of the legendary high-end brasserie le Fouquet's and the ransacking of other shops along the Champs-Elysées Avenue on 16 March 2019 made news headlines worldwide. The 'Black Bloc' movement designates an insurrectional demonstration tactic used by late twentieth and twenty-first century revolutionary left-wing militants and anarchists, who conceal their faces and dress in black, thus forming an ephemeral procession before confronting the police force (Dupuis-Déri, 2013; Carley, 2019). While some *gilets jaunes* welcome the convergence of their respective struggles (*convergence des luttes*), others distanced themselves from the violent actions of the Black Blocs.

The extent of human casualties is unprecedented in contemporary French social movements. Eleven people lost their lives during the demonstrations, including an elderly woman hit by a tear gas canister in her apartment. The Ministry of the Interior reported 2,500 wounded among the law enforcement forces and firefighters and 1,800 among demonstrators. While the media kept record of the protesters' casualties (Dufresne, 2019), comprising hand mutilations and several hundred head and eye injuries, a survey published in *The Lancet* showed the correlation in France between the usage of intermediate force, or so-called less-lethal weapons, and the increase of severe and blinding eye traumas (Chauvin et al., 2019). For healthcare professionals involved, the extent of the physical injuries observed during the demonstrations of the Yellow Vests is unique.

In its 2018 Annual Activity Report, the General Inspectorate of the National Police (IGPN, 2019) reported 'an unprecedented and significant rise' in the use of flash ball launchers (19,071 munitions drawn) and of sting-ball grenades (5,420 grenades drawn): a 61 per cent and 296 per cent increase respectively compared with 2017 (ibid., p. 29). The IGPN report explains this stark increase by the 'operations of law and order maintenance' carried out in the context of demonstrations or urban violence linked to the movement of 'Yellow Vests' and 'high school students', during the period from 17 November to 31 December 2018 (ibid.).

The methods of the law enforcement forces during the Yellow Vests protests were subject to an outcry in France and worldwide. A month after Act

I of the YVM, Amnesty International (2018) warned against the excessive use of force. Petitions circulated online. Journalists having felt particularly targeted, lodged a group complaint, and 450 academics collectively declared themselves 'accomplices of the Yellow Vests' against 'the State's authoritarian inclinations' in an open letter published in March 2019 (*Collectif des universitaires contre les repressions policières*, 2019), and which had gathered close to 2,000 signatures by January 2020. The then French Defender of Rights, Jacques Toubon, asked the executive power to ban the usage of flash balls (*Défenseur des droits*, 2019). This request was echoed by United Nations experts as well as members of the Parliament of the European Union and the Council of Europe (2019); Michelle Bachelet, the UN High Commissioner for Human Rights, also called for a 'full investigation of all reported cases of excessive use of force' during the Yellow Vests demonstrations (Bachelet, 2019). Faced with these developments, Emmanuel Macron declared that one 'could not speak of "repression" or "police violence"', adding: 'These words are unacceptable in (the context of France's) rule of law' (Macron, 2019a). In its 2018 report, the IGPN reported that, out of the 957 complaints against police violence brought to its attention, 90.5 per cent failed to demonstrate any police misconduct, despite allegations that the police had used force illegitimately or unnecessarily brutally (IGPN, 2018, p. 16). However, smartphones and social media allowed protesters, journalists and witnesses to instantly capture the forceful interventions, and thus openly challenge the official versions of the law enforcement forces. In late March 2019, Nicole Belloubet, the Minister of Justice, said in a televised interview that since Act I on 17 November, there had been 12,000 arrests, amongst which 11,000 people had been held in police custody, leading to over 2,000 convictions: 40 per cent were given jail sentences and the rest were convicted to community work or conditional sentences.

Police violence has increasingly become a subject of concern since the late twentieth century; it has supposedly caused 676 deaths between January 1977 and December 2019 (Dufresne, 2007; *Basta!*, 2019). Because these fatalities are largely limited to the suburban areas and their marginalized population, and usually imply young male residents from an immigrant background, suspected of troublemaking and delinquency (Pregnolato, 2019), the media and the public view them rather as isolated unfortunate incidents. However, the scale of the Yellow Vest protests and the widespread circulation on social media of robust and allegedly abusive policing cases led to wide public uproar and rekindled controversy over the French doctrine of policing. Elaborated in the aftermath of the 1871 Paris Commune, the French policing method (Bruneteau, 1996) was subject to the scrutiny of an inquiry committee of the National Assembly in spring 2015, following the death of environmental activist Rémi Fraisse in October 2014. Fraisse had been killed by the explosion of a stun grenade, fired by a military police officer (*gendarme*) in a skirmish during the protest against the construction of the Sivens Dam, near Toulouse in Southern France. Legislators Mamère and Popelin (2015), respectively chair and rapporteur of the inquiry committee, pointed out the difficulties encountered by the authorities in identifying and maintaining a dialogue with the organizers of demonstrations. The report also blamed the lack of personnel reserves among the specialized units for maintaining order (i.e. the CRS and mobile military police), which had forced the authorities to call on non-specialized units who lack adequate training. Another aggravating factor is the role of graphic images taken by journalists that had fuelled criticisms against the police. Last but not least, the above-mentioned investigation led by the National Assembly cautioned against the higher risks of injuries linked to the use of flash balls and grenades. Having been temporarily forbidden after Fraisse's death, stun grenades were definitively abandoned in 2017. In 2018–19, the Yellow Vests movement served, thus, to illustrate and amplify pre-existing issues (Restelli, 2019).

The fragmentation of the law enforcement forces has, moreover, led to a greater diversity of units that intervene during demonstrations. It is no longer just the security (*CRS*) and military police (*les gendarmes*), but also other mobile units, such as the anti-crime brigade (*la Brigade anti-criminalité, BAC*). Unlike the CRS who are defensive units favouring static positions aimed at exhausting protesters, the BAC is an offensive corps, which policed during the 2005 and 2007 suburban riots (*émeutes*) (Cicchelli et al., 2007). Their task is to identify troublemakers and delinquents and to actively engage them. At the beginning of the YVM, police violence was not an issue, but in the weeks before Christmas 2018, posters and signs denouncing abusive police repression appeared. Whereas the equipment used by the protesters against the police had not changed for decades – mainly street furniture, steel balls, sticks and Molotov cocktails – the equipment of the police had significantly evolved. Their weaponry is also more diversified, as evidenced by the defence ball launchers, and sting-ball grenades, along with a massive usage of tear gas canisters. The way the Yellow Vests have been using the streets is atypical. Precisely because the movement is leaderless and horizontal, there was no top-down supervision of the demonstrations or any form of the self-policing that traditional unions do when they stage protests. Besides, the Yellow Vest demonstrations were not necessarily registered beforehand with the authorities, as rallies were collectively decided through calls on social media. Therefore, the law enforcement forces did not know whom to address before and during demonstrations to de-escalate violence or redirect the flow of people, which makes law and order all the more challenging to restore.

Political outcome and significance

The Great National Debate

As early as 27 November 2018, President Macron decided to hold a three-month-long major field consultation to listen to the demands and expectations of the French people. Macron's proposal came before the government's decision to abandon the 2019 planned carbon tax increase that had sparked the Yellow Vests movement. That move to drop the contentious tax was made on 5 December 2018, after the third consecutive Saturday rally and while calls for an Act IV were still gathering momentum. Although back in 2009, there had been such a territory-wide debate, initiated by Nicolas Sarkozy on the matter of national identity (Martigny, 2009), Macron's Great National Debate (GND) was unprecedented in its scale and the personal involvement of the president.

On December 14, the government asked the National Commission for Public Debate (*la Commission nationale du débat public, CNDP*) in the person of its president, Chantal Jouanno, to carry out the organization of that unprecedented consultation exercise. In agreeing to it, Jouanno nonetheless made it clear, in a letter published in the *Official Journal*, that her acceptance 'presupposes a commitment by the government to respect the fundamental principles of the National Commission for Public Debate' (JORF, 2018), a precautionary warning that reflected a growing divergence between the government and the president of the CNDP over guarantees of independence, neutrality and impartiality in the holding of the debate. In parallel, a controversy broke out over Chantal Jouanno's salary, which ultimately led her to withdraw from the Great National Debate. Indeed, it was revealed that her gross monthly income of 14,700 euros was close to that of the President of the Republic, and substantially more than the Defender of Rights, or the president of the national data protection authority. Subsequently, two then recently appointed members of Édouard Philippe's second cabinet, whose portfolio reflected the issues at the heart of the Yellow Vests movement, were put in charge of the GND: Emmanuelle Wargon, Secretary of State to the Minister for the Ecological and Inclusive Transition, and Sébastien Lecornu, Minister for Local Authorities, attached to the Minister for Territorial Cohesion and Relations with Local Authorities.

The field consultation unfolded in two stages. From mid-December 2018 to mid-January 2019, citizens communicated their concerns and grievances to their respective mayors, who compiled 'complaint books' (*cahiers de doléances*). On 13 January 2019, Emmanuel Macron then published a *Letter to the French* (Macron, 2019b), a five-page text in which he presented his own understanding of the context, and laid out his four proposed topics for debate: ecological transition; the tax system; democracy and citizenship; and organization of the state and public services. Two days later, on 15 January, the president launched the GND itself in Grand Bourgtheroulde in Normandy, a small-size city of 3,500 inhabitants, located 30 kilometres from

Rouen, that had seen clashes between Yellow Vests protesters and the police, hence being emblematic of the movement's struggle. The Great Debate website (granddebat.fr) shows that more than 10,000 meetings were organized locally, and each brought together an average of 45 participants. The total number of participants was estimated at 500,000; 50 per cent of the meetings were organized by elected officials, 30 per cent by citizens, and 20 per cent by associations and NGOs, while 282 meetings took place outside of France, in 82 countries where the overseas French reside. There were 21 citizens' conferences, seven of which were also held overseas. The GND website also recorded more than one million online contributions. Indeed, there had not been such a nation-wide massive consultation ever since the 1788 General Estates' registers of grievances (*cahiers de doléances des Etats généraux*). All these discussions produced more than 629,000 pages. Unsurprisingly, complaints about excessive taxes topped the list of claims: 28 per cent of participants wanted a VAT decrease, and 19 per cent an income tax decrease. The contributions on sustainable development shared a sense of urgency. On governance, participants expressed their deep distrust towards elected officials and favoured a reduced number of legislators, as well as proportional voting. The GND cost 12 million euros in total. Although the exercise officially ended on 15 March 2019, online participation remained possible until 18 March and Emmanuel Macron also continued to meet mayors beyond this date. On 25 April 2019, the President concluded the national consultation with a press conference at the Élysée Palace, during which he announced a series of socio-economic measures, amongst which the reduction of income tax, and the re-indexing of modest pensions to inflation.

Pressured by a movement he had failed to foresee, Emmanuel Macron had thus swiftly responded, by initiating a nation-wide participative exercise aimed at bolstering a lively democracy, allowing virtually everyone to chip in with his or her own take on critical issues to the French people. But in so doing, the President also tried to gain the upper hand: not only did he set the debate topics, but also his own timeline by opening and closing himself the Great Debate. In doing so, Macron re-asserted that he wanted to remain 'the master of time' (Cole, 2019, pp. 81–3). In order to ensure the fairness of the consultation, a college of guarantors and observers had been constituted, composed of five members: two appointed by the government; one by the President of the National Assembly; one by the President of the Senate; and one by the President of the Economic, Social and Environmental Council, a constitutional consultative assembly comprising 233 members from various sectors of the civil society. Although the college made an overall positive assessment, both their report (Bailly et al., 2019), as well as in press conferences and media interviews, pointed to several limits of the consultation process that had concerned them: a tight schedule and extremely constrained organization; complicated questions, at times ambiguous and oriented; a maze-like website that failed to evolve despite the college's early recommendations, thus generating a great deal of frustration from the participants.

There were also issues with representativeness since it proved difficult to recruit citizens drawn by lot, so most of those who participated in the Great Debate did so on a voluntary basis, but they might not have been a representative reflection of the French society. The guarantors insisted on the precautions to be taken when interpreting the results of this consultation, as the synthetic renditions of the debates by definition were likely to leave out a number of ideas and words and to overlook nuances.

But the college's harshest criticisms were directed against the government and the President of the Republic himself. Despite repeated warnings from the college to step back from the Great Debate, communications and media interventions from members of the government, as well as the widely publicized Macron meeting tours, created repeated interference throughout the three-month consultation, thus attempting to frame and influence the debates. According to Loïc Blondiaux (*Le Monde*, 2019), such tactics fuelled the people's mistrust, ultimately transforming this never seen before participative exercise into a communication campaign. Some went further and referred to the GND as a democratic sham (Le1Hebdo, 2019). Indeed, the barometer of political trust released in January 2019 revealed a record level of distrust from the French *vis-à-vis* political actors, political institutions, trade unions and the media (CEVIPOF and OpinionWay, 2019). An opinion poll conducted at the closing of the Great Debate (Elabe and BFMTV, 2019a) showed that two-thirds of the French population believed that the consultation would not solve the political crisis: 55 per cent thought the consultation would not improve citizens' participation in public policy decision-making, against 45 per cent in agreement with this statement, while 63 per cent believed that Emmanuel Macron and his administration would not take into account the views expressed, and 37 per cent only thought otherwise. Almost four months after the start of the Yellow Vests movement, 61 per cent of the respondents continued to express their sympathy and support for the protesters and their demands, while only 28 per cent said they were hostile, and 11 per cent were indifferent to it. If there was genuine sympathy, only 10 per cent actually identified themselves as Yellow Vests, against 49 per cent who did not call themselves Yellow Vests, but still supported their actions and their claims. In November 2019, a year after the first rally, 55 per cent of the French people continued to have a positive outlook towards the Yellow Vests movement with 22 per cent supporting it and 33 per cent expressing their sympathy; 16 per cent opposed it and 13 per cent said they were against it. Fifteen per cent were indifferent to the movement. Compared with the first weeks of mobilization, when the level of support had fluctuated between 40 per cent and 50 per cent and that of sympathy between 25 and 30 per cent, the positive reception gradually declined from the end of December, to stabilize at around 20 per cent of support and 30 per cent of sympathy around March–April 2019, and has remained relatively stable since then (Elabe and BFMTV, 2019b).

The Yellow Vests and other social movements

For six months, the Yellow Vests enjoyed lasting public support and dominated the political agenda and media landscape, shaking the powers that be; in these respects, the movement was compared to May 68. As Pigenet and Tartakowsky (2012) showed in their monumental French history of social movements from 1814 to the present day, France is certainly no stranger to disruptive mass protests, and the Yellow Vests stepped into a series of historical grassroots uprisings against tax injustice: the 1358 peasants' revolt (*la jacquerie*) (Gauvard, de Libera and Zink, 2006); the 1841 Red Summer (*Été rouge*) (Caron, 2002); the late eighteenth century *sans-culottes* (Soboul, 1968); and the 1950–60s Poujadists (Souillac, 2007). However, as historian Gérard Noiriel (2018) argued in his popular history of France from the Hundred Years' War to the present day, grassroots movements cannot be comprehended by solely looking at the frontline protesters, because any social movement always involves a large number of actors interconnected in a network of roles and social relations: there are those who initiate the movement, those who coordinate the actions, those who emerge as spokespersons for their comrades, as well as the observers and commentators who learn from the movement. In his interview with *Le Monde* journalist Nicolas Truong, Noiriel (2019) cautioned that it requires an understanding of all ends of the chain to genuinely understand the Yellow Vests movement.

Admittedly, the non-hierarchical feature of the Yellow Vests movement prevented it from morphing into an organization with the usual forms of representation. Yet, the Yellow Vests managed to structure their action, coherently articulating multi-centred roundabout rallies, both physically throughout metropolitan France and also virtually in the digital age. In line with the 2010s' social movements, from the Jasmine revolution in Tunisia, also referred to as the 'Facebook Revolution', down to the 2019 Hong Kong's Be Water movement, the Yellow Vests demonstrated once again the mobilization potential of the Internet and social media (Bennett and Segerberg, 2013). These are powerful incubators and accelerators of protests, instantaneously connecting strangers, thus creating sociability, solidarity and socialization, while aggregating slogans and support. In no time at all, social media, be it Facebook for Tunisia and France or Telegram for Hong Kong, turn these movements into lively permanent general assemblies, carrying their own communication outside of traditional media channels, and gradually imposing their demands on the elites and traditional organizations who had controlled the agenda before. While the horizontality of the Yellow Vests movement encouraged citizens to come out, express, share and make public their personal socio-economic hardships, the intermediation of social media allowed them to translate their sense of their own households' deprivation into a collective coherent cause, embedded in principles of social justice, dignity and participatory democracy, despite temptations to slide towards xenophobic themes. These intense communications, be it online or actual at roundabout rallies, nurtured new social relationships that constituted the learning process of politicization for hundreds of thousands of women and men who typically shunned public speaking and politics.

The fact that the government conceded to the demands of the Yellow Vests by offering 17 billion euros to increase their purchasing power is doubly unprecedented: firstly, because the mobilization across France succeeded in pushing back the government; and secondly because of the large sum allocated to meet the protesters' concerns.

Despite its considerable achievements, the movement nonetheless failed to appeal to voters in the May 2019 elections of Eurodeputies. The two Yellow Vests lists, 'Yellow Alliance' and 'Citizen Evolution', garnered respectively 0.57 per cent and fewer than 0.01 per cent of votes. There were also Yellow Vests candidates in the lists led by the Gaullist and sovereignist (*souverainiste*) Nicolas Dupont-Aignan (*Debout la France*), and by Florian Philippot (*Les Patriotes*), the former strategic director of Marine Le Pen's presidential campaign. However, none of those lists managed to secure the 5 per cent threshold that would have allowed them to send elected representatives to the European Parliament, whereas the presidential party LREM ultimately came second with 22.42 per cent of the vote, behind Le Pen's National Rally. The European elections undeniably exposed the limits of the Yellow Vests movement by showing that the transition from the social to the political sphere failed, because of, as Rémy Lefebvre (2019) put it, 'disintermediation', i.e. the process that consists of by-passing intermediaries, the latter having been deeply discredited. As Yves Mény explained:

'Democracy as it works is based on representation and presupposes a general mediation of social and political relations. Groups, unions, parties gather, structure, organize, mobilize and act on behalf of individuals, consumers, citizens who do not necessarily have the necessary qualities, means, will or availability of time to act themselves. These filters are disappearing or in any case going through a deep crisis' (Mény, 2019, p. 232).

The key point of Mény and Lefebvre is that the Yellow Vests and similar movements are limited by their own unwillingness to negotiate with intermediaries. This is part of their essence, but limits their long-term effectiveness, at least in the case of the Yellow Vests. One may add that the act of creative destruction undertaken by Macron himself in terms of delegitimizing the '*corps intermediaires*' has itself contributed to this state of affairs. Symptomatic of this crisis, the Yellow Vests movement demonstrated that their initial refusal, then incapacity, to morph into an organized body; their disaffiliation *vis-à-vis* the elites and civil society at large; and their rejection of electoral politics eventually led to their own demise. One year after the Yellow Vests' Act I, mobilization still went on every Saturday but went relatively unnoticed, and all the more since the government's proposed legislation to reform the French pension system ignited massive inter-union strike actions in December 2019. Whereas in fall 2018, it would have been unthinkable for the Yellow Vests to join other social movements or organizations, and unions in particular – their protests never involved any strike days – it appears that the Yellow Vests subsequently changed their views, supporting these inter-union strikes against the pension reform. Their later politicization led them to realize that their demands – lowering the value added tax on necessity goods, introducing the citizens' referendum initiative and re-introducing the solidarity tax on wealth (*l'impôt de la solidarité sur la fortune, ISF*) – could actually converge with other grassroots' struggles. To mark the first year anniversary of the movement, the Yellow Vests issued an appeal on 2–3 November 2019 in Montpellier saying, 'We, the Yellow Vests from all over France, address all peoples in revolt… as brothers and sisters, and allies of movements worldwide'.

Conclusions

Although the Yellow Vests movement has died out, exemplifying Todd Gitlin's Occupy Nation (2012) that deemed the new global activism more moment than movement, the Yellow Vests insurgency was a potent and unconventional moment and movement that will yet leave a lasting imprint on French society and politics. By any standards, the Yellow Vests movement is, indeed, unique and novel in France's social movements, because of the scale of its mobilization outside any existing organizational framework; its longevity; its achievements in politicizing the fringes of French society and forcing the government to meet some of their terms; and finally the multiple forms of its expression: social networks, high-visibility vests displayed on windshields, recurrent weekly rallies, and even participation in elections.

At the same time, the Yellow Vests movement shares some common features with recent grassroots revolts worldwide. Sparked by wealth inequalities, these movements gather ordinary people who reject the established representative democracy and its elites, whom they consider to be disconnected from reality. Ignited by one factor – be it increasing fuel taxes in France and in Lebanon leading to the 2019–20 'October Revolution'; rising subway fares in Chile; an extradition law in Hong Kong; or the decision of the incumbent president to run for a fifth term in Algeria – these movements swiftly changed scale, and the withdrawal of the controversial announcement no longer sufficed to stop them. Faced with increased and evolving police use of force, they also connect with and learn from one another with regard to their strategy in demonstrations. While Jason Ng (2018), a Hong Kong-based lawyer and author, entitled his op-ed column 'What France's 'yellow vests' can teach Hong Kong activists about political protests and the use of violence', various national news outlets report about how the Hong Kong protests have in their turn been inspiring movements worldwide from Indonesia and India, to Catalonia and Chile (Daily Mail, 2019; DW, 2019; Japan Times, 2019; The Strait Times, 2019; Reuters, 2020).

Meanwhile on French news channels (France24, 2019; RTL, 2020; *La Dépêche*, 2020), scholars and commentators spoke of the 'Yellow Vest-ization' (*gilet jaunisation*) of the social mobilization that had appeared in December 2019 against President Macron's broad reform of the French pension. By 'Yellow Vest-ization' they mean a leaderless movement fuelled by social media that becomes more radical and totally unpredictable, and can potentially last a long time. Giving their name to a type of social movement is certainly an unwitting outcome of the Yellow Vests movement. Although the term 'Yellow Vest-ization' might not go beyond the borders of metropolitan France, the Yellow Vests have certainly contributed to a reshaping of social scientists' conceptualization of social movements in the twenty-first century.

12 IS FRANCE BACK (AGAIN)? EUROPEAN GOVERNANCE FOR A GLOBAL WORLD

Helen Drake and Sophie Meunier

'My key message is that France is back. France is back at the core of Europe because there can be no French success without European success', stated, in English, French President Emmanuel Macron at the 2018 World Economic Forum in Davos, Switzerland (Macron, 2018). 'Being back' at its most literal signifies a conviction that France has a fixed, rightful place in Europe and the world from which it has temporarily and mistakenly deviated. 'Being back' also suggests that France might be rekindling its traditional 'politics of prestige', which have enclosed and constrained French thinking about France's relations with the European Union (EU) in particular, and global governance in general (Sonntag, 2008; Drake, 2013; Parsons, 2017).

For decades before Macron's presidency, France's engagement with the world was guided by these 'politics of prestige', born out of the Gaullist dogma of *grandeur* and a historical 'French obsession with distinction, hierarchy and rank' (Sonntag, 2008, pp. 85–7; see also Drake, 2008). This explains the traditional emphasis placed by France on its cultural diplomacy (see Rieker, 2018, p. 433), on maintaining an active diplomatic service and, more broadly, on treating its role in the world as an indicator of status (see Lequesne, 2017). Successive French Presidents in the Fifth Republic have, in sum, approached France's international relations from the perspective of preserving its prestigious place in the world.

This chapter argues that Macron has articulated, both in substance and in style, a different vision of the necessity for France to be back at the centre of European and world affairs. This is a vision less grounded in prestige and more in a pragmatic understanding that the fate of France's domestic reforms is inextricably linked to some degree of control over its external environment. Vice versa, Macron's ambitious European agenda and efforts to take control of France's external environment were conceived by the new president as a pre-condition for internal reforms. As argued by Rieker (2018,

p. 419), 'President Macron may be right in arguing that "France is back", but it is important to note that modern French power protection or status seeking takes place through a set of very different mechanisms'.

In what follows we evaluate the extent to which the arrival of President Macron may have signalled a shift in the politics of prestige that had increasingly dogged French efforts to lead in Europe and the world (Rieker, 2018). First, we review the legacy of the interplay of domestic politics and international governance during the Hollande years. What internal and external challenges did Hollande face? What results did he achieve? Why was France deemed a 'flawed democracy' (EIU, 2013) in his time, particularly with respect to France's handling of Eurozone constraints? And why did France retreat from its traditional central role in Europe and the world under his watch?

Second, we focus on the 2017 election that brought President Macron to power. We argue that this was the first French presidential contest fought so primarily and explicitly over a new cleavage, broadly defined as an open versus a closed society (see Evans and Ivaldi, 2018, pp. 179–84). How significant were 'Europe' and global affairs in this context? Already in 2012, Europe and the world were seen to be both 'everywhere and nowhere' (Drake, 2013a) in the presidential electoral contest: apparently lacking salience for voters, but woven into any number of candidates' policy proposals. By 2017, had Euroscepticism become mainstream? How serious was the threat of 'Frexit'? As Bedock argues in Chapter 3, the 2017 electoral sequence 'confirms that the traditional left–right cleavage that had structured French political space before that year could not, in 2017, fully explain the main political attitudes of the various groups of voters. The reinforcement of the anti-globalization/Euroscepticism cleavage, taken together with more 'traditional' issues such as immigration and the economy, blurred the dividing lines' [page numbers to add].

Third, we critically reflect on Macron's first years in power, up to and including the 2019 European Parliament elections, with specific reference to his articulation, both in rhetoric and policy, of the symbiotic relation between France's internal and external dimensions. We conclude by asking whether Macron's strategy for bringing France 'back' into 'the core of Europe' – which is to politicize the issue at both the domestic and European levels – is highly risky in a climate of Euroscepticism and domestic dissent.

A disappearing act? The single term of François Hollande

When it comes to France's role in Europe and the world, the presidency of François Hollande (2012–17) looks ex post like a disappearing act, even if it contributed to some important policies and developments. A combination of internal and external challenges, coupled with weak presidential leadership (see Chapters 2 and 3) resulted in a mixed record and a relative retreat of France from the European scene.

Socialist Party contender Hollande had come to the presidency with ambitions for France's role in Europe and globalization. Above all, France was to be an agent of change. During his presidential campaign, Hollande had pummelled the slogan 'change is now'. He argued that he wanted to transform Europe to make it less liberal and more social, less focused on reducing deficits and more focused on growth. This in itself was hardly original for a French president, but Hollande's rhetorical demonization of capital (he decried finance as the 'true enemy') was a departure from the norm. Indeed, the world financial crisis of 2008–09 was fresh in the minds of French politicians and voters alike, and the idea of European integration as a Trojan horse for globalizing forces continued to stoke populist Eurosceptic and anti-globalization movements on both the radical right (the *Front National* as it was then) and the far left (*La France Insoumise*). The 2012 presidential elections, a 'game-changer' in these respects according to Chris Reynolds (2017), revealed the extent of resistance to France's openness to the world. These opposition movements contesting mainstream views of what exactly France's rightful place in the world was and should be (see Drake, 2013a; and Meunier, 2012) won a vote share close to 30 per cent in the first round. By 2017, this trend had been confirmed, as seen below (and see Chapters 3 and 4).

Like all French presidents before him in the Fifth Republic, Hollande had also wanted France to 'recover' France's international place and voice. Wishing to 'be back' in the international game is indeed a recurring trope for French presidential contenders, and Hollande was no exception. His predecessor, Nicolas Sarkozy, had attracted domestic criticism for being a hyperactive leader, deaf to dissenting voices in the French policy-making machinery, and forever in crisis mode to the detriment of strategically repositioning France in a changing world. As Jolyon Howorth (2013, p. 266) argues, under Sarkozy, 'French policy was beset with incoherence at best, irrelevance at worst'. Sarkozy's failure to muster EU support for a hastily hatched plan for a 'Union for the Mediterranean' during France's EU Council Presidency in 2008 was a liability on the balance sheet (Howorth, ibid., p. 259), as was his struggle to develop consensual governance regimes for migration and the Eurozone without breaking existing EU rules. But Hollande's presidential ambitions for restoring French influence in the world were indistinct, and he was relatively inexperienced in the policy field.

At the European level, France made many policy proposals for change during Hollande's presidency, but its voice was inaudible at times, in part because of inherent internal contradictions, and also due to unforeseen circumstances. While campaigning, as seen above, Hollande had branded 'finance' his enemy, only, as President, to subsequently preside over deep splits in his party as some (*les frondeurs*) rebelled against what they branded his neo-liberal remedies to economic woes. For many supporters and analysts, this was the original sin from which Hollande could never recover (Davet and Lhomme, 2019); for others, evidence of a dastardly scheme on Hollande's part to enact labour reform, amongst other things, under the cover of rhetorical commitments to 'more social justice' (Smith, 2013, p. 202). Symptomatic of this presidential response to the constraints of power was Hollande's approach to the EU25's Treaty on Stability, Growth and Governance (the 'Fiscal Compact Treaty') signed in 2011 by President Sarkozy. As candidate, Hollande had promised renegotiation, notably to include a growth stimulus and the creation of Eurobonds. As president, however, he oversaw its ratification, in its original form, by the French Parliament in 2012. Hollande did manage to get a 120 billion euro commitment from other Europeans to add a 'European Growth Pact', but ultimately the member states only added 10 billion euros to this end: the rest of the money was reshuffled from various existing sources.

These contradictions weakened France's standing as one of the two 'engines' of Europe alongside Germany, even though Hollande subsequently argued that his greatest achievement was to have kept Greece in the Eurozone: 'I enabled Greece to stay in the eurozone. It was so riddled with tensions and crises that it would otherwise have pulled the eurozone apart' (Hollande, 2016). As the Greek financial crisis came to a head and Alexis Tsipras was elected Prime Minister on an anti-austerity platform in 2015, Greece's participation in the Eurozone came into serious question. Hollande took the lead in mediating between Greece's creditors, chief among them Germany, and the Greek government. If this was a political success for Hollande, who indeed played a decisive role in brokering a deal, it also ultimately widened the divergences between France and Germany. For the remainder of Hollande's term, France and Germany, whose governments hailed from different political families, clashed often, and the Franco–German couple, which had been central to decades of progress towards further European integration, seemed to unravel. Hollande tried, instead, to make an alliance with like-minded Mediterranean countries, especially Italy, but their domestic economic difficulties made it impossible to counterbalance Germany and weakened French standing *vis-à-vis* Germany. Hence, German Chancellor Merkel seemed to be confirmed as the de facto leader of the EU, albeit as a 'reluctant hegemon' as *The Economist* put it, during that period (Minton Beddoes, 2013).

While Hollande was able to influence European policy in some areas, most of his proposals were not followed through. In addition to handling the Greek crisis, the Hollande legacy in the EU also includes progress on the banking union and on energy infrastructure projects throughout the EU. However, most of the proposals made by the French president were unsuccessful, such as: a common budget for the Eurozone, fiscal harmonization, a permanent president for the Eurogroup, Eurobonds, the creation of a Eurozone Parliament, a minimum wage in each Member State, protection of public services, a European carbon tax, and a New Deal for European youth employment. By the time Hollande left office, none of these proposed reforms and policy innovations had been implemented. For French political scientist Bruno Cautrès, Hollande had become ensnared in a trap of his own making: wishing to lead the EU28 on the condition that they accepted French proposals for a more 'social' Europe. These conditions could not be met, amounting to an automatic marginalization of the French voice (*Toute l'Europe*, 2016).

On the EU's relations with Russia, France joined Germany in leading the European response to the invasion of Crimea and imposing economic sanctions on Russia. Hollande was instrumental in re-establishing the dialogue between Russia and Ukraine at the height of the crisis in June 2014, leading to the cease-fire known as the Minsk Agreements. Many analysts recognize France's leadership in this regard and consider this a major policy achievement (e.g. Le Corre, 2017).

However, under Hollande, France ceded the moral and political high ground in two major EU crises: migration; and the upholding of the rule of law in its member states' domestic politics. On the migration crisis, France did not play a major leadership role. Neither did it welcome many refugees. Faced with a massive humanitarian crisis, the country of human rights offered asylum to the bare minimum: about 30,000 refugees, compared with over a million in Germany during the same period. Even before the 2015–16 terror attacks, the French population was quite negative towards refugees, and critical of the Schengen area and EU framework. Outgoing President Sarkozy had himself pitched a case for a complete overhaul, if not dismantling, of the Schengen arrangements. As for the budding rule of law crisis, Hollande did declare that the EU had the legal tools to suspend countries that violate democratic principles (Euractiv, 2016), but this was a development that took the French president and his EU counterparts into uncharted territory. Tensions between member states over their differing interpretations of democratic governance added stress to already serious fault lines.

The voice of France in Europe, already weakened by its downward economic slide relative to Germany and other member states, was further damaged by an unforeseen development that would consume the remainder of Hollande's presidency – the terrorist attacks endured in France in 2015 and 2016 (see Chapter 13). The intense, emotional pressures of the dreadful terror attacks forced a policy turn inward and a refocusing of internal and external policies towards short-term management and prevention. Domestic policy began to drift, and international ambitions to fade. France was, inevitably, the object of horrified international attention. Alongside splits in the governing party over socio-economic policy, angry fissures appeared over the appropriate response to the terror attacks and threats. President Hollande was weakened by a series of policy failures in this regard, notably his inability to persuade parliament to give constitutional force to the idea that binationals found guilty of terror offences could be stripped of their French nationality (*la dechéance de nationalité*; see Zalc, 2018). France had already, for a third year running, been branded a 'flawed democracy' by the Economist Intelligence Unit's democracy index for its transfers of sovereignty, particularly in economic governance, to the EU level (EIU, 2013). And in the 2014 European Parliament elections, the Eurosceptic *Front national* had come in first place, winning one-quarter of all votes. By the end of the Hollande years, a convincing case for further European integration had thus yet to be made.

A similar dynamic was at play in France's efforts to be a major actor in global governance more broadly, though the French voice under Hollande turned out to be stronger in international than in European politics (Howorth, 2013; Lecorre, 2017). Hollande's ambitions were to restore the prestige and reputation of France, while serving as a progressive voice for change in the international liberal order. The crowning achievement of the Hollande presidency in this latter respect was the organizing and hosting of the United Nations Climate Change Conference (COP21), an ambitious climate conference that resulted in the signing of the Paris Agreement by 174 countries (see Lecorre, 2017).

In the end, however, the Hollande presidency did not live up to either its European or global ambitions. France's strong activism in foreign affairs, such as the negotiation of the Iran nuclear deal and Operation Serval in Mali, did not compensate, in the mind of French voters, for Hollande's perceived crippling weaknesses (see Howorth, *op. cit.*). The combination of personal style (lack of charisma and authority, vague on policy positions), infighting among his government and parliamentary majority, and the series of terror attacks irremediably weakened Hollande's support at home. His loss of domestic support, coupled with the absence of structural reforms and sluggish economic growth, which scuppered his rash campaign promise to halt the rise in unemployment ('*inverser la courbe du chômage*') within a year of taking office, reverberated negatively on his ability to influence the European agenda. Brexit, following the UK's decision by referendum on 23 June 2016 to 'Leave' the EU, could have provided an opportunity for France, in the final months of Hollande's first term, to reclaim a central lead in co-piloting the EU. Yet Hollande's announcement in December 2016 that he was not running again for president further muffled his voice, and that of France, at the European level. Some observers were scathing in their assessment, such as the daily newspaper *Libération*'s EU correspondent Jean Quatremer, who concluded that 'All presidents of the French Republic have left their mark on Europe, for the best and, sometimes, the worst. All? No, only one distinguished himself by his vacuity, François Hollande. He, who presented himself as Jacques Delors' heir, will leave at best a footnote in the history of European integration' (Quatremer, 2017).

The 2017 presidential election: the consecration of an open versus closed cleavage?

The 2017 presidential election was interpreted by many analysts as a surprising fluke, the improbable result of a series of lucky breaks for Macron, including the self-destruction of François Fillon and, with him, the hopes of the UMP (now *Les Républicains*) to return to power; the implosion of the Socialist Party following Hollande's abdication as the party's natural presidential candidate; and the ultimately lacklustre performance by the National Front candidate Marine Le Pen. However, as Camille Bedock argues in Chapter 3, the fact that it was Macron and Le Pen who made it through to fight the second round of the 2017 presidential contest owed as much to *structural* as contingent factors: the 'long-term trends' in party politics and voters' values experienced not only in France but elsewhere in Europe – and beyond. Whether this open–closed distinction that marked the 2017 contest would supplant the conventional left–right cleavage is actively debated and a work in progress, inevitably. For Kriesi (2018, p. 61), Macron and his movement had merely moved into the space previously occupied by 'the old centre-left which it largely replaced', leaving the 'structure of the party system that emerges from these elections (…) largely the same' (*op. cit.*). For Gougou and Persico (2017, p. 318), '[t]he 2017 French presidential election resulted in a fragmented political space. It was structured by one main conflict dimension – immigration and authoritarianism – and one less important one – economy and environment – leading to what could be seen as a new four-party system.' Only time will tell whether the *structure* of the French party system has indeed accommodated new players and shifting priorities (and the Bedock and Murray chapters above open discussions on these questions).

Nonetheless, it is not too soon to suggest that, in 2017, Macron's victory resulted from a binary choice, for French voters, between two radically opposed visions of France's engagement with the world, an opposition which had now become the defining contemporary cleavage. The status of France in the world did not play an obvious or explicit role in determining the result of the presidential contest; neither did the traditional 'politics of prestige', nor foreign policy per se. But the question of the role of France in European integration and, more broadly, in global governance was nonetheless a structuring factor both in the campaign itself, and in the primaries that preceded it (see Reynolds, 2017, p. 130; Schön-Quinlivan, 2017).

Macron actively embraced this new cleavage both as candidate and, to date, as president. He was the only overtly pro-EU candidate in the 2017 election and one of the first politicians in France for some time to run on an unabashedly pro-EU platform, in both style and substance. His predecessors from the centre left had been far more timid when addressing European integration. Indeed, the 2005 referendum on the EU Constitution had left scars on the Socialist Party, which had split between supporters of the

Constitutional Treaty on the one hand; and partisans of an elusive 'Plan B', led by former Prime Minister Laurent Fabius, on the other (Hanley, 2017, pp. 143–6). That division contributed to France's rejection of the Draft Treaty, thereby ending its life. Reynolds (*ibid.* 120) argues that both the Ségolène Royal presidential campaign in 2007 and the François Hollande campaign in 2012 expressly avoided any serious focus on European affairs, so aware were they of the ambient Euroscepticism gathering pace since that 2005 referendum result (and also see Rieker, 2018, p. 429). By contrast, Macron projected a 'visceral attachment to the European project' (Amiel and Emelien, 2019, p. 14) and went all in, as candidate, with rhetoric and symbolism. While the National Front promised to remove all EU flags from French official buildings and Marine Le Pen had insisted that broadcasters remove the EU colours from the background of her TV appearances, Macron's campaign was heavy on European symbols: EU flags at campaign rallies, the European banner and anthem at his victory party being obvious examples.

There was substance too: candidate Macron articulated a series of ambitious measures reinforcing European integration with the objective of protecting France from the vagaries of globalization through more control at the supranational level. These proposals included the creation of a common Eurozone budget and Finance Minister; the passage of a 'Buy European Act'; the harmonization of corporate taxes across the EU; an extension of the Erasmus program; the establishment of a European Security Council; and the election of some members of the European Parliament through pan-EU lists (Macron, 2016). Whilst these ambitions, summed up in a keynote electoral message of '*une France forte dans une Europe forte*', were anything but new (we saw similar themes in Hollande's 2012 presidential bid), its intensity and clarity were.

The last two remaining candidates in May 2017 were thus offering a well contrasted, highly differentiated vision of Europe. Macron's European proposals stood in sharp contrast to those of Le Pen, who had promised to put France first by freeing it from the tyrannies of globalization and the European Union, as she saw them, and even toyed with the idea of a wholescale Frexit; or, at least, an exit of France from the eurozone. Her programme and performance on these very points were seen to falter in the face of Macron's clarity, and were indeed toned down significantly before the 2017 legislative elections, and again in the 2019 European Parliament elections (see below; also Ivaldi, 2018; and van Kessel et al., 2020. Indeed, Gerard Colomb, mayor of Lyon, argued that the second round of the presidential election had become a referendum for or against the EU (Mabille, 2017). Contrary to the common wisdom that France had turned Eurosceptic and even Europhobic, Macron's victory suggested that a sizeable portion of the French population was perhaps eager for a forward-looking, positive message on European integration; this was certainly a recurring and dominant interpretation in press coverage, outside of France, of Macron's victory (see Anderson, 2017 for a critical review of such coverage). A more sobering analysis is that, whilst it is the case that Macron's electorate ranked 'Europe' as a salient factor in their choice, French voters overall did not place it high among their concerns. Moreover, Macron's electorate was far from cohesive (Strudel, 2017).

Is France back? Articulating domestic and European reforms in tandem

In both substance and style, and without delay, newly elected President Macron set about injecting some optimism and ambition into the European project. His grand vision for the EU was articulated in his September 2017 speeches in Athens and the Sorbonne (Macron, 2017a, 2017b). These ambitious proposals were based on the central notions of European sovereignty and protection, which implied further integration of the Eurozone (e.g. finance Minister, Eurozone Parliament, budgetary capacity); a push towards a precautionary stance on foreign direct investments, especially from China, at the EU level with the creation of a pan-European FDI screening framework; the taxation of digital companies; the enforcement of strong borders, including a tough stance on immigration; stronger coordination in foreign policy and defence to protect the EU from external shocks and become less dependent on the USA; European efforts towards preserving the environment by 'making our planet great again' at the international level, even in the absence of American support; and a new EU architecture characterized by differentiated integration. In May 2018, President Macron received the International Charlemagne Prize of Aachen, 'the oldest and best-known prize awarded for work done in the service of European unification' (www.karlspreis.de/en/).

Simultaneously, comprehensive domestic reforms were devised by Macron as a precondition for succeeding in his EU-level ambitions for reasserting French influence and credibility in Europe, especially *vis-à-vis* Germany. The main thrust of his domestic reforms has been the modernization and opening, as he would see it, of the French economy. The levers, for him, and as discussed in Milner's Chapter 10, were the transformation, notably, of unemployment insurance, the pension system and the public bureaucracy. Macron and his team also insisted that these reforms respect the EU's Growth and Stability Pact, a move designed in particular to revive the Franco–German partnership. This had been weakened during the presidency of Hollande, as seen above, who had tried to find allies inside the EU to counterbalance Germany.

The envisaged synchronicity of domestic and EU-level governance reforms was for Macron driven by two principal criteria. First, his vision of EU-level 'sovereignties' was temporal: only the EU could take and enforce the big, long-term orientations that cannot be left to the vagaries of constant national electoral campaigns, such as climate change, artificial intelligence and the systemic challenges posed by China's economic and political development. Second, invoking 'Europe' to make domestic reforms palatable, or indeed justify them, has a long pedigree in the Fifth Republic, and Macron here is no exception. Indeed, implementing a 'Europe that protects' at the EU level, which can be characterized as a centre-left policy and also represents strong continuity with most if not all of Macron's predecessors, was envisaged as a precondition for domestic reforms, which many observers and critics have characterized as 'centre-right' (as discussed in several other chapters in this volume). In Macron's interpretation, as in Lionel Jospin's interpretation in the late 1990s, the EU is not a Trojan horse of globalization but a buffer against it.

... but has Europe (and France) been receptive?

Two years into Macron's presidency, how did the reality of the exercise of power compare with his grand ambitions? Initially, Macron was lucky and found favourable conditions in the EU. The combination of Brexit, which was all-consuming in UK politics, and the waning power of 'lame duck' Merkel inside Germany, left France without serious competition to retake the initiative, let alone exercise leadership, at the EU level. We see in Chapter 2 how leaders in general, and French leaders specifically, are doomed to disappoint such high expectations of the executive function and of the 'great man'. Nevertheless, the worst of the eurocrisis was over, and economic conditions had improved overall throughout the EU. Macron even scored a minor, symbolic victory early in his presidency with the October 2017 adoption by the EU of the reform on posted workers, which regulates the social regimes under which workers from a member state are employed in a different member state. Another early success was in European defence cooperation, with the creation of Permanent Structured Cooperation (PESCO) in December 2017 and the launching of the 'European Intervention Initiative' (EI2) in June 2018. Both initiatives were designed to develop joint defence capabilities and to facilitate the participation of member states in joint European actions in crises; both chimed with Macron's understanding of the EU's role in global governance.

But President Macron's domestic challenges weighed down his European ambitions. For several months, Macron's effectiveness and even legitimacy were challenged by the Yellow Vests (*gilets jaunes*) movement, which temporarily sank his popularity to new lows (see Chapter 11 in this volume). A nebulous, spontaneous mobilization of French citizens from lower middle classes and upper lower classes took place, weekend after weekend, to protest tax hikes, the lowering of purchasing power and, more generally, the arrogance of the political, Parisian elite. This new form of contestation, escaping easy classification, left Macron and his government at a loss for the appropriate response, plunging approval ratings and consuming all political capital (Fassin and Defossez, 2019).

In this context, Macron's ambitious programme bumped against German and Nordic frilosity, especially given the domestic effacement of Chancellor Merkel, Macron's most logical political ally. Scandinavian countries were fearful that French atavistic dirigisme and protectionism were underlying proposed EU reforms of foreign direct investment screening and competition policy, as well as a push towards more industrial policy at the European level (Meunier, 2020). Tensions also escalated between France and Italy, traditional allies inside the EU, who found themselves on opposite sides of the open–closed cleavage at the European level, with the liberal, elitist, Europhile Macron pitted against the far-right nationalist, populist, Eurosceptic Matteo Salvini (Hall, 2018). As for Central and Eastern Europe, relations were tense between Macron and several leaders whom he had denounced for democratic backsliding, especially in Hungary and Poland.

As the campaign for the May 2019 European elections got under way, Macron had made only modest progress on the core of his European program, vital as an accompaniment to his French reforms program: there was still no Eurozone minister, no transnational lists for electing members of the European Parliament, little fight against social dumping within the EU, and no strategic autonomy in European defence.

The European elections of May 2019

Macron's *La Republique en Marche!* competed in an unprecedently crowded field for the election to the European Parliament of May 2019 – an election that typically is low stakes, triggers low voter participation, and turns out anti-government protest votes. While 34 lists were actually fielded, of which only 6 eventually secured seats in the European Parliament, competition for voters was fierce. Many billboards for this election were left eerily empty, and the abstention rate ended up at 50 per cent. Still, the turnout was the highest since the 1994 election (only 42 per cent had voted in the 2014 election).

Like the presidential election two years earlier, the European election consecrated and pitted two main political forces that offered a stark political and ideological contrast. This time, President Macron was even more forceful and explicit in adopting the narrative of an existential fight between progressist Europhiles and nationalist Eurosceptics. The French president was personally invested in the campaign, even though the LREM list was led by his then Europe Minister, Nathalie Loiseau. He used the opportunity to explain to voters why it was crucial for France to pursue an integrationist agenda and move the protection of sovereignty to the EU level. Appealing directly not only to the French, but more broadly to the 'citizens of Europe', he proposed a 'European Renaissance' – the name of the electoral list itself – articulated around the concepts of liberty, protection and progress (*Renaissance soutenue par La République en marche, le Modem et ses partenaires*; Macron, 2019). This renaissance was to occur through institutional change at the EU level designed to cement a European demos and prevent democratic backsliding; through deeper integration of the Single Market and greater integration in defence and foreign policy; through more geopolitical voice in trade and investment; and by the EU taking the reins of environmental regulation and governance. Once again, the French president was inserting himself at the centre of EU politics, seeking to take control of the European agenda not, it would appear, for status or prestige in their own right, but rather to ease the passage of domestic reforms in France. By migrating social protection to the EU level while arguably removing protections at the domestic level, this proposed European Renaissance looked strongly like a typical neo-liberal agenda to his leftist critics. At the same time, Macron's proposals had some elements reminiscent of old French *dirigisme*, notably with respect to foreign investment screening and competition policy; and as discussed in Chapter 2, on numerous dimensions, President Macron's leadership defies conventional classification.

By contrast, Marine Le Pen turned the European elections into a referendum on Macron's presidency and into a mandate for getting French sovereignty back. The *Rassemblement National's* list, led by young newcomer Jordan Bardella, denounced France's surrendering of sovereignty to the EU and brandished a slogan ('*Prenez le pouvoir*' – take control) that was strongly reminiscent of the UK's 'Leave' mantra in the 2016 referendum ('Take back control'). Importantly, it also echoed the first of Marine Le Pen's 144 presidential election commitments from 2017, namely '*Retrouver notre liberté et la maîtrise de notre destin en restituant au peuple français sa souveraineté*' (restore our freedom and control of our destiny by returning sovereignty to the French people) (*Rassemblement National*, 2017).

In the end, while the *Rassemblement National* came in first, the result was seized upon by the Elysée as a defeat of sorts for Le Pen, and a victory of sorts for Macron. The president himself proclaimed himself pleased with the turnout across the EU, which he interpreted as a 'democratic spurt, an interest in Europe, a determination of Europe's peoples to change things and to come together to make progress' (Elysée, 2019). The RN's list had topped the results with 23.34 per cent of the vote share, which was lower than its 2014 result (24.86 per cent). Moreover, the RN obtained only 23 seats in the European Parliament – one fewer than in 2014 and the same number as the seats won by the presidential list, which garnered 22.42 per cent of the votes. Macron's policies were boosted by that second place but equal number of seats, especially since the mid-term, second-order European election rarely favours the incumbent party. Indeed, in 2014, the ruling Socialist Party and allies had come third, beaten both by the FN and the UMP. Macron's momentum was also boosted by the apparent collapse of the other political lists that competed for the remainder of the vote, with the exception of Europe Ecology-the Greens (EELV), led by Yannick Jadot, which received 13.5 per cent of the votes and 13 seats on an agenda centred around green protectionism at the EU level and a zero-carbon emission economy. The *Republicains* (LR) came in fourth with a disastrous 8.5 per cent of the vote, which lost them 12 out of 20 MEPs and represented a historical defeat. Jean-Luc Melenchon's *La France Insoumise* came in fifth place, with 6.3 per cent of the votes and six MEPs. The Socialist Party, for its part, fragmented across at least two lists and returned only five members to the EP's second largest political group, the Socialists and Democrats.

The result of Macron's Renaissance movement in the European election was also, wishful thinking or otherwise, framed as success at the EU level. As many analysts and publications reported, Macron found himself as 'the unofficial winner of the European elections, or at least the kingmaker. Then he was the chief engineer at the EU summit that decided the top jobs for the next five years' (Robert et al., 2019). Macron took advantage of a vacuum in European leadership: the UK was all-consumed with Brexit and in no position to play a constructive EU role; Merkel was on the way out, while it was not clear how much clout or leeway her successor would have; other countries, such as Italy and Spain, were enmeshed in complicated domestic electoral politics. The combination of relative success at home, especially given the Yellow Vests context, and the lack of clear leadership elsewhere in Europe amplified the French voice in Brussels and enabled Macron to play a decisive role in selecting a new EU team in tune with French interests and Macron's priorities, such as industrial policy, environmental protection and European defence. Nonetheless not all went the French President's way, when his nominee for the European Commission, Sylvie Goulard, was rejected by secret ballot following two hearings by the European Parliament (Euractiv, 2019).

Macron as international kingmaker?

Macron conveys a deep consciousness that the liberal international order is living through an historical juncture, 'marked by a very profound crisis of democracy, both in representativity and efficiency' (Semo, 2019). Demographic and economic forces have shrunk the relative weight of advanced industrialized democracies, challenging Western hegemony. The resurgence of Russia and the rapid growth of China are posing an existential challenge to the stability and desirability of liberal democracy. At the same time, the United States, the historical pillar of the liberal international order, has disengaged from the multilateral governance of global issues such as climate change, and in some cases is even actively sabotaging traditional alliances and multilateralism, such as NATO and the WTO. As some analysts have noted, these are ripe international conditions to make this a 'French moment' (Laidi, 2019). Some have gone further with hyperbole, arguing that 'The West may no longer be the leader of the world. But the EU has a new leader and it's no longer Merkel: it's French President Emmanuel Macron (Robert et al., 2019).

Indeed, Macron has seemed ubiquitous in trying to repair and protect multilateral governance of the liberal international order. These efforts were on display for instance during the 2019 G7 summit in Biarritz, where Macron's agenda included mediation on Iran, discussions on climate change and forest fires in the Amazon, reform of the WTO, and a commitment to modernize the taxation regime for large digital multinational companies. Whether these efforts will succeed is dubious, but Macron, at least, has tried to seize the moment.

Conclusions

We have argued that the Macron presidency has inextricably linked the internal and external dimensions of policy to put France back at the centre of Europe, not for its own sake – in order to gain back its lost prestige or its rightful place in the world – but rather to take control of France's external environment as a pre-condition and a shield for internal reforms. Both a European France and French Europe are expected to have a stronger voice on the world stage to promote their interests and vision, especially in the current context where the traditional pillars and guardrails of the liberal international economic order are crumbling.

This articulation of the necessity to proceed domestically and internationally in tandem has put additional spotlight on a new open–closed, progressist–nationalist cleavage now structuring French politics, as mentioned above (and in earlier chapters in this volume). According to an IPSOS/*Le Monde* study published in October 2019, 76 per cent of respondents agree that the left–right cleavage is no longer relevant (Grunberg, 2019). This number keeps growing, up from 71 per cent in 2017. The traditional left–right cleavage is particularly spurned by LREM and RN voters, among both of whom only 11 per cent believe that this is still the main explanatory cleavage in French politics. The difference between LREM and RN voters is particularly pronounced when it comes to assessing globalization: 78 per cent of Macron supporters see globalization as an opportunity and source of progress, versus only 24 per cent of Le Pen supporters (Grunberg, 2019).

This strategy of putting European integration and global governance at the centre of the political agenda carries dangers. First, nationalist and populist parties, which have been on the rise throughout liberal democracies, especially France, seem to support each other across national boundaries. Many ideological and personal linkages have been documented between the alt-right in the United States and European far-right parties, for instance. The RN now promotes a vision of an EU that needs to be reformed from the inside, instead of by leaving like Brexit. This is the far-right version of a federal Europe: a European alliance of nations with flexible governmental cooperation. By contrast, it is harder for the liberal, progressist vision carried by Macron to find international support and alliances in the current context.

As former French Ambassador to the USA Gerard Araud argued, Emmanuel Macron, like Barack Obama, is a 'hyper-realist in a world of passion' (2019). Realism per se does not excite crowds, although insofar as it is experienced as an assault on the status quo and the removal of certainty, it can incite hatred and fury, viz. the ferocity of the *gilets jaunes* movement in France (Araud, op. cit.; and Drake, 2018). This is a vision more complex, more long-term in scope, and harder to articulate in a world of instant feedback and gratification (see Fieschi, 2019).

Second, the greatest danger in making the EU and global governance a structuring cleavage in French domestic politics is that, with each election, leaders and parties are typically voted out of office and replaced with the other side: the *alternance* of power that has marked contemporary French politics for decades. Prior to the 2017 election, we have said, the EU was not central to national voting behaviour. Parties would come and go in and out of power, but a general, national consensus dominated the issue of European and global governance. If openness is the cleavage, it means that eventually and logically, pro-EU parties will be replaced by anti-EU parties. As Evans and Ivaldi have argued (2017, p. 202), the second round 'presidential run-off in 2017, unlike 2012, was conducive to Europe separating further from the traditional left–right basis of opposition, thus finding its own way into France's presidential politics'. Such politicization of European governance is a risky bet for the future of the EU.

13 IN WHOSE NAME? FRENCH SOCIETY, TERRORISM AND FOREIGN POLICY

Christopher Hill

Introduction

As the recent history of France has demonstrated all too clearly, domestic society and international politics in the modern world are deeply connected. The only issues are the nature of the two-way flow and the extent to which decision-makers acknowledge the process. In the case of the 'Hexagon', its citizens have been forced to realize that events far from home are reverberating within their country in the form of the dramatic and tragic terrorist attacks which began in 2012. Conversely, choices made by the French people through their elected representatives about how the country should be run – such as that on '*le voile*' – have not gone unnoticed abroad, creating links between domestic opponents and foreign sympathizers. The French word for the veil itself epitomises some of the difficulties the country has in coming to terms with Islam and its practices, as in general use it is a blanket term for the headscarf and for full face coverings such as the burka or niqab (Joppke, 2009).

What follows expands on this analysis through more detailed reference to the challenges which President Emmanuel Macron inherited from Presidents François Hollande and Nicolas Sarkozy in relation to both terrorism at home and foreign policy in France's near abroad. The chapter begins with a brief summary of events in both domains before turning to the central problem: how to unravel the complex knot of causal factors at play, and indeed the direction of influence – from outside in, or inside-out? Or must we just accept there is an indecipherable fluidity of interaction? Attention is given to four factors which represent plausible explanations for the troubles which have afflicted France since 2012: (1) the existence of a sizeable group of

I am grateful to the editors for their invitation to write this chapter, and for their careful scrutiny of its content. I am also indebted to Keith Banting for his perceptive advice. All translations of quoted material are mine.

déraciné young people, concentrated in the *banlieues*, among whom a small but important number is willing to attack their own society; (2) the impact of fundamentalist Islam, at odds with France's secular civic nationalism and capable of radicalizing the already alienated young; (3) a turbulent external environment in which slow-burning resentments of the country's imperial past undermine its *tiers-mondiste* self-image; (4) a more assertive national foreign policy, increasingly locked into the vicious circle of attempts to counter terrorism which then breed more hostility to France. Arguably, if any one of these factors had not existed, or been different, then events in France might have turned out very differently. If several had been absent or different then it is quite likely that that they would have done.

The events

The most obvious, and immediately serious, manifestation of the interplay of these processes has been the outbreak of terrorism within France since 2012. After the attacks inflicted by the Algerian Armed Islamic Group in the mid-1990s, the country was free of terrorist incidents until March 2012, when Mohamed Merah murdered three soldiers with Arab names in Montauban and four Jewish civilians (of whom three were children) in Toulouse. Merah was an alienated French Muslim of Algerian extraction who claimed he was avenging Palestinian and Afghan deaths – for which he saw French policy in the Middle East as having a responsibility. Hence, he posted on social media the words he addressed to his victims: 'that's the nature of Islam, my brother: you kill my brothers and I'll kill you' (cited in Kepel and Jardin, 2015, p. 118). After a lull during which many concluded that Merah was simply a deranged individual, attacks continued with increasing frequency and ferocity. The year 2015 will go down in French history as one of extraordinary tension and darkness, because of a series of grotesque 'spectacles' (Debord, 1967). In January the slaughter at *Charlie Hebdo*, accompanied by the killing of two police officers, was followed by the taking of hostages at a kosher supermarket in Paris and the murder of four of them, all Jews – the crisis being transmitted on live TV. The events drove unprecedented numbers onto the streets of French cities in solidarity, under the banner of '*je suis Charlie*' – which in turn led to hostile reactions by some Muslim youngsters in schools (a minority of Muslim pupils did not observe the minute's silence for victims, and began to give voice to conspiracy theories). In February and April of the same year there were two unsuccessful attacks by individuals, but in June an attempt was made to blow up a gas factory and a man was decapitated. On 21 August a mass shooting was foiled on the Amsterdam–Paris Thalys express train. As those who subdued the assailant were US ex-military personnel, this attracted huge international attention, encouraging those who wished to see a fight-back against the terrorists.

What happened less than three months later, however, completely dispelled any optimism. On a normal Friday evening in November, a combination of mass shootings and suicide bombing at a rock concert and restaurants in Paris left 130 people dead and 413 injured, while an attack on the *Stade de France*, where the home country was playing Germany in a prestigious friendly football match, was successfully forestalled. These clearly coordinated attacks were claimed by ISIS and indeed could only have been mounted after careful preparation involving cells inside and outside the country. It had become clear that what had happened in January amounted to far more than just revenge on a group of outspoken satirists. Indeed President François Hollande declared it to be an act of war. Whether he was tactically wise in so raising the stakes, as the US had done in 2003 with its 'war on terror', might be doubted, but from the point of view of the jihadists this was the correct description. Their capacity to repeat such sophisticated undercover operations was clearly diminished thereafter, as indicated by the public appeals to kill infidels wherever the opportunity arose, by whatever means and on a random individual basis if necessary.

It seemed that there were limits to the carnage which could be inflicted by a lone individual, even when armed with an automatic weapon. But the use of a vehicle raised the stakes considerably, as Mohamed Lahouaiej Bouhlel demonstrated on Bastille Day 2016 when he drove a lorry down the pedestrianized *Promenade des Anglais* in Nice, killing 86 and wounding 458 of those in his path. It turned out that Lahouaiej Bouhlel had not in fact acted alone, as five suspected accomplices were subsequently charged. This action had the desired traumatic effect not just in Nice but in France as a whole, and indeed more widely. It fulfilled the basic terrorist requirements of creating a huge media spectacle and of leaving scars on civil society in terms of fear, distrust, divisions and securitization. It meant that France, more than any other Western country, had suffered (in just over 18 months) three mass killings, all hitting places of great national symbolic value and, in the last case, occurring on France's most important national holiday – July 14 – marking the revolutionary event which inaugurated its modern secular history.

While this domestic upheaval was taking place, France was also engaged in looking outwards. Its foreign policy became dramatically active in the Maghreb, the Levant and sub-Saharan Africa, partly in an attempt to stop the very kind of terrorism which was being inflicted upon it. In 2011, Nicolas Sarkozy's government had combined with the United Kingdom and the United States first to prevent a massacre in Benghazi and then to make possible the fall of the Ghaddafi regime. The resulting chaos in Libya has preoccupied Paris ever since, given the opportunities it provides for an ISIS base, and for people-trafficking northwards, with the potential to act as cover for jihadists. Less than two years later, President François Hollande sent troops into a 'little war in Mali' to combat the spreading Jihadist movement there, only a short time after announcing the end of France's belief in

'Françafrique', its networks of influence so often criticized as neo-colonialism (Cristiani and Fabbiani, 2013). One Western diplomat then predicted that, as Al Qaeda would not be able to defeat France on the battlefield, it would turn to 'an asymmetrical terror campaign' (cited in *The Washington Post*, 28 January 2013). Finally, France took a leading role in the air attacks in Iraq and Syria against Daesh. Indeed, Paris was seriously put out by the failure of then UK Prime Minister David Cameron to get the support of the House of Commons for a military intervention after Bashar al-Assad had used chemical weapons in 2013, as it was by Barack Obama using Britain's decision as an excuse for failing to uphold his own 'red line' on the matter. The coalition re-formed more successfully over the following year, with all three countries committed to the use of air power against 'terrorism' in Syria, even though that extraordinarily complex conflict hardly admits of precise targeting.

In short, although French foreign policy covers a far wider range of activity than this brief summary indicates, it has had a notably higher profile since 2011 in terms of military interventions in its near abroad, mostly against targets with majority Muslim populations (Pannier and Schmitt, 2019). These actions might conceivably have limited the blow-back into the Hexagon from existing conflicts by inflicting costs on jihadist enemies, but they have certainly not stopped it. Indeed it is arguable that they have made things worse.

Juxtaposing the horrific attacks on French civil society between 2012 and 2018 with the more forward foreign policy conducted in the Middle East and North Africa since 2011 seems to suggest a simple argument about cause and effect. That is not the intention here. The purpose of this chapter is rather to disentangle the various causal processes at work in producing the unprecedented wave of violent attacks in France, which had been relatively untouched by terrorism for 15 years before 2012. The aim is also to clear away some of the polemical fog from what is understandably a highly emotional set of issues, where even academics have allowed their passions to run away with them. To that end, this chapter will proceed first by providing an overview of the various factors which have combined to create the interlinked challenges currently facing France in foreign and domestic policy. It moves on to a brief discussion of the seminal, if unnecessarily polarized, debate between the country's two leading experts on political Islam in France – Gilles Kepel and Olivier Roy – before analysing the complex issues involved in trying to explain both the course of French foreign policy during this period and the evolution of French society with respect to the challenge of multiculturality. The aim is to throw light on the reasons for the wave of terrorism which has hit France since 2011 and the nature of its links to the country's international role. The initial hypothesis is that the state is in danger of becoming trapped in an ever more vicious cycle, comprising terror attacks, the reassertion of secularist values and strongly assertive counter-terror policies at home and abroad.

A complex knot to unravel

If we start from the assumption that there is no single factor explanation for the jihadist challenge in France since 2012, then we are obliged both to map the variables involved and to make an attempt at explaining how they interact. It is important to note that the *explanandum* here is the overall phenomenon of terrorism in France. The micro-level of analysis, that of attempting to explain why an individual engaged in a terrorist act, or why it took place in this place, or that time, is not the issue – even if those multiple specificities are necessarily linked to the higher level of generalization. From a philosophical point of view, a satisfactory account of a specific event is necessary but not sufficient if we are to explain the general class of events into which it fits – as with the debate about the causes of wars, as opposed to the causes of war. Conversely, a satisfactory explanation of a broader phenomenon must be compatible with the evidence generated from specific instances which are described using the same or similar language. If, for example, an act of terrorism turns out to have been committed by a mentally deranged person with no connections to, or even knowledge of, the political issues at stake in the country, then it cannot be adduced as evidence for a general interpretation of those issues. It is, however, relevant to a full account of terrorism, so long as it is weighted against the evidence for other motivations and characteristics. It might well also be relevant to theories about other phenomena, relating for example to socio-psychological dynamics.

We now address in turn the four main factors at stake in attempts to explain the re-emergence of terrorism in France during the last seven years.

The *déracinés*

There is no doubt that France, like most societies, contains a significant number of alienated young people of all backgrounds. In part that is simply the condition of youth. Furthermore, the atomized nature of modern life, together with the expectations and pressures created by mass media, is bound to create dissatisfactions. That said, France has a further significant problem. It is not one of immigration as such. Although France has also probably taken in almost one million Muslim migrants since 2010, immigration was not even a major issue in the presidential election of 2017 (Gomart and Hecker, 2019). More significant is its large Muslim population, growing from the 1960s, which amounts to 7–9 per cent of the total population, making it the largest proportion in any EU member state except Bulgaria and Cyprus. The Muslim community now contains a number of young people with second- and third-generation minority origins, for the most part Maghrebian, many of whom still do not see themselves as enjoying the full rights of French citizenship (Hackett, 2017). The vast majority of these people wants only to make a living and to live a peaceful life. They may not self-identify in terms of religion or ethnicity, which is how the French state requires it. Yet in practice they cannot help being, to varying degrees, hyphenated French men and women. And it is by now well understood that it can be a very difficult experience growing up in a society whose attitudes and customs are at odds with those of their older relations. Young people wish to assimilate with their peer group and to respect their family traditions – although some may come both to hate the prejudices their parents have suffered as first-generation immigrants and to be scornful of their wish to conform.

The psychological and social pressures thus created, which can even shape the third or later generations if practices of social exclusion continue to affect them, can lead to alienation from conventional society and in extreme cases to hatred of it. That in turn can lead to politicization and the attractions of a fundamentalist, even violent ideology. More often it begins by leading to criminal behaviour of a less dramatic kind, and to prison for minor offences which can then radicalize the individual through contact with fellow-inmates, and preachers, or simply through the yearning for a set of beliefs which will provide direction and values in what is perceived to be a meaningless existence, lived in the headwinds of hostility from the majority. As Durkheim argued, *anomie* finds its own solutions, of which one can be suicide. Modern terrorists often explicitly choose self-destruction, but any terrorist action represents an implicit acceptance of the high likelihood of one's own death.

The problem is compounded by the oppressive character of France's *banlieues*. In one respect these are suburbs in the English sense, as they are usually on the periphery of a city, far from the chic historic centre. But they are very different from the dull but mostly safe areas of middle-class commuter housing famously symbolized by London's Metroland. Rather they tend to be isolated – if not always run-down – estates largely populated by poor people of minority origins who feel cut off in terms of both distance and culture from *les français de souche*, whose way of life they observe with ambivalence on national television.

The product of this cocktail of social, economic and psychological elements is a not insignificant pool of young people – mostly but not exclusively men – capable of being attracted into the jihadist cause against their fellow-citizens. Unemployment and housing difficulties make a major contribution, as does the existential factor of identity and not uncommonly also a painful childhood history, through bereavement, abandonment or brutality. Various cases in point are described in a rich body of recent works (Hussey, 2014; Kepel, 2015; Roy, 2017; Leiken, 2012).

The religious factor

Religion enters into the equation in two ways: on the one hand through prejudice, usually on the part of right-wing groups against Muslims and Jews, but also evident in the anti-Semitism of some radical Muslim groups (see Chapter 9); on the other it is an issue because of the elements of incompatibility between the beliefs and practices of faith communities and the secularist consensus which has evolved in French society since the Revolution. These two things are naturally connected.

In the current context, prejudice is perceived and experienced by French Muslims on a daily basis. Even those who do not practise their religion tend to object to the ban on the wearing of the female headscarf in public places, and to the fuss made over the use of the 'burkini' to preserve the modesty of Muslim women while swimming. These issues of daily life link together the two phenomena referred to above: thus a political culture strongly attached to the idea that religion is a potential threat to the values of the Republic provides legitimacy for conservative views on a 'certain idea of France'. Furthermore the idea of integration disguises the survival in many parts of society of the politically more toxic idea of 'assimilation', namely that newcomers should adopt the 'traditional' French way of life, and that they should not be surprised if their distinctive practices – whether dress, halal food in schools or the noise of the call to prayer – are resisted by the majority.

While any society contains a huge variety of distinctive practices, in France those deriving from faith and organized religion touch on a historical nerve: the angry debates in the nineteenth century over education between the Catholic church and anti-clericals, only resolved by the law of 9 December 1905 which definitively separated Church and State (Laborde, 2010). This victory for secularist reformers – at least on paper – had been assisted by the way the unjust persecution of Captain Alfred Dreyfus over twelve years from 1894 had exposed anti-Semitism at the highest levels of the Christian establishment. It is the legislation of 1905 to which such measures as the 2004 headscarf ban harken back, despite the fact that it pre-dates the arrival of the first Mosque in France (opened in Paris in 1926 as an act of gratitude for the sacrifice of Muslim soldiers in the Great War). When the Islamic community grew significantly from the 1960s on, and became a highly visible presence in the country, serious difficulties were inevitable. For as Christian Joppke (2009, p. 27) has said, 'If Islam sternly denies the very distinction of private-public, which is the essence of republicanism, how could one ever expect the two systems to co-exist peacefully?' That they mostly do rub along together on an everyday level is credit to thousands of ordinary people practising co-existence and tolerance and to the fact that the 1905 law itself insists on official neutrality between different communities of faith (Joppke, 2009, p. 41). But there is no doubt that many French Muslims perceive *laïcité* as an act of hostility towards them, just as it is used by right-wing extremists to attack both Muslims and Jews. On the other side of the argument, many French citizens see even moderate Islamic practices as a threat to human rights, in particular those of women (Laborde, 2010).

The external environment

If the existence of a significant minority of people alienated from mainstream society, most of them young and identifying as Muslim, has provided the tinder for the terrorist flames which broke out in France from 2012 on, the sparks have tended to come from events in the outside world. The general conflagration in the Middle East and the rise of ISIS created the conditions out of which anti-Western jihadism has arisen, although there have also been elements which have been particular to France. The historical context shows that the Arab–Israel dispute, which became the Israeli–Palestinian conflict, has caused problems for Europeans from 1948 on, as have the troubles of Iran, Iraq, Lebanon and Libya, to name only a few trouble spots in the region. Most dramatic were the hijackings, assassinations and airport attacks after 1969 which culminated in the downing of PanAm flight 103 over Lockerbie in 1988. But it was the outbreak of the 'war on terror', bringing a major Western military presence to Afghanistan and then Iraq after 9/11, still ongoing, which created a close nexus between events in the Middle East and European societies, 'bringing war home' for ordinary people (Hill, 2005). This was in part through the global furore created by the attacks in New York and Washington, and in part the result of the ease with which fundamentalists could exploit the openness and diversity of European societies to hit at the soft underbelly of the Western coalition. It seemed as if Samuel Huntington's grandiloquent talk of the early 1990s about a clash of civilizations was finally coming true, with European powers being drawn back into war in places they had retreated from with the end of empire.

At first France was spared what came to be known as 'blowback'. It was Spain in March 2004 and Britain in July 2005 whose capital cities were hit hard by devastating bomb explosions, claimed by Al Qaeda as reprisals for the loss of Muslim lives in the invasion and occupation of Iraq (Reinares, 2016; Hill, 2013; Pantucci, 2015). It took another seven years for France to become a major target, through the murders committed by Merah in Toulouse, probably not by coincidence at the start of the campaign for the presidential and parliamentary elections of 2012. Over the previous 15 years, since 1997, France had been free of politically inspired killings, leading some to conclude that its approach to the integration of its Muslim population was producing positive results (Laurence and Vaisse, 2006). This conclusion should not now be completely dismissed; there is still evidence that the majority of Muslims in the country regard themselves as French and are not particularly at odds with its dominant republican values. But it cannot be denied that the alarm and fear caused by attacks such as those in Paris and Nice have dispelled complacency and called into question the basic assumptions of the French model of social cohesion.

Foreign policy

To what extent has foreign policy played a part in this dramatic change? In general terms it is clear that the prolonged series of conflicts in the Middle East from October 2001 onwards have created fertile ground for jihadist antagonism towards most Western countries, given the interventions in Iraq, Afghanistan, Libya, Mali and Syria. It is also the case that terrorist attacks in Europe are often determined by mere opportunity, in terms of vulnerable targets and the residence of sleeper cells. This means that every state might find itself having to cope with a bomb attack justified in terms of the decadence of the infidel West and its collective responsibility for war in 'Muslim lands'. Furthermore many plots are foiled by the authorities, sometimes even without the publicity of a prosecution, which can give the misleading appearance of a state not being targeted. For example Spain did not suffer seriously after the 2004 atrocity until the attack in Barcelona in 2017, but between 2006 and 2010 it put 916 people on trial for terrorism, although more were on charges related to separatism than to jihadism (Hill, 2013). But none of this can fully explain either why some societies suffer more plots, more attacks and more damage than others, or why there are particular periods in which certain countries are targets.

In the case of France, no one has argued that it was in the front line of jihadist anger between 9/11 and 2012. '[A]bout a dozen' groups were 'neutralized' by the authorities between 2000 and 2008, but it was the very fact that the threat was not perceived to be great that produced the shock and subsequent security failings when attacks did begin in earnest' (Jean-François Clair, then head of the *Direction de la Surveillance du Territoire*, cited in Leiken (2012) pp. 111–12). After all, France had stayed out of the Iraq invasion and subsequent imbroglio in 2003, maintaining a relatively positive image in the Middle East and wider Muslim world. Paris had always been keen to maintain a reputation in the Middle East of being the United States' main critic within the Western camp (Boniface, 2018; Védrine, 2018). This was preserved despite – under President Nicolas Sarkozy – rejoining the military structures of NATO and eventually committing France to a more significant military role in Afghanistan. In quietly rebuilding its relations with the United States after the public clash over the Iraq war without seeming to suffer reputational damage in the Arab world, France had thus lived up to the history of adroit diplomacy so evident in the rapidity with which it had regained its standing in the Middle East after the difficult years of Suez and Algeria (1956–62). By 1963, de Gaulle was reasserting French independence in all directions, *'aux mains libres'*, including in particular acquiring a progressive image in the Third World (Vaisse, 2015; Bozo, 2012, pp. 98–100).

The realities of French *realpolitik* were not lost on Al Qaeda or on the emerging forces of ISIS, both more than capable of exploiting the growing numbers of *deracinés* among the Muslim young in France. In 2014 the ISIS spokesman called for Muslims in the West to kill their countrymen – 'especially the spiteful and filthy French' (cited in Gerges, 2017). The country's historical entanglement with the Maghreb ensured it could never have achieved the kind of immunity from attack that Italy seems to have secured. In certain quarters, at home and abroad, hostility was never far from the surface. Sarkozy's quinquennat from 2007 had certainly stoked anger among the *beurs* (the term used to refer to the children of North African immigrants) (Hussey, pp. 41–2). After all, as Minister of Interior during the riots of 2005, he had provoked an angry response by referring to young rioters as '*la racaille*' (scum) and adding: '*on va nettoyer au Kärcher la cité*' [We are going to hose down that estate].

The former president raised his country's profile significantly in the cauldron of Middle East politics by adopting a much more assertive foreign policy in 2011 with the attack on Libya which led to the fall of Muammar Qaddafi. This is an example of the law of unintended consequences, in that the intervention (with the United Kingdom, and with the US in support) was not the result of a decision to participate in the 'war on terror' – long criticized by France. It was in the first instance an attempt to live up to the UN's new doctrine of the 'responsibility to protect' by saving the population of Benghazi from Qaddafi's murderous rage. Behind the scenes, it is true, there were plenty who welcomed the opportunity for regime change in Libya, given long-running quarrels over Chad and the bringing down of a French airliner, but given the chaos of these first months of the Arab Spring, and Paris's embarrassment over its missteps in Egypt, these were hardly decisions made on the basis of a considered, rational, strategy. The fall-out from them, however, was to affect not Sarkozy but his successor, François Hollande.

Indeed, the halo effect of the 'humanitarian' intervention did not last long. Libya's descent into chaos simply exacerbated the image of arrogant Westerners misunderstanding Arab realities, while the power vacuum drew in jihadists from the Levant and elsewhere, creating a new base for terror attacks even closer to the European mainland. Soon afterwards Hollande expanded French foreign policy further, beginning the cycle of events from which it was to be almost impossible to escape, with the decisions to attack jihadism in its foreign bases rebounding through its own heightened profile and the consequent calls for French Muslims to take revenge at home. The first of these decisions came in January 2013 with what the strategic expert François Heisbourg dubbed 'a surprising little war' in Mali (Heisbourg (2013). In a short period over 4000 French troops joined Chadian and Malian forces to reclaim an area the size of Texas from jihadist groups which were setting up a pseudo-state in the north of Mali. They acted under the UN charter after a request from Mali's president. This seemed to be an example of swift, decisive and effective action. At the time of writing, however, the war has still not ended, justifying some of the early press questions about a possible quagmire. As Pezard and Shurkin (2017) have put it re Mali, 'France can't "go home", but it can't "go big" either'. It is locked into joint actions under the UN flag with Mali's neighbours in a fight against terror across the Sahel.

Then came the decision to fight ISIS in Iraq and Syria. President Hollande was thwarted by the British parliament in his wish to respond militarily to Bashar al-Assad's use of chemical weapons in 2013, but by September 2014 (after ISIS massacres of Assyrians and Yazidis) he had launched the air strikes of Operation Chammal against ISIS in Iraq. Given its historic interest in the Levant, Paris had become seriously alarmed by the success of the self-styled caliphate in controlling a wide swathe of territory, as well as by its inherent savagery. From September 2015 these strikes were extended to parts of Syria. When ISIS then claimed that the Bataclan killings in Paris of November that year had been ordered as a retaliation, Hollande immediately stepped up the air war. French forces also have been on the ground in Iraq and Libya, both for training purposes, but almost certainly also to conduct special operations, and as part of the regional struggle against jihadism in the Sahel.

This narrative shows clearly how French foreign policy, never inactive in the Mediterranean and Middle East, not only took on a much more forward character after 2011, but added four more areas of military intervention to that in Afghanistan – which was soon terminated, not least to release resources for the new combat zones. It will be noted that the new activism began before the wave of terrorist attacks on the Hexagon began in March 2012. Equally, while the decisions to act in Mali and against the Islamic State in Iraq and Syria arose out of a geopolitical strategy consistent with the campaign against the Afghan Taliban, they were subsequently given huge impetus by the new concern for security at home. The Merah killings in Toulouse had raised the alert to high levels, especially as there were further, smaller, incidents through 2013–14, but it was the shocking murders in January 2015 of *Charlie Hebdo* staff, followed by the killing of Jewish hostages at the *Hypercacher* kosher supermarket, that changed everything. This started the chain of events which led to 10,000 troops being directed to homeland security (one-seventh of the army's deployable force), and to a perception of serious crisis as the attacks on the Thalys express, in Paris again (the Bataclan and other locations) and then Nice in the summer of 2016 began to seem unstoppable (International Institute for Strategic Studies, 2016). By 2017 the Ministry of Defence's strategic review, under the heading 'A France exposed and engaged', was identifying jihadist terror and instability to the country's south as the main threats facing the state (Pannier and Schmitt, 2017).

Among the knock-on effects was the boost given to anti-Islamic feeling in France, and to the populist parties keen to exploit it. The fear also arose of terrorists using the cover of illegal immigration to arrive in the country (even if 'home-grown' terrorists turned out to be a greater problem). This in turn was exacerbated by the Syrian refugee crisis of September 2015 and the EU's failure to achieve a collective response to it. France de facto suspended the Schengen agreement on open borders, leading to persistent quarrels with Italy over the entry point at Ventimiglia. Foreign and domestic policies were becoming entangled in a series of dangerous feedback loops (Pezard and Shurkin, 2017).

Competing explanations

The two theatres of war – home and abroad – thus fed off each other, and continue to do so. This does not mean that there is a simple process of causation at work – at least beyond the determination of the French government to strike back at the perpetrators of terror wherever it can find them, and the wish of ISIS to hit the soft underbelly of its perceived enemies whenever there is the opportunity. The questions of why France was hit in 2012, and why it only then began to suffer from the problem which the UK had encountered seven years before – the violent alienation of some of its own young people – are complex ones. Yet at the same time they are problems which all too easily provoke polemics and binary positions, given how loaded they are with political baggage. Feelings about terror attacks, about social cohesion, about Islam and about foreign policy run high, affecting national and academic debate. This has been most visible in the debate between, and centred on, two French scholars who come at the issue from radically different starting points. Olivier Roy, Professor of Mediterranean Studies at the European University Institute in Florence, is an expert on comparative religions with particular reference to political Islam. He has field experience of Afghanistan and Tajikistan. Gilles Kepel is a professor in Paris at the *Institut d'études politiques*. He is an Arabist who specializes in political Islam. Both Roy and Kepel are leading international figures in their fields. They disagree strenuously, to the point where the debate has become personal and at times poisonous. Their personal antagonism is not relevant here, but their intellectual differences do provide an entry point into any attempt to understand the impact of foreign policy on French society, with specific reference to terrorism (Daumas, 2016; Nossiter, 2016).

In this context it is not possible to do justice to the subtleties on both sides, but at base the debate centres on whether Islam in France has simply been the vessel into which political, social and personal discontents have been poured; or, in contrast, whether it has an inherently political dimension which taken to extremes has necessarily subversive effects on a democracy such as France. Are French Muslims tragically misrepresented through the terrorist acts of a tiny minority of petty criminals and no-hopers, often personally disturbed and/or looking for salvation through religion – often discovered in prison – especially given that around 25 per cent are converts to Islam? Or should they be seen as providing a permissive environment for Salafism and jihadism, in part because of reactions against discrimination but also through an identification with the global Muslim *umma* in its struggles against Western hegemony?

The temptation for a detached observer is to split the difference between these two interpretations, or at least to emphasize their points of compatibility. Roy is right that many terrorists are lonely individuals rather than sophisticated strategists. They are often not even good Muslims, let alone informed Salafists. On the other hand they do self-identify as Muslims, and tend to resort to the battle cry '*Allahu Akbar*' (the Arabic words meaning 'God is the Greatest') when in action. Most also justify themselves in terms of resistance, both internationally and to the French state. Roy sees this as superficial, disguising the essential nihilism of the terrorist, half in love with death and revolt for their own sakes (Roy, 2017). Yet it is surely a mistake not to listen to what people say, about the world and about themselves. However shallow these self-understandings, they do inform us about motives, if not causes.

To be fair to Olivier Roy, he does not deny the relevance of Islam to the violence which has descended on France in recent years. But he argues that the driving force is not some form of radical Islam, as Kepel believes, but rather the converse, the 'Islamization of radicalism' (Roy, 2016, p. 6). The significant minority of converts among the jihadists is a key part of this argument, as it suggests that it is Islam's ability to offer a sense of purpose to a troubled life, plus the validation from a supportive group, which leads a young person to move from micro-criminality to taking up arms. Roy explicitly says that these youngsters are fundamentally no different from those in the United States who commit massacres in schools or universities. In other words, those in France with sociopathic or narcissistic tendencies have drifted into Jihadism instead of expressing their violence in other ways (Roy, 2016, p. 36). There is logic here, but it goes too far. Just as we need to find explanations for the fact that the USA stands out for its exceptionally high murder rate, so it is of great importance to understand the *pattern* of jihadist violence which has occurred in France to a higher degree than most other developed states, even those with significant Muslim populations, as well as its periodization – that is, its sudden recrudescence after 15 quiet years.

Kepel tends to explain the change in terms of the 'third generation' of Islam in France, stuck in an impasse after the lack of serious response to the (non-religious, non-political) riots of 2005 and unimpressed by inaction from established Muslim leaders. This new generation was thus susceptible both to inflammatory rhetoric from some imams at home and to the influence of international jihadism, which was moving away from Al Qaeda's geopolitical struggle against the United States towards an attempt to use the large numbers of poorly integrated young Muslims in Europe to hit the West in a different and easier way. The wars in Afghanistan and Iraq fostered this change of strategy and the networks needed to implement it, drawing a number of theatres of conflict together, culminating in the rise of ISIS (Kepel and Jardin, 2015, pp. 29–31).

But this argument too needs qualifying. As Kepel acknowledges, the elections of 2012, soon after Merah's attacks in Montauban and Toulouse, saw an unprecedented level of participation by Muslim voters, including from the 'third generation', helping the Socialist François Hollande into the Élysée Palace as president (Kepel, 2015; *Hexagone*, pp. 76–80, 106–10; Kemilat, 2017). They remembered Sarkozy's reaction to the riots of 2005 and hoped that Hollande would prove both more able to provide resources for the *banlieues* and more flexible on issues like the veil. As it turned out, he was to be seriously distracted by homeland insecurity. Hollande alone can scarcely be held responsible for the devastating attacks which occurred during his quinquennat. Even Sarkozy's combative attitude towards young rioters and hard line on the headscarf, designed to stop voters turning to the *Front National* but inevitably fomenting anger in the Muslim community, are not enough to explain the explosion of violence which followed his term in office. Indeed no single factor is enough, as both Kepel and Roy understand very well, notwithstanding their polemics.

One helpful approach to the complex issues of causation involved here is what has been termed the 'funnel approach'. 'This metaphor sees various explanations for a phenomenon as not mutually exclusive but instead as interdependent and ordered in terms of proximity in a causal chain'. At one end of that chain are foundational factors which are difficult to tie to the variations between particular cases. Their effects are felt, directly and indirectly, through processes which are nearer to events (Dennison and Talò, 2017). Thus the broad background factors are placed at the mouth of the notional funnel, which narrows through various intervening variables before arriving at its tip, where the outcome is to be found.

In the current context a simplified model would place at the mouth of a funnel the 'distal' or structural factors of the international and transnational environment, together with the fundamental characteristics of French society. One step closer in from the mouth of the funnel would be the variable of the specific socio-economic conditions of the present, including the lived experience of growing up as marginalized in a society and trying to make one's way in it. Here those with problems deriving from childhood and the family might either find solutions, or have further negative experiences which lead them to become seriously alienated from others, and perhaps the law. If, as has clearly been the case for many French *beurs*, deprivation and discrimination have placed serious obstacles before finding a job and a home, then even well-adjusted people can become alienated from majority French life, to say nothing of the already unbalanced.

Also to be conceptualized as intervening variables are the theatres of politics and policy – at home and abroad. At home a government can either be doing things to support an alienated minority or it can be neglectful, even hostile, while it is how policies are perceived, independent of their content or intentions, which can be decisive. In the case of France, as we have seen, from the riots of 2005 onwards the Muslim community became quickly disillusioned with Nicolas Sarkozy, leading to hopes being vested in voting him out of office (Kepel, 2017). This was the reaction of those with enough faith in the institutions of the State, and in their status as citizens, to participate in the electoral process. Unfortunately the same was not true of all the younger *banlieusards*, long disillusioned with the whole French establishment and seeing the rising influence of the *Front National* as an indication of Islamophobia in the wider population (Hussey, 2014, pp. 1–10, 43–4).

As for the theatre of international politics, for most people most of the time it remains a backcloth painted in broad colours, and emotionally distant. At certain times, however, and for certain groups, it comes into sharper focus and can act as a catalyst for events on the home front, as was the case after 2011 when French foreign policy became more assertive in the Middle East and North Africa. This is not to deny that France had a finger in most pies in the region before that. But its determination to operate below the horizon in the Algerian civil war of the 1990s, and its decision to stay out of the Iraq war in 2003, meant that it was not the focus of resentment with the West. When its profile changed therefore Al Qaeda and the rising force of ISIS immediately took notice, stirring up the latent hostility in many quarters to the way in which Paris had managed to maintain its influence in the region by siding with autocratic governments, made all too evident at the start of the Arab Spring by its patronizing dismissal of the uprising against Ben Ali in Tunisia.

The fast-moving events which followed the start of the Arab Spring and the scramble by Paris to adapt focused the minds of externally based jihadis on France as a target, leading them to activate sleeper cells inside the country. Mohammed Merah and those supporting him were the first such. But they also raised the consciousness of those alienated individuals who might have been searching for a reason to rebel against the State – or just to express their anger. Reports of French warplanes in action over Arab and/or Muslim countries, with the inevitable consequence of civilian casualties, made for easy jihadist propaganda. It also meant that the dedicated and professional cells were bound to find more recruits to their cause, in prisons, in radical mosques or simply in localities where the numbers of the disaffected were already high – as in the small town of Lunel in the Camargues, with a population of 25,000, from which around 20 young people left for the front in Syria (Kepel, 2015). Over France as a whole perhaps 1000 went to fight for the caliphate (Kepel, 2015, p. 16, pp. 176–201; Roy, 2016, pp. 20–1; Thomson, 2014).

International events, and France's own foreign policy actions, thus impacted upon an already unstable domestic environment in terms of the attitudes of the young *déracinés*, the sharp divisions over Muslim rights and *laïcité*, the growth of radical Islam in certain quarters, and an increasingly widespread lack of trust in the country's political leadership. Major terrorist attacks might have occurred again in any case as the result of slow-maturing resentments, but the interventions of 2011, and then 2013–14, probably acted as the triggers and intensifiers of the attacks. France had dramatically become the front line in Europe. Once the atrocities had begun, it was impossible to control or to predict the effects. A series of chain reactions led the government both to crack down hard at home and to redouble its efforts to hit at jihadist bases abroad. For their part the jihadists welcomed the chance to create a new order of problems for French society, and upped the ante, so far as resources allowed. They were probably surprised at the enormity of the spectacles they had been able to create, in part through attracting the kind of nihilist individual described by Olivier Roy. The scale of murder which proved possible in Paris at the Bataclan and in Nice on the *Promenade des Anglais* harkened back to the atrocities a decade or more before, in New York, Washington, Madrid and London.

At the tip of the funnel lie the 'proximate' causes of the outcome to be explained – in this case the wave of terrorism which hit France after 2012. Attacks cannot happen without human beings willing to carry them out. Some people who inflict horrific suffering for what they see as rational and moral reasons – like Mohammed Atta of 9/11 – are professional revolutionaries. Not even suicide bombers can be categorized as ipso facto disturbed. Others, however, do get drawn into violence through personal inadequacies and grievances. Their beliefs and psychological dispositions are important to understand. Still, simply noting post facto the existence of an undefined group of individuals with a propensity to violence is to beg the question of how big that group is and why attacks happen when they do. The extent of this very propensity is itself a reflection of the socio-political factors described above, both from the broad background and the intervening events and policy responses. Circumstances will determine whether, how and where the anger they feel will impact on society. Conversely, many narcissistic or nihilistic people exist in society without ever breaking the law, let alone engaging in political violence.

Conclusion

In recent years France has been subjected to a political maelstrom – not just that relating to the election of the Republic's youngest president in Emmanuel Macron, whose *En Marche!* then swept away the traditional political parties in parliamentary elections. It was the wave of terror attacks beginning in Montauban in 2012 that plunged both government and civil society into the period of fear and uncertainty which continues. It was also a period in which French foreign policy took some significant forward steps through military interventions in Libya, Mali, Iraq and Syria. As we have seen, the causal relationships between these two sets of events are complicated and not to be reduced to a simple model of A causing B. Yet it is equally clear that the two theatres of action are not wholly distinct and independent of each other. France's new activism drew the attention of jihadists and made it a natural target, while the war in Syria and Germany's decision to open its doors led to large numbers of refugees and other migrants heading for Europe, under the cover of which some jihadis were able to move freely. Equally, the presence of a significant minority of alienated young within France, both Muslims and non-Muslims seeking spiritual and practical meaning in their lives, meant that the dramas of international conflict quickly reverberated within the Hexagon. Such conditions did not make terror inevitable, but they certainly made it more likely.

The levels of causation between the domestic and the international are therefore at the same time separate and interrelated. Part of the problem is that while any given event, whether the bombing of a restaurant or of a jihadist camp, is likely to produce a specific reaction or retaliation, actions also flow from longer term processes. Domestically, that might mean the gradual accumulation of anger within a minority community, or the slow cultivation of sleeper groups. Externally, foreign policy traditions and patterns of commitment exist, such as France's African relationships, which do not fade away easily and thus condition choice when decisions have to be made. But *choice* is still a critical variable. It might have been likely that some disaffected cell would seek to kill the *Charlie Hebdo* staff, but it was not inevitable that the Kouachi brothers should have done so, or indeed that they would have succeeded, with the dramatic consequences which then flowed. There was always a good deal of contingency about who became involved, and who not. This is evident from the detailed data assembled by both Olivier Roy (2016) and Gilles Kepel (2015). Equally, one can imagine a version of recent history in which France had not intervened in either Libya or Mali. It might still have suffered devastating incidents on home soil, possibly triggering a military response abroad, but the particular chain of events with which we are familiar, and thus our debate about causes, would have been different.

The same is true of the related problem of micro versus macro analysis. It is a category mistake to focus on the psychology of individuals as a possible explanation for patterns of events like terrorist attacks, for that does not tell us why France suffered attacks later than Britain, and far more than Germany, also with a large Muslim population. Contextual issues, such as the Turkish origin of German Muslims, and the nature of German foreign policy, are key to understanding why rebels and psychotics in that country usually find other outlets than terrorism. Conversely, at the macro end of the scale, no generalization about the impact of France's foreign policy, its colonial history or its relationship with Islam can ever suffice to tell us why a particular individual came to sacrifice his or her life for the ISIS cause, or why Lunel or Strasbourg have been greater hotbeds of disaffection than Arles or Bordeaux. We need to combine the two levels of analysis, structural and close-grained, if we are to get beyond slogans and polemics.

We are left with two important and incontrovertible observations arising from the events of the last seven years. First, France now has a set of external policy commitments of greater significance than at any other time in the post-Cold War era. These not only will be difficult in themselves to resolve, but are immensely complicated by their domestic reverberations – the terrorist attacks which have already taken place and the possibility of others to come, putting the army on the streets just at the time of new commitments overseas. There is also the issue of the returning French jihadists, with its serious implications – for security, the law, and morality, to say nothing of integration into a society that is diverse but which resists the project of multiculturalism. Given these complexities, it is no surprise that President Macron has eschewed any go-it-alone version of foreign policy in favour of a pragmatic realism superficially in the tradition of 'Gaullo-Mitterandisme' popularized by Hubert Védrine. Both partners, and flexibility, are indispensable (Vaisse, 2017; Zaretsky, 2019).

This leads to the second observation, which comes from inverting the image: France also has to face up to some major challenges on the home front, on problems which in some respects have been ducked for years but in others are shockingly new. On the one hand both the place of Islam in a determinedly secular state and the condition of the *banlieues* demand urgent attention if the crumbling cement of civil society is not to lead to further disasters. The persistent *gilets jaunes* protests of 2019 are another indication of the pressure the system, and central government, is under (see Chapter 11). Each is shaped by the international context: ideas, preachers and third states in relation to French Muslims, and transnational contacts and media impacting on the young in their soulless suburbs. Yet ultimately these problems have to be resolved internally by public policy, at a time when trust in the institutions of the Fifth Republic has never been lower, and when the capacity of the presidency to effect change seems reduced (as discussed in Chapter 2). It is paradoxical that, in an era when *souverainiste* ideas are regaining popularity, France is no longer finding it so easy to pursue its distinctive approach to diversity and integration in isolation from wider trends. The elite consensus on the national interest is being undermined from within and without.

GUIDE TO FURTHER READING

CHAPTER 1

For a wide coverage of French politics and culture, Marion Demossier, David Lees, Aurélien Mondon and Nina Parish's (eds.) 2020 *Routledge Handbook of French Politics and Culture* is a good place to start. Alistair Cole's 2017 *French Politics and Society* (Routledge) provides complementary reading. Jocelyn Evans and Gilles Ivaldi's *The 2017 French Presidential Elections. A Political Reformation?* (2018, Palgrave) focuses more specifically on various aspects of the 2017 changing of the guard; and Robert Elgie, Emiliano Grossman and Amy G. Mazur's edited *Oxford Handbook of French Politics* (2020, paperback edition, Oxford University Press) is a uniquely wide-ranging work that provides a 'framework for a comparative politics of France'. Pascal Perrineau's 2017 edited volume *le Vote disruptif* (Sciences Po Les Presses) offers a series of French-language analyses of the 2017 elections that brought Emmanuel Macron to power.

CHAPTER 2

Alistair Cole's (2019) *Emmanuel Macron and the Two Years That Changed France* (Manchester University Press) and Sophie Pedder's (2019) *Revolution Française: Emmanuel Macron and the Quest to Reinvent a Nation* provide very good coverage and analysis of Macron's leadership. An even earlier publication on Macron's rise to power is journalist Adam Plowright's 2017 *The French Exception. Emmanuel Macron, the Extraordinary Rise and Risk* (Iconbooks). Grint's 2010 *Leadership: a Very Short Introduction* (Oxford University Press) covers a usefully wide range of leadership theories in a very accessible form. Marc Frangi offers an in-depth analysis of the French presidency, its powers and constraints (2018, l'Harmattan), and Christian Salmon's 2014 *Les derniers jours de la Ve République* (Fayard) depicts François Hollande's presidency as a sign of an institution – and regime – running out of steam.

CHAPTER 3

We refer readers to the following sources in particular: Clift and McDaniel (2017), Cole (2019), Haegel (2019), Lefebvre and Treille (2019) and Martinache and Sawicki (2020).

CHAPTER 4

We refer readers to the following sources in particular: Clift and McDaniel (2017), Durovic, (2019), Elgie (2018), Gil (2019), Gougou and Persico (2017), König and Waldvogel (2018), Ollion (2019) and Rescan (2019b).

CHAPTER 5

On the renewal of national identity in the RN (FN) and more generally far-right ideologies, we recommend Sylvain Crépon (2017) and Nicolas Lebourg (2017). For an overview of what the French social sciences say about the RN (FN), see Alexandre Dézé (2016). On how the *Rassemblement national* (*Front national*) appropriated the theme of secularism, we refer the reader to Sylvain Crépon (2020). On the radical right gender gap in France we refer to Amengay, Durovic and Mayer (2017).

CHAPTER 6

We refer readers to the following sources in particular: Raison du Cleuziou (2019), Raison du Cleuziou and Nicolas de Brémond d'Ars (2015) and Carnac, R. (2020).

CHAPTER 7

We refer readers to the following sources in particular: Bergström (2019), Borrillo and Lascoumes (2007), Borrillo and Fassin (2014), Butler (2002), Fassin and Memmi (2004), Gunther, Scott E. (2008), Lépinard (2020), Mossuz-Lavau (2002), Paternotte (2011), Perreau, Bruno (2014), Perreau, Bruno (2016) and Robcis, Camille (2013).

CHAPTER 8

We refer readers to the following sources in particular: Béal V., Renaud E. and Gilles P. (2015), Bezes and Le Lidec (2016), Cole, Harguindeguy, Pasquier, Stafford and de Visscher (2015), Dupuy and Pollard (2012), Epstein (2013), Evrard and Pasquier (2018), Hooghe and Marks (2003), Le Galès and Vezinat (2014), Pasquier, Simoulin and Weisbein (2013) and Poupeau (2017).

CHAPTER 9

We refer readers to the following sources in particular: Galonnier, J. (2019), Ghiles-Meilhac, S. (2015), Galonnier and Naudet, J. (2019), Anon (2019) and Legros, O. and Vtitale, T. (2011).

CHAPTER 10

On reform of labour law under the Hollande presidency, see Béroud (2018a) and Milner (2017). Howell (2011) provides a longer-term look at the politics of industrial relations regulation. Emmenegger et al. (2012) place labour law reform within a broader European context, using the concept of labour market dualisation. Béthoux and Mias (2019) use employer–employee panel data to show the impact of the recent trends in state regulation of collective bargaining, which the Macron labour reforms build upon and intensify. Palier (2010) provides an authoritative account of welfare reform in France and other European countries. For an assessment of the politics of pensions reform within a broader European context, see Naczyk (2016).

CHAPTER 11

The Yellow Vests movement has led to a wide array of publications, mostly in French at the time of writing, from different disciplinary angles, authored by scholars, collectives, but also activists and journalists. One English-language book is Turley (2019). To supplement Turley's exploration of the movement and larger resurgent populism, Cole (2019) provides an enlightening contextual analysis of France. Turning to French-language books, two are particularly useful for first-hand materials, comprising photographs, chronicles, texts of petitions, songs, slogans, spontaneous testimonies etc.: Grody and Hardoy (2020) and Patrick Farbiaz (2019). Confavreux (2019) offers another documents-based book, but enriched with the insights of 15 prominent French intellectuals such as Pierre Rosanvallon and Thomas Picketty. Finally, Adary (2019) and Huyghe, Desmaison and Liccia (2019) are two books that examine the role that social media and communication have played in bringing the once 'invisible' women and men under the spotlight.

CHAPTER 12

A recent, online-only overview of the subject can be found in Lequesne and Behal (2019). Rozenberg (2020) provides complementary reading. Various chapters in Elgie, Grossman and Mazur (2018, 2020) cover dimensions of France in the EU and the world, including Sabine Saurugger on 'The Europeanization of Public Policy in France: Actor-Centred Approaches'; Michel Goyer and Miguel Glatzer's 'Globalization: French Ambivalence as a Critical Case'; Bastien Irondelle, Jean Joana and Frédéric Mérand's 'Defense and Security Policy: Beyond French Exceptionalism'; Gordon D. Cumming's 'French Aid through the Comparative Looking Glass: A Representative, Deviant, or Agenda-Setting Case?'; and Craig Parson's 'France and the Evolution of European Integration: The Exemplary and Pivotal Case for

Broader Theories'. Samuel Faure (2020) takes an in-depth look at a specific dimension of France's international action – the politics and economics of its arms policy.

CHAPTER 13

We recommend the following sources in particular: Hill (2013), chapters 3, 7 and 9; Hussey (2014), pp. 391–405; Joppke (2009); Kepel with Jardin (2015), especially pp. 111–296; Laurence and Vaisse (2006), pp. 193–270; Leiken (2012), pp. 110–158; Roy (2017); and Vaisse (2017).

REFERENCES

Achin, C. and Lévêque, S. (2017) '"Jupiter is back": gender in the 2017 French presidential campaign', *French Politics*, 15, pp. 279–289.

Adary, A. (2019) *République-Bastille: sous les manifs, la com!* Du Palio.

Aghion, P., Bozio, A., Martin, P. and Pisani-Ferry, J. (2019) 'Réforme des retraites: l'alerte des économistes proches de Macron', *Le Monde*, 9 December.

Alemagna, L. (2019) 'Gilets jaunes: les 17 milliards à la loupe', *Libération*, 16th November.

Algan, Y., Beasley, E., Cohen, D., Foucault, M. and Péron, M. (2019) 'Qui sont les Gilets jaunes et leurs soutiens?', *Observatoire du Bien-être du CEPREMAP et CEVIPOF*, 2019 (3), pp. 1–13.

Allport, G. (1954) *The Nature of Prejudice*. Cambridge, Addison-Wesley.

Amengay, A., Durovic, A. and Mayer, N. (2017) 'L'impact du genre sur le vote Marine Le Pen', *Revue française de science politique*, 6, p. 67.

Amiel, D. and Emelien, I. (2019) *Le progrès ne tombe pas du ciel*. Paris, Fayard.

Amnesty International (2018) 'France: usage excessif de la force lors des manifestations des "Gilets jaunes"'. www.amnesty.fr/liberte-d-expression/actualites/usage-excessif-de-la-force-lors-des-manifestations (accessed 25 January 2020).

Andersen, R. and Evans, J-A. (2003) 'Values, cleavages and party choice in France, 1988–1995', *French Politics*, 1, pp. 83–114.

Anderson, P. (2017) 'The Centre can hold. The French Spring' *New Left Review*, May/June, 105. https://newleftreview.org/issues/ll105/articles/perry-anderson-the-centre-can-hold (accessed 21 October 2019).

Anon (2019) « Sonder et comprendre les opinions sur les immigrés et les minorités, *De Facto*, n°7, Mai 2019. http://icmigrations.fr/defacto/defacto-007/

Anon (2019) 'Marlène Schiappa: La PMA sera mise sur l'agenda parlementaire avant cet été', *Le Parisien*, 7 March.

Anses (2017) 'Étude individuelle nationale des consommations alimentaires 3 (INCA3)'. www.anses.fr/fr/system/files/NUT2014SA0234Ra.pdf (accessed 25 January 2020).

Araud, G. (2019) 'Invité de Léa Salamé, le 7/9, France Inter', 30 September. www.franceinter.fr/emissions/le-7-9/le-7-9-30-septembre-2019 (accessed 21 October 2019).

Arzheimer, K. (2009) 'Contextual factors and the Extreme right vote in Western Europe, 1980–2002', *American Journal of Political Science*, 53 (2), pp. 259–275.

Arzheimer, K. and Carter, E. (2006) 'Political opportunity structures and right-wing Extremist party success', *European Journal of Political Research*, 45 (3), pp. 419–443.

Asal, H. (2014) ' Islamophobie: la fabrique d'un nouveau concept. État des lieux de la recherche', *Sociologie*, 5 (1), pp. 13–29.

Assemblée nationale (2019) ' Rapport d'information sur les coûts économiques, sociaux et budgétaires des blocages, violences et dégradations commis en marge du mouvement des « gilets jaunes »'. 2167. www.assemblee-nationale.fr/15/pdf/rap-info/i2167.pdf (accessed 25 January 2020).

Assemblée nationale (2020) 'Projet de loi n°474 relatif à la bioéthique', 31 July. www.assemblee-nationale.fr/dyn/15/textes/l15t0474_texte-adopte-provisoire.pdf (accessed 8 August 2020).

Audureau, W. (2019) 'Le difficile comptage des rassemblements de 'gilets jaunes', *Le Monde*, 21 January. www.lemonde.fr/les-decodeurs/article/2019/01/21/le-difficile-comptage-des-rassemblements-de-gilets-jaunes_5412352_4355770.html (accessed 25 January 2020).

AutoPlus (2019) 'Top 5 des articles les plus lus sur Auto Plus'. www.autoplus.fr/actualite/Top-5-Actualites-2018-80-kmh-Radars-Controle-Technique-1534345.html (accessed 25 January 2020).

Bachelet, M. (2019) 'High Commissioner Bachelet calls on States to take strong action against inequalities'.

Badinter, R. and Lyon-Caen, A. (2015) *Le travail et la loi*. Paris, Fayard.

Bailly, J-P., Ballaoui, N., Canivet, G., Falque-Pierrotin, I. and Perrineau, P. (2019) *Rapport du Collège des garants du grand débat national*. https://granddebat.fr/media/default/0001/01/ee2712c96c5035c3c2913174a7b5535fc52642a4.pdf

Barthélémy, J. and Cette, G. (2015) *Réformer le droit du travail*. Paris, Odile Jacob.

Basta ! (2019) 'Base de données'. https://bastamag.net/webdocs/police/ (accessed 25 January 2020).

Baturo, A. and Elknick, J. A. (2017) 'On the importance of personal sources of power in politics: comparative perspectives and research agenda', *French Politics*, 15, pp. 505–525.

Baverez, N. (2005) *La France qui tombe*. Paris, Perrin.

BBC News (2015) 'Charlie Hebdo attack: teachers tell of classroom struggle', 30 January. www.bbc.co.uk/news/world-europe-31037598 (accessed 25 January 2020).

Béal, V., Epstein, R. and Pinson, G. (2015) 'La circulation croisée. Modèles, labels et bonnes pratiques dans les rapports centre/périphérie', *Gouvernement et action publique*, 3 (1), pp. 103–127.

Béatrice, M. (2020) 'Face à la crise, les régions se mobilisent', *Le Monde*, 7 May.

Beauregard, J. and Lebourg, N. (2012) *Dans l'ombre dès Le Pen. Une histoire des numéros 2 du FN*. Paris, Nouveau Monde Éditions.

Bedock, C. (2017) *Reforming Democracy: Institutional Engineering in Western Europe*. Oxford, Oxford University Press.

Bell, D. S. and Gaffney, J. (eds.) (2013) *Political Leadership in France: From Charles de Gaulle to Nicolas Sarkozy*. Basingstoke, Palgrave.

Benedek, T. (1959) 'Parenthood as a developmental phase: a contribution to the Libido theory', *Journal of the American Psychoanalytic Association*, 7, pp. 389–417.

Bennett, W. L. and Segerberg, A. (2014) *The Logic of Connective Action. Digital Media and the Personalization of Contentious Politics*. New York, Cambridge University Press.

Bensimon, D. and Verdès-Leroux, J. (1970) 'Les Français et le problème juif. [Analyse secondaire d'un sondage de l'I.F.O.P]', *Archives de Sciences Sociales des Religions*, 29, pp. 53–91.

Béraud, C. and Portier, P. (2015) *Métamorphoses catholiques: acteurs, enjeux et mobilisations depuis le mariage pour tous*. Paris, MSH.

Berger, M. (2014) 'Homoparentalité et développement affectif de l'enfant', *Le Débat*, 180 (3), pp. 139–146.

Bergström, M. (2019) *Les nouvelles lois de l'amour. Sexualité, couple et rencontres au temps du numérique*. Paris, La Découverte.

Bernard, M. (2018) 'La reconstruction de la droite selon Laurent Wauquiez ou les risques de l'affirmation identitaire', *Cités*, 74 (6), pp. 189–197.

Béroud, S. (2018a) 'French trade unions and the mobilisation against the El Khomri law in 2018: a reconfiguration of strategies and alliances', *Transfer*, 24 (2), pp. 179–193.

Béroud, S. (2018b) 'Macron et les syndicats: Il y a une volonté de réduire les bastions syndicaux', *Le Monde*, 30 June.

Béroud, S. and Pernot, J-M. (2018) 'Trade union expertise in public policy'. In C. Halpern, P. Hassenteufel and P. Zittoun (eds.) *Policy Analysis in France*. Bristol, Policy Press, pp. 261–275.

Béroud, S., Giraud, B. and Yon, K. (2018) *Sociologie politique des syndicats*. Paris, Armand Colin.

Besson, P. (2017) *Un personnage de roman*. Paris, Juillard.

Béthoux, E. and Mias, A. (2019) 'How does state-led decentralization affect workplace employment relations? The French case in a comparative perspective', *European Journal of Industrial Relations*, pp. 1–17 (online).

Bezes, P. and Le Lidec, P. (2010) 'L'hybridation du modèle territorial français: RGPP et réorganisations de l'Etat territorial', *Revue française d'administration publique*, 136, pp. 919–942.

Bezes, P. and Le Lidec, P. (2016) 'Politiques de la fusion. Les nouvelles frontières de l'État territorial', *Revue française de science politique*, 66 (3), pp. 507–541.

Bioulac, B. (1992) *Rapport d'information déposé par la Commission des affaires culturelles, familiales et sociales et la Commission des lois constitutionnelles, de la législation et de l'administration générale de la République sur la bioéthique*. Paris, Assemblée Nationale, p. 2565.

Blondiaux, L. (2019) ' Le grand débat a démontré qu'ouvrir le champ de la participation ne mène pas forcément au chaos', *Le Monde*, 8th April 2019.

Bonoli, G. and Palier, B. (2000) 'How do welfare states change? Institutions and their impact on the politics of welfare state reform in Western Europe', *European Review*, 8 (3), pp. 333–352.

Borne, D. (2014) *Quelle histoire pour la France?* Paris, Gallimard.

Bornschier, S. and Kriesi, H. (2012) 'The populist right, the working class and the changing face of class politics'. In J. Rydgren (ed.) *Class Politics and the Radical Right*. London, Routledge, pp. 10–29.

Bornschier, S. and Lachat, R. (2009) 'The evolution of the French political space and party system', *West European Politics*, 32 (2), pp. 360–383.

Borrillo, D. (2014) 'Biologie et filiation: les habits neufs de l'ordre nature', *Contemporary French Civilization*, 39 (3), pp. 303–319.

Borrillo, D. (2018) *La Famille par contrat. La construction politique de l'alliance et de la parenté*. Paris, Presses universitaires de France.

Borrillo, D. and Fassin, É. (eds.) (2014) *Contemporary French Civilization*, 39 (3), special issue, 2014.

Borrillo, D. and Lascoumes, P. (2007) *Amours égales? Le PACS, les homosexuels et la gauche*. Paris, La Découverte.

Borrillo, D. and Pitois, T. (1998) 'Adoption et homosexualité: analyse critique de l'arrêt du Conseil d'État du 9 octobre 1996'. In D. Borrillo (ed.) *Homosexualités et droit*. Paris, Presses universitaires de France, pp. 141–151.

Boudou, B. (2018) *Le Dilemme des frontières. Éthique et politique de l'immigration*. Paris, Éditions de l'EHESS.

Bourmaud, F-X. (2017) *Emmanuel Macron – Les Coulisses D'une Victoire*. Paris, L'archipel.

Bozo, F. (2012) *La Politique Étrangère de la France*. Paris, Flammarion.

Braibant, G. (1988) 'De l'éthique au droit', *Notes et études documentaires*, 4588. Paris, La Documentation française.

Bréchon, P., Gonthier, F. and Astor, S. (eds.) (2019) *La France des valeurs. Quarante ans d'évolutions*. Grenoble, Presses universitaires de Grenoble.

Breteau, M. and Sénécat, A. (2018) 'Un an après son élection, Emmanuel Macron tient-il ses promesses de campagne?', *Le Monde*, 7 May.

Broqua, C. (2006) *Agir pour ne pas mourir ! Act Up, les homosexuels et le sida*. Paris, Presses de Sciences Po.

Brouard, S. and Tiberj, V. (2011) *As French as Everyone Else?* Philadelphia, Temple University Press.

Brouard, S., Vasilopoulos, P. and Foucault, M. (2018) 'How terrorism affects political attitudes: France in the aftermath of the 2015–2016 attacks', *West European Politics*, 41 (5), pp. 1073–1099.

Brubakers, R. (2017) 'Between nationalism and civilizationism. The European Populist Movement in comparative perspective', *Ethnic and Racial Studies*, 40 (8), pp. 1191–1226.

Bruneteaux, P. (1996) *Maintenir l'ordre*. Paris, Presses de la fondation nationale des sciences politiques.

Bueno de Mesquita, Bruce, Alastair Smith, Randolph M. Siverson, et James D. Morrow. 2005. *The Logic of Political Survival*. Cambridge: MIT Press. Braconnier : online interview of Céline Braconnier for *Le Monde*: www.lemonde.fr/election-presidentielle-2017/article/2016/11/30/on-entend-beaucoup-dire-que-cette-fois-ci-aller-voter-n-ira-pas-de-soi_5040952_4854003.html

Burns, J-M. (1978) *Leadership*. New York, Harper Collins.

Butler, J. (2002) 'Is kinship always already heterosexual?', *Differences: A Journal of Feminist Cultural Studies*, 13 (1), pp. 14–44.

Calavrezo, O., Duhautois, R. and Walkowiak, E. (2009) 'Chômage partiel et licenciements économiques, Centre d'études de l'emploi', *Connaissance de l'emploi*, 63.

Camus, J-Y. and Lebourg, N. (2015) *Les droites extrêmes en Europe*. Paris, Seuil.

Carley, R. F. (2019) *Autonomy, Refusal and the Black Bloc. Positioning Class Analysis in Critical and Radical Theory*. London and New York, Rowman & Littlefield.

Carnac, R. (2020) 'Imaginary enemy, real wounds: counter-movements, 'gender theory', and the French Catholic church', *Social Movement Studies*, 19 (1), pp. 63–81.

Caron, J-C. (2002) *L'été: chronique de la révolte populaire en France (1841)*. Paris, Aubier.

Castelli, G. and Morales, L. (2017) 'The politicization and securitization of migration in Europe: public opinion, political parties and the immigration issue'. In P. Bourbeau (ed.) *Handbook on Migration and Security*. Cheltenham, Edgar Elgar Publishing, pp. 273–295.

Cerny, P. (1997) 'Paradoxes of the competition state: the dynamics of political globalization', *Government and Opposition*, 32 (2), pp. 251–274.

CEVIPOF and OpinionWay (2019) 'Baromètre de la confiance en politique. Vague 10. Janvier 2019'. www.opinion-way.com/en/opinion-political-surveys/published-surveys/politique/barometre-de-la-confiance-en-politique.html (accessed 25 January 2020).

Chabal, E. (2015) *A divided Republic: Nation, State and Citizenship in Contemporary France*. Cambridge, Cambridge University Press.

Chabas, C. (2019) 'Grève aux urgences: c'est la révolte des petites mains de l'hôpital', *Le Monde*, 10 August.

Chapuis, N. (2018) 'Macron et les mots choisis de la réforme', *Le Monde*, 23 March.

Chauvin, A., Bourges, J-L., Korobelnik, J-F., Paques, M., Lebranchu, P. and Villeroy, F. (2019) 'Ocular injuries caused by less-lethal weapons in France', *The Lancet*, 394 (10209), pp. 1616–1617.

Chiche, J., Le Hay, V., Chanvril, F. and Lascoumes, P. (2010) 'Du favoritisme à la corruption: les définitions concurrentes de la probité publique'. In P. Lascoumbes (ed.) *Favoritisme et corruption à la française*. Paris, Presses de Sciences Po, pp. 73–106.

Chirac, J. (1997) 'Remise au Président de la République du rapport du Comité consultatif national d'éthique sur le clonage humain', 29 April. http://discours.vie-publique.fr/notices/977012800.html (accessed 12 June 2018).

Chopin, T. (2018) 'Emmanuel Macron, la France et l'Europe', « Le retour de la France en Europe »: à quelles conditions? Fondation Robert Schuman, Questions d'Europe 473, 14 May. www.robert-schuman.eu/fr/doc/questions-d-europe/qe-473-fr.pdf (accessed 13 August 2019).

Cicchelli, V., Galland, O., de Maillard, J. and Misset, S. (2007) 'Retour sur les violences urbaines de l'automne 2005: Émeutes et émeutiers à Aulnay-sous-Bois', *Horizons stratégiques*, 3 (1), pp. 98–119.

Clift, B. and McDaniel, S. (2017) 'Is this crisis of French socialism different? Hollande, the rise of Macron, and the reconfiguration of the left in the 2017 presidential and parliamentary elections', *Modern & Contemporary France*, 25 (4), pp. 403–415.

Cole, A. (ed.) (1990) *French Political Parties in Transition*. Aldershot, Dartmouth.

Cole, A. (2006) 'Decentralization in France: central steering, capacity building and identity construction', *French Politics*, 4 (1), pp. 31–57.

Cole, A. (2012a) 'The French state and its territories', *Public Administration*, 90 (2), pp. 335–350.

Cole, A. (2012b) 'The Fast Presidency? Nicolas Sarkozy and the political institutions of the Fifth Republic', *Contemporary French and Francophone Studies*, 16 (3), pp. 311–321.

Cole, A. (2014) 'Not saying, not doing: convergences, contingencies and causal mechanisms of state reform and decentralisation in Hollande's France', *French Politics*, 12 (2), pp. 104–135.

Cole, A. (2017) *French Politics and Society*. Routledge.

Cole, A. (2019) *Emmanuel Macron and the Two Years That Changed France*. Manchester, Manchester University Press.

Cole, A. and Pasquier, R. (2017) 'Réforme régionale et gouvernance multi-niveaux: la défiance des Français', *Pouvoirs Locaux*, 109 (1), pp. 3–7.

Cole, A. and Raymond, G. (eds.) (2006) *Redefining the French Republic*. Manchester, Manchester University Press.

Cole, A., Harguindéguy, J-B., Stafford, I., Pasquier, R. and de Visscher, C. (2015) 'States of convergence in territorial governance', *Publius: The Journal of Federalism*, 45 (2), pp. 297–321.

Cole, A., Pasquier, R. and de Visscher, C. (2016) 'Les régions européennes face à la crise: une grille de lecture comparative', *Revue internationale de politique comparée*, 23 (3), pp. 285–300.

Cole, A., Fox, S., Pasquier, R. and Stafford, I. (2018) 'Political trust in France's multi-level government', *Journal of Trust Research*, 8 (1), pp. 45–67.

Collectif des universitaires contre les répressions policières (2019) 'Universitaires, nous nous déclarons « complices » des gilets jaunes'. www.change.org/p/emmanuel-macron-undefined-6f0c402e-d2b0-4163-9a87-25e5ee065f14?source_location=petitions_browse

Combrexelle, J-D. (2015) *La négociation, le travail et l'emploi*. Paris, La Documentation Française.

Comité Consultatif National d'Éthique (2005) *Avis no90. Accès aux origines, anonymat et secret de la filiation*. Paris, Comité Consultatif National d'Éthique.

Comité Consultatif National d'Éthique (2017) *Avis no126 sur les demandes sociétales de recours à l'assistance médicale à la procréation*. Paris, Comité Consultatif National d'Éthique.

Comité Consultatif National d'Éthique (2018) *Rapport de synthèse du Comité Consultatif National d'Éthique, Opinions du Comité Citoyen*. Paris, Comité Consultatif National d'Éthique.

Comité des Constructeurs Français d'Automobiles (2019) *L'Industrie automobile francaise. Analyse et statistiques 2019*. https://ccfa.fr/wp-content/uploads/2019/09/ccfa-2019-fr-web-v2.pdf (accessed 31 January 2020).

Confavreux, J. (ed.) (2019) *Le fond de l'air est jaune: comprendre une révolte inédite*. Paris, Seuil.

Conseil Constitutionnnel (n.d.-a) 'Texte intégral de la Constitution du 4 octobre 1958 en vigueur'. www.conseil-constitutionnel.fr/le-bloc-de-constitutionnalite/texte-integral-de-la-constitution-du-4-octobre-1958-en-vigueur (accessed 21 April 2020).

Conseil Constitutionnnel (n.d.-b) 'Texte intégral de la Constitution du 4 octobre 1958 en vigueur'. www.conseil-constitutionnel.fr/le-bloc-de-constitutionnalite/texte-integral-de-la-constitution-du-4-octobre-1958-en-vigueur (accessed 21 April 2020).

Conseil d'État (2014) *Association Juristes pour l'enfance et autres*, 12 December. Paris, Conseil d'Etat.

Conseil d'État (2019) *Arrêt n°411984*, 2nd and 7th Chambers, 31 July.

Conseil d'Orientation des Retraites (COR) (2018) *Évolutions et perspectives des retraites en France. Rapport annuel 2018*. Paris, COR.

Corlay, A. (2017) 'Election présidentielle: Ve ou Vie République?', 5 April.

Council of Europe (2019) *Mémorandum sur le maintien de l'ordre et la liberté de réunion dans le contexte du mouvement des « gilets jaunes » en France*. Strasbourg, Council of Europe.

Cour de cassation (1989) 'Chambre sociale', *Juris-Classeur, Semaine Juridique*, 90, II, 21553, 11 July.

Cour de cassation (2006) *Affaire Peter*, Ist civil chamber, 7 April.

Cour de cassation (2014) *Avis n°15011*, 22 September.

Cour de cassation (2015) *Arrêt n°619*, Plenary Court, 3 July.

Cour de cassation (2019a) *Arrêt n°648*, 4 October.

Cour de cassation (2019b) *Arrêt n°1113*, 18 December.

Courtois, G. (2018) 'Après un an de présidence Macron, l'optimisme s'est dissipé', *Le Monde*, 9 July.

Crépon, S. (2012) *Enquête au cœur du nouveau Front national*. Paris, Nouveau Monde Editions.

Crépon, S. (2015) 'La politique des mœurs au Front national'. In S. Crépon, A. Dézé and N. Mayer (eds.) *Les faux semblants du Front national. Sociologie d'un parti politique*. Paris, Presses de Science Po, pp. 185–205.

Crépon, S. (2017) 'Faces of the national front (1972–2015)'. In P. Blanchard, N. Nicolas Bancel and D. Thomas (eds.) *The Colonial Legacy in France. Fracture, Rupture and Apartheid.* Indiana University Press, pp. 341–350.

Crépon, S. (2020) 'Le Front national et la laïcité. Retour sur des usages contradictoires'. In V. Amiraux, D. Koussens and C. Mercier (eds.) *Nouveaux vocabulaires de la laïcité.* Paris, Classiques Garnier, pp. 37–57.

Cristiani, D. and Fabbiani, R. (2013) *From Disfunctionality to Disaggregation and Back? The Malian Crisis, Local Players and European Interests*, IAI Working Paper, 13 (8). Rome, Istituto Affari Internazionali, p. 13.

CSA (2018) *Évaluation du niveau de connaissance des ordonnances travail et perception des leur déploiement*, Study no. n°1800160, June, CSA/ France Stratégie.

Cuchet, G. (2018) *Comment notre monde a cessé d'être chrétien. Anatomie d'un effondrement.* Paris, Seuil.

Daily Mail (2019) 'Coming soon to a protest near you: Chilean demonstrators use LASERS on police as they copy dazzling tactics from Hong Kong protestors', 16 November. Available at www.dailymail.co.uk/news/article-7692483/Chilean-demonstrators-use-LASERS-police-copy-dazzling-tactics-Hong-Kong-protestors.html (consulted 4 March 2020).

Damon, J. (2017) 'Le paritarisme: définitions et délimitations', *Regards*, 52 (2), pp. 85–97.

Daumas, C. 'Olivier Roy et Gilles Kepel, querelle français sur le jihadisme', *Libération*, 15 April 2016.

Davet, G. and Lhomme, F. (2016) *Un Président ne devrait pas dire ça.* Paris, Stock.

Davet, G. and Lhomme, F. (2018) *Inch'Allah, l'islamisation à visage découvert.* Paris, Fayard.

Davet, G. and Lhomme, F. (2019) 'Francois Hollande, la faute originelle', *Le Monde*, 27 August.

de Jarcy, X. and Remy, V. (2010) 'Comment la France est devenue moche', *Télérama*. Available at: www.telerama.fr/monde/comment-la-france-est-devenue-moche,52457.php (consulted 4 March 2020).

Debord, G. (1967) *La Société du spectacle.* Paris, Buchet-Chastel.

Decharme, B. (2018) 'En cinq ans, 40 000 couples homosexuels se sont mariés', *Le Monde*, 23 April.

Défenseur des droits (2019) 'Décision du Défenseur des droits no. 2019-029'. Available at: https://juridique.defenseurdesdroits.fr/doc_num.php?explnum_id=18403 (consulted 4 March 2020).

Della Pergola, S. (2016) *World Jewish Population 2016.* https://doi.org/10.1007/978-3-319-46122-9_17

Della Sudda, M. and Avanza, M. (eds.) (2017) 'Ripostes catholiques', *Genre, sexualité & société*, n°18, Autumn.

Deloye, Y. (2006) *Les voix de Dieu.* Paris, Fayard.

Demossier, M., et al. *The Routledge Handbook of French Politics and Culture.* London, Routledge.

Dennison, J. and Talò, T. (2017) *Explaining Attitudes to Immigration in France.* Robert Schuman Centre for Advanced Studies, working paper 2017/25. Fiesole, European University Institute, p. 7.

Derrien, C. and Nedelec, C. (2017) *Les Macron.* Paris, Fayard.

Dézé, A. (2012) *Le Front national: à la conquête du pouvoir?* Paris, Armand Colin, 192 p.

Dézé, A. (2015) 'La construction médiatique de la "nouveauté" FN'. In S. Crépon, A. Dézé and N. Mayer (eds.) *Les faux semblants du Front national. Sociologie d'un parti politique*. Paris, Presses de Science Po, pp. 455–504.

Dézé, A. (2016) *Comprendre le Front national*. Paris, Bréal.

Dignan, A. (2019) *Brave New Work: Are You Ready to Reinvent Your Organisation?* Penguin.

Donegani, J-M. (1993) *La liberté de choisir. Pluralisme religieux et pluralisme politique dans le catholicisme contemporain*. Paris, FNSP.

Dovidio, J., Gaertner, S., and Pearson, A. (2016) 'Aversive racism and contemporary bias'. In C. Sibley and F. Barlow (eds.) *The Cambridge Handbook of the Psychology of Prejudice*. Cambridge, Cambridge University Press, pp. 267–294.

Drake, H. (2000) *Jacques Delors: Perspectives on a European Leader*. London, Routledge.

Drake, H. (2004) 'France in free fall? French perspectives on the Astérix complex', *French Politics*, 2, pp. 221–233.

Drake, H. (2008) 'The European fifth republic', *Contemporary French and Francophone Studies*, 12 (2), pp. 193–201.

Drake, H. (2011) *Contemporary France*. London, Red Globe Press.

Drake, H. (2013a) 'Everywhere and nowhere: Europe and the World in the French 2012 elections', *Parliamentary Affairs*, 66 (1), pp. 124–141.

Drake, H. (2013b) 'France and the European Union'. In *Developments in French Politics 5*. London, Red Globe Press, pp. 310–332.

Drake, H. (2017) 'France, Britain and Brexit'. In U. Staiger and B. Martill (eds.) *Brexit and Beyond: Rethinking the Futures of Europe*. UCL Press, pp. 97–104.

Drake, H. (2018a) 'What if it's not all about Macron'? Loughborough University London, 7th December. https://blog.lboro.ac.uk/london/diplomatic-studies/what-if-its-not-all-about-macron (accessed 21 October 2019).

Drake, H. (2018b) 'Is France having a moment? Emmanuel Macron and the politics of disruption', *Political Quarterly Blog*, 14 September. https://politicalquarterly.blog/2018/09/14/is-france-having-a-moment-emmanuel-macron-and-the-politics-of-disruption/

Drake, H. (2020) 'Political leadership in contemporary France: the case of Emmanuel Macron'. In A. Horvath, A. Szakolczai and M. Marangudakis (eds.) *Modern Leaders. In Between Charisma and Trickery*. Routledge.

Dudink, S. (2013) « Les nationalismes sexuels et l'histoire raciale de l'homosexualité », *Raisons politiques*, n°49, février, pp. 43–54.

Dufresne, D. (2007) *Maintien de l'ordre*. Paris, Hachette.

Dufresne, D. (2019) 'Six mois d'«Allô Place Beauvau»: chronique des violences d'Etat', *Mediapart*. www.mediapart.fr/journal/france/170519/six-mois-d-allo-place-beauvau-chronique-des-violences-d-etat

Dupoirier, E. and Sauger, N. (2010) 'Four rounds in a row: the impact of presidential election outcomes on legislative elections in France', *French Politics*, 8 (1), pp. 21–41.

Dupré, R., Jaxel-Truer, P. and Laurent, S. (2020) 'Les ARS, boucs émissaire de la crise sanitaire', *Le Monde*, 26 April.

Dupuis-Déri, F. (2013) *Who's Afraid of the Black Blocs? Anarchy in Action Around the World*. Toronto, Between the Lines.

Dupuy, C. and Pollard, J. (2012) 'La comparaison de politiques publiques infranationales: méthodes et pratiques', 19 (2), pp. 7–14.

Durovic, A. (2019) 'The French elections of 2017: shaking the disease?', *West European Politics*, 42 (7), pp. 1487–1503.

Duverger, M. (1964) 'L'éternel marais. Essai sur le centrisme français', *Revue française de science politique*, 14 (1), pp. 33–51.

DW (2019) 'How Hong Kong protests are inspiring movements worldwide'. www.dw.com/en/how-hong-kong-protests-are-inspiring-movements-worldwide/a-50935907

Écoiffier, M. (2013) 'Frigide Barjot mobilise les antis pour le 26 mai', *Libération*, 31 March.

Ehrhard, T. (2016) 'Le Front national face aux modes de scrutin: entre victoire sous conditions et influences sur le système partisan'. *Pouvoirs*, no. 157 (April), pp. 85–103.

EIU (Economist Intelligence Unit) (2013) 'Democracy Index 2011: democracy under Stress'. Available at www.eiu.com/public/topical_report.aspx?campaignid=DemocracyIndex2011 (accessed 13 August 2019).

Elabe & BFMTV (2019a) Les Français et la restitution du « Great débat national », *L'opinion en direct*. https://elabe.fr/emmanuel-macron-ne-parvient-pas-a-convaincre/ (accessed 31 November 2019).

Elabe & BFMTV (2019b) 'Les Français et les « gilets jaunes » un an après', *L'opinion en direct*. https://elabe.fr/gilets-jaunes-1an-apres/ (accessed 31 November 2019).

Elgie, R. (1995) *Political Leadership in Liberal Democracies*. London, Red Globe Press.

Elgie, R. (ed.) (2000) *Semi-Presdientialism in Europe*. Oxford: Oxford University Press.

Elgie, R. (2004) 'The political executive'. In A. Cole, P. Le Gales and J. Levy (eds.) *Developments in French Politics 3*. London, Red Globe Press, pp. 95–123.

Elgie, R. (2013) 'The French presidency'. In A. Cole, S. Meunier and V. Tiberj (eds.) *Developments in French Politics 5*, pp. 19–35

Elgie, R. (2018) 'The Election of Emmanuel Macron and the New French Party System: a return to the Éternel Marais?', *Modern & Contemporary France*, 26 (1), pp. 15–29.

Elgie, R., Grossman, E. and Mazur, A. (eds.) (2018; 2020 paperback) *The Oxford Handbook of French Politics*. Oxford, Oxford University Press.

Elysée (2017) 'Discours du Président de la République devant le Parlement réuni en congrès'. www.elysee.fr/emmanuel-macron/2017/07/03/discours-du-president-de-la-republique-devant-le-parlement-reuni-en-congres

Elysée (2019a) 'Lettre aux Français'. www.elysee.fr/emmanuel-macron/2019/01/13/lettre-aux-francais

Elysée (2019b) 'Une nouvelle donne pour l'Europe', 28 May. www.elysee.fr/emmanuel-macron/2019/05/28/elections-europeennes-nouvelle-donne-europe (accessed 21 October 2019).

EM! (2017) 'Emmanuel Macron. Discours du Congrès, 3 juillet'. https://en-marche.fr/articles/discours/emmanuel_macron_discours_du_congrés_3_juillet

Emanuele, V., De Sio, L. and Michel, E. (2017) 'A shared agenda, with a right-wing slant: public opinion priorities towards the French Presidential Election'. In L. De Sio and A. Paparo (eds.) *The Year of Challengers? The CISE e-Book on Issues, Public Opinion, and Elections in 2017*. Rome, CISE, pp. 63–68.

Emmenegger, P. (2014) *The Power to Dismiss. Trade Unions and the Regulation of Job Security in Western Europe*. Oxford, Oxford University Press.

Emmenegger, P., Häusermann, S., Palier, B. and Seeleib-Kaiser, M. (eds.) (2012) *The Age of Dualization: The Changing Face of Inequality in Deindustrializing Societies*. Oxford, Oxford University Press.

Epstein, R. (2005) 'Gouverner à distance. Quand l'Etat se retire des territoires', *Esprit*, 11, pp. 96–111.

Epstein, R. (2013) *La rénovation urbaine*. Paris, Presses de Sciences Po.

Eribon, D. (2004) *Sur cet instant fragile... Carnets. Janvier-août 2004*. Paris, Fayard.

États généraux de la bioéthique (2018) 'Procréation et société', *Site des États généraux de la bioéthique*, 31 January.

Euractiv (2016) www.euractiv.com/section/elections/news/hollande-in-favour-of-expelling-member-states-with-right-wing-governments/ (accessed 24 February).

Euractiv (2019) 'Why the European Parliament rejected Sylvie Goulard', 11 October. www.euractiv.com/section/future-eu/news/why-the-european-parliament-rejected-sylvie-goulard/ (accessed 21 October 2019).

European Court of Human Rights (2014) *Mennesson contre France* n°65192/1 and *Labassee contre France*, n°65941/11, 26 June.

European Court of Human Rights (2016) *Foulon v. France* n°9063/14 and *Bouvet v. France* n°10410/14, 21 July.

European Research Council (2019) 'The Effect of Manifestations of Religion in the Public Space on Sociopolitical Integration of Minority-Religion Immigrants' (European Commission). Available at https://cordis.europa.eu/project/id/804031/fr

European Union (EU) (2017) 'Council Recommendation of 11 July 2017 on the 2017 National Reform Programme of France and delivering a Council opinion on the 2017 Stability Programme of France', *Official Journal of the European Union*, C231/36.

Evans, J., and Ivaldi, G. (2017) 'An atypical "honeymoon" election? Contextual and strategic opportunities in the 2017 French Legislative Elections', *French Politics*, 15 (3), pp. 322–339.

Evans, J., and Ivaldi, G. (2018) *The 2017 French Presidential Elections. A Political Reformation?* Basingstoke, Palgrave.

Evrard, A. and Pasquier, R. (2018) 'Territorialiser la politique de l'éolien maritime en France. Entre injonctions étatiques et logiques d'appropriation', *Gouvernement & action publique*, 4 (4), pp. 63–91.

Evans, J. and Ivald, G. (2018a) 'Campaign Events and Political Change'. In *The 2017 French Presidential Elections: A Political Reformation?*, by Jocelyn Evans and Gilles Ivaldi, 97–122. London: Palgrave Macmillan.

Farbiaz, P. (2019) *Les Gilets jaunes: Documents et textes*. Croquant.

Fassin, D. and Defossez, A-C. (2019) 'An Improbable Movement? Macron's France and the rise of the Gilets Jaunes', *New Left Review*, no. 115 (February 2019), pp. 77–92.

Fassin, D. and Memmi, D. (eds.) (2004) *Le gouvernement des corps*. Paris, Éd. de l'EHESS.

Faucher, F. and Truc, G. (eds.) (2019) *Réagir aux attentats*. Paris, PUF.

Faure, S. (2020) *Avec ou sans l'Europe. Le dilemme de la politique française d'armement*. éditions de l'Université de Bruxelles.

Faye, O. (2020) 'Macron en première ligne face à l'opinion', *Le Monde*, 14 April.

Ferras, B. (2017) 'Le financement de la Sécurité sociale et de la protection sociale: entre autonomie et indépendance, une gouvernance particulière, et des innovations constantes', *Regards*, 52 (2), pp. 59–75.

Fieschi, C. (2019) *Populocracy*. Newcastle Upon Tyne, Agenda.

Financial Times (2020) 'FT Interview: Emmanuel Macron says it is time to think the unthinkable', 16 April. www.ft.com/content/3ea8d790-7fd1-11ea-8fdb-7ec06e-deef84 (accessed 17 April).

Floc'h, B. (2020) 'Les préfets pourront déroger à la réglementation nationale', *Le Monde*, 9 April.

Foerster, M. (2012) *Elle ou Lui? Une histoire des transsexuels en France*. Paris, La Musardine.

Foucault, M. (1988) 'Technologies of the self'. In P. H. Hutton, H. Gutman and L. H. Martin (eds.) *Technologies of the Self. A Seminar with Michel Foucault*. Amherst, The University of Massachusetts Press, pp. 16–49.

Fourquet, J. (2018) *A la droite de Dieu*. Paris, Cerf.

Fourquet, J. and Manternach, S. (2018) 'Les "Gilets Jaunes": Révélateur fluorescent des fractures françaises', *Fondation Jean Jaurès*. https://jean-jaures.org/nos-productions/les-gilets-jaunes-revelateur-fluorescent-des-fractures-francaises

France Stratégie (2018) *Comité d'évaluation des ordonnances Travail – réunion plénière du 22 juin 2018*. Paris, France Stratégie.

France24 (2019) 'Contestation sociale: Les raisons de la colère'. www.france24.com/fr/20191114-politique-hopital-public-sante-reforme-etudiants-precarite-gilets-jaunes-manifestations-mac (consulted 14 November 2019).

François, S. (2012) *L'écologie politique: une vision du monde réactionnaire?* Paris, Cerf.

Frangi, M. (2018) *Le président de la République*. Paris, édition l'Harmattant, 2nd edition.

Furet, F., Julliard, J. and Rosanvallon, P. (1988) *La République du Centre. La fin de l'exception française*. Paris, Calmann-Levy.

Gaffney, J. (2015) *France in the Hollande Presidency: The Unhappy Republic*. Basingstoke, Palgrave.

Galonnier, J. (2019) 'Discrimination religieuse ou discrimination raciale? L'islamophobie en France et aux États-Unis', *Hommes et Migrations*, 1324 (1), pp. 29–37.

Galonnier, J. and Naudet, J. (eds.) (2019) 'Polémiques et controverses autour de la question raciale', *La vie des idées*. https://laviedesidees.fr/Polemiques-et-controverses-autour-de-la-question-raciale.html

Garcin, J. (2017) 'Emmanuel Macron sur la Manif pour tous: « On a humilié cette France-là » ' *L'Obs*, 16 February.

Garnier, J. (2018) '« Gilets jaunes »: le manque à gagner serait de 2 milliards d'euros pour le commerce', *Le Monde*, 14 December.

Gauthier, J. and Jobard, F. (2018) *Police: Question Sensible*. Paris, PUF.

Gauvard, C., Libera, A. and Zink, M. (eds.) (2006) *Dictionnaire du Moyen-Age*. Paris, PUF.

Geisser, V. (2003) *La nouvelle islamophobie*. Paris, La Découverte.

Geisser, V., Marongiu-Perria, O. and Smaïl, K. (2017) *Musulmans de France, la grande épreuve*. Ivry-Sur-Seine, Les éditions de l'atelier.

Genschel, P. and Seelkopf, L. (2014) 'The competition state: the modern state in a global economy'. In S. Leibfried, E. Huber, M. Lange, J. D. Levy and J. M. Stephens (eds.) *The Oxford Handbook of Transformations of the State*. Oxford, Oxford University Press.

Gerges, F. (2017) Abu Mohammed al-Adnani, cited in *Isis: A History*. Princeton, Princeton University Press, p. 230.

Germain, J-M. (2016) *Mission d'information relative au paritarisme. Rapport d'information*. Paris, Assemblée Nationale.

Geva, D. (2020) 'A double-headed hydra: Marine le Pen's charisma, between political masculinity and political femininity', *NORMA (International Journal for Masculinity Studies)*, 15 (1), pp. 26–42.

Ghiles-Meilhac, S. (2015) 'Mesurer l'antisémitisme contemporain: enjeux politiques et méthode scientifique', *Revue d'histoire moderne & contemporaine*, 62-2/3 (2), pp. 201–224.

Gil, C. (2019) 'Spatial analysis of La République En Marche and French Parties, 2002–2017', *French Politics*, 17, pp. 184–210.

Givens, T. (2004) 'The radical right gender gap', *Comparative Political Studies*, 37 (1), pp. 30–54.

Goar, M. (2020) 'L'exécutif français plus durement jugée que ses homologues', *Monde*, 4 May.

Gomart, T. and Hecker, M. (2018) 'Macon, an I. Quelle politique étrangère?' *Etudes de l'IFRI*, April. Paris, Institut français des relations internationales.

Gouard, D., Audemard, J., Boyadjian, J., Marchand-Lagier, C., Mathieu, R., Olivier, L. and Theviot, A. (2017) 'Les trois électorats de la primaire de la droite et du centre: Mobilisation et production des votes aux limites de l'entre-soi', *Revue française de science politique*, 67 (6), pp. 1113–1130.

Gougou, F. and Labouret, S. (2013) 'La fin de la tripartition?', *Revue française de science politique*, 63 (2), pp. 279–302.

Gougou, F. and Martin, P. (2013) 'L'émergence d'un nouvel ordre électoral?' In *Des votes et des voix. De Mitterrand à Hollande*. Paris, Champ Social, pp. 121–132.

Gougou, F. and Mayer, N. (2013) 'The class basis of extreme right voting in France: generational replacement and the rise of new cultural issues (1984–2007)'. In J. Rydgren (ed.) *Class Politics and the Radical Right*. London, Routledge, pp. 156–172.

Gougou, F. and Persico, S. (2017) 'A new party system in the making? The 2017 French Presidential Election', *French Politics*, 15, pp. 301–321.

Gougou, F. and Sauger, N. (2017) 'The 2017 French Election Study (FES 2017): a postelectoral cross-sectional survey', *French Politics*, 15 (3), pp. 360–370.

Gouvernment.fr (2019) '2000 maisons France Service d'ici à 2022'. www.gouvernement.fr/2-000-maisons-france-service-d-ici-a-2022

Griffin, R. (2000) 'Interregnum or endgame? Radical right thought in the "Post-Fascist" era', *The Journal of Political Ideologies*, 5 (2), pp. 163–178.

Grint, K. (2010) *Leadership. A Very Short Introduction*. Oxford, OUP.

Grody, J. and Hardoy, Y. (2020) *Gilets jaunes: Une année d'insurrection et de révolte dans Paris 2020*. Yellowsphere.

Grossman, E. and Sauger, N. (2014) '"Un président normal"? Presidential (in-)action and unpopularity in the wake of the great recession', *French Politics*, 12 (2), pp. 86–103.

Grossman, E. and Sauger, N. (2017) *Pourquoi détestons-nous autant nos politiques?* Paris, Presses de Sciences Po.

Grunberg, G. (2019) 'France: Clivages Politiques et Clivages Sociaux', *Telos*, 10 October.

Grunberg, G. and Schweisguth, E. (1997) 'Vers Une Tripartition de l'espace Politique'. In D. Boy and N. Mayer (eds.) *L'électeur a Ses Raisons*. Paris, Presses de Sciences Po, pp. 179–218.

Grunberg, G. and Schweisguth, É. (2003) 'La tripartition de l'espace politique'. In P. Perrineau and C. Ysmal (eds.) *Le vote de tous les refus*. Paris, Presses de Sciences Po, pp. 339–362.

Guerrina, R. (2018) 'Does European Union studies have a gender problem? Experiences from researching Brexit', *International Feminist Journal of Politics*, 20 (2), pp. 252–257.

Guilly, C. (2013) *Fractures françaises*. Paris, François Bourin Éditeur.

Guilly, C. (2014) *La France périphérique. Comment on a sacrifié les classes populaires*. Paris, Flammarion.

Guilly, C. and Noyé, C. (2004) *Atlas des Nouvelles fractures sociales: Les Classes moyennes oubliées et précarisées*. Paris, Editions Autrement.

Guisnel, J. (2018) 'Comment Macron fait la guerre', *Le Point*, 5 July.

Gunther, S. E. (2008) *The Elastic Closet. A History of Homosexuality in France. 1942– Present*. London, Palgrave Macmillan.

Hackett, C. (2017) '5 facts about the Muslim population of Europe', *Fact Tank*, Pew Research Center, 29 November.

Hadas-Lebel, M. (2015) 'Les juifs de France, quelques leçons de l'histoire. Leçon de clô-ture du Forum « L'année vue par l'histoire »', *La Croix*, 28 May.

Haegel, F. (2013) 'Political parties: the UMP and the right'. In Cole, Meunier and Tiberj (eds.) *Developments in French Politics 5*, pp. 128–150.

Haegel, F. (2019) 'Les transformations du système partisan sont-elles (encore) déter-minées par les institutions?'. In Duhamel, Foucault, Fulla and Lazar (eds.) *La Ve République démystifiée*. Paris, Presses de Sciences Po, pp. 149–156.

Hajjat, A. (2012) *Les frontières de « l'identité nationale ». L'injonction à l'assimilation en France métropolitaine et coloniale*. Paris, La Découverte.

Hajjat, A. and Mohammed, M. (2013) *Islamophobie. Comment les élites françaises constru-isent le « problème musulman*. Paris, La Découverte.

Hall, B. (2018) 'Macron v Salvini: the battle over Europe's political future', *Financial Times*, 28 December. www.ft.com/content/79d1d422-f3e4-11e8-9623-d7f9881e729f (accessed 31 November 2019).

Hamelin, F. (2018) '80km/h: pourquoi tant de haine?', *The Conversation*. https://the-conversation.com/80-km-h-pourquoi-tant-de-haine-98861 (accessed 31 November 2019).

Hanley, D. (2017) 'From "la petite Europe vaticane" to the Club Med: the French Socialist Party and the challenges of European integration', *Modern and Contemporary France*, 25 (2), pp. 135–151.

Harcourt, B. (2015) 'The mortification of the self'. In B. Harcourt (ed.) *Exposed. Desire and Disobedience in the Digital Age*. Cambridge, MA, Harvard University Press, pp. 217–233.

Harribey, J-M. and Marty, C. (2018) 'La volonté du gouvernement est d'éviter un débat sur la repartition des fruits du travail', *Le Monde*, 23 June.

Hayward, J. (ed.) (1993) *De Gaulle to Mitterrand: Presidential Power in France*. London, Hurst.

Heath, A. and Richards, L. (2016) 'Attitudes towards immigration and their antecedents. Topline Results from Round 7 of the European Social Survey', *ESS7 Topline Results Series*, 7. www.europeansocialsurvey.org/docs/findings/ESS7_toplines_issue_7_immi-gration.pdf (accessed 8 March 2020).

Heath, A., Davidov, E., Ford, R., Green, E. G. T., Ramos, A. and Schmidt, P. (2019) 'Contested terrain: explaining divergent patterns of public opinion towards immigra-tion within Europe', *Journal of Ethnic and Migration Studies* (Published online 22 February 2019. https://doi.org/10.1080/1369183X.2019.1550145

Heinich, N. (2014) 'L'extension du domaine de l'égalité', *Le Débat*, 180 (3), pp. 123–129.

Heisbourg, F. (2013) 'A surprising little war: first lessons of Mali', *Survival*, 55 (2), pp. 7–18.

Henry, E. (2007) *Amiante: un scandale improbable. Sociologie d'un problème public*. Rennes, Presses universitaires de Rennes.

Hervieu-Léger, D. (2003) *Catholicisme, la fin d'un monde*. Paris, Bayard.

Hill, C. (2007) 'Bringing war home', *International Relations*, 21 (3), pp. 259–283.

Hill, C. (2013) *The National Interest in Question: Foreign Policy in Multicultural Societies*. Oxford, Oxford University Press.

Hofferbert, R. (1974) *The Study of Public Policy*. New York, Bobbs-Merrill.

Hoffman, S. (1994) 'Les français, sont-ils ingouvernables?', *Pouvoirs*, 68, pp. 7–14.

Hoffmann, S. (1967) 'Heroic leadership: the case of modern France'. In L. J. Edinger (ed.) *Political Leadership in Industrialized Societies: Studies in Comparative Analysis*. New York, Wiley.

Hoffmann, S. (1990) 'De Gaulle as an Innovative Leader', *French Politics and Society*, 8 (4 Fall), pp. 78–92.

Hollande, F. (2016) 'Verbatim: ce qu'a dit Francois Hollande dans son discours de renoncement', *L'Obs*, 1 December 2016.

Hollande, F. (2018) *Les leçons du pouvoir*. Paris, Stock.

Hooghe, L. and Marks, G. (2003) « Unraveling the Central State, but how? Types of multi-level governance », *American Political Science Review*, 97 (2), pp. 233–243.

Horvath, A., Szakolczai, A. and Marangudakis, M. (eds.) (2020) *Modern Leaders. Between Charisma and Trickery*. London, Routledge.

Houdayer, G. (2018) 'Levothyrox: une analyse révèle le sous-dosage de la molécule active et un composant cache', *France Bleu Website*, 14 June. www.francebleu.fr/infos/sante-sciences/levothyrox-une-analyse-revele-le-sous-dosage-de-la-molecule-active-et-un-composant-cache-1528964861 (accessed 15 June 2018).

Howell, C. (2011) *Regulating Labor: The State and Industrial Relations Reform in Postwar France*. Princeton University Press.

Howorth, J. (2013a) 'French foreign and security policy: in search of coherence and impact'. In A. Cole, S. Meunier and V. Tiberj (eds.) *Developments in French Politics 5*. London, Red Globe Press, pp. 250–266.

Howorth, J. (2013b) 'French foreign and security policy: in search of coherence and impact'. In Cole, Meunier and Tiberj (eds.) *Developments in French Politics 5*. London, Red Globe Press, pp. 250–266.

Hussey, A. (2014) *The French Intifada: The Long War Between France and Its Arabs*. London, Granta.

Huyghe, F-B., Desmaison, X. and Liccia, D. (2019) *Dans la tête des gilets jaunes*. Va Press.

Iacub, M. (2004) *L'Empire du ventre. Pour une autre histoire de la maternité*. Paris, Fayard.

Ifop & Fondation Jean Jaurès (2017) 'Emmanuel Macron et les catégories populaires', *Ifop Focus*, No. 169. www.ifop.com/wp-content/uploads/2018/03/994-1-document_file.pdf (accessed 8 March 2020).

Ignazi, P. (2018) 'Emmanuel Macron entre Jupiter et Minerve'. In R. Brizzi and M. Lazar (eds.) *La France d'Emmanuel Macron*. Rennes, Presses Universitaires de Rennes, pp. 195–216.

IGPN (2019) *Rapport Annuel de l'IGPN 2018*. Paris, Inspection General de la Police nationale.

Inglehart, R. (1990) *Cultural Shift in Advanced Industrial Societies*. Princeton, Princeton University Press.

INSEE (2018a) *Note de conjoncture. Décembre 2018*. Paris, INSEE.

INSEE (2018b) 'Les pacs de même sexe n'ont pas pour autant été remplacés. Leur nombre est stable'. www.insee.fr/fr/statistiques/2381498#tableau-Donnes (accessed 15 June 2018).

INSEE (2018c) 'Naissances hors mariage en 2017'. www.insee.fr/fr/statistiques/2381394 (accessed 15 June 2018).

INSEE (2019a) *Chômage – emploi, chômage, revenus du travail*. Paris, Insee.

INSEE (2019b) *Insee Informations rapides*. 2019-120, 9 May. Paris, INSEE.

INSEE (2020) 'Tableau de la conjoncture'. www.insee.fr/fr/statistiques/2381498# tableau-Donnes (accessed 15 June 2018).

Institut Montaigne and Elabe (2019) *La France en morceaux – Baromètre des territoires 2019*. Paris, Institut Montaigne.

International Institute for Strategic Studies (2016) *The Military Balance, 2015*. London, Taylor and Francis, pp. 64–65.

IPSOS-SOPRA-STERIA (2018) 'Fractures françaises 2018'. www.ipsos.com/fr-fr/fractures-francaises-2018-10-mois-des-elections-europeennes-des-francais-ambivalents-vis-vis-de-lue (consulted 8 August 2018).

Ivaldi, G. (2015) 'Du néo-libéralisme au social-populisme? La transformation du programme économique du Front national (1986–2012)'. In S. Crépon, A. Dézé and N. Mayer (eds.) *Les faux semblants du Front national. Sociologie d'un parti politique*. Paris, Presses de Science Po, pp. 163–183.

Ivaldi, G. (2018) 'Contesting the EU in times of crisis: the Front National and politics of Euroscepticism in France', *Politics*, 38 (3), pp. 278–294.

Japan Times (2019) 'How Catalan protest tactics are inspired by Hong Kong'. www.japantimes.co.jp/news/2019/10/21/world/catalan-protest-tactics-hong-kong/#.XiloXFMzZTY (accessed 30 November 2019).

Jérôme, B., Sellami, Y., Desmazes, Z. and Marchal, C. (2019) 'Gilets jaunes: les commerces des Champs-Élysées passent à la caisse', *Le Parisien Mazagine*, 31 August. www.leparisien.fr/economie/gilets-jaunes-les-commerces-des-champs-elysees-passent-a-la-caisse-31-08-2019-8142741.php (accessed 31 November 2019).

Joppke, C. (2009) *Veil: Mirror of Identity*. Cambridge, Polity Press.

JORF (*Journal Officiel de la République francaise*) (2016) 'Loi no.2016-1088 du 8 août 2016 relative au travail, à la modernisation du dialogue social et à la sécurisation des parcours professionnels', *JO*, 9 August.

JORF (Journal Officiel de la République francaise) (2018) 'Décision n° 2018/121/GDN/1 de la séance exceptionnelle du 17 décembre 2018 relative au grand débat national', *Journal Officiel de la République francaise*. No. 0294 du 20 décembre 2018. Text No.154. www.legifrance.gouv.fr/affichTexte.do?cidTexte=JORFTEXT000037833929 (accessed 8 March 2020).

Keating, M. (2008) 'Thirty years of territorial politics', *West European Politics*, 31 (1–2), pp. 60–81.

Kellstedt, P. (2003) *The Mass Media and the Dynamics of American Racial Attitudes*. Cambridge, Cambridge University Press.

Kepel, G. with Jardin, A. (2015) *Terreur dans L'Hexagone: Genèse du Djihad Français*. Paris, Gallimard.

Kernalegenn, T. and Pasquier, R. (eds.) (2018) *30 ans de démocratie régionale: des régions pour quoi faire?* Paris, Berger-Levrault.

Kinder, D. R. and Sears, D. O. (1981) 'Prejudice and politics: symbolic racism versus racial threats to the good life', *Journal of Personality and Social Psychology*, 40 (3), pp. 414–431.

Kokoreff, M. (2008) *Sociologie des émeutes*. Paris, Payot.

König, P. and Waldvogel, T. (2018) 'Ni gauche ni droite? Positioning the candidates in the 2017 French election', *French Politics*. https://doi.org/10.1057/s41253-018-0059-8

Kriesi, H. (2018) 'The 2017 and 2018 French and German elections', *Journal of Common Market Studies Annual Review*, 56, pp. 51–62.

Krysan, M. and Moberg, S. (2016) *A Portrait of African American and White Racial Attitudes.* University of Illinois, The Institute of Government and Public Affairs. https://igpa.uillinois.edu/report/portrait-african-american-and-white-racial-attitudes (accessed 8 March 2020).

Kuhar, R. and Paternotte, D. (eds.) (2017) *Anti-gender Campaigns in Europe Mobilizing Against Equality.* London and New York, Rowman & Littlefield.

Kuhn, R. (2020) 'The media and presidential elections'. In M. Demossier, et al. (eds.) *The Routledge Handbook of French Politics and Culture.* London, Routledge, pp. 236–245.

La Dépêche (2020) 'Il y a une gilet-jaunisation des luttes', 19 January.

Laborde, C. (2010) *Critical Republicanism: The Hijab Controversy and Political Philosophy.* Oxford, Oxford University Press.

Lagrange, H. (2006) 'Autopsie d'une vague d'émeutes'. In H. Lagrange (ed.) *Émeutes urbaines et protestations: Une singularité française.* Paris, Presses de Sciences Po, pp. 37–58.

Laïdi, Z. (2019) 'France seizes its moment on the world stage', *Financial Times,* 29 September.

Laurence, J. and Vaisse, J. (2006) *Integrating Islam: Political and Religious Challenges in Contemporary France.* Washington, DC, Brookings Institution Press.

Le Bras, H. (2014) *Atlas des inégalités: Les Français face à la crise.* Paris, Editions Autrement.

Le Corre, P. (2017) 'François Hollande's Legacy: Strong Abroad, Weak at Home', *Brookings,* 21 April. www.brookings.edu/blog/order-from-chaos/2017/04/21/francois-hollandes-legacy-strong-abroad-weak-at-home/ (consulted 8 March 2020).

Le Foll, C. (2017) 'Quels professions exercent nos députés?', Le Monde, 26 June.

Le Galès, P. and Vezinat, N. (eds.) (2014) *L'Etat recomposé.* Paris, Presses Universitaires de France.

Le Gallou, J-Y. (1985) *La préférence nationale. Réponse à l'immigration.* Paris, Albin Michel.

Le Monde (2017) 'Décryptage. Le discours d'Emmanuel Macron', 30 April–2 May.

Le Monde (2019a) 'L'Arc de triomphe entièrement restauré, cinq mois après sa dégradation pendant une manifestation des « gilets jaunes »', 3 May.

Le Monde (2019b) 'Assurance-chômage, une réforme punitive'. Editorial. *Le Monde,* 31 October.

Le Monde (2020) 'La France entre en récession, avec une économie plombée par l'épidémie et le confinement', 8 April.

LE1Hebdo (2019) « Un simulacre de démocratie ». https://le1hebdo.fr/journal/numero/236/un-simulacre-de-dmocratie-3185.html (accessed 8 March 2020).

Lebaron, F. (2017) 'Une affaire d'ethos', *Savoir/Agir,* 39 (6), pp. 6–10.

Lebourg, N. (2017) 'Cultural orientalization or political occidentalism?' In P. Blanchard, N. Nicolas Bancel and D. Thomas (eds.) *The Colonial Legacy in France. Fracture, Rupture and Apartheid.* Indiana University Press, pp. 330–340.

Lecorre, P. (2017) 'France: a critical player in a weakened Europe', Center on United States and Europe at Brookings, April. www.euractiv.com/section/elections/news/hollande-in-favour-of-expelling-member-states-with-right-wing-governments/ (consulted 8 March 2020).

Lefebvre, R. (2019) 'Les Gilets jaunes et les exigences de la représentation politique', *La Vie des idées,* 10 Septembre.

Lefebvre, R. and Treille, E. (eds.) (2019) *Les primaires ouvertes: Un nouveau standard international?.* Lille, Presses Universitaires du Septentrion.

Legros, O. and Vtitale, T. (2011) 'Les migrants roms dans les villes françaises et italiennes: mobilités, régulations et marginalités', *Géocarrefour*, 86 (1), pp. 3–14.

Leiken, R. S. (2012) *Europe's Angry Muslims: The Revolt of the Second Generation*. New York, Oxford University Press.

Lemaire, B. (2018) *France, the UK and the EU: What the Future Holds*. Chatham House. www.chathamhouse.org/file/france-uk-and-eu-what-future-holds-0

Lemarié, A. (2017), 'Le coup de "blues" d'une partie des députés LRM', *Le Monde*, 14 December.

Lemarié, A. and Mutelet, A. (2018) 'François Bayrou réitère ses critiques contre la réforme des institutions', *Le Monde*, 13 June.

Lenoir, N. and Sturlèse, B. (1991) *Aux frontières de la vie. Rapport au Premier ministre*. Paris, La Documentation française.

Lepage-Saucier, N., Schleich, J. and Wasmer, E. (2013) 'Le contrat de travail unique: quid pro quo ou simple quiproquo?', *Regards Croisés sur l'Économie*, 1 (13), pp. 263–277.

Lépinard, É. (2020) *Feminist Trouble. Intersectional Politics in Post-Secular Times*. Oxford, Oxford University Press.

Lequesne, C. (2017) *Ethnographie du Quai d'Orsay. Les pratiques des diplomates français*. Paris, CNRS éditions.

Lequesne, C. and Behal, A. (2019) 'France and the European Union', *Oxford Research Encyclopedias, Politics*. https://oxfordre.com/politics/view/10.1093/acrefore/9780190228637.001.0001/acrefore-9780190228637-e-1146?rskey=O0khhh&result=1

Lespinet-Morel, I. (2019) 'Le mouvement gréviste de 1995 est le dernier à avoir eu une telle ampleur', *Le Monde*, 6 December.

Levy, J. (ed.) (2008) *The State After Statism*. Cambridge, MA, Harvard University Press.

Levy, J-D., Potéreau, J. and Hauser, M. (2018) *Les responsables RH et leur perception des réformes d'Emmanuel Macron en matière droit du travail*. Louis Harris. Available at: http://harris-interactive.fr/opinion_polls/les-responsables-rh-et-leur-perception-des-reformes-demmanuel-macron-en-matiere-de-droit-du-travail/ (consulted 8 March 2020).

Lewis-Beck, M. S. and Nadeau, R. (2015) 'Explaining French elections: the presidential pivot', *French Politics*, 13 (1), pp. 25–62.

Lindell, H. (2014) *Les Veilleurs: enquête sur une résistance*. Paris, Salvador.

Louis, É. (2018) *Qui a tué mon père*. Paris, Seuil.

Mabille, P. (2017) 'L'Europe, on La Change Ou Elle Meurt', *La Tribune*, 25 April.

Mack, C. S. (2010) *When Political Parties Die. A Cross-National Analysis of Disalignment and Realignment*. Santa Barbara, Praeger.

Maclean, M. (ed.) (1998) *The Mitterrand Years: Legacy and Evaluation*. Basingstoke, Macmillan.

Macron, E. (2016a) 'Entretien avec Emmanuel Macron', *Challenges.fr*. www.challenges.fr/election-presidentielle-2017/interview-exclusive-d-emmanuel-macron-je-ne-crois-pas-au-president-normal_432886 (consulted 5 August 2018).

Macron, E. (2016b) 'Discours de la Porte de Versailles', 10 December. Paris, EM. https://en-marche.fr/articles/discours/meeting-macron-porte-de-versailles-discours (accessed 7 October 2019).

Macron, E. (2016c) *Révolution*. Paris, XO éditions.

Macron, E. (2017a) 'Speech by the President of the French Republic in Athens', *France Diplomatie*, 7 September. www.diplomatie.gouv.fr/en/french-foreign-policy/

european-union/events/article/european-union-speech-by-the-president-of-the-french-republic-athens-07-09-17 (accessed 8 March 2020).

Macron, E. (2017b) 'Entretien avec Emmanuel Macron', *Le Point*, 31 August.

Macron, E. (2017c) 'Transcription De Discours Du Président De La République Au Salon Vivatech 2017'. www.elysee.fr/emmanuel-macron/2017/06/15/discours-du-president-de-la-republique-au-salon-vivatech-201. Paris, Elysée (consulted 8 March 2020).

Macron, E. (2017d) 'Discours du Président de la République devant le Parlement réuni en congrès', 3 July. Paris, Elysée. www.elysee.fr/emmanuel-macron/2017/07/03/discours-du-president-de-la-republique-devant-le-parlement-reuni-en-congres (accessed 8 March 2020).

Macron, E. (2017e) 'Speech on new initiative for Europe', 26 September. Paris, Elysée. www.elysee.fr/emmanuel-macron/2017/09/26/president-macron-gives-speech-on-new-initiative-for-europe.en (consulted 25 May 2020).

Macron, E. (2018a) 'Discours du Président de la République devant le Parlement réuni en congrès', 9 July. www.elysee.fr/emmanuel-macron/2018/07/12/discours-du-president-de-la-republique-devant-le-parlement-reuni-en-congres-a-versailles (consulted 8 March 2020).

Macron, E. (2018b) 'Speech by the French President at the World Economic Forum in Switzerland, on January 24, 2018', Elysée. www.elysee.fr/emmanuel-macron/2018/01/24/speech-by-the-french-president-at-the-world-economic-forum-in-switzerland-on-january-24-2018.en (consulted 8 March 2020).

Macron, E. (2019a) '"Gilets jaunes": Macron juge "inacceptable dans un Etat de droit" de parler de "violences policières"', 7 March. www.francetvinfo.fr/economie/transports/gilets-jaunes/video-gilets-jaunes-macron-juge-inacceptable-dans-un-etat-de-droit-de-parler-de-violences-policieres_3222835.html (consulted 8 March 2020).

Macron, E. (2019b) *Lettre aux Français*. Paris, Élysée.

Macron, E. (2019c) 'Pour une Renaissance européenne' *Le Parisien,* 4 March.

Macron, E. (2020) 'Adresse aux Français', 13 avril 2020'. www.elysee.fr/emmanuel-macron/2020/04/13/adresse-aux-francais-13-avril-2020 (consulted 14 April 2020).

Mandel, M. S. (2014) *Muslims and Jews in France: History of a conflict*. Princeton, Princeton University Press.

Manif pour tous (2018) 'Laurent Wauquiez et l'adoption,' *Site de La Manif pour tous*, 26 January. www.lamanifpourtous.fr/les-chroniques/chronique-laurent-wauquiez-ladoption

Manow, P. (2010) *In the King's Shadow. The Political Anatomy of Democratic Representation*. Cambridge, Polity Press.

Marcou, G. (2006) « La « clause générale de compétence » dans les régimes d'autonomie locale des Etats européens », *Pouvoirs Locaux*, 68 (1).

Martigny, V. (2009) 'Le débat autour de l'identité nationale dans la campagne présidentielle 2007: Quelle rupture?', *French Politics, Culture & Society*, 27 (1), pp. 23–42.

Martin, P. (2000) *Comprendre les évolutions électorales. La théorie des réalignements revisitée*. Paris, Presses de Sciences Po.

Martin, P. (2007) 'Les scrutins de 2007 comme "moment de rupture" dans la vie politique française'. *Revue politique et parlementaire*, no. 1044: 167–75.

Martin, P. (2016) 'Les élections régionales de décembre 2015'. *Commentaire* Numéro 153 (1): 89–96.

Martin, P. (2015) 'L'avenir du tripartisme'. *Revue Politique et Parlementaire*, no 1075 (juin): 103–8.

Martinache, I. and Sawicki, F. (2020) *La fin des partis?* Paris, PUF.

Marzouki, N., McDonnell, D. and Roy, O. (eds.) (2016) *Saving the People: How Populists Hijack Religion*. London, Hurst.

Mayer, N. (1993) 'L'antisémitisme français à l'aune des sondages'. In M. Wieviorka (ed.) *Racisme et modernité*. Paris, La Découverte, pp. 278–288.

Mayer, N. (2004) 'Nouvelle judéophobie ou vieil antisémitisme?', *Raisons politiques*, 16 (4), pp. 91–103.

Mayer, N. (2015) 'Le plafond de verre électoral entamé, mais pas brisé'. In S. Crépon, A. Dézé and N. Mayer (eds.) *Les faux semblants du Front national. Sociologie d'un parti politique*. Paris, Presses de Science Po, pp. 299–321.

Mayer, N. and Druez, E. (2018) 'Antisemitism and Immigration in Western Europe Today. Is There a Connection? The case of France'. In F. Feldman (ed.) *Antisemitism and Immigration in Western Europe Today. Is there a Connection? Final Report*. Pears Institute for the Study of Antisemitism, Birkbeck University, London. Available at https://www.pearsinstitute.bbk.ac.uk/resources/item/antisemitism-and-immigration-in-western-europe-today-is-there-a-connection/

Mayer, N. and Tiberj, V. (2015) 'Who were the 'Charlie' in the Streets? A socio-political approach of the January 11 Rallies', *International Review of Social Psychology*, 29, pp. 59–68.

Mayer, N., Michelat, G., Tiberj, V. and Vitale, T. (2019) 'Le regard des chercheurs: Evolution et structure des préjugés'. In CNCDH (ed.) *La lutte contre le racisme, l'antisémitisme et la xénophobie. Année 2018*. Paris, La Documentation française, pp. 73–159.

Mayer, N., Michelat, G., Tiberj, V. and Vitale, T. (2020) 'Le regard des chercheurs'. In CNCDH (ed.) *La lutte contre le racisme, l'antisémitisme et la xénophobie. Année 2019*. Paris, La Documentation française, pp. 33–121.

McConahay, J., Hardee, B. and Batts, V. (1981) 'Has racism declined in America? It depends on who is asking and what is asked', *The Journal of Conflict Resolution*, 25 (4), pp. 563–579.

McGarry, A. (2017) *Romaphobia. The Last Acceptable Form of Racism*. London, Zed Books.

Méda, D. (2019) 'La réforme de l'assurance-chômage est extraordinairement punitive', *Le Monde*, 23 November.

Mendras, H. (1987) *La deuxième révolution française*. Paris, Seuil.

Mény, Y. (2017) 'A Tale of Party Primaries and Outsider Candidates: The 2017 French Presidential Election'. *French Politics* 15 (3): 265–78.

Mény, Y. (2019) *Imparfaites démocraties*. Paris, Presses de Sciences Po.

Meunier, S. (2012)'The French don't know their place (in the global economy). Parsing the deglobalization debate', *Foreign Affairs 2012*, March 30 and April 23. www.foreignaffairs.com/articles/137372/sophie-meunier/the-french-dont-know-their-place-in-the-global-economy (accessed 13 August 2019).

Meunier, S. (2020, forthcoming) 'Le Mécanisme de filtrage des investissements directs étrangers en Europe: Une réponse à l'essor des investissements chinois?' In O. Delas (ed.) *l'Union Européenne et l'Amérique du Nord à l'heure des nouvelles routes de la soie*. Editions Bruylant.

Michelat, G. and Dargent, C. (2012) *Le vote catholique, Les électorats sociologiques*. Paris, CEVIPOF, n°12.

Michelat, G. and Dargent, C. (2015) 'Système symbolique catholique et comportements électoraux', *Revue française de science politique*, 65 (1), pp. 27–60.

Michelat, G. and Simon, M. (1977) *Classe, religion et comportement politique*. Paris, FNSP.

Milner, S. (2011) 'France and its exceptional social model'. In T. Chafer and E. Godin (eds.) *The End of French Exceptionalism?* Basingstoke, Palgrave, pp. 55–71.

Milner, S. (2012) 'Fixing France's broken social model? An assessment of employment and labour market policy under the Sarkozy presidency', *French Politics*, 10 (3), pp. 290–305.

Milner, S. (2014) 'The politics of unemployment policy in an age of austerity: France in comparative perspective', *French Politics*, 12 (3), pp. 197–217.

Milner, S. (2017) 'Employment and labour market policy during the Hollande presidency: a tragedy in three acts?', *Modern and Contemporary France*, 25 (4), pp. 429–443.

Milner, S. and Mathers, A. (2013) 'Membership, influence and voice: a discussion of trade union renewal in the French context', *Industrial Relations Journal*, 44 (2), pp. 122–138.

Ministère de l'Économie et des Finances (2019) 'Flash conjoncture France -L'INSEE confirme son estimation de la croissance du 3ème trimestre (+0.3%)'. www.tresor.economie.gouv.fr/Articles/2019/11/29/flash-conjoncture-france-l-insee-confirme-son-estimation-de-la-croissance-du-3e-trimestre-0-3 (consulted 31 December 2019).

Ministère de la Justice (2013) 'Circulaire relative à la délivrance des certificats de nationalité française', 25 June. Paris, Ministère de la Justice.

Ministère de la Justice (2018) 'Statistiques du ministère de la justice 2016'. Paris, Ministère de la Justice. www.justice.gouv.fr/statistiques-10054/references-statistiques-justice-12837/justice-civile-et-commerciale-donnees-2016-31191.html (accessed 12 June 2018).

Ministère de la Transition écologique et solidaire (2017) *Fiscalité carbone*. Paris, Ministère de la Transition écologique et solidaire. www.ecologique-solidaire.gouv.fr/fiscalite-carbone (accessed 12 June 2018).

Ministère de la Transition écologique et solidaire (2019) *Fiscalité des énergies*. Paris, Ministère de la Transition écologique et solidaire.

Ministère du Travail (2018) *Projet de loi pour la liberté de choisir son parcours professionnel*, NOR: MTRX1808061L/Bleue-2. Paris, Ministère du Travail.

Minton Beddoes, Z. (2013) 'Europe's Reluctant Hegemon', *The Economist*, 13 June.

Moreau, C. (2018) 'Adoption par les couples homosexuels: 'Uniquement pour des enfants atypiques' en Seine-Maritime', 18 June. www.francebleu.fr/infos/societe/adoption-par-les-couples-homosexuels-uniquement-pour-des-enfants-atypiques-en-seine-maritime-1528997253 (accessed 21 June 2018).

Mosse, G. L. (1985) *Nationalism & Sexuality. Respectability and Abnormal Sexuality in Modern Europe*. New York, Howard Fertig.

Mosse, G. L. (1997) *L'Image de l'homme. L'invention de la virilité moderne*. Paris, Éditions Abbeville.

Mossuz-Lavau, J. (2002) *Les Lois de l'amour. Les politiques de la sexualité en France (1950–2002)*. Paris, Payot.

Mouffe, C. (2005) *On the Political*. London, Routledge.

Mudde, C. (2007) *Populist Radical Right Parties in Europe*. Cambridge, Cambridge University Press.

Mudde, C. and Kaltwasser, C. R. (2018) 'Studying populism in comparative perspective: reflections on the contemporary and future research agenda', *Comparative Political Studies*, pp. 1–27.

Naczyk, M. (2016) 'Creating French-style pension-funds: business, labour and the battle over patient capital', *Journal of European Social Policy*, 26 (3), pp. 205–218.

Ng, J. (2018) 'What France's 'yellow vests can teach Hong Kong activists about political protests and the use of violence", *South China Morning Post*, 11 December. www.scmp.com/comment/insight-opinion/hong-kong/article/2177366/what-frances-yellow-vests-can-teach-hong-kong (accessed 8 March 2020).

Noiriel, G. (2018) *Une histoire populaire de la France – De la guerre de Cent Ans à nos jours.* Marseille, Agone.

Noiriel, G. (2019) *Les Gilets jaunes à la lumière de l'histoire – dialogue avec Nicolas Truong.* Paris, Editions de l'Aube.

Nossiter, A. (2016) '"That ignoramus": 2 French scholars of radical Islam turn bitter rivals', *New York Times*, 12 July.

Obsershall, A. (1973) *Social Conflicts and Social Movements.* Englewood Cliffs, Prentice Hall.

OCDE (2014) *France. Les réformes structurelles: impacts sur la croissance et impact du l'avenir.* Paris, OCDE. www.oecd.org/france/FRANCE_ReformesStructurelles.pdf (accessed 8 March 2020).

OECD (2018a) *Employment Database.* OECD. Available at: www.oecd.org/els/emp/onlineoecdemploymentdatabase.htm (accessed 8 March 2020).

OECD (2018b) *Temporary Employment.* OECD. Available at: https://data.oecd.org/emp/temporary-employment.htm (accessed 8 March 2020).

OFCE (2019) 'Perspectives économiques 2019–2021', *Revue de l'OFCE.* No. 162.

Olivera, M. (2010) 'Les Roms comme « minorité ethnique»? Un questionnement roumain', *Études tziganes*, 39–40, pp. 128–150.

Ollion, É. (2019) 'Changer de vie. Les députés novices et la condition politique au XXIᵉ siècle', *Politix*, 128 (4), pp. 91–114.

Organization for Economic Cooperation and Development (OECD) (2017) *OECD Economic Surveys.* Paris, OECD.

Ouest-France (2019) 'Gilets jaunes. La dégradation des radars a coûté 'un peu moins de 500 millions d'euros à l'État'. www.ouest-france.fr/societe/gilets-jaunes/gilets-jaunes-la-degradation-des-radars-coute-un-peu-moins-de-500-millions-d-euros-l-etat-6494496

Palier, B. (2005) 'Ambitious agreement, cumulative change: French social policy in the 1990s'. In W. Streeck and K. Thelen (eds.) *Beyond Continuity: Institutional Change in Advanced Political Economies*, pp. 127–141.

Palier, B. (2010) *A Long Goodbye to Bismarck? The Politics of Welfare Reform in Western Europe.* Amsterdam University Press.

Pannier, A. and Schmitt, O. (2019) 'France between the fight against terrorism and future warfare', *International Affairs*, 95 (4), p. 907.

Pantucci, R. (2015) *'We Love Death as You Love Life': Britain's Suburban Terrorists.* London, Hurst.

Parsons, C. (2017) 'France and the evolution of European integration'. In R. Elgie, E. Grossman and A. Mazur (eds.) *The Oxford Handbook of French Politics.* Oxford, Oxford University Press, pp. 585–605.

Pascual, J. (2015) 'GPA: la filiation reconnue, le débat continue', *Le Monde,* 4 July.

Pasquier, R. (2012) *Le pouvoir régional. Mobilisations, décentralisation et gouvernance en France*. Paris, Presses de Sciences-Po.

Pasquier, R. (2013) 'Gouvernance territoriale: quelles articulations entre régions et métropoles?', *Pouvoirs Locaux*, n°96, pp. 34–41.

Pasquier, R. (2016a) 'Crise économique et différenciation territoriale. Les régions et les métropoles dans la décentralisation française', *Revue internationale de politique comparée*, 23 (3), pp. 327–353.

Pasquier, R. (2016b) 'Les régions dans la réforme territoriale. Des colosses aux pieds d'argile?', *Cahiers Français*, n°391, pp. 20–25.

Pasquier, R. (2018) 'Les fractures territoriales en France: construction d'un problème public', *Cahiers Français*, n°402, pp. 2–7.

Pasquier, R. and Perron, C. (2008) 'Régionalisme et régionalisation dans une Europe élargie: les enjeux d'une comparaison Est/Ouest', *Revue d'études comparatives Est/Ouest*, 39 (3), pp. 5–18.

Pasquier, R., Simoulin, V. and Weisbein, J. (eds.) (2013) *La gouvernance territoriale. Pratiques, discours et théories*. Paris, LGDJ-Lextenso éditions.

Paternotte, D. (2011) *Revendiquer le "mariage gay": Belgique France, Espagne*. Brussels, Éditions de l'ULB.

Paternotte, D. (2015) 'Habemus gender! Autopsie d'une obsession vaticane', *Sextant*, 31, pp. 7–22.

Pedder, S. (2018) *Emmanuel Macron and the Quest to Reinvent a Nation*. Bloomsbury Continuum.

Pedder, S. (2019, paperback) *Revolution française. Emmanuel Macron and the Quest to Reinvent a Nation*. London, Bloomsbury.

Pelinka, A., Bischof, K. and Stögner, K. (eds.) (2015) *Handbook of Prejudice*. Amherst, Cambria.

Pénicaud, M. (2017) 'Signature des ordonnances. Discours de Muriel Pénicaud, French Government'. Available at: http://travail-emploi.gouv.fr/actualites/presse/discours/article/signature-des-ordonnances-discours-de-muriel-penicaud (consulted 8 March 2020).

Pèrez-Agote, A. (2012) *Portraits des catholicismes. Une comparaison européenne*. Rennes, Presses universitaire de Rennes.

Perona, M. (2018) 'Le Bien-être des Français – Décembre 2018', *Observatoire du Bien-être du CEPREMAP*, No. 2019-02.

Perona, M. (2019) 'La France Malheureuse', *Observatoire du Bien-être du CEPREMAP*, No. 2019-01.

Perreau, B. (2014) *The Politics of Adoption. Gender and the Making of French Citizenship*. Cambridge, MA, MIT Press.

Perreau, B. (2016) *Queer Theory: The French Response*. Stanford, Stanford University Press.

Perrineau, P. (2003) 'La surprise lepéniste et sa suite législative'. In P. Perrineau and C. Ysmal (eds.) *Le vote de tous les refus. Les élections présidentielles et législatives de 2002*. Paris, Presses de Science Po, pp. 199–222.

Perrineau, P. (ed.) (2017) *le Vote disruptif*. Paris, Presses de Sciences Po.

Pettigrew, T. F. and Meertens, R. W. (1995) 'Subtle and blatant prejudice in Western Europe', *European Journal of Social Psychology*, 25 (1), pp. 57–75.

Pezard, S. and Shurkin, M. (2017) 'Mali is France's Afghanistan, but with a difference', *War on the Rocks*, 1 December 2017. https://warontherocks.com/2017/12/mali-is-frances-afghanistan-but-with-a-difference/ (consulted 8 March 2020).

Pietralunga, C. (2016), Macron, les électeurs de droite ont le choix entre "le statut quo ou le retour en arrière"', *Le Monde*, 21 November.

Pigenet, M. and Tartatowsky, D. (eds.) (2012) *Histoire des mouvements sociaux en France de 1814 à nos jours*. Paris, Éditions La Découverte.

Plowright, A. (2017) *The French Exception. Emmanuel Macron, the Extraordinary Rise and Risk*. Iconbooks.

Portier, P. (2016) *L'Etat et les religions en France. Une sociologie historique de la laïcité*. Rennes, Presses universitaires de Rennes.

Poulat, E. (2003) *Notre laïcité publique*. Paris, Berg.

Poupeau, F-M. (2017) *Analyser la gouvernance multi-niveaux*. Grenoble, PUG.

Preciado, P. (2008) 'Pharmaco-pornographic politics: towards a new gender ecology', *Parallax*, 14 (1), pp. 105–117.

Preciado, P. (2014) *Pornotopia: An Essay on Playboy's Architecture and Biopolitics*. Cambridge, MA, MIT Press/Zone Books.

Pregnolato, A. (2019) 'La contestation des violences policières ont une histoire', *The Conversation*, 4 January. https://theconversation.com/les-contestations-des-violences-policieres-ont-une-histoire-109272 (consulted 8 March 2020).

Prissette, N. (2016) 'Exclusif. Les patrons prient Hollande d'agir pour l'emploi', *Le Journal du Dimanche*, 9 January.

Prissette, N. (2017) *Emmanuel Macron: Le président inattendu*. Paris, First.

Quatremer, J. (2017) 'Coulisses de Bruxelles – François Hollande, l'homme sans Conviction (Européenne) – Libération.Fr', *Libération Coulisses de Bruxelles* (blog), April 16, 2017. http://bruxelles.blogs.liberation.fr/2017/04/16/francois-hollande-lhomme-sans-conviction-europeenne/

Raffy, S. (2011) *François Hollande. Itinéraire secret*. Paris, Fayard.

Rain, A. (2018) 'Le choix du temps long donne l'opportunité de penser aux grandes questions', *Le Monde,* 23 June.

Raison du Cleuziou, Y. (2019) *Une contre révolution catholique. Aux origines de La Manif pour tous*. Paris, Seuil.

Raison du Cleuziou, Y. and de Brémond d'Ars, N. (2015) *French Catholics and Their Church. Pluralism and Deregulation*. Washington, DC, CRVP. www.crvp.org/publications/Series-VIII/16-master-frenchrevuYRC.pdf

Raison du Cleuziou, Y. (2018) 'La structuration interne du catholicisme français: une description sociologique en deux enquêtes successives', *Bulletin de littérature ecclésiastique*, 473, January-March, pp.9–37.

Rassemblement national (2017) '144 engagement présidentiels'. https://rassemblement-national.fr/pdf/144-engagements.pdf (accessed 15 August 2019).

Raymond, G. (2006) 'The republican ideal and the reality of the Republic'. In A. Cole and G. Raymond (eds.) *Redefining the French Republic*. Manchester: Manchester University Press, pp. 5–24.

Raymond, G. (2013) 'Le diesel et la France: une histoire d'amour qui dure depuis 30 ans', *The HuffPost*. www.huffingtonpost.fr/2013/03/04/diesel-france-taxe-fiscalite-psa-pollution-montebourg_n_2804743.html (accessed 8 March 2020).

Reinares, F. (2016) *Al-Qaeda's Revenge: the 2004 Madrid Train Bombings*. Washington, DC, Woodrow Wilson Center Press.

Rémond, R. (2000) *Le christianisme en accusation. Entretiens avec Marc Leboucher*. Paris, DDB.

Renaud-Garabedian, É. (2019) 'Violences en marge des gilets jaunes: des commerçants en danger, un soutien minimal de l'État', *Sénat. Rapport d'information n° 605 (2018–2019)*. www.senat.fr/rap/r18-605/r18-605.html (accessed 8 March 2020).

Rescan, M. (2018) 'Agenda, taxis, rythme… le lent apprentissage de l'Assemblée par des députés de LRM', *Le Monde*, 16th June.

Rescan, M. (2019a) 'Quand les deputés LRM redecouvrent la vie locale', *Le Monde*, 19 August.

Rescan, M. (2019b) *Les grandes illusions: enquête sur les soldats de la macronie*. Paris, Editions Robert Laffront.

Restelli, A. (2019) 'Le maintien de l'ordre français mis à l'épreuve par les gilets jaunes?', *Droit & Société. Théorie et sciences sociales du droit*. https://ds.hypotheses.org/6045 (consulted 8 March 2020).

Reungoat, E. (2015) 'Le Front national et l'Union européenne. La radicalisation comme continuité'. In S. Crépon, A. Dézé and N. Mayer (eds.) *Les faux semblants du Front national. Sociologie d'un parti politique*. Paris, Presses de Science Po, pp. 225–245.

Reuters (2020) 'To skirt police restrictions, some Indian protesters take a page from Hong Kong and beyond', 4 January. www.reuters.com/article/us-india-citizenship-protests-tactics/to-skirt-police-restrictions-some-indian-protesters-take-a-page-from-hong-kong-and-beyond-idUSKBN1Z3061 (consulted March 2020).

Reynolds, C. (2017) 'Presidential elections and Europe: the 2012 game changer', *Modern and Contemporary France*, 25 (2), pp. 117–134.

Reynolds, C. (2020) 'La France dans la rue'. In *The Routledge Handbook of French Politics and Culture*. London and New York, Routledge, pp. 121–132.

Riché, P. (2018) 'La carte des "gilets jaunes" n'est pas celle que vous croyez', *L'Obs*, 21 November. www.nouvelobs.com/politique/20181121.OBS5815/la-carte-des-gilets-jaunes-n-est-pas-celle-que-vous-croyez.html (consulted 8 March 2020).

Rieker, P. (2018) 'French status seeking in a changing world: taking on the role as guardian of the liberal order', *French Politics*, 16, pp. 419–438.

Robcis, C. (2013) *The Law of Kinship: Anthropology, Psychoanalysis, and the Family in France*. Ithaca, Cornell University Press.

Robert, A., Gotev, G. and Morgan, S. (2019) 'Macron, the EU's New Leader', *EURACTIV*, 28 August 2019. www.euractiv.com/section/politics/news/the-brief-macron-the-eus-new-leader/ (consulted 8 March 2020).

Roger, P. (2020a) 'Début d'idylle entre l'Etat et les collectivités', *Le Monde*, 1 May.

Roger, P. (2020b) 'Les élus locaux sur le devant de la scène', *Le Monde*, 4 May.

Roger, P. (2020c) 'Au second tour des élections municipales 2020, abstention record et percée écologiste', *Le Monde*, 29 June. Available at: www.lemonde.fr/politique/article/2020/06/29/au-second-tour-des-municipales-abstention-record-et-percee-ecologiste_6044563_823448.html (consulted 9 August 2020).

Romei, V. (2017) 'The numbers that prompted France's labour law plan', *Economist*, 7 July.

Rouban, L. (2018) *Le paradoxe du macronisme*. Paris: Presses de Sciences Po.

Roux, G. (2006) 'Quelle évolution de la xénophobie en France?', *Futuribles*, 319, pp. 19–42.

Roy, O. (2017) *Jihad and Death: The Global Appeal of Islamic State*. London, Hurst.

Roy, O. (2019) *L'Europe est-elle chrétienne?*. Paris, Seuil.

Rozenberg, O. (2020) "France is back'...in a French Europe'. In S. Bulmer and C. Lequesne (eds.) *The Member States of the European Union*. Oxford University Press, 3rd edition, pp. 73–100.

Rozès, S. (2018) 'Mouvements sociaux: '2018 n'est pas 1995', *Le Monde*, 4 March.

RTL (2018) 'INFO RTL – "Gilets jaunes": Bruno Le Maire annonce une perte de 0,1 point de croissance', 10 December. www.rtl.fr/actu/politique/gilets-jaunes-bruno-le-maire-annonce-sur-rtl-une-perte-de-0-1-point-de-croissance-en-2018-7795869162 (consulted 8 March 2020).

RTL (2020) 'Réforme des retraites: assiste-t-on à une "gilet-jaunisation" du mouvement?', 20 January (consulted 8 March 2020).

Sauger, N. (2007) 'Un Système Électoral Vecteur d'instabilité ? L'impact Du Système Électoral Sur La Structuration Du Système Partisan Sous La Cinquième République'. In *Les Partis Politiques En France*, edited by Florence Haegel, 359–391. Paris: Presses de Sciences Po.

Sauger, N. and Sarah-Louise, R. (2014) 'Économie et vote en 2012, The economy and the vote in 2012. An election of crisis?' *Revue française de science politique* 63 (6): 1031–49.

Sala Pala, V. (2006) 'Novembre 2005: Sous les émeutes urbaines, la politique', *French Politics, Culture Society*, 24 (3), pp. 111–129.

Salmon, C. (2014) *Les derniers jours de la Ve République*. Fayard.

Sartori, G. (1976) *Parties and Party Systems*. Cambridge, Cambridge University Press.

Sawicki, F. (2013) 'Political parties: the socialists and the left'. In A. Cole, S. Meunier and V. Tiberj (eds.) *Developments in French Politics 5*, pp. 151–172.

Schön-Quinlivan, E. (2017) '"The elephant in the room" no more: Europe as a structuring line of political cleavage in the 2017 presidential election', *French Politics*, 15, pp. 290–302.

Semo, M. (2019) 'A Biarritz, le difficile G7 de Macron', *Le Monde*, 23 August 2019.

Serre, D. (2009) *Les Coulisses de l'État social. Enquête sur les signalements d'enfants en danger*. Paris, Seuil.

Shepard, T. (2018) *Sex, France, and Arab Men, 1962–1979*. Chicago, University of Chicago Press.

Siméant, J. (1998) *La cause des sans-papiers*. Paris, Presses de Sciences Po.

Simon, P. and Tiberj, V. (2013) *Sécularisation ou regain religieux: la religiosité des immigrés et de leurs descendants*, Documents de travail, 196. Paris, Institut National d'Études Démographiques (INED), 47pp.

Sineau, M., and Bruno Cautrès. 2013. 'Les Attentes Vis-à-Vis Du Nouveau Président'. In *La Décision Électoale En 2012*, edited by Pascal Perrineau, 229–42. Paris: Armand Colin.

Sirinelli, J-F. (2017) *Les Révolutions françaises. 1962–2017*. Paris, Odile Jacob.

Smith, T. B. (2013) 'France in crisis? Economic and welfare policy reform'. In A. Cole, S. Meunier and V. Tiberj (eds.) *Developments in French politics 5*, pp. 186–202.

Soboul, A. (1968) *Les sans-culottes parisiens de l'An II: mouvement populaire et gouvernement révolutionnaire (1793–1794)*. Paris, Editions du Seuil.

Sonntag, A. (2008) 'The Burdensome Heritage of prestige politics'. In M. Maclean and J. Szarka (eds.) *France on the World Stage. Nation State Strategies in the Global Era*. Basingstoke, Palgrave, pp. 77–90.

Soroka, S. and Wlezien, C. (2010) *Degrees of Democracy: Politics, Public Opinion, and Policy*. Cambridge University Press.

Souillac, R. (2007) *Le mouvement Poujade: de la défense professionnelle au populisme nationaliste (1953–1962)*. Paris, Presses de Sciences Po.

Stenner, K. (1997) 'Perceived threat and authoritarianism', *Political Psychology*, 18, pp. 741–770.

Stenner, K. (2005) *The Authoritarian Dynamic*. Cambridge, Cambridge University Press.

Stephens, P. (2019) 'The rights and wrongs of Emmanuel Macron's vision for Europe', 21 November.

Stimson, J. (2004) *Tides of Consent: How Opinion Movements Shape American Politics*. Cambridge, Cambridge University Press.

Stimson, J., Tiberj, V. and Thiébaut, C. (2010) 'Le mood, un nouvel instrument au service de l'analyse dynamique des opinions: application aux évolutions de la xénophobie en France (1999–2009)', *Revue française de science politique*, 60 (5), pp. 901–926.

Strudel, S. (2017) 'Emmanuel Macron: un oxymore politique?' In P. Perrineau (ed.) *Le vote disruptif. Les élections présidentielle et législatives de 2017*. Paris, les Presses de Sciences Po, pp. 206–219.

Taguieff, P. A. (1985) 'Le néo-racisme différentialiste. Sur l'ambiguïté d'une évidence commune et ses effets pervers', *Langage et société*, 34, pp. 69–98.

Taguieff, P. A. (1992) *Les protocoles des sages de Sion*. Paris, Berg International.

Taguieff, P. A. (2002) *La nouvelle judéophobie*. Paris, Fayard/Mille et une nuits.

Taguieff, P. A. (2004*) Rising from the Muck: The New Anti-Semitism in Europe*. Chicago, Ivan R. Dee.

Taguieff, P. A. (2010) *La nouvelle propagande antijuive*. Paris, PUF.

Tajfel, H. (1978) *Differentiation Between Social Groups: Studies in the Social Psychology of Intergroup Relations*. London, Academic.

Tartakowsky, D. (2014) *Les droites et la rue. Histoire d'une ambivalence de 1880 à nos jours*. Paris, La Découverte.

The Guardian (2017) 'Emmanuel Macron under fire for plan to give wife 'first lady' role', 6 August.

The Guardian (2020) 'Managing a crisis: why do female leaders seem to be more successful?' 25 April.

The Strait Times (2019) 'How Catalan protest tactics are inspired by Hong Kong'. www.straitstimes.com/world/europe/how-catalan-protest-tactics-are-inspired-by-hong-kong

Thelen, K. (2003) 'Comment les institutions évoluent: perspectives de l'analyse comparative historique', *L'Année de la régulation*, 7, pp. 13–43.

Théry, I. (1997) 'Le CUS en question', *Notes de la fondation Saint Simon*, October.

Théry, I. (2007) *La Distinction de sexe*. Paris, Odile Jacob.

Théry, I. (2016) *Mariage et Filiation pour tous*. Paris, Seuil.

Théry, I. and Leroyer, A-M. (2014) *Filiation, origines, parentalité. Le droit face aux nouvelles valeurs de responsabilité générationnelle*, Rapport du groupe de travail Filiation, origines, Parentalité installé par le Ministère des affaires sociales et de la santé et le Ministère délégué chargé de la famille.

Thomson, D. (2014) *Les Français jihadistes*. Paris, Les Arènes.

Tiberj, V. (2008) *La crispation hexagonale: France fermée contre France plurielle, 2001–2007*. Plon.

Tiberj, V. (2012) 'Two-Axis Politics'. *Revue Française de Science Politique* Vol. 62 (1): 71–106.

Tiberj, V. (2017) 'Running to stand still. Le clivage gauche/droite en 2017', *Revue française de science politique*, 67, 6, pp. 1089–1112.

Toute l'Europe (2016) 'Europe: quel bilan pour François Hollande?' www.touteleurope. eu/actualite/europe-quel-bilan-pour-francois-hollande.html (accessed 27 August 2017).

Trierweiler, V. (2014) *Merci pour ce moment*. Paris, Les Arènes.

Truc, G. (2016) *Sidérations. Une sociologie des attentats*. Paris, PUF.

Turley, S. (2019) *Uprising: How the Yellow Vest Protests Are Changing France and Overturning the World Order*. Turley Talks.

Vail, M. (2004) 'The myth of the frozen welfare state and the dynamics of contemporary French and German social-protection reform', *French Politics*, 2, pp. 151–183.

Vaisse, M. (2005) 'La puissance ou l'influence'. In Jean-Claude Allain, et al. (eds.) *Histoire de la Diplomatie Française*. Paris, Perrin, pp. 868–871.

van Kessel, S., Chelotti, N. Drake, H. Roch Gonzalez, J. and Rodi, P. (2020) 'Eager to leave? Populist radical right parties' responses to the UK's Brexit vote', *British Journal of Politics and International Relations*.

Vauchez, A. (2009) 'Quand les juristes faisaient la loi...' Le moment Carbonnier (1963–1977), son histoire et son mythe', *Parlements*, 11 (1), pp. 105–116.

Vaudano, M. and Breteau, P. (2017), 'Mandats, professions, études des députés...la nouvelle Assemblée en douze infographies', *Le Monde*, 26 June.

Veltz, P. (2008) *Des lieux et des liens. Politiques du territoire à l'heure de la mondialisation*. Paris, Edition de L'Aube.

Venturi, R. (2015) *Collective Bargaining to Drive Labour Law Reform*. France Stratégie Policy Brief, September.

Verjus, A. and Boisson, M. (2005) 'Quand connaître c'est reconnaître. Le rôle de l'expertise familiale dans la production d'un sens commun du parent', *Droit et société*, 60 (2), pp. 449–467.

Vie Publique (2019) 'Interview de M. Christophe Castaner, ministre de l'intérieur, à BFMTV-RMC le 28 août 2019, sur les violences lors des manifestations de "Gilets jaunes" et la police', 28 August. www.vie-publique.fr/discours/270240-christophe-castaner-28082019-police (consulted 8 March 2020).

Vie publique (2020a) 'Projet de loi pour une démocratie plus représentative, responsable et efficace'. www.vie-publique.fr/loi/20800-pour-une-democratie-plus-representative-responsable-et-efficace-projet

Vie publique (2020b) 'Projet de loi pour un renouveau de la vie démocratique'. www. vie-publique.fr/loi/273301-reforme-constitutionnelle-2019-pour-un-renouveau-de-la-vie-democratique

Walt, V. (2019) 'I'm in this Death Valley'. Interview with Emmanuel Macron. *Time Magazine*, 19 September.

Washington Post (2013) 'In northern Mali's war Al Qaeda affiliate is directing the fight', *Washington Post*, 28 January.

Wlezien, C. (1995) 'The public as thermostat: dynamics of preferences for spending', *American Journal of Political Science*, 39, pp. 981–1000.

www.ohchr.org/EN/NewsEvents/Pages/DisplayNews.aspx?NewsID=24265& LangID=E (accessed 25 January 2020).

www.sciencespo.fr/cevipof/fr/content/le-barometre-de-la-confiance-politique

Zalc, C. (2018) 'La déchéance de nationalité. Eléments d'histoire d'une révision constitutionnelle ratée', *Pouvoirs*, 3 (166), pp. 41–57.

Zaretsky, R. (2019) 'Macron is going full de Gaulle', *Foreign Policy*, 11 February.

Zick, A., Wolf, C. and Küpper, B. (2008) 'The syndrome of group-focused enmity: the interrelation of prejudices tested with multiple cross-sectional and panel data', *Journal of Social Issues*, 64 (2), pp. 363–383.

Zick, A., Küpper, B. and Hovermann, A. (2011) *Intolerance, Prejudice and Discrimination A European Report*. Berlin, Friedrich Ebert Stiftung.

Zucker-Rouvillois, É. (1999) 'Éléments pour une chronologie scientifique, juridique et politique: l'expertise familial'. In D. Borrillo, E. Fassin and M. Iacub (eds.) *Au-delà du PaCS. L'expertise familiale à l'épreuve de l'homosexualité*. Paris, Presses universitaires de France, pp. 130–144.

INDEX

Printed by Printforce, United Kingdom